Splendor of the True

SUNY series in Western Esoteric Traditions

David Appelbaum, editor

Splendor of the True

A Frithjof Schuon Reader

Selected, translated, and with an introduction by
James S. Cutsinger

Foreword by
Huston Smith

SUNY PRESS

Cover image: Photograph of Frithjof Schuon (c. 1958). Courtesy of World Wisdom, Inc.

Published by State University of New York Press, Albany

Printed in the United States of America

For information, contact State University of New York Press, Albany, NY
www.sunypress.edu

Production by Eileen Meehan
Marketing by Fran Keneston

Library of Congress Cataloging-in-Publication Data

Schuon, Frithjof, 1907–1998.
[Selections. English. 2013]
Splendor of the true : a Frithjof Schuon reader / selected, translated, and introduced by James S. Cutsinger ; foreword by Huston Smith.
p. cm.
Includes bibliographical references and index.
ISBN 978-1-4384-4611-0 (hardcover : alk. paper)
ISBN 978-1-4384-4610-3 (pbk. : alk. paper)
1. Religion—Philosophy. 2. Religions. 3. Philosophy. I. Cutsinger, James S., 1953– II. Title.

BL51.S463213 2013
210—dc23 2012017394

10 9 8 7 6 5 4 3 2 1

Socrates
Do you think Truth is akin to moderation and proportion or to disproportion?

Glaucon
To proportion.

Socrates
Then in addition to our other requirements we must look for a mind endowed with moderation and grace and drawn by nature to see the Truth in all things.

Plato, *Republic*, 486d

CONTENTS

V. SPIRITUALITY

ILLUSTRATIONS

POEMS

FOREWORD

Anyone who wants to escape from the culture of despair that seems to have overtaken America in recent years can do no better than to read this book. In his famous 1978 Commencement Address at Harvard University, Alexander Solzhenitsyn attributed this despair to the West's "spiritual exhaustion." More and more people are recognizing that this exhaustion is not serving our society well—to say the least!—but its cultural barons give us no suggestions as to how to extricate ourselves from it. This book does just that, and it does so by weaving a tapestry from judiciously selected passages in the vast corpus of Frithjof Schuon, whom I join the editor in regarding as the spiritual prophet of our time *par excellence*. The easiest way I can explain my side of that estimate is to address it personally.

Early in life I realized that what I most wanted was to understand the ultimate nature of things—God, Truth, Reality, the Big Picture, the Infinite, whatever we choose to call it. Next came the realization that, since there is no commensurability between the Real and the unreal, I could accomplish my objective only by taking Revelation seriously, since this is the way in which the Real makes itself known to human beings. So I turned my attention in that direction—to Revelation as it appears in all the great religions, for they were all set in motion by revealed Truth. But this brought me to an impasse: the problem of the one and the many, as philosophers call it. Truth, capitalized, has to be single—"Hear O Israel, the Lord thy God, the Lord is One"—whereas the world's wisdom traditions (as I have come to think of them) are incontestably plural. They are alike in many respects, but they also contradict one another on important points. How could I uncompromisingly affirm the singularity of the Real and at the same time believe that all the authentic religions have stemmed from its single Source? To put the matter starkly, how could I believe in "Revelations"—using the capitalization to validate their ultimacy—without dropping the word's plural ending? The standard way to finesse that problem is to change the capital "R" to lower case when speaking in the plural, but the deeper I moved into the profundities of the wisdom traditions, the more singular their presiding Truth appeared.

I am not sure that if I had been left to my own devices I could have ever solved this problem, which would have meant knocking my head against its wall for my entire career. Frithjof Schuon rescued me from that fate. I will not steal the thunder of the book in hand by saying how he cut the Gordian knot and squared the circle, to mix my metaphors. It is enough if I say that when his position came into focus for me—it took some time, for though passages in his writing are so inspiringly beautiful as to make the reader interrupt his reading and pause to pray, others are as difficult as any passage in philosophy one can name—I realized that I was in the presence of a metaphysical genius, a man who was doing exactly what I was trying to do: honor equally religion's breadth, embracing its manifold historical expressions, and its vertical height, anchored in the One Living God. And he was doing it with a flair that I could admire only from a very great distance. I apprenticed myself to Schuon and will keep on doing so for the rest of my life.

It remains for me to say in closing that in the translator and editor of this collection, Schuon has found the perfect amanuensis. No one alive understands his outlook better than James Cutsinger, and in this labor of love he does a remarkable job of making Schuon accessible to a much wider audience than this extraordinary writer has thus far enjoyed.

—Huston Smith

INTRODUCTION

Few religious writers of recent times have had as polarizing an effect on those acquainted with their work as Frithjof Schuon.

A first group of readers have competed to see who can praise him in the grandest terms. One of them tells us that Schuon's books offer "completely new perspectives in every aspect of religious thought,"[1] while another asserts that "*à propos* religion, equally in depth and breadth," he was "the paragon of our time."[2] Yet a third prolific and highly respected scholar has elevated his own superlatives to the level of the superhuman, comparing Schuon to "the cosmic Intellect itself."[3] It is important to note that these are not the words of marginal thinkers or cultish sycophants. On the contrary they represent the considered judgment of several of the academy's most prestigious and influential names. Schuon—who was at once a philosopher, an authority on the world's religions, a spiritual guide, and a gifted poet and painter—seemed to many of his most learned readers not just a man but a providential phenomenon, a many-sided genius with a God-given spiritual role for our age.

At the same time, however, his work has been severely criticized—when not simply ignored—by a second and admittedly much larger group, and this includes academics who might have otherwise been expected to benefit most from his insights: philosophers of religion, authorities on mysticism and spirituality, and comparative religionists. In fact scholarly dismissals began many years ago when a prominent reviewer of one of this author's first books complained that "Schuon glories in his contempt for human reason" and that his writings are little more than "a disconnected series of

1. Jacob Needleman, *The Sword of Gnosis: Metaphysics, Cosmology, Tradition, Symbolism* (London: Routledge and Kegan Paul, 1974), 14–15.

2. Huston Smith, commenting on Schuon's book *Logic and Transcendence* (London: Perennial Books, 1975).

3. "Schuon seems like the cosmic Intellect itself . . . surveying the whole of the reality surrounding man and elucidating all the concerns of human existence in the light of sacred knowledge" (Seyyed Hossein Nasr, *Knowledge and the Sacred: The 1981 Gifford Lectures* [Albany, New York: State University of New York, 1989], 107).

private thoughts";[4] another critic has charged Schuon with a "subtle arrogance which is hardly becoming in those who desire religious unity,"[5] while a third objects that "the very manner in which Schuon's thesis is developed suggests that the theoretical is the basis for what is. . . . The course of philosophy (and theology, too) over the past two centuries is precisely one of questioning such an approach."[6] For a number of reasons, the opinions of those in this second group have tended to carry the day. As a result Schuon's books are seldom read in college or university classrooms, and his name therefore remains comparatively unknown among students of religion and philosophy, as well as among those in the wider public whose choice of reading is influenced by what the pundits say.[7]

My aim in compiling this anthology has been to redress this imbalance by offering its readers a glimpse of the full scope of Schuon's philosophy in order that they might be able to judge for themselves what to make of this provocative, and obviously controversial, writer. It should be understood from the outset that I am by no means an indifferent observer. Having studied and written about Schuon for the past quarter century, I have long been convinced that he is an author whose work deserves a much larger audience and much fairer hearing, and this book has been quite deliberately designed to persuade others to think the same. Colleagues in the field who are accustomed to maintaining neutrality may fault me for adopting the role of an advocate, and if so they are kindly invited to bring their preferred methodology to the table and to be as critical as they wish. For my part, I cannot but agree with Schuon that "knowledge saves only on condition that it engages all that we are,"[8] and since—as I see it—the only good reason for seeking knowledge in the domain of religion is that

---

4. R. C. Zaehner in a review of Schuon's *Spiritual Perspectives and Human Facts* in *The Journal of Theological Studies*, Vol. 6 (1955), 341.

5. Richard Bush, "Frithjof Schuon's *The Transcendent Unity of Religions*: Con," *Journal of the American Academy of Religion*, Vol. 44, No. 4 (1976), 717.

6. Shunji Nishi in a review of Schuon's *Transcendent Unity of Religions* and *Logic and Transcendence* in *The Anglican Theological Review*, Vol. 60 (1978), 120.

7. Or if not unknown at least unnamed. "One rarely encounters academic specialists in the spiritual dimensions of religious studies who have not in fact read several of the works of Schuon, but this wide-ranging influence is rarely mentioned in public because of the peculiar processes of academic 'canonization'" (James W. Morris, "Ibn ʿArabī in the 'Far West': Visible and Invisible Influences," *Journal of the Muhyiddin Ibn ʿArabī Society*, No. 29 [2001], 106). Noting the "profound effect of the abundant writings of Frithjof Schuon" on "several generations of philosophers and theologians seeking to develop a comprehensive, non-reductive 'philosophy of religions,'" Morris attributes scholarly unwillingness to acknowledge this influence to the "vagaries of academic opinion and respectability" (105–106).

8. *Prayer Fashions Man: Frithjof Schuon on the Spiritual Life*, ed. James S. Cutsinger (Bloomington, Indiana: World Wisdom, 2005), 24.

it might in fact save us, I have chosen to remain as fully engaged with the Schuonian message as possible.

My task as editor has not been an easy one. The complete corpus of Schuon's writings is extensive and imposing: more than two dozen books, some four thousand poems, and nearly two thousand letters, as well as approximately twelve hundred short spiritual texts, which were privately circulated among his friends and close associates.[9] My goal here is simply to present a small cross-section of the evidence that has led Schuon's defenders to draw what must otherwise seem excessively flattering conclusions concerning his stature and significance, while at the same time challenging his critics—and the religious studies community as a whole—to give his work a much fuller and more sustained examination than it has so far received.

But words of both praise and blame aside, who exactly was Frithjof Schuon,[10] and why, if his perspective has seemed to some so immensely important, has he been so disparaged when not neglected by others?

PERENNIALIST

A first response is to say that Schuon was the leading spokesman for a contemporary school of religious thought known as perennialism,[11] the

9. Compiled in his later years as "The Book of Keys" (*Le Livre des clefs*), these texts were initially composed as *mudhākarat* or "sermons" for Schuon's Sufi disciples (see below for a discussion of his role as a *shaykh*). With the exception of a first volume in German—*Leitgedanken zur Urbesinnung* [Guiding Thoughts for Primordial Meditation] (Zürich: Orell Füssli Verlag, 1935); revised edition: *Urbesinnung: Das Denken des Eigentlichen* [Primordial Meditation: Contemplating the Real] (Freiburg im Breisgau: Aurum Verlag, 1989)—the author's books were compiled from articles originally written in French and published in such journals as *Le Voile d'Isis*, *Études traditionnelles*, and *Connaissance des religions*. Schuon wrote poetry in Arabic, English, and German; a sampling of his English poems can be found in *Road to the Heart* (Bloomington, Indiana: World Wisdom Books, 1995), and the German poems appear in a number of collections, including *Songs for a Spiritual Traveler: Selected Poems* (Bloomington, Indiana: World Wisdom, 2002), *Adastra & Stella Maris: Poems by Frithjof Schuon* (Bloomington, Indiana: World Wisdom, 2003), and *Autumn Leaves & The Ring: Poems by Frithjof Schuon* (Bloomington, Indiana: World Wisdom, 2010). For further information, see the Bibliography of Works by Frithjof Schuon, pp. 277–86.

10. A much more complete picture of Schuon than this brief introduction intends to supply can be found in Jean-Baptiste Aymard and Patrick Laude, *Frithjof Schuon: Life and Teachings* (Albany, New York: State University of New York, 2004) and Michael Fitzgerald, *Frithjof Schuon: Messenger of the Perennial Philosophy* (Bloomington, Indiana: World Wisdom, 2010).

11. The label "traditionalism" is also sometimes used; see for example Kenneth Oldmeadow, *Traditionalism: Religion in the Light of the Perennial Philosophy* (Colombo, Sri Lanka: Sri Lanka Institute of Traditional Studies, 2000). The term "traditionalism" underscores the importance of fidelity to the revealed doctrines and rites of the major religions, whereas "perennialism" points to the metaphysical unanimity of these religions.

distinctive teaching of which is that the world's great religious traditions are all expressions or crystallizations of a single, saving Truth.

Born in Basle, Switzerland in 1907, Schuon writes that even as a young boy

> I saw with my eyes and my heart the beauty, grandeur, and spirituality of other civilizations . . . and I could never believe that one religion alone in the whole world was the true one and that all other religions were false. . . . How could God, wishing to save every human soul, have given the saving truth to only one people and thus condemned so many others, who are no worse than these, to remain forever in deadly darkness?[12]

Comparing this Truth to a perennial flower, a perennialist teaches that there is one divine Source of all wisdom—itself timeless and universal—which has repeatedly blossomed forth at different moments of history. The major religions, including Hinduism, Buddhism, Taoism, Confucianism, Judaism, Christianity, and Islam, are different blooms on that wisdom—or, to change the metaphor, different paths leading to the same summit or different dialects of a common language.

Schuon's early signature work, *The Transcendent Unity of Religions*, first published in 1948, was a key to defining the perennialist standpoint, a standpoint often associated with two other especially noteworthy spokesmen, René Guénon and Ananda K. Coomaraswamy.[13] As the word "transcendent" implies, the unity or unanimity of the world's wisdom traditions is not to be found in the "human atmosphere" but in the "divine stratosphere"—to borrow one of Schuon's more memorable metaphors—and for the perennialist this means that a careful distinction must be drawn between two levels of religious meaning and interpretation. Outwardly or exoterically the doctrines of the major traditions are clearly different, even contradictory, a fact not surprisingly stressed by scholars whose approach to religion is strictly historical and empirical. The Hindu tradition, for example, includes

---

12. Letter to Benjamin Black Elk (7 October 1947); see the Appendix, pp. 202–203 (Selection 2).

13. The French metaphysician René Guénon (1886–1951), with whom Schuon corresponded and collaborated for nearly twenty years, may be regarded as the founder of the perennialist school; Guénon articulated the first principles of this perspective in such books as *An Introduction to the Study of Hindu Doctrines* (1921) and *Man and His Becoming according to the Vedānta* (1925). Ananda K. Coomaraswamy (1877–1947), for many years curator of Indian art at the Boston Museum of Fine Arts, was the author of numerous books and articles on metaphysics, art, religion, and traditional civilizations; see especially his *Selected Papers* on *Metaphysics* and *Traditional Art and Symbolism*, ed. Roger Lipsey (Princeton: Princeton University Press, 1977).

many Gods, Judaism insists there is only one God, and Buddhism declares the question of God to be moot. Or again, Christians believe that God is a Trinity and that the divine Son of God was incarnate as Jesus Christ, beliefs explicitly rejected by Islam.

According to Schuon, however, such outwardly divergent teachings, providentially adapted to the spiritual, psychological, and cultural needs of different peoples at different periods of history, can be inwardly or esoterically reconciled by those who are sensitive to the metaphysical and symbolic meanings of revealed doctrines and rites and who are prepared to follow the golden thread of the dogmatic letter to the deepest—or highest—level of Spirit. From the perennialist point of view, this is why one finds such a remarkable "stratospheric" consensus among the greatest mystics and sages, such as Shankara in Hinduism, Ibn Arabi in Islam, and Meister Eckhart in Christianity.[14]

Schuon's perennialism embraces three distinct dimensions, which are reflected in his use of three Latin phrases: *Sophia Perennis* (perennial wisdom), *Philosophia Perennis* (perennial philosophy), and *Religio Perennis* (perennial religion). When speaking of the *Sophia Perennis*,[15] what he has in mind above all is metaphysical Truth as such—eternal, immutable, and supra-formal Wisdom—which he would occasionally sum up by citing the advaitic teaching of Shankara: "God is real; the world is unreal; the soul is not different from God." *Philosophia Perennis* on the other hand refers in the Schuonian lexicon to the conceptual approximations and elaborations of this Wisdom that are to be found in the West among such figures as Plato, Plotinus, the Church Fathers, and the medieval Scholastics,[16] although Schuon also uses this phrase to refer more generally to "the connecting link between different religious languages."[17] Finally, *Religio Perennis* is an expression he employs in order to accentuate the "quintessence of all spirituality," the "underlying universality in every great spiritual patrimony," or simply the "underlying religion" (*la religion sous-jacente* in his original

---

14. See Reza Shah-Kazemi, *Paths to Transcendence: According to Shankara, Ibn Arabi, and Meister Eckhart* (Bloomington, Indiana: World Wisdom, 2006).

15. For example, in "Axioms of the *Sophia Perennis*," *The Transfiguration of Man* (Bloomington, Indiana: World Wisdom Books, 1995).

16. *Stations of Wisdom* (Bloomington, Indiana: World Wisdom Books, 1995), 33; see also Schuon's article "The Perennial Philosophy" in *The Unanimous Tradition: Essays on the Essential Unity of All Religions*, ed. Ranjit Fernando (Colombo, Sri Lanka: Sri Lanka Institute of Traditional Studies, 1991). The phrase *philosophia perennis* appears to have been used for the first time by Agostino Steuco (1496–1549), a Vatican librarian, and it was given currency in the early eighteenth century by the philosopher Leibniz.

17. See below Ch. 1, "The Sense of the Absolute in Religions," p. 14.

French).[18] Reduced to its perennial essentials, every genuine religion is doctrinally based on a salvific descent of the Real into the illusory and, at the operative level of practice, on a metaphysical discernment between the Real and illusory and a contemplative concentration on the Real.

The perennialist perspective is sometimes classified as a kind of pluralism, but in fact it is fundamentally different, and this difference places Schuon worlds apart from many contemporary comparativists and philosophers of religion. Most pluralists, working inductively from the data presented by ethnographers and historians of religion, envision the diversity of religious traditions as the *natural* effect of a corresponding variety among human beings and cultures: Different people at different times and in different places have endeavored to reach out to the divine Reality—a Reality, many pluralists would insist, that can never be known as it is in itself[19]—and the religions, which are the results of their collective efforts, are therefore as varied as they are.

Schuon teaches by contrast that the great traditions are this Reality's own self-disclosures, each a *supernatural* effect resulting from direct revelation. The differences between them, together with certain fundamental divergences between the types of people to whom the revelations were given, correspond in the first instance to distinct archetypes in the divine Mind and distinct intentions in the divine Will, with each religion reflecting—as Schuon puts it—one of the "confessional Faces" of God.[20] In other words

18. See below "*Religio Perennis*," p. 192, where the author presents this "quintessence" or "underlying universality" in light of the Patristic maxim: "God became man that man might become God." See also the Appendix, pp. 226–27 (Selection 32).

19. Pluralist thinking is often undergirded by the Kantian assumption that knowledge is inevitably mediated by conceptual categories, which means that we can never experience Reality *an sich*, as it is in itself. I shall return to the question of cognitive limits below.

20. "There is not only a personal God—who is so to speak the 'human Face,' or the 'humanized Face,' of the supra-personal Divinity—but there is also, beneath this first hypostatic degree and resulting from it, what we may term the 'confessional Face' of God: It is the Face God turns toward a particular religion, the Gaze He casts upon it, *without which it would not even exist*" (see Ch. 4, "The Mystery of the Hypostatic Face," p. 33 [italics added]). I say "in the first instance" because Schuon was not so blind as to think that the religions as we actually find them in history are immune to a variety of adaptive, and sometimes distorting, forces. "In every religious cycle four periods are to be distinguished: first the 'apostolic' period, then the period of full development, after which comes the period of decadence, and last the final period of corruption" (Schuon, *Christianity/Islam: Perspectives on Esoteric Ecumenism*, ed. James S. Cutsinger [Bloomington, Indiana: World Wisdom, 2008], 10). The divine origin of the orthodox traditions notwithstanding, each of them nonetheless includes what he calls a "human margin"; see the chapter by that title in his book *In the Face of the Absolute* (Bloomington, Indiana: World Wisdom Books, 1989).

religions are not human creations, and they should not be understood to comprise merely partial or complementary truths, which then need combining with those of other traditions in order to achieve a more complete—but still always imperfect—picture of the Real. On the contrary, each tradition is integrally true in that it provides its adherents with everything they need for reaching the highest or most complete human state, a state in which they may come to know and participate in the Supreme Reality itself.

Three consequences follow from Schuon's position, each of which is bound to be problematic for pluralists of a more typically historicist, empiricist, and "democratic" mindset. First, a merely abstract respect for the great wisdom traditions or a purely theoretical acknowledgment of their "transcendent unity" is not enough. Those intent on penetrating, and not merely appreciating, the religions must be concretely engaged in the practice of one of them, a practice prescribed in that religion's sacred scriptures and followed by its own saintly authorities. "A spirituality deprived of these bases," Schuon warned, "can only end up as a psychological game without any relation to the unfolding of our higher states."[21] The syllogism is perennialist through and through: Whoever knows one religion knows implicitly all the others as well, for each of the orthodox faiths of the world is the manifestation of a single, underlying Essence. But the only way truly to know a given religious tradition—deeply and experientially and in such a way as to understand its very reason for being—is by believing in it and doing what it requires. Therefore, only those who are fully living the life required by their own religion, opening themselves to its doctrinal vision and submitting themselves to its moral and sacramental precepts, are qualified to speak with authority about any religion.[22]

Second, the validity or spiritual legitimacy of a religion is not to be measured by something as subjective as the personal testimony of any given believer, however learned or faithful, but rather by objective criteria. "In order for a religion to be considered intrinsically orthodox," Schuon writes,

> it must be founded upon a doctrine which, taken as a whole, is adequate to the Absolute . . . and it must promote and bring to fulfillment a spirituality proportioned to this doctrine, which

21. See below Ch. 19, "The Nature and Function of the Spiritual Master," p. 172. Schuon clearly parts company with a growing number of people who prefer to call themselves "spiritual" outside the context of a traditional religion.

22. One is reminded of the saying of Evagrios the Solitary: "The theologian is one who prays, and the one who prays is truly a theologian."

> means that it must include both the idea and the fact of sanctity. The religion must therefore be of divine and not philosophical origin, and as a result it must convey a sacramental or theurgic presence, manifest above all in miracles and—though this may be surprising to some—in sacred art.[23]

As for a given branch or spiritual community within a larger tradition, it too must be evaluated on the basis of objective factors, above all the scriptures and other revealed sources of the religion in question as these are interpreted by that tradition's "apostolic" and "patristic" authorities.[24] Readers who are accustomed to stressing the importance of tolerance and open-mindedness will doubtless wince, but Schuon did not hesitate to bring these criteria to bear in denouncing what he regarded as pseudo-religions and "intrinsic heresies," and he was prepared to name names.[25]

Finally, a third result of his perennialism—and this may take the reader by surprise—is that Schuon was deeply skeptical of interfaith dialogue, at least in its most common forms. I do not mean to suggest that he was some sort of religious "isolationist"; on the contrary his personal friendships with believers and spiritual authorities in many different traditions were varied and extensive and included Hindu *gurus* and pundits, Pure Land Buddhist priests and Zen masters, Christian monks and abbots, and Native American chiefs and shamans.[26] But he knew very well that contemporary ecumenical discussions are too often dominated by interlocutors who fail to take seriously their own tradition's theology and who therefore end up reducing whole religions to an ethical least common denominator in the interest of promoting peace and harmony. Laudable as such a goal might seem, for

23. Schuon, *Forme et substance dans les religions* [Form and Substance in Religions] (Paris: Dervy-Livres, 1975), 19. I should point out that when Schuon speaks here of doctrinal "adequacy" he is not referring to a teaching that is merely "acceptable"; he is alluding instead to the Scholastic definition of truth as the "adequation of reality and mind" (*adaequatio rei et intellectus*).

24. Certain pluralists on the other hand prefer to "demythologize" the scriptures and dismantle traditional doctrines on the pretext that they can no longer be understood, let alone believed and practiced, by modern people; see for example John Hick, *The Metaphor of God Incarnate: Christology in a Pluralistic Age* (Louisville, Kentucky: Westminster/John Knox, 1993).

25. For example, the Transcendental Meditation movement of Mahesh Yogi (see the Appendix, Selection 12). In Schuon's terminology an "intrinsic heresy" is incompatible with metaphysical Truth as such; an "extrinsic heresy" on the other hand is a valid dogmatic perspective, which only appears to be false from the point of view of another such perspective. See the important chapter "Orthodoxy and Intellectuality" in Schuon's *Stations of Wisdom*.

26. Schuon took a special interest in the religious traditions of the Plains Indians, twice visiting the American West, in 1959 and 1963. He also enjoyed longstanding friendships with Benjamin Black Elk, son of the Oglala Sioux elder Black Elk, and Thomas Yellowtail, a Crow Sun Dance chief.

Schuon this deliberate blurring of dogmatic differences involved—at least potentially—a kind of "blasphemy against the Holy Spirit," for if differences between the religions are indeed willed by God and if they manifest the various facets or "faces" of the Supreme Reality, these differences must be salvifically necessary.[27] And this being so, one is obliged to respect the integrity of each orthodox tradition as an irreplaceable repository of the sacred, honoring the formal structure of its distinctive dogmas, rites, and symbols so as to ensure that these unique "dialects" not be confused or collapsed into a kind of "religious Esperanto."[28]

"If all men were metaphysicians and contemplatives," Schuon notes,

> a single Revelation might be enough; but since this is not how things are, the Absolute must reveal itself in different ways, and the metaphysical viewpoints from which these Revelations are derived—according to different logical needs and different spiritual temperaments—cannot but contradict one another on the plane of forms. . . . The great evil is not that men of different religions do not understand one other, but that too many men—due to the influence of the modern spirit—are no longer believers.

Given this situation, his advice was that people should "return to faith, whatever their religion may be, provided that it is intrinsically orthodox and in spite of dogmatic ostracisms."[29] Better in other words to worship God in a religiously exclusivistic but orthodox environment than to run the risk of diminishing or disparaging, however unintentionally, one of Heaven's gifts.

---

27. Schuon occasionally cited the Koran in this regard: "For each We have appointed a divine law and a traced-out way. Had God willed He could have made you one community. But that He may try you by that which He hath given you (He hath made you as ye are). So vie one with another in good works. Unto God ye will all return, and He will then inform you of that wherein ye differ" (*Sūrah* "The Table Spread" [5]:48).

28. The phrase is Coomaraswamy's; see "Sri Ramakrishna and Religious Tolerance," *Coomaraswamy, 2: Selected Papers: Metaphysics*, ed. Roger Lipsey, 40. In a recent book, *God is Not One: The Eight Rival Religions That Run the World—and Why Their Differences Matter* (New York: HarperCollins, 2010), Stephen Prothero alleges that perennialist writers treat all the religions as if they were the same, but this is a complete misrepresentation of Schuon's position, whom Prothero never bothers to cite or even mention.

29. Letter of 29 May 1964. For the complete letter, see *Gnosis: Divine Wisdom: A New Translation with Selected Letters*, ed. James S. Cutsinger (Bloomington, Indiana: World Wisdom, 2006), 133–34. Schuon's observation concerning "how things are" will perhaps be taken as an example of the "subtle arrogance" mentioned by one critic above. If so, surely the only response can be that Schuon was right, whether we like the way he puts things or not. The majority of religious believers need a formal, and relatively simple, expression of Truth in which they can put their entire trust without being troubled by metaphysical subtleties.

SHAYKH

This insistence on a serious, sacramental commitment to an orthodox tradition is one of the hallmarks of Schuon's teaching. There are of course many writers on the subject of religion who believe in God and say their prayers and who encourage others to do the same—though their numbers have been sharply reduced over the last several decades among academic religionists, as we shall be discussing shortly. What one finds in Schuon's case, however, is a writer who takes the further step of insisting that only those who do believe and pray,[30] and who do so moreover on the canonical basis supplied by an authentic revelation, can speak on the subject of religion, any religion, with true authority.

Schuon did not exempt himself from this rule, a fact that brings us to a second answer to the question of who he was, why he has provoked such divergent responses among his readers, and why so many remain unaware of his work. Since his death in 1998, it has become a matter of public record that his own spiritual practice was undertaken within the framework of Islam, specifically within the mystical tradition of Sufism. Some of his closest associates have published biographical reminiscences in recent years,[31] and we now know that this perennial philosopher served for more than sixty years as the *shaykh*, or spiritual master, of a traditional Sufi brotherhood in the *Shādhilīyyah-Darqāwīyyah* lineage.[32]

Growing up in Western Europe in the early years of the twentieth century, Schuon had been raised first as a Protestant and later received confirmation as a Roman Catholic. Nowhere in these Christian contexts, however—as he explains in several letters as well as in his unpublished memoirs[33]—did he encounter spiritual teaching and guidance of the same kind and caliber as he had discovered, during his early teens, in the scriptures and sacred art of the East.[34] "Being *a priori* a metaphysician," he recalls,

30. "Even if our writings had on average no other result than the restitution for some of the saving barque that is prayer, we would owe it to God to consider ourselves profoundly satisfied" (Schuon, *The Play of Masks* [Bloomington, Indiana: World Wisdom Books, 1992], vii).

31. For example, Martin Lings, *A Return to the Spirit: Questions and Answers* (Louisville, Kentucky: Fons Vitae, 2005), 1–19.

32. This is an unbroken line of initiatic transmission tracing its origin to the thirteenth-century master Abu al-Hasan al-Shadhili (1196–1258) and including among its subsequent branches an order founded in the early nineteenth century by Mawlay al-Arabi al-Darqawi (1760–1823).

33. *Erinnerungen und Betrachtungen* (Lausanne: privately circulated, 1974); English translation: "Memories and Meditations" (Bloomington, Indiana: privately circulated, 1982).

34. "In my childhood I was first a Protestant and later a Catholic; to the simple and sincere piety of my first teacher, who lived wholly on the Bible, I owe much. In Catholicism I loved the

> I had since my youth a particular interest in *Advaita Vedānta*, but also in the method of realization of which *Advaita* approves. Since I could not find this method—in its strict and esoteric form—in Europe, and since it was impossible for me to turn to a Hindu *guru* because of the rules of the castes, I had to look elsewhere; and since Islam *de facto* contains this method in Sufism, I finally decided to look for a Sufi master; the outer form did not matter to me.[35]

This search took him eventually, in 1932, to Mostaganem, Algeria, where he met and was soon initiated by one of the most celebrated of twentieth-century Sufi masters, the *shaykh* Ahmad al-Alawi.[36] This aspect of Schuon's personal background, together with his own subsequent role as a *shaykh* in his own right—the Shaykh Isa Nur al-Din Ahmad al-Shadhili al-Darqawi al-Alawi al-Maryami—was kept in the strictest confidence until his death, and those who had the privilege of approaching him for spiritual direction, including perhaps as many as a thousand disciples throughout the world, were asked to do their part in protecting his privacy.[37]

There were at least two reasons for the veil of anonymity surrounding Schuon's person and for the relative secrecy of his Sufi brotherhood. First, like any other such authority—whether Hindu *guru*, Buddhist *roshi*, or Christian *geronda*—he was obliged by his office to take into careful consideration the moral and other qualifications of those who sought to become his disciples. "In former times," he writes,

> when an aspirant presented himself at the door of a *zāwiyah* [a Sufi center for prayer] he was at first left to knock in vain; one was wary of opening the door to him right away, and it

liturgical manifestation of the holy, the beauty of the divine service in the Gothic-style churches, the cult of Mary and the Rosary. But I could not stop with this, for at an early age I had read the *Bhagavad Gītā* and profoundly experienced the sacred art of the Far East" (Letter of 21 December 1980; see footnote 76 below).

35. Letter of January 1996.

36. See Martin Lings, *A Sufi Saint of the Twentieth Century: Shaikh Ahmad al-Alawi: His Spiritual Heritage and Legacy* (Berkeley and Los Angeles: University of California, 1973). "To meet such a one," Schuon later wrote, "is like coming face to face in mid-twentieth century with a medieval Saint or a Semitic Patriarch, and this was the impression made on me by the Shaikh Al-Hajj Ahmad Bin-Aliwah, one of the greatest Masters of Sufism, who died a few months ago at Mostaganem" ("*Rāhimahu 'Llah*," *Cahiers du Sud*, August–September, 1935).

37. In addition to his Sufi disciples, Schuon also gave counsel to a number of seekers from other religions, including Hindus, Buddhists, Jews, and Christians; regarding this unusual role, see Ch. 19, "The Nature and Function of the Spiritual Master," pp. 175–77.

> sometimes happened that he was left to wait many days. . . . One wanted to be sure of his sincerity, humility, capacities, and good character. I do not say that things were always like this or that we must do things this way; I simply indicate a traditional point of view, which is as obvious as it is indispensable. Needing no one, we are not interested in strangers who simply wish to make our acquaintance.[38]

Although Schuon devoted considerable time and attention to those who were in earnest about their spiritual lives and who exhibited the persistence necessary to seek him out, he had no interest at all in proselytizing or attracting newcomers. His personal guidance was destined for a relatively small number of people, and he took very seriously his responsibilities for protecting their privacy and providing them with a congenial environment for their spiritual work—"a little garden of the Holy Virgin," as he liked to call it, hidden from the public gaze.[39]

But a second, and for our purposes more important, reason for his circumspection was an abiding concern that the message he sought to convey in his books—a perennial, hence universal, message precisely—not be confused or identified with a single religion. He knew that those who were aware of his Christian background might falsely conclude from his Sufi affiliation and function that he had renounced the religion of his youth and "converted" to Islam, whereas in fact his initiatic link with the Muslim tradition in no way conflicted with his remaining throughout his long life an adamant defender of traditional Christianity against its own modernist critics nor with his having a special affinity for the Christian East and the Hesychast method of prayer.[40] He

38. Letter of 8 June 1984.

39. "One must live in a little garden of the Holy Virgin, without unhealthy curiosity and without ever losing sight of the essential content and goal of life" ("Message to a Disciple," undated document). It is useful to note in this regard that Schuon's branch of the *Shādhilīyyah* Sufi line came to be known as the *Tarīqah Maryamīyyah*, having been blessed, he informed his disciples, with the celestial patronage of the Virgin Mary. "The coming of Sayyidatna Maryam [as the Virgin is called in Islam] did not depend on my own will but upon the will of Heaven; it was a totally unexpected and unimaginable gift" (Letter of September 1981). For further insight into the distinctively Marian aspects of his teaching, see my article "Colorless Light and Pure Air: The Virgin in the Thought of Frithjof Schuon," *Sophia: The Journal of Traditional Studies*, 6:2 (Winter 2000); reprinted in *Maria: A Journal of Marian Studies*, 3:1 (August 2002) and in *Ye Shall Know the Truth: Christianity and the Perennial Philosophy*, ed. Mateus Soares de Azevedo (Bloomington, Indiana: World Wisdom, 2005).

40. Schuon's brother was a Trappist monk, and his numerous other Christian contacts included the Russian Orthodox archimandrite Sophrony Sakharov (1896–1993), who was a noted disciple of Saint Silouan of the Holy Mountain of Athos, and the widely influential Roman Catholic

therefore felt it was necessary to avoid not only "the curiosity of Westerners," who might well have flocked to his door in hopes of finding something strange and exotic, but even more the misunderstandings of "Muslim Easterners, for whom a *shaykh* embodies not only what is most lofty and mysterious in Islam but also what is narrow and sentimental—when in reality I wished to represent above all the *Religio Perennis*."[41] Moreover Schuon was perfectly aware of the political implications of being a Muslim in the West, to say nothing of a *shaykh*, and he was quick to recognize—even in a "pre-9/11" context—the importance of distancing himself and his philosophy from the misleading associations such terms and categories could easily lead to:

> If we present ourselves in the Western world as "Muslims," people will think quite logically that we are converts, apostates, and traitors, given that Islam rejects Christianity. . . . Muslims on the other hand will welcome us as "brothers" and will congratulate us on having rejected the false religion that is Christianity, whereas in reality we are Vedantists who have sought an initiation and a spiritual method. What this means is that we shall appear in a false light in regard to both the East and the West. It is therefore important to keep silent to the extent we can.[42]

These facts go some further way in helping answer the question of why Schuon's name is not better known among scholars of religion nor cited as often as one might have expected in the pertinent bibliographies. Despite

writer Thomas Merton (1915–1968), who near the end of his life was in regular correspondence with several of Schuon's disciples about the possibility of meeting with "the Shaykh" and asking him for spiritual guidance; see *The Hidden Ground of Love: The Letters of Thomas Merton on Religious Experience and Social Concerns*, ed. William H. Shannon (New York: Harcourt, 1993), 476–77.

41. Letter of 21 August 1971. "Our starting point is *Advaita Vedānta* and not the voluntarist, individualist, and moralist anthropology with which Sufism is unquestionably identified" (Letter of 29 April 1989).

42. Letter of January 1992. Schuon adds, "In the Muslim world religion is becoming more and more politicized, which makes our position all the more precarious in the Western world—although we would have nothing to fear if people knew what we are in reality, not 'believers' of this or that faith but esotericists, who are by definition universalists, open to every orthodox credo." It should be emphasized that Schuon had nothing but the highest respect for the revealed forms of Islam and for traditional Islamic law as such: "Admittedly, one has the right to criticize those who, by an excessive and possibly absurd legalistic zeal, refuse to benefit from the simplifications that the Law itself offers, but one does not have the right to scorn in the least a given prescription of the Law or to take advantage of simplifications with a feeling of superiority or triumph. The Law is sacred" ("The Book of Keys," No. 887, "On the Subject of the Notion of Exotericism").

being a much-published author, his role as a *shaykh* led him to maintain a deliberate public anonymity, far from the halls of academia and the lecture and conference circuits where he might otherwise have gained a wider hearing.

Silence, circumspection, and relative anonymity notwithstanding, it was only natural for an author who was so deeply immersed in an intense contemplative practice and in the day-to-day life of a spiritual community to bring at least something of that side of himself to his written expositions, and this was certainly true for Schuon. From first to last—from *The Transcendent Unity of Religions* in 1948 to *The Transfiguration of Man* in 1995—his books testify to a continuing interest in the scriptures, doctrines, symbols, rites, and sacred arts of the Muslim tradition. *Understanding Islam*—first published in 1961 and translated into Arabic, Persian, and Urdu, as well as many European languages—remains his most often reprinted and most widely read title, though *Sufism: Veil and Quintessence* and *Christianity/Islam: Perspectives on Esoteric Ecumenism* should also be mentioned.[43] These books continue to attract a small but highly receptive audience in the Islamic world as well as in the West. At the same time, it is not surprising that a significant number of his Muslim readers, including at least a few other Sufi authorities, have found much to object to in Schuon's work. His uncompromising defense of a pure or integral esotericism "uncolored" by the viewpoint of any specific religion or formal spiritual framework,[44] his perennialist insistence on the validity and salvific efficacy of all the world's major traditions, and his trenchant criticisms of what he called the "moralizing metaphysics" of "average Sufism"[45] made him an unusual *shaykh*, to say the least, and it has

43. *Understanding Islam*, ed. Patrick Laude (Bloomington, Indiana: World Wisdom, 2011), foreword by Annemarie Schimmel; *Sufism: Veil and Quintessence*, ed. James S. Cutsinger (Bloomington, Indiana: World Wisdom, 2006), foreword by Seyyed Hossein Nasr; *Christianity/Islam: Perspectives on Esoteric Ecumenism*, ed. James S. Cutsinger (Bloomington, Indiana: World Wisdom, 2008); two anthologies of Schuon's writings on Islam should also be noted: *Dimensions of Islam*, trans. P. N. Townsend (London: Allen and Unwin, 1969) and *Islam and the Perennial Philosophy*, trans. J. Peter Hobson (London: World of Islam Festival, 1976).

44. "The word 'esotericism' designates not only the total truth insofar as it is 'colored' by entering a system of partial truth but also the total truth as such, which is colorless" (see Ch. 2, "Two Esotericisms," p. 17). Schuon described his perspective as that of "Islamic esotericism," where "the esotericism comes first and Islam afterward," and not that of "esoteric Islam," where "Islam comes first and esotericism afterward" ("The Book of Keys," No. 1008, "Islamic Esotericism and Esoteric Islam").

45. "The Quintessential Esoterism of Islam," *Sufism: Veil and Quintessence*, 102. Critical though he could be of confessional or "contingent" expressions of Islamic spirituality, Schuon was adamant in his defense of a "quintessential Sufism" consisting of three key elements: discernment between the Real and illusory—between *al-Haqq*, the True, and *al-hijāb*, the veil—as expressed by the *Shahādah*; permanent concentration on the Real by means of *Dhikru 'Llāh*, the Remembrance or Invocation of God; and conformity to the Real through *Ihsān*, beauty of soul or virtue.

sometimes been difficult for those of other Sufi lineages, let alone the exoteric Muslim majority, to understand and accept his full perspective, however impressed they might otherwise be with particular aspects of his teaching.

Some of his critics have gone so far as to suggest that Schuon was not really serious about his Islamic affiliation and practice and that he gradually drifted away from an initially firm footing in traditional *Tasawwuf*, but this claim appears to be belied by the facts. In this respect, as in others, he seems on the contrary to have undergone virtually no intellectual or spiritual change or development. Having as a young man made the decision to enter Islam, he continued to practice within that framework for the rest of his life, and yet he remained simultaneously a "pure esotericist" from start to finish. In a letter written when he was just twenty-five—several months before meeting the *shaykh* al-Alawi—he said to a friend,

> If there were any essential difference between a path that passes through Benares and one that passes through Mecca, how could you think that I would wish to come to God "through Mecca" and thereby betray Christ and the *Vedānta*? Is the Nirvana of Mecca different from the Nirvana of Benares simply because it is called *fanā*ʾ and not *nirvāna*? Either we are esotericists and metaphysicians who transcend forms . . . and do not distinguish between *Allāh* and *Brahman*, or else we are exotericists, "theologians," or at best mystics, who consequently live in forms like fish in water and who do make a distinction between Mecca and Benares.[46]

Precisely the same metaphysical accentuation remains evident nearly fifty years later in another letter, written to one of his disciples when Schuon was seventy-four:

> Our *Tarīqah* is not a *Tarīqah* like the others. . . . Our point of departure is the quest after esotericism and not after a particular religion—after the total Truth, not a sentimental mythology. To renounce and forget the religion of our [Christian] forefathers simply to immerse ourselves in another religion . . . could never be our perspective.[47]

Here we begin to see yet another reason, or rather set of reasons, why Schuon's writings may have failed to gain a wider readership and why they

46. Letter of 15 May 1932.

47. Letter of 18 May 1981.

will doubtless never be popular even among those who in other ways are prepared to appreciate many of the key elements in his philosophy, including his defense of revelation and tradition, his movingly poetic descriptions and explanations of religious symbols and art, his penetrating criticisms of the modern world, and his insistence on the practice of virtue and prayer. As attractive as Schuon's work might be for the serious person of faith, whether Muslim or otherwise, his message refuses to be domesticated in the interest of any sectarian aim and cannot be limited by any formal enclosure—even the "mystical enclosure" of traditional Sufism.[48]

GNOSTIC

The difficulties certain of the faithful may have in appreciating Schuon's teaching are nothing, however, compared to the problems modern scholars must face in coming to terms with his work. For if he has seemed insufficiently partisan from the point of view of some fellow Sufis, he is undoubtedly much too partisan for the taste of most contemporary religionists, who are trained to be wary of mixing personal commitment with scholarly discourse.[49] His frequent references to God and not merely to what people *say* about "God," his confident asseverations as to the esoteric significance of sundry doctrines and symbols, and his continual talk about "pure" metaphysics and Truth—with a capital "T" after all!—are bound to leave many of the professoriate feeling nonplussed if not irritated, or else embarrassed to have been caught reading such an author. What will one's colleagues think?

Asked in a 1991 interview why his books had not received more attention in university circles, Schuon quickly cut to the chase with a reply that was at once abrupt and revealing: "The reason is that I am not a relativist. Today all the scholars are relativists, and I am an absolutist. I believe in Truth, and the official scholars do not believe in Truth."[50] Anyone who

---

48. Schuon discusses the uniqueness of his perspective, and the differences between his teaching and that of other Sufis, at several points in the Appendix, notably in selections 6, 19, and 29.

49. Jan G. Platvoet gives voice to what is for many academics the default methodology: "Scholars of religion . . . can only take an agnostic position in respect of the truth or falsehood of the beliefs of the faithful. They must, therefore, confine themselves to investigating what is empirical about these beliefs and rituals i.e. to those elements and aspects of them that belong squarely to our own world and are parts of its empirical, cultural, and historical realities" ("Rattray's Request: Spirit Possession among the Bono of West Africa," *Indigenous Religions: A Companion*, ed. Graham Harvey [London and New York: Cassell, 2000), 81). Mircea Eliade's complaint that contemporary religionists often "take refuge in a materialism or behaviorism impervious to every spiritual shock" (*The Quest* [Chicago: University of Chicago, 1969], 62) still rings true.

50. "Frithjof Schuon: Messenger of the Perennial Philosophy" (biographical video featuring interviews with Schuon in 1991 and 1992; Bloomington, Indiana: World Wisdom, 2012).

has had a religion course in a secular university setting—or for that matter in any number of "church-related" institutions of higher learning—is well aware of what Schuon is talking about and knows that he is largely right, not perhaps about any given scholar as an individual person of faith but about virtually all the scholars *qua* scholars. For with few exceptions most academic religionists decided long ago to adopt the public posture of agnostics, obediently doing their part to uphold the opinion that opinions—more or less well informed by historical and other empirical data—are all we can hope for when it comes to God and other ultimate issues.

Into such a climate of assumptions and professional protocols the words of this "absolutist" inevitably descend like a thunderbolt, shattering preconceptions, flouting conventions, and often offending the sensibilities of those who might otherwise have been sympathetic to his ecumenical outlook. Even readers who admit to finding themselves powerfully attracted by Schuon often report having experienced a certain shock on first contact with his work. For here one is confronted by an approach to religion and spirituality that eschews, indeed strongly denounces, the pervasive "contextualism" of today's university, refusing to justify itself by any of the usual standards of academic research while at the same time conveying a clear and unmistakable note of authority and total certainty.[51]

But where does this authority come from? And what are the foundations, if any, for Schuon's certainty?

In order to begin addressing these questions, one must dig deeper than we have thus far—deeper certainly than a discussion of perennialism as a school of thought and deeper too than an acknowledgment of this author's connection with Sufism. Something of the depth in question was suggested many years ago in a review of Schuon's third book, *Spiritual Perspectives and Human Facts* (1953). Noting that this volume possessed "the intrinsic authority of a contemplative intelligence," the reviewer went on to suggest that its author "speaks of grace as one in whom it is operative and as it

---

51. "We grew up at a time when one could still say—without blushing on account of its naiveté—that two and two make four, when words still had a meaning and said what they meant to say, when one could conform to the laws of elementary logic or of common sense without having to pass through psychology or biology or so-called sociology and so forth, in short when there were still points of reference in the intellectual arsenal of men. By this we wish to point out that our way of thinking and our dialectic are deliberately out of date; and we know in advance, for it is only too evident, that the reader to whom we address ourselves will thank us for it" (Schuon, *Survey of Metaphysics and Esoterism* [Bloomington, Indiana: World Wisdom Books, 1986], 2). As one scholar has noted, "If the premise of the Perennial Philosophy is conceded, then much of the apparatus of modern scholarship . . . stands condemned" (Carl Ernst, "Traditionalism, the Perennial Philosophy, and Islamic Studies," *Middle East Studies Association Bulletin*, Vol. 28, No. 2 [December 1994], 181). For Schuon's further thoughts on authority, certainty, and infallibility, see Ch. 7, "Tracing the Notion of Philosophy," pp. 67–68.

were in virtue of that operation."[52] If this observation is to be regarded as anything more than hyperbole—and similar comments on the part of other learned readers oblige us, if we are honest, at least to consider that option—a radical shift in assumptions is going to have to take place. We must entertain the possibility, if only as an experiment in thought, that Schuon was someone who actually *knew* what he was talking about, someone who had apprehended the Truth—with that capital "T" once again—in a way that cannot be accounted for in terms of sheerly natural causes or purely human phenomena.

I realize how inflated such language will sound to many readers. It is, therefore, of the greatest importance that in approaching Schuon's work from this angle we be exceedingly cautious, for the last thing I want to do is to give the impression that his faithful defenders are nothing more than mere fideists, whose appreciative response to his books is based on a prior conviction concerning his spiritual station. By all accounts Schuon was indeed an exceptional human being, and his "presence" was such that many who knew him were inclined to describe him in quite extraordinary terms; such testimonials in fact abound, and not only on the part of injudicious disciples.[53] But it would be a mistake to suppose that the validity of his philosophy somehow rested on his charisma or other personal qualities. In fact one of the characteristic and most frequently noted features of his books is how rigorously impersonal they are; autobiographical allusions are extremely rare, and one finds no references at all to his own spiritual attainments, whatever those may have been. This is no accident, for though Schuon certainly wished for his readers to put their trust in God, he was not in the business of soliciting their trust in himself or in promulgating his insights as it were *ex cathedra*. On the contrary, his explicit and often stated aim was to teach his readers "how to think"[54] so that they might

---

52. Bernard Kelly, "Notes on the Light of the Eastern Religions: With Special Reference to the Writings of Ananda Coomaraswamy, René Guénon, and Frithjof Schuon," *Dominican Studies*, Vol. 7 [1954]), 265.

53. To give but one instance, we may quote the distinguished author of the foreword to this anthology: "With the possible exception of His Holiness the Dalai Lama, Frithjof Schuon is the only person I have known who invariably made me feel, on leaving him, that I had been in the presence of a different order of human being" (Huston Smith, *Sophia: The Journal of Traditional Studies*, Vol. 4, No. 2 [Winter 1998], 31).

54. "I have the impression of living in a world where almost no one knows how to think anymore; this does not encourage me to share my thoughts. One of the reasons I write articles is that I hope to influence not only the intelligence but also the soul or sensibility of readers and to teach them how to think" (Letter of 9 September 1970).

come to know God for themselves. As a *shaykh,* Schuon was unquestionably a master to those in his charge, but as an author, he was always careful to maintain the stance of a logician and diagnostician.

Of course, even after the bugbear of authoritarianism has been put to rest, there will remain for many an even greater obstacle: the claim that it is possible for anyone—Schuon or otherwise—truly to know things of a spiritual or supernatural order. The question of whether he himself might have been a "gnostic" or *jnānin* pales to insignificance before the more radical question of whether there really is such a thing as genuine *gnosis* in the first place—whether "spiritual knowledge" or a "science of the Real" is anything more than an idle dream and hence unworthy of the attention of the serious reader.[55] When Schuon tells us that "human intelligence coincides in its essence with certainty of the Absolute,"[56] that "the real and the knowable coincide,"[57] that "everything that exists is inscribed *a priori* in the theomorphic substance of our intelligence,"[58] or that "real knowledge has no history"[59] because it is dependent instead on the sudden and supersensible "grasping of a truth already latent within us,"[60] the testy response of many scholars will no doubt be to say: Did this latter-day Platonist know nothing about the philosophy of the last two or three hundred years? Was he really so naive as to be unaware of what any undergraduate knows, that human knowledge is strictly dependent on sensory experience and irrevocably conditioned by cultural categories? Had he never heard of Kant, to say nothing of the numerous postmodern reminders that we are all in epistemological

---

55. Schuon often uses the term *gnosis* as a synonym for metaphysical knowledge, as in his book *Gnosis: Divine Wisdom*; see below, pp. 14–15, 66. "We say *gnosis* and not 'Gnosticism,' " he clarifies, "for the latter is most often a heterodox mythological dogmatism, whereas intrinsic *gnosis* is not other than what the Hindus mean by *jnāna* and *Advaita Vedānta.* To claim that all *gnosis* is false because of Gnosticism amounts to saying, by analogy, that all prophets are false because there are false prophets" (Schuon, *Roots of the Human Condition* [Bloomington, Indiana: World Wisdom Books, 2002), 10–11). Christian readers of Schuon sometimes balk at this word, but Saint Irenaeus of Lyons, the greatest of the early cataloguers of heresy, made a point of denouncing all "*gnosis* falsely so called" (1 Tim. 6:20), which obviously implies the existence of a *gnosis* "rightly so called."

56. *Logic and Transcendence*, ed. James S. Cutsinger (Bloomington, Indiana: World Wisdom, 2009), 49.

57. *In the Face of the Absolute*, 37.

58. See Ch. 6, "Consequences Flowing from the Mystery of Subjectivity," p. 52.

59. *Spiritual Perspectives and Human Facts*, ed. James S. Cutsinger (Bloomington, Indiana: World Wisdom, 2007), 10.

60. Schuon, *Stations of Wisdom*, 15.

bondage—however subtle and unconscious—to our gender, race, social class, period, and climate of opinion?[61]

As a matter of fact Schuon was well aware of such Kantian and post-Kantian "critiques," and much of his work was devoted to exposing the radical inconsistency involved in every such claim to *know* the limits of knowledge. "In times past it was the object that was sometimes doubted," he writes,

> but in our day no one fears the contradiction of doubting the knowing subject in its intrinsic and irreplaceable aspect; intelligence as such is called into question, even "examined," without wondering "who" examines it . . . and without taking account of the fact that philosophic doubt is included in this same devaluation, that it falls with the fall of intelligence, and that at the same stroke all science and philosophy collapse.[62]

It is not my aim in this short introduction to attempt to justify Schuon's position; whatever else one might say about him, this is clearly an author who is able and ready to speak in his own defense, and these opening words of mine are no more than a prelude to letting him do just that in the pages that follow. But perhaps I could venture just a hint as to what this defense will consist in by underscoring the phrase "knowing subject" in the passage above. For Schuon, learning "how to think" means above all learning how to come to grips with the "who" of the subject or self—not just *ab extra* but in its "intrinsic and irreplaceable aspect"; and what this in turn involves is the sudden realization—however demanding and protracted the preparation may prove—that in knowing That which is we must be That which knows. This is what it means to be a gnostic, no more but at the same time no less.

Gnosis thus understood is the prerogative of a faculty that Schuon calls the Intellect and that he describes, following the medieval Christian mystic

---

61. Schuon anticipates these criticisms: "There are few things that . . . 'a man of our times' endures less readily than the risk of appearing naive; everything else can be sacrificed as long as the feeling of not being duped by anything is safeguarded. . . . Those who reproach our ancestors with having been stupidly credulous forget first of all that one can also be stupidly incredulous and second that the self-styled destroyers of illusion live on illusions that exemplify a credulity second to none; for a simple credulity can be replaced by a complicated one, adorned with the arabesques of a reflexive doubt forming part of the style, but it is still credulity. Complication does not make error less false or stupidity less stupid" (See Ch. 3, "Naiveté," p. 23).

62. Schuon, *Light on the Ancient Worlds*, ed. Deborah Casey (Bloomington, Indiana: World Wisdom, 2006), 111. See also "The Contradiction of Relativism" in Schuon's *Logic and Transcendence*.

Meister Eckhart, as "uncreated" and "uncreatable."[63] Largely dormant in most and yet present in all, it is a power of immediate or intuitive discernment, unobstructed by the boundaries of physical objects and unaffected by the limitations of historical circumstance. In contrast with the reason or discursive intelligence, the Intellect enables us to *see* what is so, not as a conclusion conceptually derived from a premise, but with the immediacy of perception—or "combustion" perhaps, to recall Plato's "leaping spark."[64] It is a direct apprehension of being as object by virtue of being as subject, an apprehension that "comes into being" when the mind attends to itself and to what makes it attend, and when in this way it enters into an "other" that is essentially inward, there to know God. But not just any God or God in any mode: To see God truly is to see that there is within Him something other than God that "is" God nonetheless, which is our seeing—and which our thinking, even in its most skeptical forms, has involved all along, though we "knew Him not" (John 1:10).

Schuon's ultimate goal was not to promulgate truths in the propositional plural; it was to bring about a direct engagement with Truth in the ineffable singular. To read him otherwise, as if his main interest were in advancing some hermeneutical theory that the rest of us are simply obliged to accept or as if his insights were tied to certain formulations of language whose incompleteness or fragility the suspicious postmodernist may eventually hope to expose, is to misinterpret the evident authority of his work and to misconstrue virtually every sentence he wrote. "Every doctrine," Schuon readily admits—and this clearly includes even that of the gnostic—"is only error when confronted with the divine Reality in itself, but a provisional, indispensable, salutary 'error,' containing and communicating the virtuality of Truth."[65]

63. Eckhart: "There is something in the soul [*anima*] which is uncreated and uncreatable; if the whole soul were such, it would be uncreated and uncreatable, and this is the Intellect [*Intellectus*]" (as quoted in the papal Bull *In agro dominico* [1329]). According to Schuon the Intellect amounts to a microcosmic revelation, even as Revelation is a macrocosmic intellection.

64. *Epistle VII*, 341d. As Schuon writes, "When the heat produced by rubbing two pieces of wood together—or by a lens capturing a ray of sunshine—reaches the precise degree that is its culminating point, a flame suddenly bursts forth; in just the same way intellection, as soon as the mental operation is capable of supplying an adequate support, instantly grafts itself onto this support" (see Ch. 17, "Modes of Spiritual Realization," p. 162).

65. *Spiritual Perspectives and Human Facts*, 173. This is an important key to understanding the nature of the author's mode of argument, and it provides one response to the critic mentioned above who complained of Schuon's "contempt for human reason" (see footnote 4). As Schuon notes elsewhere, "Logic is nothing other than the science of mental coordination, of rational conclusion; it is therefore unable to reach the universal and transcendent by its own means; a supra-logical—but not 'illogical'—dialectic based on symbolism and analogy, and thus descriptive rather than ratiocinative, may be more difficult for some people to assimilate, but it conforms more closely to transcendent realities" (*Les Stations de la sagesse* [Stations of Wisdom] [Paris: Buchet et Chastel, 1958], 23).

THIS BOOK

There are a number of ways to navigate the landscape of Schuon's work. In an earlier volume devoted primarily to his writings on spirituality,[66] I chose to focus on four key elements—truth, prayer, virtue, and beauty—which he himself repeatedly emphasized in his unpublished "Book of Keys"[67] and which constitute the essential ingredients of the *Religio Perennis*. According to Schuon, truth must be the starting point of one's journey toward God, prayer is its motive force, and virtue and beauty are the inward and outward fields through which the journey proceeds. "Metaphysical truth, a life of prayer, moral conformity, interiorizing beauty: This is the essential, and this is our message."[68]

In the present anthology the horizon has been considerably broadened so as to provide a more complete picture of the full scope of topics addressed in Schuon's writings, both published and private. I have given priority to selections that are relatively short in order to make the collection as accessible as possible and to keep certain of his most important and recurrent themes and ideas front and center. Some chapters in the author's published corpus run to nearly forty pages—clearly too long if one is also seeking both balance and range—and I was reluctant to reduce these longer pieces to a more manageable size, especially since Schuon's articles are in many cases "small independent treatises, which often summarize the entire doctrine."[69] Respecting his decisions as to the integrity and length of his published chapters seemed the wiser course. It is important to add that these "treatises" were typically prompted by questions posed by Schuon's disciples

66. James S. Cutsinger, *Advice to the Serious Seeker: Meditations on the Teaching of Frithjof Schuon* (Albany, New York: State University of New York, 1997).

67. See above, p. xvii, note 9.

68. Letter of September 1992. Accentuating the metaphysical element, Schuon summed up his perspective this way: "Our position is well known: It is fundamentally that of metaphysics, which is by definition universalist, 'dogmatist' in the philosophical sense of the term, and traditionalist; it is universalist because it is free from all denominational formalism; 'dogmatist' because it is far from all subjectivist relativism—we believe that knowledge exists and is a real and efficacious adequation; and traditionalist because the traditions are there to express—in a variety of ways and yet unanimously—this quintessential position, which is at once intellectual and spiritual and which in the final analysis is the reason for the existence of the human spirit" (*Du Divin à l'humain: Tour d'horizon de Métaphysique et d'Epistémologie* [From the Divine to the Human: Survey of Metaphysics and Epistemology] [Paris: Le Courrier du Livre, 1981], 7–8).

69. Schuon's own assessment, from the foreword to his book *The Play of Masks*, vii.

and other spiritual inquirers and are therefore largely occasional in nature; this being so they need not be read in any particular order.[70]

The chapters featured in the first section are focused on the topic of religion and tradition. Here Schuon has been given the opportunity to defend and develop several of his most important teachings concerning the supernatural origin, salvific necessity, and "transcendent unity" of the world's religions. He explains in the opening chapter—to single out just one idea of special importance to the perennialist perspective—that "the sense of the absolute is not grafted onto exactly the same organic element in one religion as it is in another";[71] for this reason commonalities or correspondences between the traditions are not to be sought, or not at least necessarily, in the same relative place or position. To cite a classic example—first articulated by Schuon himself but subsequently borrowed by many scholars—it would be a mistake to suppose that Muhammad is to Islam what Christ is to Christianity simply because they are both founders or messengers, and it would likewise be a mistake to suppose that the Bible is to Christianity what the Koran is to Islam simply because they are both sacred texts. On the contrary, Christ is to Christianity what the Koran is to Islam, for each is a manifestation of the uncreated *Logos* or Word of God. As for Muhammad, his role in Islam is analogous to that of Mary in Christianity, for his illiteracy and her virginity made each a pure medium or vehicle for divine revelation.[72] The chapters of this opening section also serve to highlight Schuon's traditionalist emphasis on the importance of religious orthodoxy in providing the essential framework for an authentic esotericism; as he insisted again and again, "It is impossible to approach God or the Absolute or the Self without the blessing and aid of Heaven."[73]

---

70. As the author himself once noted, "There are two ways of reading a book: Either the reader begins at the beginning and continues patiently to the end, or else he freely chooses the chapters that immediately arouse his interest" (*Esoterism as Principle and as Way*, trans. William Stoddart [London: Perennial Books, 1981], 9). Schuon encouraged his audience to opt for the second possibility if they wished, and I am glad to do the same.

71. See Ch. 1, "The Sense of the Absolute in Religions," p. 5.

72. *À propos* revelation, here is one further example of the "level" of correspondence Schuon discerns between traditions: "The Buddha wished at first to keep the Revelation—or corresponding Knowledge—to himself, and it was only after the thrice repeated insistence of the Gods that he decided to communicate it; this initial hesitation is profoundly symbolic, for it manifests an aspect of the revelatory process itself, as does the breaking of the first Tables of the Law on Sinai" (*L'Œil du cœur* [The Eye of the Heart] [Paris: Dervy-Livres, 1974], 83).

73. See Ch. 19, "The Nature and Function of the Spiritual Master," p. 172.

The second section is devoted to the perennial philosophy. Here the reader will find selections representative of the author's metaphysical and epistemological teachings. Worthy of special note is the distinctively Schuonian conception of *Māyā in divinis*—"relativity in God"—as well as the closely related idea of the "relative Absolute." According to Schuon, the divine Principle embraces two distinct levels. The higher is the Absolute as such, which transcends every possible category and is thus "Beyond-Being"; in Hindu terminology this is *Para-Brahma* or *Brahma nirguna*. The lower is the "relative Absolute," a distinct level within God Himself which, though absolute in relation to creatures, is nonetheless relative in relation to the pure Absolute; in Schuon's lexicon this is "Being" or the personal God, corresponding to the Hindu *Apara-Brahma* or *Brahma saguna*. The presence of *Māyā in divinis* or "relativity in God" is crucial for both cosmology and theodicy, according to Schuon, for without this idea one can explain neither why there is a world nor why that world contains evil. Other topics discussed in this section include the miracle of intelligence; the Greco-Hindu idea of "universal manifestation" as contrasted with the Semitic idea of creation; the Pythagorean symbolism of principial numbers; differences between philosophy, theology, and *gnosis*; and the relationship between knowledge, faith, love, and the *religio cordis* or religion of the heart.

The third section highlights Schuon's perspective on human nature and destiny. What does it mean to say that human beings were created in God's image and likeness? What are the respective "messages" of the male and female bodies? Given that men and women are equally "theomorphic," how are we to account for the misogyny of early Buddhism? How does the human form differ from that of animals, and in what ways does Darwinism fall short in explaining our distinctive nature? What is the difference between intellection and ratiocination, and what is the justification for saying that within the Intellect "resides the mystery in which knowing is being and being is knowing"? What is the meaning of the Sufi concept of *fitrah* or "primordial norm," and how is it related to "intrinsic morality," which is the law of right action implicit in the ethical teachings of all the major traditions? These are just a few of the questions Schuon will address in these chapters. Of particular interest is his perennialist effort to reconcile the eschatologies of the world's religions. Borrowing both Western and Eastern terminology—and drawing "from human subjectivity all the immediate and far-reaching consequences it implies"[74]—the author distinguishes five possible outcomes of human life on earth: Paradise, "limbo–lotus," purgatory, "limbo–transmigration," and hell.

---

74. See Ch. 12, "Universal Eschatology," p. 116.

In the fourth section we turn to some of Schuon's observations concerning sacred art and symbolism. It would be difficult to exaggerate the significance of aesthetic intuition for this author, and equally difficult to overstate its importance as a corrective to the characteristically modern idea that beauty is merely subjective or relative. Often citing the *hadīth* "God is beautiful, and He loveth beauty," Schuon taught that the "Beauty of God corresponds to a deeper reality than His Goodness"[75] and that the beauty one finds in virgin nature and sacred art is theophanic in character—no less than a divine revelation for those with the discernment to recognize what he called the "metaphysical transparency of phenomena."[76] The chapters included here treat a wide range of subjects, among them the principles of traditional art, the errors of naturalism, the meaning of dreams, the relationship between symbols and initiatic rites, and ways of distinguishing among the various degrees of Reality—from the Absolute as such to matter. Also discussed are the criteria necessary for judging the authenticity of visions, auditions, divinations, healing powers, and other miraculous phenomena.

Finally, the fifth section introduces a few of the author's key teachings on spirituality. Here my aim is to highlight the operative or methodic side of his perspective, aptly summed up in his maxim that "the unicity of the divine Object requires the totality of the human subject."[77] As discussed earlier, Schuon was adamant that the Truth should be lived and not merely thought about, and that in order to live it fully and faithfully we must accept the theological doctrines, follow the moral precepts, and engage in the spiritual practices of one of the world's orthodox religious traditions. Human beings are temperamentally different, however, and when it comes to spiritual practice what may be best or most appropriate for one type of person is not necessarily so for another. The author was therefore keenly interested in the relationship between temperament and spiritual discipline, and in the opening and closing chapters of this section he borrows from the Hindu tradition in distinguishing three possible paths—those of knowledge

---

75. See Ch. 13, "The Question of Forms in Art," p. 124.

76. Schuon speaks of being spiritually overwhelmed as a young boy by a statue of the Buddha in a Basle museum: "Our first encounter—intense and unforgettable—with Buddhism and the Far East took place in our childhood before a great Japanese Buddha of gilded wood, flanked by two images of Kwannon. Suddenly faced with this vision of majesty and mystery, we might well have paraphrased Caesar by exclaiming: *veni, vidi, victus sum*" ["I came, I saw, I was conquered"] (*Treasures of Buddhism* [Bloomington, Indiana: World Wisdom Books, 1993], 8). In his later years he confided to a friend, "I could spend hours visually assimilating the messages of traditional worlds. For me visual assimilation came before conceptual assimilation" (Letter of 8 June 1982).

77. See Ch. 5, "Summary of Integral Metaphysics," p. 48.

(*jñāna-mārga*), love (*bhakti-mārga*), and action (*karma-mārga*)—which he in turn links to three "fundamental" human types: the intellective, the affective, and the volitive. Human differences notwithstanding, Schuon nonetheless insisted that certain virtues and qualities of soul are indispensable for anyone embarking on the spiritual journey, and these he summarized in six "stations of wisdom":[78] purity and detachment, corresponding to the "north" of divine Inviolability; courage and strength, corresponding to the "east" of divine Omnipotence; contentment and simplicity, corresponding to the "west" of divine Peace; trust and compassion, corresponding to the "south" of divine Mercy; veracity and effacement, corresponding to the "height" of divine Transcendence; and sincerity and dignity, corresponding to the "depth" of divine Immanence. Also in this section is a very important chapter on spiritual guidance and the role of the spiritual master.

Following the chapter selections, readers will find an appendix featuring a variety of previously unpublished materials. These have been garnered from several private sources, including the author's "Book of Keys," his personal memoirs, and his letters.[79] Among the many topics considered here are Schuon's own early search for a master and his entry into Islam; the relationship between the *Religio Perennis* and particular religious traditions; the absence of method in the teaching of the great Hindu saint Sri Ramana Maharshi; the symbolism of chess; the principal stages of life and the steps one should take in order to age well; the relationship between laughter and spiritual dignity; matrimonial fidelity and the Adamic androgyne; why Schuon was not only a writer but also an artist, and why he chose to paint Pte San Win—the White Buffalo Calf Woman—bringing the sacred pipe to the Sioux;[80] the errors of the Mahesh Yogi movement; the sense in which Christ's Incarnation bestows a "universal blessing," and the sense in which it does not; the status of the ego or individuality in a *jīvan-mukta*; how to assess whether someone is a genuine spiritual master; Dante, Shakespeare, and the difficult art of writing poetry; the necessity of

---

78. See Ch. 20. These same "stations" provide the organizational structure for *A Treasury of Traditional Wisdom* (Louisville, Kentucky: Fons Vitae, 2000), a compilation of quotations from the sacred texts and spiritual authorities of the world's religions, assembled by one of Schuon's long-time associates, Whitall N. Perry.

79. Throughout his life Schuon carried on an extensive correspondence with scholars, religious leaders, and spiritual seekers from a variety of religious backgrounds and from all over the world, and his responses to their questions often contained the seeds of ideas that were later developed into published articles and chapters.

80. See "The Descent of the Sacred Pipe," the sixth print in the color gallery of Schuon's art (following p. 152); see also Frithjof Schuon, *The Feathered Sun: Plains Indians in Art and Philosophy* (Bloomington, Indiana: World Wisdom Books, 1990).

hell and the meaning of the unforgivable "sin against the Holy Spirit"; why the ancients preferred a geocentric cosmology even though they knew about heliocentrism; how to overcome the six principal illnesses of the soul; the importance of a traditional affiliation with a living religion; why Schuon was critical of ecumenical and interfaith dialogue; the spiritual importance of correct grammar and diction; Maryam (the Virgin Mary) as a type of the inward soul; the paradoxical actions of the pure pneumatic; and which form of Buddhism is best for a Western seeker. A number of selections deal either as a whole or in part with the practice of Invocation—whether in the form of Sufi *dhikr*, Hindu *japa*, Buddhist *nembutsu*, or the Christian Jesus Prayer or other "prayer of the heart." The rhythmic repetition of one of the revealed Names of God was for Schuon the "quintessential orison," and he regarded this practice as the most suitable form of contemplative discipline for men and women today.

In order to provide a clearer picture of the depth and variety of the author's concerns and capacities, I have included a few examples of his artwork as well as a sampling of his late German verse in English translation. Although Schuon was always careful to specify that he was a metaphysician and not an artist, his paintings and drawings nonetheless serve as an important complement to his writings, conveying as they do the same sense of the sacred—the same intuition of beauty as "the splendor of the true," to use one of his own most characteristic expressions. He was particularly fascinated by the beauty and spiritual significance of the human form, and the images featured here accentuate this fact while at the same time reflecting his interest in a wide range of traditional worlds, including those of Islam, Christianity, Hinduism, and especially the Plains Indians.[81] As for the art of painting with words, Schuon wrote poetry throughout his life, beginning in his native German when he was still a young boy, and later in both Arabic and English. In his final years, between 1995 and his death in 1998, he returned to German, composing approximately 3,500 "didactic" poems (*Sinngedichte*) in that language, and it has been remarked that these are in many ways "musical" syntheses or summaries of key ideas in

81. "What I seek to express in my paintings—and indeed I cannot express anything other—is the Sacred combined with Beauty, thus spiritual attitudes and virtues of the soul. And the vibration that emanates from the paintings must lead inward" (from a letter, quoted in the editor's introduction to *Images of Primordial and Mystic Beauty: Paintings by Frithjof Schuon*, ed. Michael Pollack (Bloomington, Indiana: Abodes, 1992), 4. Schuon's artwork included approximately two hundred oil paintings as well as many sketches and drawings. Although the earliest of the color images presented here, "Maghreb," dates from the 1930s, he regarded his later work, which was focused primarily on scenes from Plains Indian life and on the celestial Feminine, as more mature and "essential."

his earlier metaphysical prose. The poems included here, each linked more or less thematically to the chapter that follows, have been taken from two bilingual collections of this late German verse, *Songs for a Spiritual Traveler* and *Adastra & Stella Maris*.[82]

In translating the prose selections in this volume from the author's original French, I have tried to respect his own explicit rules and admonitions as set forth in a chapter called "On the Art of Translating."[83] Schuon was well aware of the fact that this delicate art always involves something of a balancing act, in which fidelity to the original language and clarity in the language of translation frequently pull the translator in opposite directions. He insisted that a "translation ought to be literal to the extent that it can be," but at the same time he warned against "an over-accentuation of the style at the expense of the thought." Most pointedly for our purposes here, he noted that "a French author is not supposed to be an Englishman," and yet he was quick to add that when a given French idiom or syntactical construction is rendered into English the translator must be certain that it remains "perfectly understandable."[84]

With these strictures in mind, I have endeavored wherever possible to follow the literal flow of Schuon's wording so as to preserve its characteristic cadence, tone, and texture. But when faced with difficult choices, my approach has been to err on the side of clarity, privileging the message itself over its original linguistic form. Although I have benefited greatly from the efforts of previous English translators, including Lord Northbourne, G. E. H. Palmer, Gustavo Polit, William Stoddart, and Peter N. Townsend, I have felt obliged to depart from them in significant ways whenever I sensed that their decisions had resulted in unnecessary complication, turgidity, or confusion or in misleading associations. Everyone agrees about the importance of allowing Schuon's distinctive "voice" to be heard; my goal has been to do precisely that while at the same time ensuring that each and every sentence makes good sense to the English-speaking reader.

A word or two should be added, finally, concerning my notes and glossary. The breadth of Schuon's erudition can be somewhat daunting, even for the seasoned scholar. The pages of his books contain numerous

82. See the Bibliography of Works by Frithjof Schuon, p. 286.

83. In *To Have a Center* (Bloomington, Indiana: World Wisdom Books, 1990).

84. *To Have a Center*, 149, 150, 152. In this same chapter the author calls attention to yet another balancing act: While precedence should be given to "simple, concrete, and everyday words," one must beware of watering down difficult ideas and thus becoming "an accomplice of the democratic and demagogic destruction of language" (151). As usual Schuon pulls no punches: "A thought ought to maintain its level: A book addressed to readers that are intelligent does not have to be 'adapted' for foreign readers who are not" (153).

allusions to traditional theological doctrines, important philosophers and spiritual authorities, and the sacred scriptures of the world's religions, but a citation or other reference is seldom provided. A series of translator's notes, organized by chapter and keyed to the relevant page numbers, has therefore been included near the end of this volume: Dates are given for historical figures, brief explanations are offered as to the significance of their teachings in relation to the points Schuon is making, and chapter and verse sources are indicated for his frequent quotations from and allusions to the Bible, Koran, and other sacred texts. The Authorized (King James) Version of the Bible, his preferred English translation, has been used throughout; since Schuon made his own translations from the Koran, I have chosen to render his French for these passages directly into English, though the Pickthall interpretation of the Arabic has been used when Koranic quotations appear in my notes. As new readers will quickly discover, it was customary for Schuon to employ a number of technical terms in his writings, drawn from a multitude of religious traditions and involving several languages, including Sanskrit, Arabic, Greek, and Latin, and he sometimes makes use of these terms in rather surprising ways, independently of their traditional contexts. A glossary has therefore been provided as well; textbook translations of foreign terms and phrases are given, but where appropriate I have also included somewhat more detailed explanations in an effort to convey at least something of Schuon's own specific usage.

*
* *

I have tried to be as frank as I can about the difficulties as well as the benefits presented by Schuon's perspective. My goal of course is to persuade not dissuade—to pique curiosity and not merely raise hackles—and I shall be disappointed if these opening hints as to this author's significance, subtlety, and scope have failed to attract at least a few adventurous readers. In bringing this introduction to a close I would like to extend a special invitation to three groups of such readers in particular—groups that clearly overlap in a variety of important ways.

First are proponents of interfaith dialogue. It seems to me obvious that anyone interested in promoting understanding between religious believers will find Schuon invaluable. This should prove especially true for those interlocutors who have grown dissatisfied with the reductionist tenor of the current conversation—its tendency to force the religions into a Procrustean bed of scientistic assumptions and liberal social platitudes—and who are therefore open to the prospect of an ecumenism that is at once deeply esoteric and yet fully traditionalist. In pondering the insights of Schuon the *perennialist,* they will gradually begin to discern a transcendent unity among the world's religions while at the same time respecting and safeguarding the revealed integrity of their immanent or exoteric forms.

Second are my fellow academics. Anyone who studies religion stands to learn from this author, but the scholars whom I most have in mind—and their numbers increase every day—are those who have found themselves wondering whether there might be an intellectually respectable way of bridging the divide between their personal religious commitments, which they have been trained to keep private, and their public work as historians, philosophers, social scientists, and critical interpreters of texts. Such an audience cannot but profit from its encounter with Schuon the *shaykh,* a man who realized that spiritual methods are considerably more rigorous than their scientific counterparts and whose religious affiliation and contemplative discipline made him a more, and not less, scrupulously objective thinker.

Third and finally are spiritual "seekers." Here I include anyone who has ever been told that intelligent people no longer talk about Truth but who has nonetheless been unable to shake the conviction that there must be something More, something *knowably* More. As a university professor for more than thirty years, I have repeatedly witnessed the disheartening effects of academic skepticism, and I confess to having a special affection and sympathy for this disillusioned multitude. If they will give the admittedly demanding work of Schuon the *gnostic* the attention it requires and deserves, I promise them that he will provide in abundance precisely the resources they need for constructively doubting the fashionable doubts of our day and calling the bluff on de-mythologizers and debunkers of every size and stripe.

Needless to say, I would be delighted if the doubters and debunkers themselves would take this book in hand and submit themselves to some Schuonian dialectic. What I can promise *them* is that their minds will be stretched in ways they had never imagined.

ACKNOWLEDGMENTS

Numerous people have contributed to making this a better book than I could have possibly managed with my own meager resources.

My primary debt of gratitude is to the author of the foreword. Indeed without Huston Smith there might have been no book at all, for it was he who first brought Schuon's name to my attention—over three decades ago, at the annual meeting of the American Academy of Religion in 1980, my first year in the profession. Professor Smith has been a wise and generous friend in countless ways ever since, and I am delighted to have this opportunity to acknowledge his many kindnesses.

I would also like to express my sincere thanks to Michael Fitzgerald, together with his entire staff at World Wisdom, publisher of several of my new editions of Schuon's books; without his encouragement, support, and personal example my scholarly work would have taken a very different and much less spiritually rewarding turn. Special words of appreciation also go to Mark Perry, whose assiduous reviews and critiques of my work, here and elsewhere, have resulted in much more faithful and compelling translations; to Clinton Minnaar, whose eagle-eye proofreading has always struck me as little short of miraculous; and to Judy Fitzgerald, for her invaluable help in selecting and preparing the examples of Schuon's artwork.

In my quest to bring Schuon's work to the attention of a wider readership, I have been greatly assisted—over the course of many years—by the insights and criticisms of numerous students, colleagues, friends, and family members, including Michael Allen, Christopher Bamford, Jordan Bissell, Mark Bonadio, Steven Boyer, William Chittick, Leah Cutsinger, Father Cassian Dunlop, Waleed El-Ansary, Antoine Faivre, Robert Fastiggi, Joseph Fitzgerald, John Granger, Veena Howard, Peter Kreeft, Jean-Pierre Lafouge, Patrick Laude, Father Mark Mancuso, Richard McCombs, Barry McDonald, Terry Moore, Seyyed Hossein Nasr, Jean-Claude Petitpierre, Scott Reeves, Joshua Robinson, Vincent Rossi, Catherine Schuon, Reza Shah-Kazemi, Carl Still, William Stoddart, Marco Toti, Charles Upton, and David Weddle.

These acknowledgments would not be complete if I failed to mention, finally, those among my Schuonian mentors and friends who have passed beyond this life, especially Martin Lings, Alvin Moore Jr., and Whitall N. Perry. *Aiōnia ē mnēmē.*

To all these spiritual and intellectual benefactors, and to others I may now be forgetting to name, my sincerest thanks.

Permission to use and quote from hitherto unpublished written documents and to reproduce copyrighted paintings, sketches, and photographs has been kindly granted by World Wisdom, Inc.

—James S. Cutsinger

Frithjof Schuon in 1965

The Gift

The splendor of the true, it is said, is in the beautiful,
Which wants to manifest the depth of wisdom;
Yet beauty also strives toward truth—
It lies in its nature to yearn for light.

The fair Queen of Sheba journeyed
To the wise King of the Hebrews:
"Thou, wise man, give me what thou knowest of God—
I shall give thee all I am."

Truth pours out God's nectar for us.
We owe it everything—our very being.

PREFACE

It has often been said, and most justly, that the ills of our time come from the scission between faith and science; paradoxically, the origins of this scission are to be found in faith itself, at least in its extrinsic and subjective aspect, and this is because faith has not been adequately buttressed by commentaries of a sapiential nature and because in the minds of most people sentimental rather than metaphysical reasons prevail; left outside the purview of faith, the intellectual element—or the need for explanations—was bound in the end to turn against this faith, though "from below" and on a purely rational and material level.

But the scission in question has other causes as well, both subjective and objective. On the one hand the "intellectual worldliness" inaugurated by the Renaissance and Descartes resulted in a weakening of contemplative intelligence and the religious instinct, and on the other hand new factors—inventions and discoveries of every kind—came to profit from this weakening and have seemed to constitute a blatant refutation of the tenets of faith. Modern man seems to be less and less capable of resisting intellectually the suggestiveness of facts which, though belonging to the natural order, lie outside the ordinary and normal experience of human beings; in order to combine the religious symbolism of Heaven and the astronomical fact of the galaxies within one and the same consciousness, an intelligence is needed that is more than just rational—unless one has a faith that is not given to everyone—and this brings us to the crucial problem of intellection and hence to that of *gnosis* and esotericism. All things considered, the hostility of the medieval Church toward the new astronomical theories is explained by this constellation of factors and is justified *a posteriori* in view of the consequences.

But skepticism does not always need the help of a Descartes to implant itself, for Cartesianism would be ineffectual without a soil already prepared to receive it; in fact, given favorable conditions, all "worldliness" provides an opening for the mentality of doubt and the denial of the supernatural. No people, however contemplative they might be, can resist for long the psychological effects of modern science—the difference in this respect between men marked by the Renaissance and the traditional collectivities of Asia and elsewhere is only relative—and this clearly shows how "abnormal" this science is in relation to the basic elements of human nature. Obviously no knowledge is bad in itself or in principle, but many forms of knowledge can be harmful in fact if they do not correspond to man's hereditary habits and are imposed on him without his being spiritually prepared; unless the soul is enlightened with metaphysical knowledge or an impregnable sanctity, it finds it difficult to accommodate facts that nature has not offered to its experience.

This is why traditional doctrines, and above all the Revelations from which they are derived, take full account of collective and "normal" human experience, for this constitutes an indisputable basis since we are in fact human beings; these doctrines provide a comprehensive and qualitative knowledge of the cosmos, while at the same time conveying the idea that this cosmos is as nothing in comparison with the Absolute and that the Absolute in any case eludes the means of investigation of a strictly human knowledge. The same principle—that of the "normal" and "providential" limitation of experience—also applies to art: Art needs the limits imposed by nature, at least insofar as the art in question concerns a collectivity, which by definition is "passive" and "unconscious"; if the resources of machines and the chemical industry are placed at the disposal of a people or their artisans, their art will be corrupted—not of course in all its manifestations but to the extent that it belongs to everyone.

The tragic impasse of the modern mind thus results from the fact that most people are incapable of grasping *a priori* the compatibility between the symbolic expressions of tradition and the material observations of science; these observations lead modern man to want to understand the "why" of everything, but he wants this "why" to be as external and as easy as that of "scientific" phenomena; in other words he wants answers on the level of his own experiences, and since these are purely material, his consciousness is closed in advance to all that goes beyond them.

Modern man is no longer willing to accept the idea of an anthropomorphic and "infinitely perfect" God who created the world "out of goodness" while foreseeing its horrors, and who created man "free" while knowing he would misuse his freedom—a God who, despite His "infinite goodness," would punish man for faults that He, the "omniscient" Creator, could not have failed to foresee. But this is to be quite uselessly hypnotized by the unavoidable defects of anthropomorphic symbolism, a symbolism that is itself unavoidable and that has been proven to be well founded by thousands of years of effectiveness; it is to contend—not without a certain pretentiousness—against ways of speaking which, though doubtless imperfect, are opportune in certain circumstances; and it is to deprive oneself of the truth, even the saving truth, merely for reasons of dialectic.[1]

We would respond to these sophistries by pointing out that the Absolute is not an artificial postulate that can be explained by psychology but rather something "pre-mental," something as self-evident and concrete as the air we breathe or the beating of our hearts; that a non-atrophied intelligence—the pure, intuitive, contemplative Intellect—allows no doubt on this subject, the "proofs" being in its very substance; that the Absolute necessarily assumes more or less human traits in relation to man, without however being intrinsically limited by them; that the possibility of human goodness is a metaphysical proof of divine goodness, which is necessarily limitless in relation to its earthly traces; that the sentimental anthropomorphism of monotheists is what it must be, given the character of the masses to which it is addressed; that in a general way the sacred Scriptures, far from being popular tales, are on the contrary highly "scientific" books by virtue of their polyvalent symbolism, which is at once cosmological, metaphysical, and mystical; and that when man trusts in his reason alone, he ends up unleashing the dark and dissolving forces of the irrational.

The Vedantic and Buddhist solution, which avoids the dilemmas posed by anthropomorphism, is certainly unsuited to the monotheistic collectivities; and yet by a tragic paradox some answer of this nature has become indispensable in order to satisfy the need for explanations found within these same collectivities once they have lost the religious instinct and begun wrestling with the logical contradictions that anthropomorphism inescapably entails. Of course, such an answer or solution is necessarily found in the West as well, but it takes a form that is in general too indirect to be capable of explaining the contradictory elements in anthropotheist symbolism in a way that can be understood by the majority of believers; as for most modern "intellectuals"—to speak without euphemism—they are not intelligent enough to understand writers like Saint Anselm or Saint Thomas Aquinas, that is, to understand them in depth and to find in their writings evidence of God. The darkening of our world—whether one means the West properly so called or its ramifications in the East and elsewhere—is clearly apparent in the fact that an extreme mental dexterity goes hand in hand with a no less excessive intellectual superficiality. It has become habitual

1. As Saint Peter clearly foresaw: "Knowing this first, that there shall come in the last days scoffers, walking after their own lusts, and saying, Where is the promise of his coming? for since the fathers fell asleep, all things continue as they were from the beginning of the creation" (2 Peter 3:3–4).

to treat concepts as if they were playthings of the mind, committing one to nothing; in other words nothing is left untouched, and yet nothing is assimilated. Ideas no longer bite into the intelligence, which glides over concepts without taking time to really grasp them. The modern mind skims the surface, all the while toying with mental images but without knowing their possibilities and function, whereas the traditional mind proceeds in depth, whence come doctrines that may seem merely "dogmatic" but that are fully sufficient and effective for anyone who knows what a doctrine is. Contemporary man has lost the sense of repose and contemplation, and living on husks he no longer realizes what fruit is.

One of the great errors of our time is to speak of the "failure" of religion or religions; this is to blame the truth for our refusal to accept it, and by the same token it is to deny man both liberty and intelligence. Intelligence depends in large measure on the will, hence on free will, and this is because free will can help to actualize the intelligence or on the contrary to paralyze it. It was not without reason that medieval theologians located heresy in the will. Intelligence can in fact fall into error, but its nature does not allow it to resist truth indefinitely; for this to happen a volitional factor must intervene—or more precisely a passional factor, namely, prejudice, sentimental bias, individualism in all its forms. There is an element of irrational "mystique" at the root of every error, a tendency not deriving from concepts but making use of them or producing them; behind every restrictive or subversive philosophy can be discerned a "taste" or "hue"; errors proceed from "hardenings," forms of dryness, and intoxications.

Far from proving that modern man "keeps a cool head" and that the men of old were merely dreamers, modern "nonbelief" and "exact science" are to be explained all told by a wave of rationalism—sometimes apparently "anti-rationalist"—which reacted against the religious sentimentalism and bourgeois Romanticism of the previous era; indeed rationalist and Romantic tendencies have existed side by side since the so-called Enlightenment. The Renaissance also knew such a wave of "false lucidity," and like our age it rejected truths along with "outworn" sentimentalities, while nonetheless replacing them with new sentimentalities that were supposedly "intelligent." To understand these oscillations properly one must remember that Christianity, as a path of love, was opposed to pagan rationalism and that it therefore placed emotional elements having a spiritual quality in opposition to the implacable but "worldly" logic of the Greco-Romans, while in time absorbing certain sapiential elements which their civilization contained.

The essays assembled in this volume do not give systematic solutions to the problems we have just outlined, but they do contribute to the answer we have endeavored to provide in all our works. At a time when the revealed forms of the spirit are threatened as much by the thoughtlessness of man as by a preconceived hostility, it is essential to place the truths by which man has always lived and should continue to live within a sapiential setting; if there is an "exact science" embracing all things, it resides above all in a consciousness of the realities underlying both traditional symbols and fundamental virtues, for these are nothing less than the very "splendor of the true."

I

RELIGION AND TRADITION

Tradition is not a childish and outmoded mythology but a science that is terribly real.

—*Understanding Islam*

Sanctuaries

Prayer in stone: such is the tall cathedral,
Long, solemn, and dark within—
A window, breaking the light into sheaves of color;
Devotion, motionless before golden images.

Islam's house of prayer, imageless and plain—
Piety's face is turned toward Mecca;
Side by side, in rows, men stand and pray,
In the perfume of faith and submission to God.

O sanctuary of virgin nature:
No stone, no carpet, only forest and field,
Mountain peaks, sun, and deep night—
And all throughout, the power of the All-Highest.

A sanctuary that God has given us:
It is not far, it is closest life;
Where are the heights where the gods are enthroned?
In man's body the Godhead wants to live.

1

THE SENSE OF THE ABSOLUTE IN RELIGIONS

The world's religions are separated from one another by barriers of mutual incomprehension. One of the principal reasons for this incomprehension is that the sense of the absolute is situated in each case on a different plane so that points of comparison often prove illusory. Elements resembling one another in form appear in such diverse contexts that their function changes from one religion to another, and their nature therefore changes as well to some extent. This diversity results from the fact that the infinitude of the possible excludes strict repetition. The sufficient reason finally for a "new" phenomenon from the point of view of the manifestation of possibilities is its difference in relation to "antecedent" phenomena. Worlds are not made for one another, and the cause of their particularities is also the cause of their diversity, hence of their reciprocal exclusion.

We might simply take note of this situation and leave each religious world to speak in its own language without trying to show that this language is precisely one among others, but we live in an age when the interpenetration of civilizations gives rise to many problems—not new, it is true, but singularly timely and urgent—and when the diversity of traditional perspectives gives a convenient pretext to those who wish to destroy the very idea of the absolute and the values connected to it. Confronted with a relativism that is growing ever more intrusive, it is necessary to restore to the intelligence a sense of the absolute, even to the point of having to underline for this purpose the relativity in which immutable things are clothed.

*

* *

It seems entirely natural for people to generalize the "structure" of their religious convictions. For example, the conviction of the Christian results from the divinity of Christ and in turn from the signs that manifest this divinity, then from Christ's power to save, and finally from the historical character of these various factors; basing themselves exclusively on these criteria and not finding their exact equivalent elsewhere, Christians will see nothing but improbability outside their own spiritual cosmos. Muslims will have the same feeling, of course, though in favor of Islam and for a more or less opposite reason: Whereas in Christianity the center of religion is the "Word made flesh," of which the Church is only the "mystical body," in the Muslim climate it is Islam as such—the divine Law enveloping man and the whole of society—which is of prime importance; here it is a question of "totality" not "center," and the Prophet is not the determining center from which everything flows but the personification of this totality. The accent is placed on the totality and not the spokesman, and it is the divine quality of this totality—this terrestrial crystallization of the celestial Will[1]—together with the inner experience that results from practicing this religion, which gives Muslims their profound conviction; and let us add that the Koran, while being the center or the "Christic" element of the religion, becomes irresistible only through its deployment—*al-islām*—which appears like a system of channels divinely proportioned to receive and direct the flow of the human will. Blessedness for Christians consists in holding fast to the saving divinity of Christ, even to the point of sharing in his cross, but blessedness for Muslims consists on the contrary in opening out into a totality, in "surrendering" (*aslama*, whence the word *islām*) their will to God, in "abandoning" it within the framework of a divine Will that encompasses the whole human personality, from the body to the spirit and from birth to the encounter with God.

If Christianity places God in man through the mystery of the Incarnation, Judaism in turn places man in God through the mystery of the "chosen People." It is impossible to dissociate the God of the Jews from His people; to speak of Jehovah is to speak of Israel, and conversely. The great Revelation of Monotheism, or the great personal manifestation of God, took place in Israel, and it is this "fact," the mystery of Sinai—together with the choosing of this people—which gives to believing Jews their unshakable conviction and constitutes for them that "element of the absolute" without which no religious faith is possible.

For the Christian the overwhelming argument is the divinity of Christ and, flowing from this, the fact that there is an intermediary between God and man in the form of God made man—not forgetting another intermediary, the Mother of God. The argument from divinity presupposes that the value of the message depends on this divinity, whereas the argument from proximity presupposes that God is remote, which is clearly true, although

1. This Will is here conceived as both "divine Word" and "uncreated Book."

not in every respect. Islam starts precisely from the idea that the infinitely transcendent God is at the same time infinitely close—"closer than your jugular vein"—so that in religious experience He surrounds and penetrates us like a sort of luminous ether, if such an imaginative expression is permissible; the only necessary intermediary in this case is our own response, *al-islām*, the central element of which is prayer in all its forms.

The Judaic God was "remote," but He dwelt among His people and sometimes spoke to them; the Christian God—as God-Man—is the "intermediary" between this remote God and man, a God who is thenceforth silent and merciful; as for the God of Islam, He is "near" (*Al-Qarīb*) but without being human. These are not different Gods, of course; it is simply a question of different perspectives and of the "divine attitudes" corresponding to them. God is always and everywhere God, and this is why each of these perspectives is to be found in its own way within the other two; in one mode or another there is always both "remoteness" and "proximity," just as there is always an "intermediary" element.

The sense of the absolute is not grafted onto exactly the same organic element in one religion as it is in another—whence the impossibility of making comparisons between the elements of religions simply from the outside—and this fact can be seen very clearly in the differing natures of conversions to Christianity and Islam. Conversion to Christianity seems in certain respects like the beginning of a great love, making all of a man's past life appear vain and trivial; it is no less than a "rebirth" after "death." But conversion to Islam is like awakening from an unhappy love or like sobriety after drunkenness, or again like the freshness of morning after a night of distress. In Christianity the soul is "freezing to death" in its congenital egoism, and Christ is the central fire that warms and restores it to life; in Islam on the other hand the soul is "suffocating" in the constriction of the same egoism, and Islam appears like the cool immensity of space, which allows the soul to "breathe" and "expand" toward the boundless. The "central fire" is denoted by the cross, the "immensity of space" by the Kaaba, the prayer rug, the abstract interlacings of Islamic art.

In a word, the faith of Christians is a "concentration" and that of Muslims an "expansion" (*bast, inshirāh*), as the Koran explicitly states,[2] but each of these modes is necessarily found somewhere within the framework of the "opposing" perspective. Concentration or "warmth" reappears in Sufic "love" (*mahabbah*), whereas expansion or "coolness" penetrates into Chris-

2. "Have We (God) not expanded [or "opened"] thy breast (O Muhammad) and removed the burden which weighed on thy back?" (*Sūrah* "Solace" [94]:1–3). Again: "He whom God desires to guide, He expands his breast for Islam, and he whom He desires to stray, He constricts his breast and shrinks it" (*Sūrah* "Cattle" [6]:126).

tian *gnosis* and in a more general way into the "peace" of Christ insofar as this peace is the basis of "purity of heart" and contemplation.

To pass from one Asian tradition—Hinduism, Buddhism, or Taoism—to another is perhaps no great matter, for the metaphysical content is everywhere quite apparent and serves to underscore the relative nature of the differences between their various "mythologies." Precisely because of their spiritual transparency, these traditions readily absorb elements of foreign traditions; for example, a Shinto divinity can become a *bodhisattva* without any change of its essence, for the names refer to universal realities. But inside the framework of the three Semitic traditions, a change of religion almost amounts to a change of planet, for in this case the divergent "alchemical positions" must rest on one and the same prophetic and messianic Monotheism, so that the particular form monopolizes the whole man; spiritual keys present themselves as exclusive "facts," for otherwise they risk becoming inoperative, and *gnosis* alone has the right to be aware that a key is a key.[3] What is metaphysically self-evident takes precedence over "physical" or "phenomenal" certainty in cases where such a question can arise; on the other hand certainty with respect to "facts" can never weaken or abolish the self-evidence of principles, the eternal "thoughts" of God.

*

* *

The differences between religions are reflected very clearly in their differing forms of sacred art. Compared with Gothic art, above all in its "flamboy-

3. When one looks closely at the intentions hidden behind the verbal formulations, it is apparent that the rejection of the divinity of Christ by Islam does not mean that the perspective of unity could deny such a fundamental reality, but rather that its intellectual structure rules out the Christian way of expressing it; in other words Islam divides the person of the God-Man into two parts according to the levels to which the two natures belong, and it does so because it considers Being only in its extra-cosmic divinity. This perspective, which cannot fail to take a dogmatic turn, at the same time aims to avoid the danger of a *de facto* "divinizing" of the human individual, that is, the danger of individualist "humanism" with all its consequences; the aim essentially is to counteract the doctrine of "deification." From the Muslim point of view, the saying of Christ, "Before Abraham was, I am," signifies that the *Logos*, the uncreated "Word" of God—hence the Intellect as such—"precedes" in a purely principial way all temporal, even prophetic and primordial, manifestation. As for the Koran's apparent denial of the crucifixion, we have always held that this is a question of theology rather than history, and we have encountered the same point of view in a work of Massignon ("Le Christ dans les Evangiles selon al-Ghazzali"): "Abu Hatim, basing himself on the opinion of one of his masters (who is not named), declares that the beginning of the Koranic verse (4:157) in no way denies the crucifixion and that it must be interpreted in light of its ending, 'and they did not kill him truly (*yaqīnā*). God raised him to Himself,' and, since Jesus died a martyr, in light of the verses on the death of martyrs (2:154; cf. 3:169): 'Do not say of those who have been killed on the path toward God that they are dead: but that they are living; although you are not aware of it.' "

ant" style, Islamic art is contemplative rather than volitive—"intellectual" rather than "dramatic"—and it places the cold beauty of geometrical design in opposition to the mystical heroism of cathedrals. Islam is the perspective of omnipresence ("God is everywhere"), which coincides with that of simultaneity ("Truth has always been"), and it aims to avoid any particularization or "condensation," any "unique fact" in time and space, although as a religion it necessarily includes an aspect of such uniqueness, without which it would be ineffective or even absurd. In other words Islam aims at what is "everywhere center," and this is why—symbolically speaking—it replaces the cross with the cube or the woven fabric; it "decentralizes" and "universalizes" to the greatest possible extent, as much in the realm of art as in that of doctrine, and it is opposed to any individualist knot and hence to any "personalist" mysticism.

To express ourselves in geometrical terms, we could say that a point that seeks to be unique, and that thus becomes an absolute center, appears to Islam—in both art and theology—as a usurpation of the divine absoluteness and therefore as a form of "association" (*shirk*). There is only one center, God, whence the prohibition against "centralizing" images, especially statues; even the Prophet, the human focus of the tradition, has no right to a Christic uniqueness and is "decentralized" by the series of other Prophets. The same is true of Islam and the Koran, which are similarly integrated into a universal fabric and a cosmic rhythm, having been preceded by other religions and other "Books," which they merely restore. The Kaaba, center of the Muslim world, becomes space as soon as one is inside the building; the ritual direction of prayer is then projected toward the four cardinal points. If Christianity is like a central fire, Islam on the contrary resembles a blanket of snow, at once unifying and leveling and having its center everywhere.

*

* *

In every religion there is not only a choice for the will between the hereafter and the here-below but also a choice for the intelligence between truth and error, though there are differences of correlation. Thus Christ is true because he is Savior—whence the importance that the phenomenal or historical element assumes in Christianity—whereas Islam aims to save by beginning with a fundamental distinction (*lā ilāha illā 'Llāh*) which is primarily metaphysical and which constitutes saving Truth. In point of fact, whether one is speaking of Christianity or Islam or any other traditional form, it is always metaphysical truth which—thanks to its universality—determines the real values of things, and because this truth envelops and penetrates everything it contains neither "here-below" nor "hereafter"; only universal essences count, and these are "everywhere and nowhere." On this plane, there is no choice for the will to make, for as Aristotle says, "The soul is all that it knows." This contemplative serenity appears in the abstract freshness of mosques as well as in many Romanesque churches and in certain elements of the best Gothic churches, particularly in the rose windows, which are like "mirrors of *gnosis*" in these sanctuaries of love.

At the risk of repeating ourselves, let us return to certain parallels. If Christianity can be at least partially defined with the help of the words "miracle," "love," and "suffering," Islam will correspond in turn to the triad "truth," "strength," and "poverty." Islamic piety makes one think less of a center filled with a sweet and vivifying warmth—this is the Christian *barakah*—than of a gift presented in a light that is white and fresh; its spiritual means are dynamic rather than affective, though the differences in this realm are doubtless far from absolute. Muslim asceticism has something about it that is dry and of the desert, possessing scarcely any of the dramatic attraction of the asceticism of the West; and yet in its climate of patriarchal poverty there is also a musical and lyrical element, which recreates the Christian climate on a different foundation.

We said above that Islam intends to base itself on the element "Truth"—in other words it places the accent there according to its own point of view and intention—and that it is the impersonal character of this element that "decentralizes" Islamic "mythology." In Christianity, it would seem on the contrary that the divine Reality—manifested by Christ—has precedence over truth, the first being "concrete" and the second "abstract." This is certainly the case when "truth" is reduced to the level of thought, though we should not lose sight of the fact that it is impossible for anyone to know the divine Reality in the absence of metaphysical truth, whatever the degree of his understanding may be. On the other hand the word "truth" is often taken to be synonymous with "reality"—"I am the way, the truth, and the life"—and this is exactly how Islam understands it; at the outset one can have no knowledge beyond the "truth," and this is precisely why we have a right to call "true" what is "real." This terminology is in no way prejudicial to the effective—and eventually "concrete"—quality of our apparently "abstract" knowledge. Be that as it may, the "subjective" manifestation of the Absolute is no less real than its "objective" manifestation: Certainty is nothing less than a miracle.

*

* *

A question that inevitably arises in this context concerns the historicity of the great religious phenomena. Should more confidence be placed in a tradition that presents a maximum of historical evidence? To this the reply must be that there is no metaphysical or spiritual difference between a truth manifested by temporal facts and a truth expressed by other symbols—for example, in a mythological form; the modes of manifestation simply correspond to the mental requirements of different human groups. If certain mentalities prefer empirically improbable marvels to historical "reality," this is because the marvelous—which no religion can do without—signifies transcendence in relation to terrestrial facts; we are tempted to say in fact that the aspect of improbability is the sufficient reason for the marvelous. This unconscious need for feeling the essence of things explains the propensity for exaggeration found among certain peoples; it is like a trace of nostalgia for the Infinite. Miracles are an interference of the marvelous in the sensory realm; whoever admits miracles must also admit the principle of the marvelous as such and even be prepared to tolerate pious exaggeration on a certain plane.

The value of "mythological" marvels and the existence of contradictions between the religions—which do not imply an intrinsic absurdity within a given religion any more than do the internal contradictions found within all religions—each show in their own way that for God truth lies above all in a given symbol's effective power of enlightenment and not in its literalness; and this is all the more evident in that God, whose wisdom surpasses all words, puts multiple meanings into a single expression.[4] An obscurity in expression—whether elliptical or antinomic—often indicates a richness or depth in meaning, and this explains the apparent inconsistencies found in the sacred Scriptures. In this way God manifests His transcendence in relation to the limitations of human logic; human language can be divine only in an indirect way, and therefore neither our words nor our logic are on the level of the divine intention. The uncreated Word shatters created speech while at the same time directing it toward concrete and saving truth.

Must one therefore conclude—on the pretext that principles are more important than phenomena—that a historical basis has in itself less justification from a spiritual perspective than a mythological or purely metaphysical basis? Most certainly not, or not at least insofar as it is a question of symbolism; what is less justifiable, however, is to attribute a significance to this historical basis it should not have or to suppose it can somehow replace the symbolic truth and metaphysical reality it expresses, though even then the importance of historical facts remains intact in relation to sacred institutions. From another point of view it should be noted that a traditional narrative is always true: The more or less mythical features that

4. Just as the blow of a hammer produces a multitude of sparks, so—according to the Cabalists—a single word of the *Torah* contains multiple meanings.

are imposed on the historical life of the Buddha are simply so many ways of expressing spiritual realities it would be difficult to describe otherwise.[5] In cases where the Revelation is most explicitly founded on history, and to the extent this is so, the historical mode is no doubt necessary. In a world that was heir to Jewish "historicism" and Aristotelian empiricism, it was inevitable that Revelation would take the form of an earthly event without the addition of any non-historical symbolism; on the other hand too great an insistence on historicity—not historicity as such—may obscure the metaphysical content of sacred facts or their spiritual "transparency" and can even end, in the form of excessive criticism, by "eroding" history itself and belittling something whose greatness is not understood.[6]

Those who favor rigorous historicity against the mythologies of Asia will no doubt object that historical truth furnishes proofs of the validity of the means of grace; but historical proofs, precisely because they are historical, could never be completely rigorous in this domain, whereas tradition as such, with all it includes in the way of symbolism, doctrine, and sanctity—not to mention other more or less indeterminate criteria—furnishes far more irrefutable proofs of the divine origin and validity of the rites it transmits. A tradition's acceptance of a means of grace—and the effective use of these means in producing sanctity—is in a certain sense a criterion far more convincing than historicity, not forgetting the intrinsic value of the Scriptures. History is often incapable of verification; it is tradition, not criticism, that guarantees it, but it guarantees at the same time the validity of non-historical symbolisms. The present and permanent miracle of tradition nullifies the objection that no man living has been a witness of sacred history, for saints are its witnesses far more than historians; to deny

---

5. The fact that the life of the Buddha—which is historical in its main features, including certain miracles—retraces the myth of Indra does not mean that it is itself a myth, any more than the prophecies concerning Christ invalidate his historical reality. If the Buddha's first steps after Enlightenment were marked by lotuses, this fact belongs to the subtle order and is in no way "unreal."

6. The more or less "democratic" depreciation of the Holy Virgin, sanctioned by Péguy and many others, is one example of this. Another example is the "criticism"—not just "archeological" but even "psychological"—of sacred facts, an error that is poles apart from intellectuality and precludes an understanding of the facts in question. Modern exegesis is only a caricature of ancient hermeneutics, if indeed there remains any relationship at all between them; it consists above all in giving doubts and prejudices the status of dogmas. According to these prejudices, it is "impossible" that a book should have been written prior to a certain date or that a scribe should have copied a book, even a sacred one, without altering it; exaggerated conclusions are drawn from the smallest facts, and the most disproportionate deductions and inductions are allowed even though all the positive data are contrary to these false principles.

tradition as the guarantor of truth amounts in the end to asserting that there are effects without causes.

There is doubtless no truth more "exact" than that of history, but what must be stressed is that there is a truth more "real" than that of facts; the higher reality embraces the "exactness," though the latter is far from comprehending the former. Historical reality is less "real" than the profound truth it expresses and that myths likewise express, and a mythological symbolism is infinitely more "true" than a fact deprived of symbolism. This brings us back to what we were saying above: The mythological or historical value of the marvelous, like the existence of dogmatic antinomies, serves to show that for God truth resides above all in the efficacy of the symbol and not in the "bare fact."

With regard to historicity or its absence, three degrees must be distinguished: mythology, qualified historicity, and exact historicity. We find the first degree in all mythology properly so called as well as in the monotheistic accounts of creation, and the second degree in other "prehistoric" narratives, whether they concern Noah or Jonah or the human *avatāras* of Vishnu.[7] In Judaism rigorous historicity starts perhaps at Sinai; in Christianity it appears throughout the New Testament[8] but not in the apocryphal writings or *Golden Legend*, though the fact that these are not canonical works has earned them a disregard that is quite undeserved, symbolism being an essential vehicle of truth. As for Islam, exact historicity belongs to the life

---

7. In our opinion the non-human *avatāras* belong to mythological symbolism, though one must avoid putting every phenomenon that is contrary to the experience of our millennium into this category. In a related vein we see no logical reason for denying historicity to the loves of the *gopīs*, for if such a symbolism is possible it has a right to exist on the plane of facts; there is something analogous in the case of the Song of Solomon, where the literal meaning, since it obviously exists, retains all its rights; moral interest must not be confused with the truth, which runs through all the levels of Existence.

8. It is true, of course, that there are a number of inaccuracies in the Gospel stories—regarding the "three Mary Magdalenes," for example—and even some contradictory features; what these seem to show us is that sacred things, though situated in time, are nonetheless beyond history. Such irregularities are in no way contrary to the divine Will; they can also be found in sacred art, where they serve as "openings," safeguarding the indefinite flux of life, for every form is inadequate in relation to Heaven. One sees the same thing in the extreme freedom with which the Old Testament is quoted in the New; in crystallizing itself the divine Speech is at the same time reluctant to commit itself to certain "fixations." Be that as it may, simply reading the Gospels is quite enough in our opinion to reduce to nothing all the artificial arguments aimed at ruining the authenticity of the texts. Those who, contrary to tradition, extol the value of "criticism" or "objective analysis" forget the essential, namely intelligence, without which the best of methods is futile. Of course, intelligence is often identified in our day with a critical attitude precisely, as if to doubt a piece of evidence were a sufficient proof of being intelligent.

of the Prophet and his Companions, as well as to those of their sayings (*ahādīth*) recognized by the tradition,[9] but not to stories concerning pre-Islamic Prophets and events; these are woven of symbols that are certainly "exact" but at the same time more or less "mythical," though to take them literally is always to be inspired by their "alchemical" virtue even when a real understanding is lacking.[10]

The historical perspective—with all its importance for a certain level of Christian doctrine—is legitimate only insofar as it can be included within Platonic non-historicity. Christian "personalism" comes from the fact of the Incarnation and then from the "bhaktic" character of Christianity, a character that in no way prevents this religion from containing metaphysics and *gnosis*, for Christ is "the light of the world"; *gnosis* is not for everyone, however, and a religion cannot be metaphysical in its actual form, whereas Platonism can be since it is not a religion. In any case, Christian historicity, which is intimately connected to Jewish historicity, implies no superiority in comparison with other perspectives—nor any inferiority, for that matter, as long as the characteristic in question is situated on the level to which it rightfully belongs.

*

* *

Does the object of faith take precedence over faith itself or does faith take precedence over its object? Normally, it is the object that has precedence over faith since it is what determines faith and provides it with a sufficient reason; but from a certain point of view and in certain cases faith can be

---

9. According to a widespread opinion, almost all the sayings and deeds of the Prophet recorded by the *sunnah* are falsifications produced by certain interested theologians. The psychological improbability of such a hypothesis is ignored, and it seems to be forgotten that the supposed falsifiers were men who believed in Islam and feared hell; no weight is given to tradition or orthodox unanimity, of course, and this proves an ignorance of what is possible in a tradition and what is not; indeed it indicates an essential misunderstanding of what tradition really is. If the Arab mentality is too scrupulous to accept a *hadīth* without knowing the chain of its reporters (*isnād*), still less would its scruples allow it to forge false texts; to pretend the contrary is to admit that there are men who risk damnation by piety. "Woe to them for what their hand has written," says the Koran (*Sūrah* "The Cow" [2]:79). The fact that Muslim traditionalists began very early to denounce certain falsifications only confirms what has just been said.

10. The shock that the Christian suffers from the Koranic version of Biblical stories in no way differs from the shock experienced by the Jew in the face of New Testament quotations from the Prophets; Christians are often strangely forgetful of Jewish exegesis even though it is essential for a proper understanding of the Old Testament and could fill many gaps.

more important than its content and can "force" the gates of Heaven despite the insufficiency of some immediate object of belief. Faith includes two "poles," one objective and dogmatic and the other subjective and mystical; the ideal is perfect faith in an orthodox truth. It is the idea that engenders faith, and the quality of the idea determines the quality of the faith; and yet the often paradoxical and unforeseeable play of universal Possibility sometimes allows the pole "faith" to predominate over the pole "idea"; this is why Tibetans can say that a dog's tooth that is mistaken for a relic and becomes the object of a sincere and ardent faith actually begins to shine.[11] There can in fact be a faith that carries in its very substance the imprint of a truth which ordinary consciousness is more or less unaware of, provided no intrinsic error compromises the quality of its ardor, for it must be of such purity and nobility as will safeguard it from serious errors; faith of this kind amounts to an "existential" intuition of its "intellectual" object. The possibility of a faith that takes precedence over the "ideological" element and compels it, so to speak, to an ultimate surrender of truth presupposes a highly contemplative mentality already freed from many obstacles; furthermore, if the quality of faith can in this way compensate for the precariousness of the idea, the idea must nonetheless appear like a light, however feeble, and not like a darkness; on this plane there are many imponderables.

It is easy to understand the slight respect shown by *bhakta*s, or at least by some of them, toward "word-for-word" exactness in belief or worship if one takes into consideration their "subjectivism"—we do not say their "individualism"—which finds all the criteria of "truth" in the intensity of faith and the negation of the ego; it is true, of course, that such an attitude is not easy to realize in just any sort of traditional climate, unless—apart from all questions of doctrine—one has in mind those simple souls who practice a touching and efficacious devotion to some pious image and who are to be found *sub omni caelo*. We certainly do not wish to confuse naiveté with intrinsic heresy, even when this heresy is passive—and even though, from the point of view of pure truth, every limited concept has a provisional aspect of heresy—for an error as such could never be correct; nonetheless, by virtue of the "exception that proves the rule," there exists in some cases a *de facto* supremacy of the magic of the soul over the correctness of the symbol, and this supremacy must be taken into account if one wishes to grasp every aspect of the eternal interchange between man and God. We are dealing in this case with a possibility that may have to do less with men

11. The story is told of Valmiki, who, invoking the divine name of Rama backward, was saved by his faith. The exaggerated character of this story underlines its intention.

themselves than with the manner in which God sees and judges them. It is the mystery of the "faith that moves mountains" and saves, whatever our ignorance. Be that as it may, a certain reversal of the normal polarity is to be found in all genuine faith in the sense that the object appears at the outset as a "dead letter"; but in this case the normal relationships of things are not affected, for the symbol that is to be assimilated retains all its value.

*

* *

Gnosis or the *philosophia perennis* is the connecting link between the different religious languages. The mode of manifestation of *gnosis* is "vertical" and more or less "discontinuous"; it is like fire and not water in the sense that fire breaks forth from the invisible and can disappear into it again whereas water has a continuous existence; but the sacred Scriptures remain the necessary and unchanging basis, the source of inspiration and the criterion of all *gnosis*.[12] Direct and supramental intellection is in reality a "remembering" not an "acquisition"; intelligence in this realm does not take cognizance of something located in principle outside itself, but all possible knowledge is on the contrary contained in the luminous substance of the Intellect—which is identified with the *Logos* by "filiation of essence"—so that the "remembering" is nothing other than an actualization, thanks to an occasional external cause or an internal inspiration, of an eternal potentiality of the intellective substance. Discernment exists only in relation to the relative even if this relative lies beyond creation and at the very level of Being, and this explains why the Intellect has been compared to a deep sleep untroubled by dreams, though a sleep eminently non-passive and supra-conscious; the Intellect coincides in its innermost nature with the very Being of things,[13] and this is why *gnosis* underscores the profound continuity between the diverse forms of consciousness of the absolute.

---

12. It is said in Judaism that esotericism was revealed by God to Moses in the Tabernacle and then subsequently lost but that wise men were able to reconstitute it, basing themselves on the *Torah*. Whatever may have been the diverse formulations of Christian *gnosis*, the pneumatological mysteries always find their scriptural basis in the New Testament, notably in the prologue to the Gospel of John and in the talk by night with Nicodemus, as well as in the Epistles. As for "eternal life," there are certainly no "second class" faithful, though "in my Father's house are many mansions"; equality before God concerns the "external" fact of salvation and not its possible "internal" modes.

13. It is in this sense that the Gospel can say of the Word-Light—the divine Intellect—that "all things were made by him; and without him was not anything made that was made" (John 1:3).

But why this consciousness at all, some will ask? Because the truth alone makes us free; or better still because there is no "why" with regard to the truth, which is our intelligence, our freedom, and our very being; if it is not, we are not.

Gnosis

Revealed faith speaks to every man;
Secret and difficult is the kernel of wisdom.
Gnosis is not form, nor is it time;
The sage is guided by a hidden star.

In one sense *gnosis* is a part
Of faith, its content finely spun;
And yet the depth of *gnosis* still remains
Beyond the yoke of Pharisaic power.

Who can fathom the word of God's wise men?
I am neither Jew nor Muslim nor Christian,
Rumi said; and my Islam is not
Dogmatic belief; it is that which is.

O light of the heart, shining before the Most High,
Which always was and nevermore shall fade.

2

TWO ESOTERICISMS

The word "esotericism" suggests in the first place the idea of complementarity, of a "half" if one might put it this way. Esotericism is the complement of exotericism, the "spirit" that completes the "letter"; where there is a truth of revelation, hence a formal and theological truth, there must also be a truth of intellection, hence a non-formal and metaphysical truth—not a legalistic or obligatory truth but a truth that flows from the nature of things and that also is vocational since not every man grasps this nature.

But in fact this second truth exists independently of the first; hence it is not a complement or half in its intrinsic reality but only extrinsically and as it were "accidentally." This means that the word "esotericism" designates not only the total truth insofar as it is "colored" by entering a system of partial truth but also the total truth as such, which is colorless. This *distinguo* is not a mere theoretical luxury; on the contrary it leads to extremely important consequences.

Thus esotericism as such is metaphysics, to which an appropriate method of realization is necessarily joined; on the other hand the esotericism of a particular religion—of a particular exotericism precisely—adapts itself to this religion and thereby enters into theological, psychological, and legalistic complexities foreign to its nature, while nonetheless preserving in its secret center its authentic and plenary nature, without which it would not be what it is.

*

* *

The monotheistic Scriptures each manifest an *upāya*, a religious perspective, which is by definition particular and limiting, and more often than not hermeneutics is affected by this perspective; this is not the case, however, for the fundamental formulations—or fundamental symbols—of the religions, which in themselves are not restrictive in any way.

In Christianity the Patristic formula of saving reciprocity is a priceless jewel: "God became man that man might become God"; it is a revelation of paramount importance, of the same rank as Scripture; this may seem surprising, but it is a "paracletic" possibility, examples of which are found—very rarely, it is true—in all traditional worlds. The saying *anā'l-Haqq* of al-Hallaj, which is so to speak the Sufic equivalent of the Vedic *aham Brahmāsmi*, is a case of this kind; al-Hallaj himself affirmed the possibility of post-Koranic sayings situated at the level of the Koran, for which other Sufis did not pardon him, at least not in his time.

In Islam the first *Shahādah*—the affirmation of Unity in the form of the *Yin-Yang*, so to speak, and "the most precious thing that I have brought to the world," according to the Prophet—expresses essential metaphysics in a way that contains no confessional limitation; in Hindu terms we could say that it is the equivalent at once of an *Upanishad* and a *mantra*. The same is true for the second *Shahādah*, which attests to the mission of the Prophet and thereby evokes the mystery of immanence; this it joins to the mystery of transcendence, which is indicated by the first *Shahādah* at least *a priori*, for the first *Shahādah* also contains an "immanentist" meaning.[1]

But there are not only formulas; there are also phenomena of another order, notably human theophanies. As a universal symbol, and from the point of view of an esoteric application, Christ represents first of all the *Logos* in itself and then the immanent Intellect—*aliquid est in anima quod est increatum et increabile*—which both enlightens and liberates; the Blessed Virgin personifies the soul in a state of sanctifying grace, or this grace itself. There is no theophany that is not prefigured in the very constitution of the human being, made as it is "in the image of God," and esotericism aims to actualize the divine element in that mirror of God that is man. Meister Eckhart spoke of immanent sacraments; "congenial" symbols can be supports, he said, no less than sacraments in the proper sense of the word.

Thus it is necessary to distinguish, we repeat, between an esotericism that is largely based on a particular theology and linked to the speculations offered us *de facto* by traditional sources—and it goes without saying that these doctrines or insights can be of the greatest interest—and another esotericism that springs from the truly crucial elements of the religion and, for that very reason, from the simple nature of things; the two dimensions can certainly be combined, and in fact they most often are. To be concrete: Christian esotericism is *de facto* Clement of Alexandria, Origen, Dionysius the Areopagite, and Meister Eckhart, as well as Boehme and his school;[2]

1. We interpret the words "immanent," "immanence," and "immanentism" according to their etymological meaning: *immanens* means "dwelling within." The modern philosophical interpretation, from Spinoza onward, is mistaken; immanence is neither identity, nor negation of transcendence, nor—all the more—epistemological subjectivism.

2. And without forgetting the esotericisms of pre-Christian origin, such as Hermeticism and the craft initiations, or chivalry, whose origin, however, seems uncertain to us.

but it is also, and even above all and *de jure*, the universal truths—and corresponding attitudes—that issue from the doctrinal, ritual, and "phenomenological" foundations of Christianity.

As for hermeneutics, which plays such an important role in the esotericism of Semitic monotheism, respect for given authors or established conventions should not allow us to forget that this science is meant to proceed according to strict rules; Ghazzali and others insist on this. But it is far from the case that this principle has always been followed in a climate of religious and mystical enthusiasm; abuses of interpretation are encountered even in someone like Ibn Arabi and even in the *Zohar*, usually because of an insufficiently restricted *bhakti*. In this domain three modes or degrees should be distinguished: first, an interpretation that springs harmoniously from a given symbolism; second, an interpretation that imposes a heterogeneous symbolism on the literal sense that this sense could not possibly imply; third, an interpretation that is actually contrary to the literal meaning but that profits from the assumption that every word of God, even if it is negative, allows for a positive interpretation—which in the opinion not only of the *ʿulamāʾ* but of many esotericists constitutes a flagrant abuse and a kind of pious perversion.

But let us return to the subject at hand: *Advaita Vedānta* is unquestionably an intrinsic esotericism and as such suffices unto itself; but it is not an esotericism-complement, that is, an esotericism found alongside a religious system of a sentimental character. This does not mean that its place within the economy of the spiritual means of Hinduism is one of complete isolation; beside it there is in fact the bhaktic *Vedānta* of Ramanuja, which corresponds to a religious mysticism in the sense that it is based on a conception of the personal God; as a result it is dualistic and voluntaristic, like the Semitic spiritualities in their general manifestation. But advaitists are the first to acknowledge that *bhakti* corresponds to a degree of the one truth, hence to a necessity, and that it is legitimate for this very reason.

*
* *

Strict and universal esotericism—of the "advaitic" type, so to speak—has always existed in the climate of Semitic monotheism, and necessarily so, and this opinion can be supported by the following arguments. First, if such an esotericism is to be found in every religious climate, it is for the simple reason that there are people everywhere whose nature requires it, people in other words whose intelligence, discernment, and contemplativity are proportioned to pure metaphysics and thus to the corresponding path. Second, if there are no documents proving the more or less traditional existence of this *gnosis*, this is because it was of necessity transmitted orally—apart from certain providential exceptions that are also required in this domain—for *gnosis* is independent of the exoteric systems that can serve as its vehicle, and it therefore inevitably contains certain aspects that are incompatible with them.

It is thus not surprising that from a strictly theological point of view *gnosis* is "enemy number one"; because of its recourse to intellection it seems to make Revelation redundant and even superfluous, which in theological language is called "submitting Revelation to the judgment of reason"; this confusion between reason and intellection—a confusion that is far from disinterested—is altogether typical. Plato's anticipated retort is the following, and it is all the more justified in that religious sentimentalism has had extremely serious consequences—consequences that are at the same time providential since "it must needs be that offenses come": "All force of reasoning must be enlisted in opposing those who try to abolish knowledge or understanding or intelligence while at the same time making dogmatic assertions" (*Sophist*, 249).

Fideist mentalities like to insist that pure intellectuality—which they confuse with the most profane philosophy since they have in mind reason alone—has as its goal and result only "speculations" and "theses," things purely "natural," whereas only religion, according to this perspective, offers "life" and the "supernatural." This is a perfect begging of the question; it is to hold that "life" and the "supernatural" are obtained only outside intelligence; in the final analysis it is to deny that man—who alone is endowed with an intelligence capable of absoluteness—is "made in the image of God."

*

* *

The rationalistic pseudo-*gnosis* of our times represents a backlash against the theological anti-*gnosis* of the first Christian centuries; and this vengeful effect of a distant cause not only comes from without, from the unbelieving world, but is produced within the very bosom of the Church. In fact, two causes combine here: hatred of *gnosis* on the one hand and thirst for novelty and need for change on the other; these are typical features of the creative and adventurous, and in its extreme effects even Luciferian, mentality of the West. This mentality has combined, both providentially and unfortunately, with what we may term Christian "innovationism" and even, although more indirectly, with Jewish Messianism.

Be that as it may, it is neither metaphysical discernment nor contemplativity that is primarily lacking in Europeans but rather a sense of the static, of the principle of immutability—in short, of the "unmoved mover." The "worldliness" of Westerners lies in their inventive hypertrophy—the

Westerner always feels the need to "burn what he has worshipped"—and in their cultural mutability, whereas the "worldliness" of Easterners lies only in the excessiveness of the ordinary passions of body and soul. This is bad enough, of course, for passions becloud the intelligence, whatever the ethnic climate in which they arise and whatever the natural gifts of a particular individual or collectivity.

The point will perhaps be made that a lack of the sense of the Immutable or of an appreciation for static values or functions evinces a corresponding lack of metaphysical intelligence; this is true for the majority—in a manner that is necessarily relative—but it in no way excludes the presence of metaphysics and contemplativity, so that it would be a mistake to conclude that the West possesses nothing in this respect and has everything to learn from the East. It is true that it would be in the greatest interest of the Western elite to draw inspiration from Vedantic doctrine and to assimilate thoroughly the key notion of *Māyā in divinis*, even though this notion is to be found in someone like Meister Eckhart and doubtless also in others in a more or less incidental manner; but in the final analysis intellectuality does not depend on this notion entirely, as is proven by Thomism and Vishnuite *Vedānta*. *Grosso modo*, the West possesses everything essential, but it does not wish to hear of it, and in this consists its drama and absurdity.

Creation's Play

Here is the lion, there the little cat;
Here is the eagle, there the little bird;
Lion and eagle did the Lord create in earnest—
The little animals are like His Smile.

There must be all kinds in the world:
Not only the powerful and nobly beautiful,
But also that which speaks of childhood innocence—
So that the Lord might reconcile us with our fear.

3

CONCERNING NAIVETÉ

Attributing a naive outlook to everyone who lived in the past is the simplest way of exalting oneself. It is all the easier and more tempting because it is founded in part on accurate although fragmentary observations, which can be readily exploited—with the help of exaggerated generalizations and arbitrary interpretations—when linked to a progressivist evolutionism. We must first of all come to some agreement as to what naiveté means. If to be naive is to be direct and spontaneous, to know nothing of dissimulation and subterfuge and doubtless also nothing of certain experiences, then non-modern peoples certainly possess—or possessed—this kind of naiveté; but if it is merely to be without intelligence or critical sense and to be open to all kinds of deception, then there is certainly no reason to suppose our contemporaries any less naive than our ancestors.

Be that as it may, there are few things the insulated being who calls himself "a man of our times" endures less readily than the risk of appearing naive; everything else can be sacrificed as long as the feeling of not being duped by anything is safeguarded. In reality the acme of naiveté is to believe that man can escape from naiveté on every plane and that it is possible for him to be fully intelligent through his own efforts; whoever seeks to gain all things by cleverness ends by losing all in blindness and ineffectuality. Those who reproach our ancestors with having been stupidly credulous forget first of all that one can also be stupidly incredulous and second that the self-styled destroyers of illusion live on illusions exemplifying a credulity second to none; for a simple credulity can be replaced by a complicated one, adorned with the arabesques of a reflexive doubt forming part of the style, but it is still credulity. Complication does not make error less false or stupidity less stupid.

Contrary to the popular image of a hopelessly naive Middle Ages and a breathtakingly intelligent twentieth century, history shows that simplicity of outlook is not abolished but merely displaced and that the most flagrant form of naiveté is not to notice this; there is nothing more simplistic than a pretension to "begin from scratch" on every plane, not to mention the systematic—and unbelievably insolent—self-uprooting that characterizes certain tendencies of the contemporary world. It is fashionable to regard not only the people of the Middle Ages but even those of fairly recent generations as having been duped in every possible way, so that to resemble them would be a cause for embarrassment; in this respect the nineteenth century seems almost as remote as the Merovingian age. Current opinions prove that people think themselves incomparably more "realistic" than anyone has ever been, even in the recent past; "our time" or "the twentieth century" or "the nuclear age" seems to hover like an uprooted island or a fabulously "clear-headed" monad above millennia of childishness and blundering. The contemporary world is like a man ashamed of having had parents and wanting to create himself and to re-create space, time, and all the physical laws or seeking to extract from nothingness a world objectively perfect and subjectively comfortable, and all this by means of a creative activity independent of God or opposed to God; unfortunately, attempts to create a new order of Being can end only in self-destruction.

The average young person of today seems to hold our fathers responsible for every ill; this is a completely absurd attitude, for not only could our fathers reproach their fathers in the same way, and so on endlessly, but there is also nothing to prove that the children of the present-day youth will not one day have solid reasons to level the same reproach at their elders. If these young people declare themselves to be innocent in principle because they have no ideology and are not interested in politics, they forget that a world can go adrift precisely for this reason; a misfortune can come about because someone does something but also because no one does anything. No one is alone in the world, and others take on the job of thinking and acting for those who wish to do neither. Contemporary man has collected a wealth of experiences, which explains a certain measure of disillusionment, but the conclusions he draws are so false that they virtually reduce to nothing all that has been gained or ought to have been gained.

*
* *

A fact that can lead to error, and that is not left unexploited, is the analogy between the childhood of individuals and that of peoples; the analogy is only partial, however, and from a certain point of view the truth is actually just the reverse, for the collectivity is in one respect the opposite—or the inverted image—of the individual. Whereas it is age that normally represents wisdom in individuals, in a traditional collectivity—as well as in humanity considered as a whole—wisdom coincides with the origin, that is, with the "apostolic period" of a civilization and with the "golden age" of humanity in general; on the other hand, just as every civilization declines as it gets further from its origins and nearer the "end times"—humanity as a whole does the same—so the individual declines at least physically with age; and just as the period of Revelation or the "golden age" is a time when Heaven and earth are in contact and when Angels speak with men, so the childhood of the individual is in some respects a time of innocence, happiness, and nearness to Heaven; there is thus a direct analogy between individual life and the cycles of the collectivity but also an inverse analogy that places wisdom at the origin of the life of the collectivity and at the end of the life of the individual. Nevertheless, it is undeniable that an old society has gathered experiences and developed arts—though this is merely an outward expression—and it is precisely this fact that leads to error when the postulates of evolutionism are accepted *a priori*.

There is clearly an important distinction between a naiveté that is intrinsic and one that is extrinsic; an extrinsic naiveté exists only accidentally and in relation to a world that is the product of certain experiences, but it is full of hypocrisy, useless cleverness, and dissimulation; how could a man who is unaware of the existence of falsehood or who knows it only as a deadly and exceptional sin appear as otherwise than ingenuous to a mean-spirited and artful society? To a pathologically crafty person every normal man seems naive; for the swindlers it is the honest people who are artless. Even where a certain critical sense exists, it is far from constituting a kind of superiority in itself, for it is merely an excrescence produced by an environment in which everything is falsified. It is thus that nature produces self-defensive reflexes and adaptations, which can be explained only by a particular environment or prevailing circumstances; there is no difficulty in admitting that the physical particularities of an Eskimo or Bushman do not in themselves constitute a superiority.

If the men of old sometimes appear ingenuous, it is often because they are considered from a distorted point of view, which is the result of a more or less generalized corruption; to accuse them of being naive amounts to applying a law to them retroactively. Likewise, if an ancient writer can give the impression of simplemindedness, this is largely because he did not have to take account of a thousand errors still unknown or a thousand possibilities of misinterpretation, and also because there was no need for his dialectic to be like the Scottish dance between the eggs, for such an author could in large measure dispense with nuances; words still possessed a freshness and fullness—or magic—which it is difficult for us to imagine, living as we do in a climate of verbal inflation.

Naiveté occurring merely from a lack of experience is of course a purely relative affair: Men in general, and collectivities in any case, cannot help being unsophisticated about experiences that they have not had and that involve possibilities they are unable to foresee, and it is easy for those who have had such experiences to sit in judgment regarding the inexperience of others and to believe themselves superior; the worth of men is not decided by their accumulation of experience, however, but by their capacity to profit from it. We may be more perspicacious than others with regard to what we have experienced but at the same time more naive with regard to what we have yet to experience—or what we are incapable of experiencing, whereas others may have done so in our place; for it is one thing to have lived through an event and another to have drawn the right conclusions from it. Playing with fire because one does not know that it burns is no doubt a kind of naiveté, but jumping into a river because one has burnt a finger is certainly no better, for to be unaware that fire burns is no more naive than to be unaware that one can escape from fire otherwise than by drowning. The great, the classic, error is that of remedying abuses by other abuses—apparently of less significance but really more fundamental inasmuch as they compromise principles; it is the error of getting rid of the disease by killing the patient.

*

* *

Our ancestors could be criticized for a form of naiveté on the plane of the physical sciences, which took the form of a certain confusion between domains. Because of a lack of experience or observation—although in itself this is certainly nothing to worry about—they were sometimes inclined to overestimate the scope of cosmic correspondences; for this reason they tended imprudently to apply to one order laws applicable to another and hence to believe, for instance, that salamanders can resist fire—and even extinguish it—owing to certain properties of these batrachians and even more to a confusion between them and the "fiery spirits" of the same name; the men of old were all the more liable to such mistakes because they still knew from experience the protean character of the subtle substance enveloping and penetrating the material world—in other words, because the barrier between the corporeal and animic states was less solidified than in later periods. Men of today are in turn relatively excusable on this same plane but in a contrary sense in that their total lack of experience of perceptible animic manifestations seems to confirm them in their materialism; nonetheless, despite the inexperience of modern man with regard to things belonging to the animic or subtle order, phenomena of this kind still exist, and they are by no means inaccessible to him in principle even though he labels them *a priori* as "superstitions" and abandons them to occultists.

Acceptance of the animic dimension is in any case a part of religion, for one cannot deny magic without straying from faith; as far as miracles are concerned, their cause surpasses the animic plane though their effects penetrate it. In the language of theologians the term "superstition" tends to be confusing because it expresses two entirely different ideas: a wrong application of religious sentiment on the one hand and a belief in unreal or ineffectual things on the other; thus spiritualism is called "superstition," but rightly so only with respect to its interpretations of phenomena and its cult and not with respect to the phenomena themselves; on the other hand sciences like astrology are perfectly real and effectual and imply no deviation of a pseudo-religious kind. The term "superstition" should really not be applied to sciences or facts that people ignore and ridicule without understanding them at all, but to practices that are either intrinsically useless or totally misunderstood and that are called on to make up for the absence of spiritual attitudes or effectual rites; no less superstitious is a false or improper interpretation of a symbol or some coincidence, often in conjunction with imaginary fears or scruples. Today the word "superstition" no longer means anything; when theologians use it—the point bears repetition—one never knows whether they are censuring a concrete diabolism or a mere illusion; for them a magical act and a pretense at magic look the same, and they do not notice the contradiction inherent in declaring in the same breath that sorcery is a great sin and that it is nothing but superstition.

But let us return to the scientific naiveté of the men of old. According to Saint Thomas Aquinas, "an error concerning the creation engenders a false science of God"; this does not mean that knowledge of God demands a total knowledge of cosmic phenomena—a completely unrealizable condition in any case—but that our knowledge must be either symbolically accurate or physically adequate; in the second case it must retain for us a symbolic intelligibility, for without this all science is vain and harmful. For example, human science has the right to stop short at, or restrict itself to, the view that the earth is flat and that the heavens revolve since the spiritual symbolism involved in this view adequately reflects a real situation; but the evolutionary hypothesis is a proposition at once false and pernicious since—besides being contrary to the nature of things—it deprives man of his essential significance and at the same stroke destroys the intelligibility of the world. In any human science dealing with phenomena, there is always an element of error; we cannot attain to more than a relative knowledge in this domain, but taken as a whole this can be sufficient in the context of our spiritual science. The ancients knew the laws of a nature that can be perceived directly: Their astronomy was founded more or less on appearances, and though it included errors in the material field—but not in the spiritual field since appearances are providential and have a meaning for us—this deficiency was largely compensated for by the comprehensiveness of traditional knowledge, which in fact takes account of Angels, Paradises, demons, hells, and the nonevolutionary spontaneity of creation—that is, the crystallization of celestial Ideas in the cosmic substance—as well as the apocalyptic end of the world and many other such facts; these facts, whatever their mythical vesture, are essential to human beings. By contrast, a science that denies them, prodigious though it may be in the material observation of sensible phenomena, can never espouse the principle enunciated by Saint Thomas; this is because a knowledge of essential things takes precedence over a knowledge of secondary things and because a knowledge that excludes the essentials of creation, both in fact and in principle, is incomparably more remote from an exact and complete adequation to truth than a science that is apparently "naive" but whole.

If it is "naive" to believe—because one sees it this way—that the earth is flat and the sky and stars revolve around it, it is no less "naive" to take the world of the senses to be the only world or the whole world and to believe that matter, or energy if one prefers, is Existence as such; such errors are indeed incomparably greater than that of the geocentric system. The materialist and evolutionist error is immeasurably harmful—we must insist on this—whereas a primitive and "natural" cosmology is nothing of the kind; this shows that there is no common measure at all between the insufficiency of the ancient cosmography and the overall—we do not say "partial"—falsity of a Promethean and titanic science, whose principle was bequeathed to us from the decadence of Greece.

And this is characteristic of the ravages of scientism and its special psychology: If one remarks to a convinced believer in progress that man could not possibly endure psychologically the conditions on another planet—and there is talk of colonizing other planets to relieve terrestrial overpopulation—he will answer without batting an eye that a new kind of man with the necessary qualities will be produced; such unawareness and insensibility are not far from the inhuman and monstrous, for to deny what is total and inalienable in man is to scoff at the divine intention that makes us what we are and that has consecrated our nature through the "Word made flesh." Tacitus laughed at the Germanic tribes who tried to stop a torrent with their shields, but it is no less naive to believe in planetary migration or to believe in the establishment by purely human means of a society fully satisfied and perfectly inoffensive and continuing to progress indefinitely. All this proves that man, though he has inevitably become less naive in some things, has nonetheless learned nothing as far as essentials are concerned; the only thing that man is capable of when left to himself is to "commit the oldest sins the newest kind of ways," as Shakespeare would say. And the world being what it is, one is doubtless not guilty of a truism in adding that it is better to go to Heaven naively than to go intelligently to hell.

*
* *

In trying to reconstruct the psychology of the men of old, our contemporaries nearly always make the serious mistake of failing to take into account the inward repercussions of the corresponding outward manifestations; what matters is not some superficial improvement but the effectiveness of our attitudes toward the Invisible and the Absolute. Ways of thinking and acting that may sometimes surprise us by their appearance of ingenuousness—especially in the lives of the saints—often conceal an efficacy that is for that very reason all the more profound; despite the fact that in more recent times man has accumulated a mass of experiences and much cleverness, he is certainly less "authentic" and less "effective," and less sensitive to the influx of the supernatural, than were his distant ancestors; though he may smile—he the "civilized" man who has become an "adult"—at some apparently simplistic piece of reasoning or at an attitude that is *a priori* childish or "pre-logical," the inward effectiveness of these points of reference eludes him. It never seems to occur to historians and psychologists that the surface components of human behavior are always relative and that a plus or a minus on this plane alone is never decisive since only the inward workings of our contact with higher states or celestial prolongations are of real importance; the mental distance between a living "primitive" and a "civilized" person is regarded as equivalent to thousands of years, but experience proves that this distance, where it exists, is equivalent to no more than a few days, for man is everywhere and always man.

*
* *

It is not naiveté and superstition alone that shift their position; intelligence does so as well, and in fact they all move together; it is possible to satisfy oneself of this by reading philosophical texts or art criticism, where an obstinate individualism strides upon the stilts of a pretentious pseudo-psychology; it is as if one wished to borrow the subtlety of a Scholastic and the sensitivity of a troubadour in order to say whether the temperature is hot or cold. A monstrous expenditure of mental ability is incurred in expressing opinions that have no relation to intelligence; those who are not intellectually gifted learn to play at thinking and cannot even manage without this imposture, whereas those who are well endowed are in danger of losing their ability to think by falling in with the trend. What looks like an ascent is really a descent: Ignorance and lack of intelligence are at ease in a wholly superficial refinement, and the result is a climate in which wisdom takes on the appearance of naiveté, uncouthness, reverie.

In our day everyone wants to appear intelligent; people would rather be accused of a crime than of naiveté if the accompanying risks could be avoided. But since intelligence cannot be drawn from the void, subterfuges are resorted to, one of the most prevalent being the mania for "demystification," which makes one look intelligent at a very small cost, for all one needs to do is assert that the normal response to a particular phenomenon is "prejudiced" and that it is high time it was cleared of the "legends" surrounding it; if the ocean could be made out to be a pond or the Himalayas hills, it would be done. Certain writers find it impossible to be content with taking note of the fact that a particular thing or person has a particular character or destiny, as everyone had done before them; they must always begin by remarking that "it has too often been said" and go on to declare that the reality is something quite different and has at last been discovered and that up until now all the world has been "living a lie." This strategy is applied above all to things that are evident and universally known; it would doubtless be too naive to acknowledge in so many words that a lion is a carnivore and that he is not quite safe to meet.

Be that as it may, there is naiveté everywhere and there always has been, and man cannot escape from it unless he can surpass his humanity; in this truth lie the key and solution to the problem. For what matters is not the question of knowing whether the dialectic or demeanor of a Plato is naive or not, or whether they are so to a certain extent and no further—and one would like to know where the absolute standards of all this could be found—but simply the fact that the sage or the saint has an inward access to concrete Truth; the simplest formulation—doubtless the most "naive" for some tastes—can be the threshold of a Knowledge as complete and profound as possible.[1]

1. "Blessed are the poor in spirit: for theirs is the kingdom of heaven" (Matt. 5:3); "But let your communication be, Yea, yea; Nay, nay: for whatsoever is more than these cometh of evil" (Matt. 5:37); "Except ye be converted, and become as little children, ye shall not enter into the kingdom of heaven" (Matt. 18:3); "Blessed are they that have not seen, and yet have believed" (John 20:29).

If the Bible is naive, it is an honor to be naive; if the philosophies that deny the Spirit are intelligent, there is no such thing as intelligence. Behind a humble belief in a Paradise situated among the clouds there is at least some basis of inalienable truth, but more than that—and this is something priceless—there is a merciful Reality that never disappoints.

Winter

Dancing crystals fall from the sky—
Each one is a little world of its own.
And soon the land is veiled with snow;
All is white—the play of colors fades.

Thus it is when illusion disappears
Beneath the snow of patience, trust in God—
Of purity, announcing Heaven's Reign;
O light-filled silence of Serenity.

4

THE MYSTERY OF THE HYPOSTATIC FACE

One encounters the rather surprising opinion in certain Muslim authors that no "Messenger" or founder of religion loved God as much as the Prophet of Islam did and that none was as much beloved by God as he. Some will say that this is merely a matter of partiality, ignorance, and lack of imagination; this is true *de facto*, but it is not an exhaustive explanation, for the opinion in question benefits—as a religious sentiment or quasi-moral act—from a background transcending the order of purely human opinions.

The key to the enigma is that there is not only a personal God—who is so to speak the "human Face," or the "humanized Face," of the supra-personal Divinity—but also, beneath this first hypostatic degree and resulting from it, what we may term "the confessional Face" of God: the Face God turns toward a particular religion, the Gaze He casts upon it, without which it would not even exist. In other words the "human Face" or "personal Face" of God assumes different modes, which correspond to a similar diversity of religious, confessional, or spiritual perspectives, so much so that it could be said that each religion has its own God, without thereby denying that God is one and that this unity can at any time pierce the veil of diversity; the fact that the God of Islam manifests—or can manifest—Himself differently from the God of Christianity could not mean that Christians and Muslims do not in substance worship the same God.

The divine Being contains all the spiritual possibilities and consequently all the religious and mystical archetypes; having projected them into existence, He looks on each of them with a particular and appropriate Gaze; in a similar way it is said that the angels speak to each person in the appropriate language. This "Gaze" or "Face" is a new kind of "divine subjectivity," subordinated to that of God as such and transmitting this subjectivity to man in a particular mode; it is thus that colorless light, without ceasing to be light, projects the colors of the rainbow and that water transformed into ice gives rise to crystallizations and hence to differentiated and even opposite manifestations. If there is a conflict between religions, denominations, and paths, it is because there is "competition" between archetypes: The archetypes could never be fundamentally contradictory—the apparent opposition of the colors red and green is resolved precisely in their colorless origin—but they are nonetheless mutually exclusive, except at their centers, which by definition are non-formal and open onto pure light.

It is important to understand that the *Hypostasis*-Face or *Hypostasis*-Gaze is not an abstraction but on the contrary a concrete divine self-determination for the sake of a particular human receptacle, whether individual or collective; and this self-determination projects into human *Māyā* a particular universe in all its completeness, with its own laws, possibilities, and wonders. In this sense, it can be said that a change of religion is a change of planets, and to understand a foreign religion as a phenomenon is above all to grasp that it is a planet and not simply a continent—even though there are degrees of remoteness or difference, of course, and thus degrees in the feeling of estrangement that a foreign religious climate can produce.

The sun is one, but it looks upon the planets in different ways and is seen differently according to their positions in space: a simplistic image perhaps and yet adequate to illustrate the point.

*

* *

It will be said exoterically—in Muslim language—that God sent Muhammad in order to found Islam; it can be said esoterically that the archetype *in divinis* of the "Islamic possibility" projected this possibility into existence and thereby became for this projection its God; the projection is not separated from God as such but "particularizes" Him in a certain fashion while nonetheless communicating all the qualities and functions of God to the human receptacle, though precisely according to the "style" required by this particularization.

Each divine Face operates by means of a governing Idea that describes it and that is all-encompassing: When one says "Christ" in a Christian setting, one has said everything; the mystery of the saving manifestation takes precedence over everything else; there is only one decisive truth: "God became man that man might become God." Now the "hypostatic specification"—the "divine Face" that projected this particular aspect of the relationship "God-man" into the world—accepts responsibility in a certain sense for all the consequences that the archetype provokes in the human world, not excluding the entirely natural phenomenon of religious prejudice; nevertheless, even within this limitation God does not cease being God—the only God there is—and He does not allow any one of His particular projections an absolute triumph. He contradicts it either *ab extra* or *ab intra*, either by another religion or by the *sophia perennis*: *Spiritus autem ubi vult spirat.*

In a Muslim setting the governing Idea—the ontologically indisputable Idea, so to speak—is the postulate of God as One: To say *Allāh* is to say everything; in a quasi-existential manner this word closes the door to any dispute. And this quality of absoluteness redounds necessarily on the Messenger and permits the assertion—in good conscience and under the gaze of the corresponding "hypostatic Face"[1]—that no one was more loved by *Allāh* than the Messenger of *Allāh*, that is, the spokesman for the governing Idea that this Name expresses and manifests. This is an example of what we have more than once called the "relative absolute"—a paradoxical expression, certainly, but indispensable on the plane of metaphysical analysis.[2]

More specifically, the governing Idea on the Christian side is the dazzling phenomenon of the unique God-Man, who is incomparable and *a fortiori* unsurpassable, and alone capable of saving souls; on the Muslim side it is the lightning-like self-evidence of the Absolute, the unique Principle, which is indivisible, inviolable, invincible. Certainty of the Absolute is absolute, just as "the doctrine of Unity is unique" (*al-Tawhīdu wāhid*) and just as faith in the Savior is salvific.

Each religion is a system, which is not only dogmatic, mythological, and methodic but also cosmic and eschatological. The values of one system cannot be measured by the standards of another,[3] but this does not contradict the evident homogeneity of their common essence.

*
* *

As a religion Christianity is an *upāya*—a "saving stratagem," hence one formal system among others—and the divinity of the Messenger does not change this fact; "God alone is good," said Christ. The limitation of the Christian system appears from the outset in its axiomatic definition of man as "sinner," who can approach God only on this basis—hence the implicit or explicit rejection of all *gnosis*; but man is also "child of God" since God is "Father," and moreover "my kingdom is not of this world,"

---

1. In an implicitly conditional manner, however, since it is a "form."

2. The *Vedānta* distinguishes between the "non-supreme" Principle (*Apara-Brahma*) and the "supreme" Principle (*Para-Brahma*); unlike the second, the first is not the Absolute in itself, but it is "practically" the Absolute in relation to the world; it is thus "relatively absolute." The personal God is "absolute" without being intrinsically "the Absolute."

3. In a similar manner, though on an entirely different plane, the values of one art cannot be measured by the standards of another; the values of Far Eastern music, for example, cannot be judged by the criteria of Western music; the needs and intentions are too different, even though the reason for the existence of every art—as *a fortiori* for the existence of spiritual paths—is the passage from accidentality to substance or from the world of shadows to that of archetypes.

which indicates an esotericism of love intended as such for a society of spiritual men but not for a human collectivity as a whole.[4] In fact the legalistic application of this "wisdom of the saints" has created a dangerous scission in the social body, as is shown in Christian history by the underlying tension—or chronic warfare—between clergy and laity, in the Catholic world above all.[5]

The "hypostatic Face" that presides over Islam "reacted" against this perspective: not only against the danger of scission and disequilibrium but also and *a priori* against the idea that "man equals sinner" and the idea that "God became man"; this second idea determined Trinitarian theology or more exactly the equation between the aspect of trinity and the Absolute, whence a "Christocentrism" dominating everything *de facto*. On the one hand Islam could be said to have brought God back to His primary meaning and to His transcendent essentiality, and on the other hand to have brought man back to his primordial and "supernaturally natural" priesthood, thereby consecrating the entire society.

For Islam God is not "Father"—at least not *a priori* and toward everyone—but rather "Lord," which is more appropriate with regard to an entire collectivity; as for man, he is "slave"—not "child," which for Muslim sentiment would presuppose a mystical intimacy—but he is also, thanks to his human dignity precisely, "vicar" on earth, hence the representative of God. According to this perspective, the love of God is an excellent thing insofar as it is founded on the postulates of Islam; now God loves most perfectly the slave-vicar, the mirror of divine Unity. Muslims cannot "reason" otherwise than within the framework of their system;[6] for them Muhammad is pre-eminently "servant" because he personifies—in keeping with the idea of "Lord"—the "prostration" of the creature, and he is also pre-eminently

---

4. This society, or *civitas Dei*, was realized by Christianity in the monastic orders, especially on Mount Athos.

5. The Orthodox world was unable to resist this movement. Be that as it may, when one examines the history of European dress picture by picture—first the princely and then the bourgeois, both feminine and masculine—it is hard to believe these are Christian costumes, so much are they marked by an increasing worldliness or even frivolity, in short by an almost total absence of any sense of the sacred; one wonders how it is possible that these could have been people who read the Gospel, knew what a crucifix is, went to confession, and received communion.

6. One should not lose sight of the fact that Christ is a relatively esoteric phenomenon—hence his disdain for the "commandments of men" and his insistence on inwardness—and that exoteric Islam, legalistic by definition, could not do otherwise than level a kind of reproach at him for this fact, at least indirectly. "Jesus was perfect," a dervish once told us, "but he was not able to prevent men from making him a god."

"vicar" because he personifies a complete legislation and exercises on this basis the function of monarch, at once spiritual and temporal.[7]

God cannot contradict Himself, certainly, but He can manifest different dimensions of His one Substance, these being differentiated by *Māyā*. The Christian system, hostile to the "flesh," "nature," and the here-below, implacably excludes all sexual *yoga* or "tantrism," whereas the Islamic system, because it is favorable to equilibrium and the natural norm, tends to sanctify what nature, at once wise and generous, offers us; for man exists not only to master and transcend the particular facts—innocent in themselves—of his surroundings and life: He also exists to ennoble and sanctify them, in short to integrate them into his "verticality," his vocation and path. There is not only a mysticism of sacrifice; there is also a mysticism of gratitude.

The "hypostatic Faces" of God "personify" diverse archetypes; hence the very notion of "love of God"—as alluded to earlier—is also affected and differentiated: Sacrificial in the Christian perspective, this same love aims to be more "inclusive" in the Islamic perspective, without thereby neglecting asceticism, since it is meant to realize all the modes granted us by existence itself. It is necessary to take this play of archetypes into account when encountering a confessional annexation of the love of God, and *a priori* of God Himself, and to understand that the hypostatic Face to which this annexation refers serves as a guarantee for the opinions or sentiments that conform to the world of possibilities it has created—even, incidentally, when this entails breaking the shell of the symbolism and manifesting, quite paradoxically, its quintessence, which is "everywhere and always" the Truth.[8] Every religion comes from God and for this reason "commits" God—to a certain degree and in certain respects—to the framework of a particular belief, but this does not make God in His aseity an adherent of any given credo: *quod absit*.

It could also be said that God operates by antinomism on the plane of diversified Revelation. He does not at the outset reveal the Truth in all its complexity but successively or sporadically sets forth antinomic aspects,[9] each of which opens at its center onto the total Truth; and this Truth does

---

7. Not to mention the specifically Islamic argument that the last of the "Messengers" must be the most eminent, for finality rejoins primordiality while realizing an unprecedented synthesis.

8. Thus the Koran readily reminds us that "God doeth what He will."

9. The role of antinomism—dialectic through contrasts—in diverse theologies, especially the Palamite, is well known. The theologian puts forward two apparently irreconcilable statements whose very contradiction provokes—like a spark flashing from flint—an enlightening, if not always expressible, intuition.

not reveal itself in a gratuitous fashion: It has its demands, which in the final analysis engage the whole of man.

*

* *

Undeniably, the claim—even indirect—that there exists a religious Messenger more perfect than Christ has something deeply shocking about it, but one must not lose sight of the fact that from the Muslim point of view the assertion that Jesus is God by virtue of an intrinsic Trinity[10]—so that in a certain fashion God is Jesus—is at least as shocking. And in a similar way, for a Hindu or Buddhist the assertion that their respective Revelations are merely "human" or "natural" in origin, that they are not at all "supernatural," and that Christianity alone can save man is just as odious as the underestimation of Christ is for Christians.[11] Or again, it is deeply offensive to Jews—and also Muslims—to hear that personages having the stature of Enoch, Noah, Abraham, Moses, or Elijah had access to Paradise only thanks to the mediation of Jesus of Nazareth, whereas they would accept in principle the intervention of a divine Power—the "divine Names" amounting in practice to *hypostases*—hence of a non-temporal and trans-historical *Logos*.[12]

All things considered, the idea that a particular religious Messenger could have loved God more perfectly than another such Messenger, or than all the others, seems to us an unnecessary luxury; in Islam—where it appears in even one of the most eminent writers—it follows neither from the Koran nor the *Sunnah*; it is therefore nothing more than pious excess. The question remains whether and to what extent such initiatives or divergences can be avoided within a religious space, seeing that religion lives in part—humanly speaking—from enthusiasm and that no one can impose boundaries on the excesses of faith, or even on theological or mystical speculation, as the case may be.

---

10. Which means that not admitting the Trinity is equivalent to denying God.

11. This underestimation can extend to the Mother of Christ: When the Koran declares that "God hath chosen thee (O Mary) and hath purified thee, and hath raised thee above all women," there are commentators who find a way of making it say merely that Mary was "the most pious woman of her time," no more and no less—an absurd minimalizing, which is explainable by the fear of Mariolatry; it is always a case of *ad majorem Dei gloriam*, which in the climate of an overly sensitive monotheism is theologically and psychologically decisive.

12. Which Christ personified in fact. Islam takes this into account in naming Jesus the "Spirit of God" (*Rūh Allāh*) but without drawing the same conclusions as Christianity. Furthermore, the question must be raised, not whether Christ "descended into hell" to raise souls to the "beatific vision," but whether this saving gesture embraced without distinction all men of good will—even outside Israel—who lived prior to the Christian era.

For us the important thing is to know not only why extreme opinions—whatever their level—exist in religious climates but also why they are encountered even among esotericists of the highest rank. No doubt one must take into account an element of *bhakti* or mystical love, which embraces things in a single flow of devotion without bothering to examine them with a critical eye, an examination that appears in such climates as a dissonance and almost as a betrayal. The mythical garden of tradition is a closed and blessed system, one which the contemplative does not willingly leave in order to enter into the cold and neutral space of such an "exact science" as "comparative religion"; if the gnostic sees himself as obliged to transcend the world of forms, he will do so preferably through the providential opening located at the very center of his own garden; he will hesitate—in a narrowly confessional climate—to penetrate into the stratosphere of truth pure and simple. This of course does not prevent a less affective and more objective outlook from maintaining its rights in all cases, and this is so *a fortiori* on the universal plane where the great initiates aim to stand and where they can stand to the extent their information is sufficient;[13] an exact knowledge of phenomena is certainly not detrimental to a profound knowledge of God.

In summary, we shall say that the extreme opinions encountered in religious climates benefit from two "extenuating circumstances": The first, which we have just been discussing, is a devotional mentality that favors a form of thinking that is more pious than logical; the second, set forth earlier, is the irresistible self-evidence—and invincible power—of a governing Idea. In the wake of this Idea, or in the shadow of this divine "Face," unilateral or even exorbitant opinions benefit at least from a certain plausibility, whether formal or implicit. They are admissible in a quite specific connection, or else they express truths independently of their literal meaning. In either case it is best to regard them as symbols, unless they are intrinsically aberrant, and not to view them outside the Idea that determines them directly or indirectly and that, if it cannot always justify—or corroborate—them without reservation, can at least excuse them. For this governing Idea projects the Absolute into human *Māyā*, and in the religious space this is everything.

---

13. One Sufi cheerfully advises his prince to oppress the Christians—which goes a bit far after all—whereas another frequents them and tends to protect them; this proves that in a climate at once esoteric and traditionally rigorous there is a margin permitting very different options. Let us note in this connection that the oppressive, anti-Christian laws of the Umayyad caliph Umar II are sometimes attributed, either ignorantly or fraudulently, to the great Umar, the companion of the Prophet and second caliph, whose magnanimity toward Christians was well known. Be that as it may, the following verse of the Koran could in many cases be applied to the disproportion that exists between the absolute Idea and relative opinions—including symbolic but ill-sounding legends: "Say *Allāh*! Then leave them to their vain discourse" (*Sūrah* "Cattle" [6]:92).

II

THE PERENNIAL PHILOSOPHY

Metaphysics cannot be taught to everyone,
but if it could be there would be no atheists.

—*Spiritual Perspectives and Human Facts*

Sophia Perennis

Worldly philosophers construct their theses—
Each one finds what no one found before;
Each one thinks that he has hit the mark
With a newly invented system.

The gnostic seeks only to explain
In new surroundings what always has been known.
Yea, since the origin of man, individual truth
In metaphysics is unknown.

Forms of thought may well be new;
The doctrine's kernel is as timeless as stone.

5

SUMMARY OF INTEGRAL METAPHYSICS

Our aim in this chapter is to examine the landscape of metaphysical doctrine. By way of introduction, we must begin with the idea that the supreme Reality is absolute and therefore infinite. That which is absolute allows for no augmentation or diminution, no repetition or division; hence it is solely and totally itself. And that which is infinite is not determined or limited by any boundary; it is in the first place Potentiality or Possibility as such, and *ipso facto* the Possibility of things, hence Virtuality. Without All-Possibility there would be neither Creator nor creation, neither *Māyā* nor *Samsāra*.

The Infinite is as it were the intrinsic dimension of plenitude proper to the Absolute; to speak of the Absolute is to speak of the Infinite, for neither is conceivable without the other. We can symbolize the relationship between these two aspects of the supreme Reality with the following images: In space the absolute is the point, and the infinite is extension; in time the absolute is the moment, and the infinite is duration. On the plane of matter the absolute is ether—the underlying and omnipresent primordial substance—and the infinite is the indefinite series of substances; on the plane of form the absolute is the sphere—the simple, perfect, and primordial form—and the infinite is the indefinite series of more or less complex forms; finally, on the plane of number, the absolute is unity or unicity, and the infinite is the unlimited series of numbers or possible quantities, or simply totality.

The distinction between the Absolute and the Infinite expresses the two fundamental aspects of Reality: essentiality and potentiality; this is the highest principial prefiguration of the masculine and feminine poles. Universal Radiation, hence *Māyā* both divine and cosmic, flows forth from the second aspect, the Infinite, which coincides with All-Possibility.

*

* *

The "Sovereign Good" is the First Cause precisely insofar as it is revealed by phenomena that we label "good," and this means that the Real and the

Good coincide. Indeed positive phenomena are what attest to the supreme Reality, not negative, privative, or subversive phenomena; these latter would manifest nothingness "if it existed," and they do so indirectly and paradoxically, for nothingness corresponds to a goal that, even though it can never be realized, tends toward realization. Evil is the "possibility of the impossible," without which the Infinite would not be the Infinite; to ask why All-Possibility includes the possibility of its own negation—a possibility continually emerging anew but never fully actualized—is like asking why Existence is Existence or why Being is Being.

Therefore, if we call the supreme Principle the Good, *Agathon*, or if we say that it is the Sovereign Good that is the Absolute and thus the Infinite, it is not because we paradoxically limit Reality but because we know that every good comes from it and manifests it essentially, thus revealing its nature. One can assuredly say that the Divinity is "beyond good and evil," but only on condition of adding that this "beyond" is in turn a "good," for it testifies to an Essence in which there can be no shadow of limitation or privation and which therefore cannot be anything else but the absolute Good or absolute Plenitude; this is perhaps difficult to explain but not impossible to conceive.

The variety of manifestations of the Good in the world clearly has its source in a principial and archetypal diversity whose root is located within the supreme Principle itself; this diversity pertains not only to the divine qualities, from which our virtues are derived, but also—in another respect—to aspects of the divine Personality, from which our faculties are derived; we shall speak of this again.

While still on the subject of the aspects or modes of the Sovereign Good and their reverberations in the world, we should also consider the relationship of transcendence and that of immanence; the first is connected more directly with the Absolute and the second with the Infinite. According to the first relationship, God alone is the Good; He alone possesses the quality of beauty, for example; compared to divine Beauty, the beauty of a creature is nothing, just as existence itself is nothing next to divine Being; this is the perspective of transcendence. The perspective of immanence also begins with the axiom that God alone possesses both qualities and reality; but its conclusion is positive and participative, and it is therefore said that the beauty of a creature—being beauty and not its contrary—is necessarily the beauty of God since there is no other; and the same is true for all the other qualities as well as for the miracle of existence, which lies at their very basis. Unlike the perspective of transcendence, the perspective of immanence does not nullify creaturely qualities but on the contrary makes them divine, if one may so express it.

*
* *

The preceding considerations lead us first to the question of the "why" of universal manifestation and second—as a result of this question—to the problem of evil. To answer the question of why there is a relativity—hence a *Māyā* and thus a manifestation—we may refer in the first place to an idea of Saint Augustine's that we have mentioned more than once, namely, that it is in the nature of the good to want to communicate itself; to speak of the good is to speak of radiation, projection, unfolding, gift of self. But to say radiation is at the same time to say distance, hence estrangement or impoverishment; the solar rays dim and become lost in the night of space. At the end of this trajectory there arises the paradoxical phenomenon of evil, which nonetheless has the positive function of highlighting the good *a contrario* and of contributing in its own way to equilibrium in the phenomenal order.

A remark is called for here concerning the divergence between the Aryan or Greco-Hindu idea of "universal manifestation" and the Semitic or monotheistic idea of "creation." The first refers to the world insofar as it results from an ontological necessity: the radiation or communication of the Good, precisely; in other words *Māyā* springs from the Infinitude of the supreme Principle, and to speak of *Māyā* is to speak of *samsāra*, the world of "transmigration." As for the Semitic idea of creation, it does not refer to the world considered in its totality but insofar as it is reduced to a single cycle and conceived as the effect of a single "free" act of God.

In reality, the creation to which we belong is but one cycle of universal manifestation, which is composed of an indefinite number of cycles, each of which is "necessary" with respect to its existence but "free" with respect to its particularity. The Universe is a fabric woven of necessity and freedom, of mathematical rigor and musical play; every phenomenon participates in these two principles.

*
* *

The first distinction to be made in a comprehensive metaphysical doctrine is between the Absolute and the relative or between the Infinite and the finite: between *Ātmā* and *Māyā*. The first term expresses *a priori* the single Essence, the Eckhartian "Godhead" (*Gottheit*), Beyond-Being; the "personal God" already pertains to *Māyā*, of which He is the "relatively absolute" summit, encompassing in a certain sense the entire domain of relativity down to the extreme limit of the cosmogonic projection.

The second "qualitative" and "descending" distinction is between the Principle and manifestation, God and the world. The Principle includes the Absolute and its reflection within relativity, Being or the personal God; the distinction in this case is between the "pure Absolute" and the "relative Absolute," which is relative in relation to the Absolute as such but absolute in relation to the world. As for Manifestation, it extends from the central reflection of the Principle—the *Logos*, and the celestial, angelic, and avataric world—to the peripheral, infra-celestial, purely "natural," and samsaric world.

A third distinction-synthesis is between "Heaven" and "earth," the word "earth" being taken in a symbolic or analogical sense: The celestial order includes on the one hand the two "degrees" of the Principle itself, namely, the pure Absolute and the Absolute colored by relativity, and on the other hand the Principle manifested at the center of the cosmos, the *Logos*; whereas the "earthly" order—whether it is a question of our earth or other similar worlds that necessarily remain unknown to us—is the purely "natural" world mentioned earlier.

A fourth fundamental distinction places the *Logos* at the center: On the one hand it is placed below the pure Absolute and above the "natural" and "profane" world, and on the other hand it combines the "celestial" and the "earthly"—or the "divine" and the "human"—because it includes the already relative dimension of the Principle as well as the manifestation of this Principle at the cosmic center. The *Logos* is the "uncreated Word"; it is "true man and true God."

What all of this means is that the total Universe comprises four fundamental degrees: the Principle as such, which is the "pure Absolute"; the Principle already included in *Māyā*, which is God the Creator, Legislator, and Savior; the Principle reflected in the created order, which is the "celestial" order and also the *Avatāra*; and the peripheral creation, which is purely "horizontal" and "natural." In other words: first, the Principle in itself; second, the prefiguration of manifestation in the Principle; third, the projection of the Principle in manifestation; and fourth, manifestation in itself. The line of demarcation changes place or level according to the perspective.

*
* *

The relationship between the Absolute and the relative—between *Ātmā* and *Māyā*—implies three situations or tendencies: first, conformity to the Principle or the "upward" tendency; second, the expansive affirmation of possibilities, hence "horizontal"—or, if one prefers, "passional"—existence; and third, nonconformity to the Principle and thus the "downward" tendency, an illusory movement in the direction of a "nothingness" that is obviously nonexistent but that is possible as a negative and subversive point of reference. These are the three *gunas* of Hindu doctrine, which penetrate and regulate all that is created.

But there is not only this hierarchy of positions or tendencies; there is also in the Universe a diversifying manifestation of the positive possibilities included in the divine Potentiality. Thus a complementarity exists between the active and passive functions, the masculine and feminine poles, as well as between the powers and qualities that we encounter everywhere in the world and that we ourselves possess to one degree or another. All the cosmic possibilities are derived from these principles and their indefinitely diverse combinations.

To be more explicit, we shall say that there is first of all, on this side of the one Substance—and in a sense as a reflection of the aspects "Absolute" and "Infinite"—a duality of the creative functions or of the masculine and feminine poles; this is the duality "Activity–Passivity," from which are derived all the analogous functions at every level of the Universe. Next—and once again at each of the levels, including the divine summit of *Māyā*—there is a trinity of divine and universal faculties: namely, "Consciousness–Power–Love"; all the capacities of knowing, willing, and loving are derived from this trinity. After this trinity, in this series of numerical conceptualizations, comes a quaternary of fundamental qualities, namely, "Purity" or "Rigor," "Life" or "Gentleness," "Strength" or "Act," and "Beauty" or "Goodness," or "Peace" or "Beatitude"; by analogy this is the quaternary "Cold–Heat–Dryness–Humidity," to which moreover correspond the cardinal points.

As we have seen, the trinity includes faculties that are at once divine and creaturely: the capacities to know, to will, and to love. In the medieval Masonic ternary "Wisdom–Strength–Beauty," these faculties are expressed by their qualitative aspects: Wisdom is the content of knowledge; Strength is the virtue of will; Beauty is the ideal object of love. In the Vedantic trinity "Being–Consciousness–Bliss," the faculties are reduced to their ontological essences; in a certain sense they are the ternary "Object–Subject–Union," the first element evoking will, the second knowledge, and the third love; the pole "Being," *Sat*, potentially contains "Power," whence its connection with will.[1] Another Hindu trinity—less fundamental than the preceding—is the *Trimūrti*, the "Triple Manifestation": On the one hand this trinity is

1. Let us note that the trinity that the Koran attributes to Christianity—the Father, the Son, the Virgin—is altogether logical in its way and corresponds to what we have just expounded; as for the Christian Trinity proper, the Holy Spirit, like the Virgin, represents the mystery of divine Love.

understood in relation to the three cosmic tendencies—ascending, expansive, and descending—in which case it represents a hierarchy or "verticality"; on the other hand, and more directly, it pertains to the point of view of "horizontality" since it represents a system of quasi-equivalent and complementary terms. Shiva is comparable to the dark and descending tendency inasmuch as he negates and destroys; but he also pertains to the divine aspect *Chit*, "Consciousness"—or "Knowledge"—inasmuch as he reduces to ashes the "Great Illusion," *Mahā-Moha*, and this represents an intrinsically positive function.

Let us summarize: The principial numbers—or the numerical symbols—are either "horizontal" or "vertical" depending on whether they indicate a differentiation reflected at every universal level or a projection that penetrates into relativity. When the duality is horizontal it expresses the "active" and "passive" poles; when it is vertical it expresses the "absolute" and "relative" degrees—first in the divine Order and then in the cosmic order. When the trinity is horizontal it expresses the faculties, which are *a priori* divine; when it is vertical it expresses the cosmic tendencies. Finally, when the quaternary is horizontal it refers to the universal qualities; when it is vertical it indicates the degrees of the Universe—the penetration into relativity—as described earlier.

Perfection and Projection: The entire structure of the Universe is expressed by these two words. The "horizontal" numbers relate to the polarizations of the divine Perfection and the "vertical" numbers to the degrees of the cosmogonic Projection.

Here a precision is called for regarding the aspects of the Sovereign Good: There is no need to consider a trinity formed by the aspects "Good," "Absolute," "Infinite"; what should be said instead is that the Sovereign Good is absolute and therefore infinite. By its very nature the divine Good "wills to communicate itself" or "radiate," and this "will" is necessarily prefigured in its intrinsic nature, if one may express it this way.

*
* *

According to a German proverb, "He who says A must say B" (*Wer A sagt, muss B sagen*), and this applies also—and indeed above all—to knowledge. The unicity of the divine Object requires the totality of the human subject; this is the principle and the key of sacred Doctrine, and it is what distinguishes it from profane philosophy, which may ask a man to inflate himself but will never ask him to transcend himself.

The all-encompassing demand of sacred Doctrine—of "theosophy" in the proper sense of the word—results from the fact that a specifically human intelligence is by definition capable of objectivity and transcendence, and this implies *ipso facto* the same capacity for the will and the feeling soul, whence the freedom of our will and the moral instinct of our soul. And just as our intelligence is fully human only through truths related to God and our final ends, so too is our will fully human only through its operative participation in these truths; and similarly our soul is human only through its morality, detachment, and magnanimity, hence also through its love of the Truth and the Way. To say that free will and moral sensibility are part of the intelligence of *homo sapiens* means that there can be no truly consistent and plenary metaphysical knowledge without the participation of these two faculties, the volitive and affective; to know completely is to be. The circle of knowledge is completed in our personality, in its death in God and in its life in God. And "where your treasure is, there will your heart be also."

"I-ness"

My mind has often dwelt on the enigma of "I."
Why is it I who thinks himself "I,"
And not another? Why is the world
Divided into many thousand mirrors?

Yet see: no one wonders at it.
One blindly lives throughout the day
And thinks on many things, but not on this;
One readily believes it cannot be otherwise.

And this is strange: the I is colored
According to age, according to experience;
Who am I then? Who has inherited my heart,
Who can lift my I out of its orbit?

And behind all is enthroned the unique Self,
Deep-hidden Sun beneath the shell
Of earthly existence.

O Sun, mayest Thou shine
Into the somber cell of our "I-ness"!

6

CONSEQUENCES FLOWING FROM THE MYSTERY OF SUBJECTIVITY

The first thing that should strike us when we reflect on the nature of the Universe is the primacy of the miracle called intelligence—or consciousness or subjectivity—and hence its incommensurability with every material object, whether a grain of sand or the sun, or any creature whatever as an object of the senses. The truth of the Cartesian *cogito ergo sum* is not that it presents thought as the proof of being but simply that it expresses the primacy of thought—hence of consciousness or intelligence—in relation to the material world that surrounds us; obviously it is not our personal thought that preceded the world, but it was—or rather is—absolute Consciousness, of which our thought is a distant reflection: a thought that reminds us, and proves to us, that in the beginning was the Spirit. Nothing is more absurd than to suppose that intelligence could come from matter, hence the greater from the lesser; an evolutionary leap from matter to intelligence is from every point of view the most inconceivable thing that could be.

We shall no doubt be told that the reality of a creator God has not been demonstrated; aside from the fact that it is not difficult to demonstrate this reality with arguments proportionate to its nature—arguments, however, which are for that very reason inaccessible to certain minds—the least that can be said is that evolution has never been proven by anyone, and with good reason; transformist evolution is accepted as a useful and provisional postulate, as almost anything will be accepted, provided no obligation is felt to accept the primacy of the Immaterial since this escapes the grasp of our senses. When one begins by acknowledging the immediately tangible mystery of subjectivity or intelligence, however, it is easy to understand that the origin of the Universe is not inert and unconscious matter but a spiritual Substance, a Substance that moves as it were from coagulation to coagulation and from segmentation to segmentation—while including other projections as well, both manifesting and limiting—and that finally produces matter by causing it to emerge from a more subtle substance, although one still remote from the principial Substance. It will be objected that there is no proof of this, to which we reply that the phenomenon of subjectivity constitutes this proof precisely, to say nothing of other possible intellectual proofs not required by Intellection; and besides, there are infinitely fewer proofs for the inconceivable absurdity of evolutionism, which supposes that the miracle of consciousness could somehow spring from a heap of earth or pebbles, metaphorically speaking.

In the same vein of thought we would argue that the ideas of a "Great Spirit" and of the primacy of the Invisible are natural to man and need no demonstration; now what is natural to human consciousness, which is distinguished from animal consciousness by its objectivity and totality—its capacity for the Absolute and the Infinite—proves *ipso facto* its essential truth, for adequation to the real is precisely the reason for the existence of intelligence.[1] From another point of view, if Intellection and Revelation are "supernaturally natural" to man, it is obvious that their rejection is also a possibility of human nature, or else it would not occur; because man is fully intelligent and thereby wholly free, it follows that he alone among terrestrial creatures is free to rebel against his own nature. But he possesses this liberty only in the wake of a fall that first of all separates him from the immanent Revelation of Intellection and then sets him against prophetic Revelation, which for its part is meant to compensate for the absence of immanent Science and which—by means of this compensation—awakens it, at least in principle.

Extrinsic arguments, taken as points of reference or keys, contribute to proving the intellectual and existential primacy of the Spirit, but—let it be said once again—we have no need of such proofs; if there are people for whom the shadow of a cat does not prove the presence of the real cat or for whom the sound of a waterfall does not prove the proximity of water, this does not mean that our knowledge of the animal or waterfall necessarily or exclusively depends on the shadow or sound. Our starting point is twofold: On the one hand everything that exists is inscribed *a priori* in the theomorphic substance of our intelligence—there is no complete consciousness that does not prolong absolute Consciousness—and on the other hand the intellectual actualization of the real or possible depends on the perfection of our nature or else on an external factor that activates this perfection or completes it if it is partial: a factor such as Revelation or, in a more particular way, an experience that provokes the archetypal remembrance of which Plato spoke.

---

1. We have heard someone say that the wings of birds prove the existence of air and similarly that the religious phenomenon, common *a priori* to all peoples, proves the existence of its content: namely, God and the afterlife; this is clearly pertinent if one takes the trouble to examine the argument in depth.

*
* *

Man's liberty is total but it cannot be absolute since the quality of absoluteness pertains to the supreme Principle alone and not to its manifestation, even one that is direct or central. To say that our liberty is total means that it is "relatively absolute," that it is complete on a particular level and within certain limits; nonetheless our liberty is real—as is that of an animal, or else a bird in a cage would not feel deprived of freedom—and this is because liberty as such is liberty and nothing else, whatever its ontological limits. We partake of absolute Liberty, that of the divine Principle, to the extent that we conform to it, and this possibility of communion with Liberty as such, or with the Absolute, originates precisely from the total, although relative, character of our liberty. This amounts to saying that in and through God man can be reunited with pure Liberty; only in God are we absolutely free.

To acknowledge that man is by definition situated between an intellection that connects him to God and a world that has the power to detach him from God, and that since he is free in proportion to his intelligence he therefore possesses the paradoxical freedom to wish to make himself God, is to acknowledge at the same time that the possibility of a rupture between Intellection and mere reason is present from the very start because of the ambiguity of the human condition; suspended between the Infinite and the finite, the *pontifex* cannot but be ambiguous, and it is therefore inevitable that "offenses come." Beginning with the original fall and passing thence from fall to fall, man arrives finally at a rationalist Luciferianism,[2] which either turns against God and thus opposes our nature or turns against our nature and thus opposes God. The rational faculty detached from its supernatural context is necessarily opposed to man, and it is bound to give rise in the end to a way of thinking and form of life that are opposed to him as well; in other words Intellection is not completely secure except in souls that are providentially exempted from certain risks inherent in human nature; but it is not—and cannot be—secure in man as such for the simple reason that man by definition includes passional individuality, and it is precisely the presence of this individuality that creates the risk of a rupture with pure Intellect and hence the risk of the fall.

What is human is what is natural to man, and what is most essentially or most specifically natural to him is what relates to the Absolute and

2. Or existentialist Luciferianism, which on the whole amounts to the same thing since there is no one who reasons more than one who denies intellectual efficacy.

requires thereby the transcending of what is earthly in man.[3] Even prior to symbols, doctrines, and rites, our very subjectivity—as we have said—points as clearly as possible to our relationship with the Spirit and the Absolute; without the absolute primacy of the Spirit, relative subjectivity would be neither possible nor conceivable; it would be an effect without a cause.

Intelligence separated from its supra-individual source is accompanied *ipso facto* by that lack of a sense of proportions called pride; conversely, when intelligence has been reduced to rationalism, pride prevents it from rising to its source; all rationalism can do is to deny the Spirit and replace it with matter, and it is thus from matter that it makes consciousness spring forth, assuming it does not succeed in denying consciousness altogether by reducing it to a particularly refined or "evolved" kind of matter—and efforts to do this are obviously far from lacking.[4] Rather than bow before the self-evidence of the Spirit, proud reason will deny its own nature, even though this is what enables it to think; in its concrete conclusions it lacks imagination and a sense of proportions as much as it does intellectual perspicacity, and this is precisely a consequence of its pride.

Corruptio optimi pessima: This proves once again the monstrous disproportion between the cleverness of a reason that has become Luciferian and the falseness of its results. Torrents of intelligence are wasted to conceal the essential and brilliantly prove the absurd: namely, that spirit ended up springing from a piece of earth—or, let us say, from an inert substance—over the course of billions of years; in relation to the supposed result, this quantity is merely laughable and proves nothing. What we find here is a loss of all common sense and a perversion of the imagination, which—strictly speaking—no longer have anything human about them and which cannot be accounted for except by the well-known scientistic prejudice that explains everything from below and erects no matter what hypothesis as long as it

3. The word "humanism" constitutes a curious abuse of language in that it expresses a notion contrary to what is fully human, hence to the human properly so called; indeed nothing is more fundamentally inhuman than the "purely human"—the illusion of constructing a perfect man starting with the individual and terrestrial—whereas the human in the ideal sense draws its reason for being and its entire content from what transcends the individual and the earthly.

4. Speaking of "energy" rather than "matter"—and other subtleties of the kind—changes nothing in relation to the root of the problem and merely transposes the limits of the difficulty. Let us mention that a so-called "socio-biologist"—this word implies a whole program—has carried ingenuity to the point of replacing matter with "genes," whose blind egoism, combined with the instinct of ants or bees, is said to have ended up forming not merely bodies but consciousness and finally human intelligence, which is miraculously capable of delivering a dissertation on the very genes that had amused themselves by producing it.

excludes real causes, which are transcendent and non-material and of which the concrete and tangible proof is our subjectivity precisely.

*

* *

Spirit is Substance, matter is accident: In other words matter is nothing more than a contingent and transitory modality of the radiation of the Spirit, which projects worlds and cycles while remaining transcendent and immutable. This radiation gives rise to a polarization into subject and object: Matter is the terminal point of the descent of the objective pole, and sensory consciousness is the corresponding subjective phenomenon. For the senses the object is matter, or let us say the perceptible physical domain; for the Intellect objective reality is the Spirit in all its forms. It is by it that we exist and know; if it were not immanent in physical substances, they could not exist for one instant. And it is in this Spirit precisely that the subject–object opposition is resolved; it is resolved in a Unity that is at once exclusive and inclusive, transcendent and immanent. While transcending us infinitely, the alpha and the omega reside in the depths of our heart.[5]

What we can and must know is what we are; and this is why we can know it infallibly, provided the veils separating us from our true nature are removed. Man imposes these veils on himself because his Luciferian will identifies itself with them, because he therefore believes that he recognizes himself in them, and because to remove them is thereby to die. This at least is what man feels as long as he has not understood that "I am black, but beautiful."

There are also extrinsic proofs of the primacy of the Spirit, and these are by no means negligible; we have often alluded to them, and they result from the very nature of man. If everything had begun with matter and if there were no Spirit, hence no God, how could we explain the fact that men were able firmly to believe the contrary for thousands of years and even put forth a maximum of intelligence in affirming it and a maximum of heroism in living up to it? It is preposterous to attribute this to progress since unbelievers of every kind are far from being superior to believers and sages, and nowhere does one see an evolutionary transition from the second to the first; materialistic ideas have manifested and spread before our eyes—since the "Age of Enlightenment"—even though it is impossible to find in this process a qualitative ascent, at once intellectual and moral; quite the contrary.

---

5. The key to the Delphic mysteries is: "Know thyself" (*Gnōthi seauton*); to know the nature of subjectivity is to know the structure of the world.

Those who hold the evolutionist belief in intellectual progress like to explain religious and metaphysical ideas by inferior psychological factors, such as fear of the unknown, childish longing for a perpetual happiness, attachment to an imagery that has become dear to them, escape into dreams, the desire to oppress others at little expense, and so forth; but how can one fail to see that such suspicions, presented shamelessly as demonstrated facts, entail psychological inconsistencies and impossibilities, which cannot escape any impartial observer? If humanity had been stupid for thousands of years, one could never explain how it ceased being so, especially since this supposedly occurred in a very short period of time; and it can be explained still less when one observes with what intelligence and heroism it was stupid for so long and with what philosophic myopia and moral decadence it has finally become "lucid" and "adult."[6]

The essence of the real is the banal or trivial, scientists and other pseudo-realists seem to say. To which we would answer: The essence of the real is the miraculous—the miracle of consciousness, intelligence, knowledge. In the beginning there was not matter but Spirit, which is both the alpha and the omega of all.

6. A characteristic trait of our times is that everywhere "the cart is put before the horse"; what should normally be the means becomes the end, and vice versa. Machines are supposed to be there for men, but in fact men are there for machines; whereas formerly roads existed for towns, now towns exist for the roads; instead of mass media being there for "culture," now "culture" is there for the mass media. The modern world is an inextricable confusion of reversals that no one can stop.

Māyā

The goddess *Māyā* sewed a garment
Of golden cloth, yet with dark stripes—
For shadow ever follows light;
Shining and darkness—who can understand?

A garment—the world. Whom did *Māyā* desire to clothe
And what to veil? That which alone is:
The hidden sun that shines unseen—
Primordial beauty: the pure and naked Real.

7

TRACING THE NOTION OF PHILOSOPHY

Were Ibn Arabi, Jili, and other theoreticians of Sufism philosophers? Yes and no, depending on the meaning given this word.

According to Pythagoras wisdom is *a priori* knowledge of the stellar world and everything above us, *sophia* being the wisdom of the gods and *philosophia* that of men. For Heraclitus the philosopher is someone who devotes himself to a knowledge of the profound nature of things, whereas for Plato philosophy is knowledge of the Immutable and the Ideas; and for Aristotle it is knowledge of first causes and principles, together with the sciences derived from them. Moreover philosophy implies for all the Ancients moral conformity to wisdom: He alone is wise, *sophos*, who lives wisely. In this particular and precise sense, the wisdom of Solomon is philosophy; it is to live according to the nature of things on the basis of piety—the "fear of God"—and for the sake of what is essential and liberating.

All this shows that the word "philosopher" in itself has nothing restrictive about it, to say the least, and that one cannot legitimately impute to this word itself the vexing associations of ideas it may elicit; the term is used for all thinkers, including eminent metaphysicians—some Sufis consider Plato and other Greeks to be prophets—so that one would like to reserve it for sages and simply use the term "rationalists" for profane thinkers. Nonetheless it is legitimate to take account of a misuse of language that has become conventional, for there can be no doubt that the terms "philosophy" and "philosopher" have been seriously compromised by ancient and modern sophists; in fact the major disadvantage of these words is that they have come to imply that the norm for the mind is reasoning pure and simple,[1] in the absence of intellection and without benefit of

1. Of course the most "advanced" of the modernists seek to demolish the very principles of reasoning, but this is simply fantasy *pro domo*, for unless he wishes to demonstrate nothing at all man is condemned to reason as soon as he uses language. In any case, one cannot demonstrate the impossibility of demonstrating something, if words are still to have any meaning.

indispensable objective data. Admittedly a person is neither ignorant nor rationalistic just because he is a logician, but he is both if he is a logician and nothing more.[2]

In the opinion of all profane thinkers, philosophy means to think "freely" and as far as one can without presuppositions, which is clearly impossible; on the other hand *gnosis*, or philosophy in the proper and original sense of the word, means to think in accordance with the immanent Intellect and not by means of reason alone. This can be confusing, for in both cases the intelligence operates independently of outward prescriptions, although for diametrically opposite reasons: The rationalist draws his inspiration if necessary from a pre-existing system, but this does not prevent him from thinking in a way he deems to be "free"—falsely so, since true freedom coincides with truth; and likewise, *mutatis mutandis*, the gnostic—in the orthodox sense of the term—may base himself extrinsically on a given sacred Scripture or some other gnostic, but this does not prevent him from thinking in an intrinsically free manner by virtue of the freedom proper to the immanent Truth or proper to the Essence, which by definition escapes formal constraints. Whether the gnostic "thinks" what he has "seen" with the "eye of the heart" or whether on the contrary he obtains his "vision" thanks to the intervention—preliminary and provisional, though never fully effective—of a thought, which then takes on the role of occasional cause, is a matter of indifference with regard to the truth or its quasi-supernatural bursting forth in the mind.

*

* *

The reduction of intellectuality to simple rationality is often rooted in the prejudice of a school: Saint Thomas is an empiricist in the sense that he reduces the cause of all non-theological knowledge to sensible perceptions in order to be able to underestimate the human mind to the advantage of Scripture—because this allows him, in other words, to attribute the glory of "supernatural" knowledge to Revelation alone; and Ghazzali inveighs against the "philosophers" because he wishes to give the Sufis a monopoly

2. A German author (H. Türck) has proposed the term "misosopher"—"enemy of wisdom"—for those thinkers who undermine the very foundations of truth and intelligence. Without mentioning some ancient precedents, we would add that misosophy begins *grosso modo* with "criticism" and ends with subjectivisms, relativisms, existentialisms, dynamisms, psychologisms, and biologisms of every kind. As for the ancient expression "misology," it designates above all a fideist hatred for the use of reason.

on spiritual knowledge, as if faith and piety, combined with intellectual gifts and grace—all the Arab philosophers were believers—did not provide a sufficient basis for pure intellection.

According to Ibn Arabi, the "philosopher"—which for him practically means the skeptic—is incapable of knowing universal causality except by observing causes in the outer world and drawing from these observations the conclusions demanded by his sense of logic. According to another Sufi, Ibn al-Arif, intellectual knowledge is merely an "indication" pointing to God: The philosopher knows God only by way of a "conclusion"; the content of his knowledge is only "for the sake of God" and not "by God" as is that of the mystic. But this *distinguo* is valid only if we assimilate all philosophy to unmitigated rationalism and forget that in the doctrinal mystics there is also an obvious element of rationality. In short, the term "philosopher" in current speech signifies nothing other than the fact of expounding a doctrine while respecting the laws of logic, which are those of language and of common sense and without which we would not be human; to practice philosophy is first and foremost to think, whatever the reasons that rightly or wrongly incite us to do so. But according to the best of the Greeks it means more precisely expressing certainties that have been "seen" or "lived" with the immanent Intellect by means of reason, as we already noted above; now an explanation necessarily takes on the character given it by the laws of thought and language.

Some will object that the simple believer who understands nothing of philosophy can derive much more from scriptural symbols than does the philosopher with his definitions, abstractions, classifications, and categories—an unjust reproach, for in the first place theorizing thought does not exclude supra-rational intuition, which is completely obvious, and in the second place it does not pretend to provide by itself anything it is unable to offer by virtue of its nature. What it can offer may be of immense value, or else it would be necessary to suppress all doctrines; Platonic *anamnesis* can have doctrinal concepts as its occasional cause as well as symbols provided by art or virgin nature. If in intellectual speculation there is a human danger of rationalism and thus—at least in principle—of skepticism and materialism, mystical speculation for its part includes, with the same reservation, a danger of excesses or even of rambling and incoherence, whatever may be said by esotericizing zealots who take pleasure in begging the question and using sublimating euphemisms.

*

* *

We must say a few words here in defense of the Arab philosophers, who have been accused among other things of confusing Plato, Aristotle, and

Plotinus. We believe on the contrary that they had the merit of integrating these great Greeks in one and the same synthesis, for what interested them was not systems but truth as such. We shall no doubt run counter to certain esotericist prejudices if we say that metaphysically orthodox philosophy—that of the Middle Ages as well as antiquity—is derived from sapiential esotericism, whether intrinsically by its truth or extrinsically in relation to the simplifications of theology; it is "thinking" certainly but not ratiocination in the void. If it is objected that the errors found in some philosophers who are otherwise orthodox prove the non-esoteric and consequently profane nature of all philosophy, this argument can be turned against theology as well as mystical or gnostic doctrines, for erroneous speculations can be found here as well on the margin of real inspirations.

To give a concrete example, which is interesting in itself and apart from any question of terminology: The Arab philosophers rightly accept the eternity of the world, for, as they say, God cannot create at a given moment without putting Himself in contradiction with His very nature and thus without absurdity;[3] most ingeniously Ghazzali replies—and others have repeated the same argument—that there is no "before" with regard to creation, that time "was" created with, for, and in the world. But this argument is invalid since it is unilateral: Though it safeguards the transcendence, absolute freedom, and timelessness of the Creator in relation to creation, it does not explain the temporality of this creation, which means that it does not take into account the temporal limitation of a unique world projected into the void of non-time, a limitation necessarily involving God since He is its cause and since it exists in relation to His eternity;[4] the very nature of duration requires a beginning. The solution of the problem is that the co-eternity of the world is not that of our "actual" world, which of necessity had an origin and will have an end; rather this co-eternity consists in the necessity of successive worlds. God being what He is—with His absolute Necessity and absolute Freedom—He cannot not create, but He is free with

3. Indeed, the unicity of God excludes that of the world in both succession and extent; the infinity of God demands the repetition of the world in both respects: Creation cannot be a unique event anymore than it can be reduced to the human world alone.

4. All the same, it can be said in favor of this argument—which is repeated by Ibn Arabi—that it is the only legitimate way of reconciling emanationist truth with creationist dogma without giving this dogma an interpretation too far removed from the "letter"; we say "emanationist truth" in order to emphasize that what is in question is an authentic metaphysical idea and not some pantheistic or deistic emanationism. Be that as it may, Ibn Arabi, when speaking of creation—at the beginning of his *Fusūs al-Hikam*—cannot help expressing himself in a temporal mode: "When the divine Reality willed to see . . . its Essence" (*lammā shā᾿a ᾿l-Haqqu subhānahu an yarā . . . ʿaynahu*); it is true that in Arabic the past tense has in principle the sense of the eternal present when it is a question of God, but this applies above all to the verb "to be" (*kāna*) and does not prevent creation from being understood as an "act" and not a "quality."

regard to the modes of creation, which never repeat themselves since He is infinite. The whole difficulty comes from the fact that Semitic peoples take into consideration only one world, namely ours, whereas the non-Semiticized Aryans either accept an indefinite series of creations—this is the Hindu doctrine of cosmic cycles—or else consider the world as a necessary manifestation of the divine Nature and not as a contingent and particular phenomenon. In this confrontation between two theses, the theological and philosophical, it is the philosophers and not the theologians—even if they were Sufis like Ghazzali—who are right; and if doctrinal esotericism is the explanation of problems posed but not clarified by faith, we do not see why those philosophers who provide this explanation thanks to intellection—for reasoning pure and simple would not succeed in doing so, and it is in any case metaphysical truth that proves the worth of the intuition corresponding to it—would not have the same merit as recognized esotericists, especially since, to paraphrase Saint Paul, one cannot testify to great truths except by the Holy Spirit.

For theologians, to say that the world is "without beginning" amounts to saying that it is eternal *a se*—this is why they reject the idea—whereas for philosophers it means that it is eternal *ab alio*, for it is God who lends it eternity. Now an eternity that is borrowed is a completely different thing from eternity in itself, and it is precisely for this reason that the world is both eternal and temporal: eternal as a series of creations or a creative rhythm and temporal by the fact that each link in this flux has a beginning and an end. It is universal Manifestation as such that is co-eternal with God because it is a necessary expression of His eternal Nature—the sun is unable to abstain from shining—but eternity cannot be reduced to a given contingent phase of this divine Manifestation. Manifestation is "co-eternal," which is to say that it is not eternal in the same way as the single Essence; and this is why it is periodically interrupted and totally reabsorbed into the Principle, so that it is at once existent and nonexistent and does not enjoy a plenary and so to speak "continuous" reality like the Eternal itself. To say that the world is "co-eternal" nevertheless means that it is necessary as an aspect of the Principle, that it is therefore "something of God," which is already indicated by the term "Manifestation"; and it is precisely this truth that theologians refuse to accept—for obvious reasons since in their eyes it abolishes the difference between creature and Creator.[5]

5. The total Universe can be compared to either a circle or a cross, the center in both cases representing the Principle; in the first image the relationship between the periphery and the center is discontinuous, this being the dogmatic perspective of theology, analogically speaking, whereas in the second image the same relationship is continuous, this being the perspective of *gnosis*. The first perspective is valid when phenomena as such are considered—something *gnosis* would not contest—whereas the second perspective takes into account the essential reality of things and the Universe.

The "co-eternity" of the world with God recalls the universal *Materia* of Empedocles and Ibn Masarrah, which is none other than the *Logos* as Substance (*ʿamāʾ* = "cloud" or *habāʾ* = "dust"):[6] It is not creation as such that is co-eternal with the Creator; it is creative virtuality, which comprises—according to these doctrines—four fundamental formative principles. Symbolically speaking, these are "Fire," "Air," "Water," "Earth,"[7] which recall the three principial determinations (*gunas*) included in *Prakriti*: *Sattva*, *Rajas*, *Tamas*, the difference in number indicating a secondary difference in perspective.[8]

*

* *

Regarding the confrontation between Sufis and philosophers, the following remark must be made: If Ghazzali had limited himself to noting that there is no possible esoteric realization without an initiation and a corresponding method and that philosophers in general require neither one nor the other,[9] we would have no reason to criticize him, but his reproach is leveled at philosophy as such; in other words it is situated above all on the doctrinal and epistemological plane. In fact the Hellenizing philosophy here in question is neutral from the initiatic point of view, for its intention is to provide an exposition of truth and nothing else; particular opinions—such as those of rationalism properly so called—do not enter into the definition of philosophy.[10] Be that as it may, the Ghazzalian ostracism makes us

6. This idea, like the terms used to express it, belongs to Islam, apart from the Greek analogies noted afterward; there is nothing surprising in this since truth is one.

7. This Empedoclean quaternity is found in another form in the cosmology of the Indians of North America and perhaps also of Mexico and other more southern regions: Here it is Space that symbolizes Substance, the universal "Ether," while the cardinal points represent the four principial and existentiating determinations.

8. *Sattva*—analogically speaking—is "Fire," which rises and illumines; *Tamas* is "Earth," which is heavy and obscure. *Rajas*—by reason of its intermediary position—includes an aspect of lightness and another of heaviness, namely, "Air" and "Water," but both considered in violent mode; it is on the one hand the unleashing of the winds and on the other that of the waves.

9. This possible silence proves nothing in any case against the rightness of a given philosophy; and besides, Plato said in one of his letters that his writings did not include all his teachings. It may be noted that, according to Synesius, the goal of monks and philosophers is the same, namely, the contemplation of God.

10. In our first book, *The Transcendent Unity of Religions*, we adopted the point of view of Ghazzali regarding "philosophy": Bearing in mind the great impoverishment of modern philosophies, we simplified the problem as others have done before us by making "philosophy" synonymous with "rationalism." According to Ghazzali, to practice philosophy is to operate by syllogisms—though he has no qualms making use of them himself—and thus to use logic; the question is whether one does so *a priori* or *a posteriori*.

think of those theologians of old who sought to oppose the "vain wisdom of the world" with "tears of repentance" but who finally did not refrain from constructing systems of their own and who in doing so could not manage without the help of the Greeks, to whom nevertheless they denied the assistance of the "Holy Spirit" and therefore any supernatural quality.

Sufis do not wish to be philosophers—that is understood; and they are right if they mean by this that their starting point is not doubt and that their certainties are not rational conclusions. But we absolutely do not see why when they reason wrongly they would do so in a manner different from philosophers nor why a philosopher when he conceives a truth whose transcendent and axiomatic nature he recognizes would do so in a manner different from the Sufis.

Ibn Arabi dealt with the question of evil not as a gnostic but as a "thinker," explaining it in terms of subjectivity and relativity with an entirely Pyrrhonic logic. The problem with this treatment is that in abolishing evil, practically speaking—since it is reduced to a subjective point of view—one ends up abolishing good by the same stroke, whether this was intended or not; and in particular one abolishes beauty by depriving love of its content, even though Ibn Arabi's doctrine insists precisely on the reality of both and on their necessary connection. It is beauty that determines love, not conversely: The beautiful is not what we love and because we love it, but what by its objective value obliges us to love it; we love the beautiful because it is beautiful even if we lack judgment, and this does not invalidate the principle of the normal relationship between object and subject. Likewise, the fact that one may love because of an inward beauty and despite an outward ugliness or that love may be mixed with compassion or other indirect motives cannot invalidate the nature of either beauty or love.

On the other hand Ibn Arabi responded to the question of freedom as a gnostic: Every creature does what it wills because every creature is basically what it wills to be—in other words because a possibility is what it is and not something else. In the final analysis, freedom coincides with possibility, and this is attested to by the Koranic story of the initial pact between human souls and God; destiny is therefore what the creature wills by his nature and thus by his possibility. One may wonder which we should regard as more admirable: the gnostic who penetrated the mystery or the philosopher who knew how to make it explicit.

But if man does what he is or if he is what he does, why strive to become better and why pray to this end? Because there is a distinction between substance and accident: Demerits as well as merits can come from either one without a man necessarily knowing from which they come, unless he is a "pneumatic" and is aware of his substantial reality, an ascending reality precisely because of its conformity to the Spirit (*Pneuma*). "Whoso knoweth his soul knoweth his Lord"; but even then the effort belongs to man and the knowledge to God; in other words it is enough for us to strive while being aware that God knows us. It is enough for us to know we are free in and through our movement toward God, our movement toward our "Self."

*

* *

In a certain respect the difference between philosophy, theology, and *gnosis* is total; in another respect it is relative. It is total when "philosophy" is taken to mean only rationalism, when "theology" means only the explanation of religious teachings, and when *gnosis* is only intuitive and intellective, thus supra-rational, knowledge; but the difference is merely relative when "philosophy" means the fact of thinking, "theology" the fact of speaking dogmatically about God and religious things, and *gnosis* the fact of presenting pure metaphysics, for then the categories interpenetrate. It is undeniable that the most illustrious Sufis, while being "gnostics" by definition, were at the same time to some extent theologians and to some extent philosophers or that the great theologians were to some extent philosophers and to some extent gnostics, this last word being understood in its proper and not sectarian meaning.

If we wish to retain the restricted or even pejorative sense of the word "philosopher," we can say that *gnosis* or pure metaphysics starts with certainty, whereas philosophy on the contrary starts from doubt and serves to overcome this doubt only with the means at its disposal, which are intended to be purely rational. But since neither the term "philosophy" as such nor the use that has always been made of the word obliges us to accept only its restrictive sense, we shall not censure too severely those who employ it with a wider meaning than may seem opportune.[11]

Theory by definition is not an end in itself; it is only—and seeks only to be—a key for becoming conscious through the "heart." If a suspicion of superficiality, insufficiency, and pretension is attached to the notion of

11. Even Ananda Coomaraswamy does not hesitate to speak of "Hindu philosophy," which at least has the advantage of making clear the "literary genre," and in any case the reader is supposed to know what the Hindu spirit is in particular and what the traditional spirit is in general. In a similar manner, when speaking of the "Hindu religion," one knows perfectly well that it is not a case—and cannot be a case—of a Semitic and western religion, hence a religion that tends to resist every differentiation of perspective; one also speaks traditionally of the Roman, Greek, and Egyptian "religions," and the Koran does not hesitate to say to the pagan Arabs: "Unto you your religion, and unto me mine," even though the religion of the pagans had none of the characteristic features of Judeo–Christian monotheism.

"philosophy," it is precisely because all too often—and in fact always in the case of the moderns—it is presented as if it were sufficient unto itself. "This is only philosophy": We readily accept this turn of phrase but only provided one does not say, "Plato is only a philosopher"—Plato who knew that "beauty is the splendor of the true," a beauty including or requiring all we are or can be.

When Plato maintains that the *philosophos* should think independently of common opinions, he is referring to intellection and not logic alone; on the other hand Descartes, who did everything to restrict and compromise the notion of philosophy, maintains the same thing while starting from systematic doubt, and as a result philosophy for him is synonymous not only with rationalism but also with skepticism. This is a first suicide of the intelligence, inaugurated by Pyrrho and others as a reaction against what was believed to be metaphysical "dogmatism." The "Greek miracle" is in fact the substitution of reason for Intellect, of the fact for the Principle, of the phenomenon for the Idea, of the accident for the Substance, of the form for the Essence, of man for God; and this applies to art as well as thought. The true Greek miracle, if miracle there is—and in this case it would be related to the "Hindu miracle"—is doctrinal metaphysics and methodic logic, providentially utilized by the monotheistic Semites.

*
* *

The notion of philosophy, with its lingering trace of human fallibility, evokes *ipso facto* the problem of infallibility and thus the question of knowing whether man is condemned by his nature to err. The human mind, even when disciplined by a sacred tradition, remains exposed to many flaws; but that such flaws are possible does not mean they are inevitable in principle; on the contrary they are due to causes that are in no way mysterious. Doctrinal infallibility pertains to the realm of orthodoxy and authority; the first element is objective and the second subjective, and each has a significance that is formal or non-formal, extrinsic or intrinsic, traditional or universal, depending on the case. This being so, it is not really difficult to be infallible when one knows one's limits; it is enough not to speak of things of which one is ignorant, which presupposes of course that one knows one is ignorant of them. This amounts to saying not only that infallibility is a matter of information and intellection but also that it includes, essentially, a moral or psychological condition, without which even men who are in principle infallible become accidentally fallible. Let us add that there is nothing wrong with offering a plausible hypothesis provided that it is not presented in the form of certainty *ex cathedra*.

In any case there is no infallibility that *a priori* encompasses all possible contingent domains; omniscience is not a human possibility. No one can be infallible about phenomena that are unknown or insufficiently known; a person may have an intuition for pure principles without having it for a given phenomenal order, that is, without being able to apply the principles spontaneously in a particular domain. The importance of this possible incapacity diminishes in cases where the phenomenal domain in question is secondary and where, on the contrary, the principles infallibly expressed are essential. One must forgive small errors on the part of someone who offers great truths—and it is these truths that determine how small or how great are the errors—whereas it would obviously be perverse to forgive great errors just because they are accompanied by many small truths.[12]

Infallibility—in a sense by definition—pertains to the Holy Spirit in one degree or another and in a way that may be extraordinary or ordinary, properly supernatural or quasi-natural; in the religious domain the Holy Spirit adapts itself to the nature of man in the sense that it is content to forestall the victory of intrinsic heresies, a victory that would falsify that "divine form" that is the religion; for the *upāya*, the "saving mirage," is willed by Heaven and not by men.[13]

12. There is certainly no reason to admire a science that enumerates insects and atoms but is unaware of God, a science that professes ignorance concerning Him and yet claims omniscience as a matter of principle. It should be noted that the scientist, like every other rationalist, does not base himself on reason as such; he calls "reason" his lack of imagination and knowledge, and the gaps in his knowledge are for him the "data" of reason.

13. Always respectful of this form, the Holy Spirit will not teach a Muslim theologian the subtleties of Trinitarian theology or those of *Vedānta*; and from another angle it will not change a racial or ethnic mentality—neither that of the Romans with regard to Catholicism or that of the Arabs with regard to Islam. Humanity must have not only its history but also its histrionics.

Bodhi

It has been said
    Nirvāna is nothingness.

Not for the wise,
    But for the ignorant.

There is a void
    Which is mere nothingness;

There is another
    Which alone is real.

And It is empty
    Because beyond the world;

Yet It is fullness
    For him who contains It—

For the Awakened,
    Who wanders no more;

O holy silence—
    Jewel in the Lotus, hail!

8

UNDERSTANDING AND BELIEVING

It is commonly accepted that a man can believe without understanding; people are much less aware of the opposite possibility—that one can understand without believing—and it may even appear to be a contradiction since faith does not seem necessary except for those who do not understand. But hypocrisy is not merely the dissimulation of a person who pretends to be better than he is; it can also be seen in a disproportion between certainty and behavior, and in this respect most men are more or less hypocritical since they claim to accept truths that they practice only feebly. On the plane of simple belief, to believe without acting on one's belief corresponds—on the intellectual plane—to an understanding that is devoid of faith and life; for real belief means identifying oneself with the truth one accepts, whatever the level of this adherence. Piety is to religious belief what operative faith is to doctrinal understanding or—we may add—what sanctity is to truth.

If we begin with the idea that spirituality consists essentially in two factors, namely, discernment between the Real and the illusory and permanent concentration on the Real—the *conditio sine qua non* in each case being the observance of traditional rules and the practice of the accompanying virtues—we can see that there is a relationship between discernment and understanding on the one hand and between concentration and faith on the other; whatever its degree, faith always means a sort of existential participation in Being or the Real; to make use of a fundamental *hadīth*, it is "to worship God as if thou sawest Him, and if thou seest Him not, yet He seeth thee." In other words, faith is a participation of the will with intelligence; just as on the physical plane a man must adapt his action to the conditions determining its nature, so also on the spiritual plane he should act in accord with his convictions, and he should do so by inward activity even more than outward activity, for "before acting one must be," and our being is nothing other than our inward activity. The soul should be to the intelligence what beauty is to truth; this is what is called "moral qualification," which must accompany intellectual qualification.

There is a relationship between faith and symbol; there is also one between faith and miracles. In the symbolic image as well as in the miraculous fact, it is the language of being and not of reasoning that speaks; man must respond with his own being to a manifestation of being on the part of Heaven, and this he does through faith or love—these are two aspects of one and the same reality—though without thereby ceasing to be a creature who thinks. Practically speaking, one might wonder what basis or justification there could be for an elementary faith that is disdainful, or nearly so, of any attempt at comprehension; but we have just provided the answer: Such a faith is based on the illuminating power that belongs in principle to the symbols, phenomena, and arguments of Revelation.[1] The "obscure merit" of this faith consists in our not being closed to a grace for which our nature is made. There is room for differences on the human side regarding modes or degrees of receptivity as well as intellectual needs; these needs do not in any sense mean that the thinking man lacks faith but merely show that his receptivity is sensitive to the most subtle and implicit aspects of the divine Message; now what is implicit is not the inexpressible but the esoteric, and this has a right to be expressed.[2] We have already drawn attention to the relationship between faith and miracles; in fact, perfect faith consists in being aware of the metaphysically miraculous character of natural phenomena and therefore in seeing in them the trace of God.

The defect of unbelief or absence of faith does not therefore lie in a natural lack of special aptitudes, nor is it due to some unintelligibility in the Message, for then there would be no defect; it lies in a passional stiffening of the will and in the worldly tendencies that bring this about. The merit of faith is fidelity to the "supernaturally natural" receptivity of primordial man; it means remaining as God made us and remaining open to a Message from Heaven that might be contrary to our earthly experience but that is nonetheless incontestable in light of subjective as well as objective criteria.[3]

It is related that Ibn Taimiyyah,[4] when coming down from the pulpit after a sermon, once said: "God comes down from Heaven to earth as I am

---

1. These are the "signs" (*āyāt*) of which the Koran speaks, and they may include even natural phenomena as seen in light of revealed doctrine. It should be pointed out that the insensibility exhibited by those who believe in an intrinsically orthodox religion toward the arguments of another religion does not in any way come into question here since the motive for refusal in this case is something positive, namely, an already existing faith that is valid in itself.

2. It goes without saying that the implicit is to be found even on the plane of the literal meaning, but this mode of instruction causes practically no problems and is not at issue here.

3. To say that Abraham and Mary had the merit of great faith means that they were sensible to divine criteria despite the apparent impossibility of the Message; this shows that the men of old were by no means credulous, if we may be allowed to make this remark in a context that clearly transcends the level of ordinary humanity, for we are speaking of prophets.

4. Arab theologian of the thirteenth century, Hanbalite by origin, and the protagonist of an extreme exotericism.

coming down now";[5] there is no reason to doubt that he meant this to be taken literally—with a literalism averse to all interpretation—but his attitude has nonetheless a symbolic value independent of his personal opinions: The refusal to analyze a symbol with discursive and separative thought—in order to assimilate it directly and as it were existentially—does in fact correspond to a possible perspective and one that is therefore valid in the appropriate circumstances. We see here a coincidence between "blind faith" and an attitude that is at once its opposite and its analogue, namely, the assimilation of truth through a symbol and by means of the whole soul, the soul as such.

*

* *

As a quality of the soul, faith is the stabilizing complement of the discerning and as it were explosive intelligence; without this complement intellectual activity—not pure intellection—can easily allow itself to be carried away by its own movement and become like a devouring fire; it loses its balance and ends either by consuming itself in an irresolvable restlessness or simply by exhausting itself and becoming sclerotic. Faith implies all the static and gentle qualities, such as patience, gratitude, trust, generosity; it offers the mercurial intelligence a stabilizing element and thus achieves—together with discernment—an equilibrium that is like an anticipation of sanctity. In Islam the complementary terms "blessing" (or "prayer," *salāh*) and "peace" (or "greeting," *salām*) are applied to this polarity at its highest level.

We have had occasion to stress more than once that an intellectual qualification is not fully valid unless accompanied by an equivalent moral qualification; this is what explains all the fideist attitudes, which seem bent on limiting the force of intelligence. The supporters of tradition (*naql*) pure and simple during the first centuries of Islam were deeply conscious of this, and Ashari himself must have sensed it—although it took him in the opposite direction, since he ventured onto the plane of theological reasoning—when he attributed to God an unintelligibility that, in the final analysis, could indicate no more than the precariousness of man's intellectual resources before the dimension of absoluteness.

One could meditate or speculate indefinitely on transcendent truths and their applications; this in fact is what we ourselves do, but we have valid reasons, and it is not for ourselves that we do it. Indeed one could spend a whole lifetime speculating on the supra-sensory and the transcendent, but

5. With reference to the *hadīth* of "the Descent" (*al-Nuzūl*): "Our Lord—Blessed and Exalted be He—cometh down each night unto the earthly heaven (*al-samā' al-dunyā*) when the last third of the night yet remaineth, and He saith: Who calleth upon Me that I may answer him? Who asketh of Me that I may give unto him? Who seeketh My forgiveness that I may forgive him?"

all that matters is the "leap into the void," which is a fixation of the mind and soul in an unthinkable dimension of the Real; this leap, which cuts short and completes in itself a chain of formulations that is in principle endless,[6] depends on a direct understanding and a grace and not on having reached a certain phase in the unfolding of doctrine, for this unfolding—we repeat—has no logical end. This "leap into the void" we can refer to as "faith"; it is the negation of this reality that gives rise to every philosophy that is simply an "art for art's sake" and to all thought that believes it can attain to an absolute contact with Reality by means of analyses, syntheses, arrangements, filterings, polishings; such thought is mundane because of this very ignorance and because it ends up becoming a "vicious circle," which not only provides no escape from illusion but even reinforces it through the lure of a progressive knowledge that is in fact nonexistent.[7]

Considering the harm that the prejudices and tendencies of ordinary piety can sometimes inflict on metaphysical speculations, it might be tempting to conclude that piety should be abandoned on the threshold of pure knowledge, but this would be a false and highly pernicious conclusion; in fact piety—or faith—should never be absent from the soul, though it is only too clear that it must be on the same level as the truths it accompanies, which means that such an extension is perfectly consistent with its nature, as is proven by Vedantic hymns, to take just one particularly conclusive example.

Hindus have been criticized for being inveterate idolators and finding in the least phenomenon a pretext for idolatry; there is even an annual festival, apparently, at which the craftsman gathers his tools together in order to worship them. The truth is that the Hindu refuses to become rooted in outwardness but instead readily looks to the divine substratum of things, whence his acute sense of the sacred and his devotional mentality; this is precisely what modern man does not want, a man who has become monstrously "adult" by conforming to the worst illusion that has ever darkened the human mind. The reflection of the sun may not be the sun, but it is nonetheless "something of the sun," and in this sense it is

6. Without this completion, there would be no such thing as doctrines since doctrines are by definition forms, delimitations, mental coagulations.

7. A valid doctrine is a "description," and its author—basing himself on a direct and supramental knowledge—is therefore under no illusion as to its inevitable formal limitations; on the other hand a philosophy that claims to be a "research" is a mere nothing, and its apparent modesty is no more than a pretentious negation of true wisdom, which is absurdly called "metaphysical dogmatism." There is obviously no humility in saying one is ignorant because everyone is ignorant.

not wrong to speak elliptically of a kind of identity since the light is always the one light and the cause is really present in the effect; whoever does not respect the effect renders himself incapable of fully respecting the cause—a cause moreover which withholds itself from anyone who despises its reflections—and whoever does understand the cause perceives it also in its earthly traces. The sense of the sacred: This phrase gives felicitous expression to a dimension that should never be absent from either metaphysical thought or everyday life; this is what gives birth to the liturgies, and without it there is no faith. The sense of the sacred, accompanied by dignity, incorruptibility, patience, and generosity, is the key to integral faith and the supernatural virtues inherent in it.

*

* *

In adopting the alchemist's distinction between a "dry path" and a "moist path," the first corresponding to "knowledge" and the second to "love," it is important to realize that the two poles to which these paths correspond—"fire" and "water"—are both reflected in each path, so that "knowledge" necessarily contains an aspect of "moisture" and "love" an aspect of "dryness."

Within the framework of a path of love, the aspect of "dryness" or "fire" is doctrinal orthodoxy, for there can be no spirituality without the implacable and immutable bulwark provided by a divine expression of salvific Truth; in a similar and yet opposite fashion, "moisture" or "water"—the feminine aspect, which is derived from the divine Substance (*Prakriti*, the *Shakti*)—is indispensable to the path of "knowledge" for the obvious and already mentioned reasons of equilibrium, stability, and effectiveness.

As for comparing the quality of "knowledge" with fire, this cannot perfectly and exhaustively account for the nature of the metaphysical intelligence and its realizational activity. Indeed, apart from its qualities of luminosity and ascension, fire in itself includes an aspect of agitation and destructiveness, and this aspect—the very one that fideist opponents of *kalām* have in mind—proves that "knowledge-fire" is not self-sufficient and therefore has an imperative need for "knowledge-water," which is none other than faith, together with all its stabilizing and soothing virtues.[8] Even the most penetrating intelligence, if it relies too much on its own strength, runs the risk of being forsaken by Heaven; forgetting that the knowing Subject is God, it closes itself to the divine influx. Any thought that is ignorant

8. "There is no lustral water like unto knowledge," says the *Bhagavad Gītā*; in this case water, not fire, is related to *jnāna*.

of metaphysical and mystical truths is profane,[9] but so also is any thought that knows these truths well enough in theory and yet approaches them in a disproportionate way, without a sufficient adaptation of the soul; unlike the first kind of thought, the second is not profane by definition, but it is so secondarily or morally and thus leaves itself seriously open to error, for man is not merely a mirror: He is a complex and fragile cosmos. The connection—often affirmed by tradition—between Knowledge and Peace shows in its own way that in pure intellectuality the mathematical element is not everything and that fire alone could never be the symbol of intellectuality.[10]

The combination of the two principles "fire" and "water" is none other than "wine," which is both "liquid fire" and "igneous water";[11] liberating intoxication comes precisely from this alchemical and as it were miraculous combination of opposite elements. Wine, not fire, is thus the most perfect image of liberating *gnosis* when this *gnosis* is considered not only in its total amplitude but also in the equilibrium of its virtual modes, for a balance between discernment and contemplation can be conceived at every level. Another image of this equilibrium or concordance is oil, for it is through oil that fire is stabilized and becomes the calm and contemplative flame of the lamps in sanctuaries. Like wine, oil is an igneous liquid, which "would almost glow forth (of itself) though no fire touched it," according to the famous Verse of Light (*āyat al-Nūr*).

From a certain elementary point of view, there is a connection between the emotional path of "warriors" and water, which is passive and "feminine," just as there is a connection between the intellectual path of "priests" and fire, which is active and "masculine"; but it is abundantly clear—we would stress this again—that water has a sacerdotal aspect of peace and that fire has a warlike aspect of devouring activity, and that each path necessarily contains a "dry" pole and a "moist" pole.

9. "Metaphysical": concerned with universal realities considered objectively. "Mystical": concerned with the same realities considered subjectively, that is, in relation to the contemplative soul insofar as they enter operatively into contact with it.

10. Shankara describes "inward Wisdom"—with which he identifies himself—as "That which is the stilling of mental agitation and the supreme consolation. . . . That which is the pool Manikarnika. . . . That which is the Ganges"; each of these images refers to water not fire. Islam for its part associates coolness, the color green, and streams with Paradise.

11. When the American Indians called alcohol "fire-water," they were expressing a profound truth without knowing it: the alchemical and quasi-supernatural coincidence of liquidity and combustion. According to the *Brihadāranyaka Upanishad* and the *Shatapatha Brāhmana*, the divine Fire (*Agni*) is engendered within the undifferentiated Self (*Ātmā*) by the tension between igneous Energy (*tejas*) and the Water of Life or the Elixir (*rasa*); *Agni* is "churned" and "born of the Waters" or "born of the Lotus"; he is the Lightning hidden in celestial Waters.

All these considerations bear upon the problem of the relationships between speculative intelligence and faith: Faith is pure and calm "water"; intelligence is active and discriminating "fire." To say that water is pure amounts to saying that it has a virtual quality of luminosity and that it is therefore predisposed to be a vehicle for fire and to be transmuted into wine, as happened at the marriage in Cana; when considered with regard to its possibilities, water is a virtual wine since it already possesses luminosity because of its purity and in this sense is comparable to oil; like wine, oil is igneous by its very nature, but at the same time it does not correspond exactly to wine except when combined with the flame it feeds, whereas wine has no need of any complement to manifest its nature.

*

* *

It follows from all we have said that faith and intelligence can each be conceived at two different levels: Faith as a quasi-ontological and pre-mental certitude ranks higher than intelligence understood as discerning and speculative thought,[12] but intelligence as pure intellection ranks higher than a faith which is no more than a sentimental adherence; this ambivalence is the source of numerous misunderstandings, but it also makes possible an exo-esoteric language that is at once simple and complex. Faith in its higher aspect is what we might call *religio cordis*: It is the "inward religion" that is supernaturally natural to man and that coincides with *religio caeli*—or *religio perennis*—that is, with universal truth, which is beyond the contingencies of form and time. This faith needs little to be contented: Unlike an intelligence that favors exactness but is never satisfied in its play of formulations—passing from concept to concept, symbol to symbol, without being able to settle on any—faith of the heart is capable of being satisfied by the first symbol that providentially comes its way and of living on it until the supreme Encounter.[13]

12. This higher faith is utterly different from the irresponsible and arrogant informality so characteristic of the profane improvisers of Zen or *jnāna*, who seek to take short cuts by omitting the essential human context of all realization, whereas in the East—and in the normal conditions of ethical and liturgical ambience—this context is largely supplied in advance. One does not enter the presence of a king by the back door.

13. In the lives of saints, the spiritual career is often inaugurated by an outward or inward incident that precipitates in the soul a particular and definitive attitude toward Heaven; the symbol in this case is not the incident itself but the positive spiritual factor that the incident serves to highlight.

The faith in question, which we have called *religio cordis*—the subjective and immanent side of *religio caeli*—includes two poles that conform to the distinction between the "dry" and "moist" paths; they are represented in northern Buddhism by Zen and *Jōdo* respectively. Both resist verbal comprehension, the first to plunge into our very being and the second to plunge into faith. For Zen, truth must coincide with reality, which is our existential and intellective substratum; whereas for *Jōdo* truth-reality is attained in perfect faith—in surrendering to universal Substance, which is Mercy and which appears to us in a given Sign or Key.[14]

The spiritual dimension symbolized by wine or intoxication is represented in *Mahāyāna* by the union of the two poles *Vajra* ("Lightning" or "Diamond") and *Garbha* ("Matrix")—or *Mani* ("Jewel") and *Padma* ("Lotus")—or by the conjunction between expressed Truth (*Upāya*) and liberating Knowledge (*Prajnā*); the "great Bliss" (*Mahāsukha*) resulting from the union of the two poles evokes the Beatitude (*Ānanda*) of *Ātmā*, in which "Consciousness" (*Chit*) and "Being" (*Sat*) meet. According to its most outward meaning, this directly or indirectly sexual symbolism expresses the equilibrium between mental knowledge and virtue; on this basis the equilibrium may be between doctrinal investigation and spiritual practice or between doctrine and method. All these modes can be brought back to the confrontation between "knowing" and "being" or between intellectual objectification and volitive or quasi-existential participation, or we might say between a mathematical or architectural dimension and an ethico-aesthetic or musical dimension, taking these terms in the most comprehensive sense they can bear and keeping in mind that phenomena have their roots in the divine order. It is true that from a certain point of view the element "being" is more than a complement; it combines the elements "knowing" and "willing," and in this case it represents the synthesis of sanctity underlying the polarity "intelligence-beauty," which brings us back to the symbolism of love and wine and to the mystery of faith coinciding with *gnosis*.

The cult of a goddess, of a *Shakti* or *Tārā*—of a "Lady," one might simply say—may indicate the predominance of a perspective of love or a dogmatic and methodic *bhakti*, but it may just as well be a sign, within the very perspective of *gnosis* or *jnāna*, that emphasis is being placed on the element "faith" in the higher sense of the term, the sense considered by Zen and *Jōdo*, precisely—the first according to the "dry path" and the second

14. In Amidism faith is ultimately based on an intuition of the essential Goodness of the Absolute, which is divinely "Other" in relation to the existence-bound subject; in Zen, on the contrary, what we call "faith" is based on an intuition of the essential reality of our "Self," our subjective, transpersonal, and nirvanic Essence.

according to the "moist path." This is also what Ibn Arabi meant—and in his case there can be no doubt that the perspective was that of *gnosis*—by the "religion of love," which he identified with *al-islām*, the essential conformation of the intelligence and soul with the divine nature, beyond all forms and oppositions.

III

HUMAN NATURE AND DESTINY

Man is "not of this world," and it is
the world that makes him aware of this.

—*Stations of Wisdom*

Samsāra

Man is the highest form of life on earth:
To become a noble human being
Is rare fortune—this is the teaching of the East;
To be a man is wholeness, to be an animal mere part.
The human state is the gate to salvation,
But not without effort, for the path is steep.

And so man roams this world of suffering,
Where everything is dying, passing, fading, crumbling.
The Buddha wishes that all should be happy:
His duty is to spread the message far and wide.
He does not do this with his word alone—

His serene being shines into the dark.

9

MAN IN THE UNIVERSE

Modern science, which is rationalist as to its subject and materialist as to its object, can describe our situation physically and approximately, but it can tell us nothing about our extra-spatial situation in the total and real Universe. Astronomers know more or less where we are in space, in what relative "place," in which of the peripheral arms of the Milky Way, and they may know where the Milky Way is situated among the other clusters of stardust; but they do not know where we are in existential "space," namely, in a state of hardening and at the center or summit of this state and, at the same time, on the edge of an immense "rotation," which is none other than the current of forms, the "samsaric" flow of phenomena, the Πάντα ῥεῖ of Heraclitus. In seeking to pierce to its depths the mystery of the things that contain—space, time, matter, energy—profane science forgets the mystery of the things contained; it seeks to explain the quintessential properties of our bodies and the intimate functioning of our souls, but it does not know what existence and intelligence are. Given its principles, it cannot but ignore what man truly is.

When we look around us, what do we see? First, existence; second, differences; third, movements, modifications, transformations; fourth, disappearances. All these things together manifest one of the states of universal Substance; this state is at once a crystallization and a rotation, a heaviness and a dispersion, a solidification and a segmentation. Just as water is in ice and the movement of the hub in a rim, so is God in phenomena; He is accessible in them and through them, and this is the whole mystery of symbolism and immanence. God is "the Outward" and "the Inward," "the First" and "the Last."[1]

God is the most dazzlingly evident of all self-evident things. Everything has a center; therefore the totality of things—the world—also has a center. We are at the periphery of "something absolute," and this something cannot be less powerful, less conscious, less intelligent than ourselves. Men

1. Koranic divine Names: *al-Ẓāhir* and *al-Bāṭin*, *al-Awwal* and *al-Ākhir*.

think they have "solid earth" beneath their feet and possess a real power; they feel perfectly at home on earth and attach much importance to themselves, whereas they know neither whence they came nor whither they are going and are drawn through life as by an invisible cord.

All things are limited. Now to say limitation is to say effect, and to say effect is to say cause; thus it is that all things, by their limitations no less than their content, prove God, the first and therefore limitless Cause.

What proves the Absolute extrinsically? In the first place the relative, which is meaningless without the absoluteness it restricts, and in the second place the "relatively absolute," which is the reflection of the Absolute in the relative. The question of intrinsic or direct proofs of the Absolute does not arise, for the evidence is in the Intellect itself and thus in our very being, and this means that indirect proofs can do no more than serve as supports or occasional causes; in the Intellect subject and object coincide or interpenetrate in a certain fashion. Certainty exists in fact, or else the word would not exist; hence there is no reason to deny it on the plane of pure intellection and the universal.[2]

*

* *

The ego is at once a system of images and a cycle; it is something like a museum, as well as a unique and irreversible journey through that museum. It is a moving fabric made of images and tendencies; the tendencies come from our own substance, and the images are furnished by the environment. We put ourselves into things, and we place things in ourselves, whereas our true being is independent of them.

Alongside this system of images and tendencies that constitutes our ego, there is a myriad of other systems of images and tendencies. Some of them are worse or less beautiful than our own, and others are better or more beautiful.

We are like foam ceaselessly renewed on the ocean of Existence. But since God has put Himself into this foam, it is destined to become a sea of stars at the time of the final crystallization of spirits. When its terrestrial contingency is left behind, the tiny system of images must become a star immortalized in the halo of Divinity. This star can be conceived on various levels; the divine Names are its archetypes; beyond the stars burns the Sun of the Self in its blazing transcendence and infinite peace.

---

2. Modern philosophy is a liquidation of evidences and therefore fundamentally of intelligence; it is no longer in any degree a *sophia* but rather a "misosophy."

Man does not choose; he follows his nature and his vocation, and it is God who chooses.

*
* *

A man who has fallen into the mire and who knows that he can get out in one way or another and with a certain effort does not think of rebelling against natural laws or cursing existence; it is obvious to him that mud can exist and that there is such a thing as gravity, and he thinks only of getting out of the mire. We are in the mire of earthly existence, and we know we can escape from it, whatever trials we may undergo; Revelation gives us this assurance, and the Intellect is able to take this into account *a posteriori*. It is therefore absurd to deny God and revile the world for the sole reason that existence presents fissures, which indeed it cannot but present, for otherwise it would not exist and would not be able to "existentiate."

We are situated as if beneath a sheet of ice that neither our five senses nor our reason enable us to pierce, but the Intellect—at once a mirror of the supra-sensible and itself a supernatural ray of light—passes through this ice without difficulty once Revelation has allowed it to become conscious of its own nature; religious belief also passes through this cosmic shell, no doubt in a less direct and more affective manner, but nonetheless often intuitively; divine Mercy, which is contained in universal Reality and which proves the fundamentally "beneficent"[3] character of this Reality, desires that Revelation should intervene wherever this sheet of ice or shell exists, and this means that we are never completely imprisoned except in our refusal of Mercy. Mistaking the ice for Reality, we do not acknowledge what it excludes, and we experience no desire for deliverance; we try to compel the ice to be happiness. On the physical level, no one thinks of refusing the Mercy that dwells indirectly in the nature of things; no man on the point of drowning refuses the pole held out to him, but too many men do refuse Mercy in the total order because it surpasses the narrow bounds of their daily experience and the no less narrow limits of their understanding. In general man does not want to be saved except on condition that he does not have to surpass himself.

The fact that we are imprisoned in our five senses contains within itself an aspect of Mercy, paradoxical though this may seem after what has just been said. If the number of our senses were multiplied—and there is no limit in principle to their multiplication—objective reality would tear

3. Although the divine nature is beyond moral specifications.

through us like a hurricane; it would rip us into pieces and at the same time crush us. Our "vital space" would become transparent; we would be as if suspended over an abyss or rushed through an incommensurable macrocosm, with its entrails exposed so to speak, and filled with terror; instead of living in a maternal, charitably opaque, and water-tight compartment of the universe—for the world is a womb and death a cruel birth—we would find ourselves ceaselessly faced with a totality of spaces or abysses and a myriad of creatures and phenomena, such that no individual being could possibly endure the experience. Man is made for the Absolute or the Infinite, not for limitless contingency.

Man, we have said, is as if buried under a sheet of ice. His experience of it takes various forms: At one time it is the cosmic ice that matter has become in its present and post-Edenic state of solidity, and at another time it is the ice of ignorance.

Goodness is in the very substance of the Universe, and for this reason it penetrates right into the matter we know, "accursed" though this matter may be; the fruits of the earth and the rain from the sky, which make life possible, are nothing if not manifestations of the Goodness that penetrates everywhere and warms the world and that we carry within ourselves, in the depths of our frozen hearts.

*
* *

The symbolism of a fountain reminds us that all things are by definition an exteriorization projected into a void, a void that is in itself nonexistent but that is nonetheless perceptible in phenomena; water in this imagery is the "stuff that dreams are made on" (Shakespeare) and that produces worlds and beings. The distance of the water drops from their source corresponds on the macrocosmic scale to a principle of coagulation and hardening and also on a certain plane to a principle of individuation; gravity, which makes the drops fall back, is the supernatural attraction of the divine Center. The image of the fountain does not take into account, however, the degrees of reality nor especially the absolute transcendence of the Center or Principle; what it is does take into account is the unity of "substance" or "non-unreality,"[4] although not the existential separation that cuts the relative off from the Absolute; the first relationship goes from the Principle to manifestation and the second from manifestation to the Principle; in other words there is unity "from the point of view" of the Principle and diversity or separation from the point of view of creatures insofar as they are only themselves.

4. What this means is that nothing can be situated outside the only Reality.

In a certain sense, worlds are like living bodies, and beings are like the blood or air that courses through them; the containers as well as the contents are "illusory" projections from the Principle—illusory since in reality nothing can be separated from it—but the contents are dynamic and the containers static; this distinction is not apparent in the symbolism of the fountain, but it is apparent in the symbolism of respiration or the circulation of blood.

The sage looks at things in connection with their necessarily imperfect and ephemeral exteriorization, but he also looks at them in connection with their perfect and eternal content. In a moral and therefore strictly human and volitive context, exteriorization coincides indirectly with the idea of "sin,"[5] and this is something that man, insofar as he is an active and passional creature, must never lose sight of.

*
* *

There has been much speculation as to how the sage—the "gnostic"[6] or *jnānin*—"sees" the world of phenomena, and occultists of all sorts have not refrained from putting forward the most fantastic theories on "clairvoyance" and the "third eye"; but in reality the difference between ordinary vision and the vision enjoyed by the sage or gnostic is obviously not of the sensory order. The sage sees things in their total context, hence in their relativity and at the same time in their metaphysical transparency; he does not see them as if they were physically diaphanous or endowed with a mystical sonority or visible aura, even though his vision may sometimes be described by means of such images. If we see before us a landscape and we know it to be a mirage—even if the eye alone cannot discern its true nature—we look at it otherwise than we would if it were a real landscape; a star makes a different impression on us from a firefly, even when the optical circumstances are such that the sensation is the same for the eye; the sun would fill us with terror if it ceased to set.[7] It is thus that a spiritual vision of things is distinguished by a concrete perception of universal relationships and not by some special sensory characteristic. The "third eye" is the faculty of seeing

5. "All that becomes deserves to perish," says Goethe in *Faust*; but he is mistaken in attributing the destructive function to the devil, whose role is in fact restricted to perversion and subversion.

6. This word, here and elsewhere, is used in its etymological sense and has nothing to do with anything that may historically be called "Gnosticism." It is *gnosis* itself that is in question and not its pseudo-religious deviations.

7. It is not for nothing that Vedantists describe ignorance as "mistaking a rope for a snake."

phenomena *sub specie aeternitatis* and therefore in a sort of simultaneity; intuitions concerning modes of being that are in practice imperceptible are often added as well, as is only natural.

The sage sees causes in effects and effects in causes; he sees God in all things and all things in God. A science that penetrates the depths of the "infinitely great" and the "infinitely small" on the physical plane and yet denies other planes, even though it is these other planes that reveal the sufficient reason of the nature we perceive and that provide its key, is a greater evil than ignorance pure and simple; it is in fact a "counter-science," and its ultimate effects cannot but be deadly. In other words modern science is a totalitarian rationalism, which eliminates both Revelation and Intellect, and at the same time a totalitarian materialism, which ignores the metaphysical relativity—and hence the impermanence—of matter and the world; it does not know that the supra-sensible, which is beyond space and time, is the concrete principle of the world and that it is therefore the origin of the contingent and changeable coagulation we call "matter."[8] The science labeled "exact"[9] is in fact an "intelligence without wisdom," just as post-scholastic philosophy is conversely a "wisdom without intelligence."

The principle of individuation produces a succession of spiritual outlooks that become ever narrower. First of all, beyond this principle, there is the intrinsic vision of Divinity, which consists in seeing only God. The next stage in descending order is to see all things in Him, and next again to see God in all things; in a certain sense these two ways of seeing are equivalent or nearly so. After this comes the wholly indirect "vision" of the ordinary man: things "and" God; and finally there is the ignorance that sees only things and excludes God, which amounts to saying that, for all practical purposes, it reduces the Principle to manifestation or the Cause to the effect. But in reality God alone sees Himself; to see God is to see by Him.

One must know what contains and not become dispersed among contents. What contains is above all the permanent miracle of existence, then the miracle of consciousness or intelligence, and then the miracle of joy, which—like an expansive and creative power—fills as it were the existential and intellectual "spaces." All that is not capable of immortality will be burned. Accidents perish; Reality alone remains.

8. Recent interpretations may perhaps "refine" the idea of matter, but they do not rise above its level in the smallest degree.

9. It is not really "exact" since it denies everything that it cannot prove on its own ground and by its own methods, as if the impossibility of material or mathematical proofs were somehow a proof of nonexistence.

There is in every man an incorruptible star—a substance called upon to become crystallized in Immortality and eternally prefigured in the luminous proximity of the Self. This star man can set free only in truth, in prayer, and in virtue.

Lalla

When Lalla Yogishwari found *ātmā*
Within herself, the outer world became
Her sole garment, a web of dreams;
Thus she went naked beneath the vault of Heaven.

And as she entered from the outward to the Inward,
So did the Inward enter her body's fullness;
And thus she went naked and dancing through the land—
In Lakshmi's ecstasy and in *ātmā*'s stillness.

10

THE MESSAGE OF THE HUMAN BODY

To say that man, and thus the human body, is "made in the image of God" means *a priori* that the body manifests something absolute and therefore something unlimited and perfect. What most distinguishes the human form from animal forms is its direct reference to absoluteness, as seen first of all in its vertical posture; it follows that if animal forms can be transcended—and they are so precisely by man—the human form cannot be: It marks not only the summit of earthly creatures but also, and for this very reason, the exit from their condition, or from *Samsāra* as Buddhists would say. To see man is to see not only the image of God but also a door open toward *Bodhi*, liberating Enlightenment, or let us say toward a blessed anchoring in the divine Proximity.

Because it is absolute, the supreme Principle is *ipso facto* infinite; the masculine body accentuates the first aspect, and the feminine body the second. On the basis of these two hypostatic aspects, the divine Principle is the source of all possible perfection; because it is the Absolute and the Infinite, it is necessarily also Perfection or the Good. Now each of the bodies, the masculine and the feminine, expresses modes of perfection evoked by the corresponding gender; all cosmic qualities are divided in fact into two complementary groups: rigorous and gentle, active and passive, contractive and expansive. The human body, as we have said, is an image of Deliverance; the liberating Path may be either "virile" or "feminine," though there is not a strict line of demarcation between the two modes, for man (*homo, anthropos*) is always man; the immaterial being that was the primordial androgyne survives in each of us.

This allusion to the primordial androgyne—which was divided well before the successive entry of its halves into matter[1]—permits us to insert a parenthesis here. The human form cannot be transcended, for its sufficient reason is to express the Absolute, hence the unsurpassable; this cuts short the metaphysically and physically aberrant imaginings of the evolutionists,

1. And which is realized *a posteriori* in sexual union.

according to whom this form is the result of a lengthy elaboration beginning with animal forms, an elaboration at once arbitrary and unlimited. Even materialists who consider transformist evolution inexplicable, and indeed contradictory, accept the hypothesis as an indispensable idea, and this of course takes us outside of science and into philosophy—or more exactly into a rationalism whose arguments are cut off from the very roots of knowledge; if the evolutionist hypothesis is indispensable to these materialists, it is because in their minds it replaces the concept of a sudden creation *ex nihilo*, which to them seems the only other possible solution. In reality, this hypothesis is as unnecessary as the creationist concept; for a creature appears on earth, not by falling from heaven, but by passing progressively—starting with its archetype—from the subtle world into the material world; its materialization comes about within a sort of visible aura that is comparable in every way to the "spheres of light" in which, according to many accounts, celestial apparitions begin and end.[2]

*

* *

It is very clear, displeasing as this may be to ancient moralists who had difficulty reconciling the feminine with the Divine, that deiformity essentially implies femininity—for reasons that are simply logical as well as metaphysical; even without knowing that femininity is derived from an "Eternal Feminine" of a transcendent order, one is obliged to take into account the fact that woman, since she is situated like the male in the human state, must be deiform precisely because this state is deiform. It is not surprising therefore that even a tradition as "misogynist" as Buddhism finally consented—within the *Mahāyāna* at least—to make use of the symbolism of the female body, which would be meaningless and even harmful if this body, or femininity as such, did not contain a spiritual message of paramount significance; according to tradition the Buddhas—and *Bodhisattvas*—do not save solely through doctrine but also through their supra-human beauty; but to speak of beauty is to speak implicitly of femininity. The beauty of the Buddha is necessarily that of *Māyā* or *Tārā*.

The "misogyny" of Buddhism is explained by the fact that its method, at its origin and in general at least, appeals essentially to the characteristics of a masculine psychology, which means that it operates fundamentally by means of intellection, abstraction, negation, and strength, and with what Amidism calls "power of oneself"; the same observation applies, if not to

2. One recalls the "chariot of fire" that lifted up Elijah and the "cloud" that veiled Christ during the Ascension.

Hinduism as a whole, at least to certain schools and to its general perspective, which culminates—as in Buddhism—in the excessive and, to say the least, schematic idea that woman as such cannot attain Deliverance, that she must first be reborn in a masculine body and follow the methods of men. Ancient discussions on the question of knowing whether a woman possesses a "soul" have a similar meaning; what is at issue is not the immortal soul itself but the Intellect in its most specifically masculine aspect. Be that as it may, the decisive point is not whether a woman is capable concretely of a specific method; it is simply that since she is human she is clearly capable of sanctity.

The anti-feminine ostracism of certain traditional perspectives has another cause, however, besides the problem of qualification for a particular *yoga* that may be considered unique: namely, the idea that the male alone is the whole man. There are in fact two ways of situating the sexes, either horizontally or vertically: According to the first perspective, man is on the right and woman on the left; according to the second, man is above and woman below. On the one hand man reflects *Ātmā* according to Absoluteness, and woman reflects it according to Infinitude; on the other hand man alone is *Ātmā*, and woman is *Māyā*;[3] but the second conception can be said to be true only if the first conception is accepted as well; indeed the first takes precedence over the second, for the fact that a woman is human is clearly more important than the fact that she is not a male.[4] An acknowledgment that spiritual methods of a specifically virile kind are scarcely suited to the feminine psyche becomes dogmatic on the basis of the second perspective; and one could perhaps also note that within the traditional surroundings here in question social conventions tend to create—at least on the surface—the feminine type that suits them ideologically and practically; humanity is made in such a way that a social anthropology is never a perfect good but on the contrary always a "lesser evil," or in any case an approximation.[5]

---

3. There are passages in the various Scriptures which would certainly permit one to believe this is so and which have to be understood in light of other passages that remove their exclusive quality. As is well known, sacred Books do not proceed by means of nuanced formulations but by antinomic affirmations; since it is impossible to accuse them of contradiction, it is necessary to draw the conclusions their antinomianism requires.

4. The *Shāstras* teach that women who serve their husbands, seeing in them their God, obtain a masculine rebirth and then attain Deliverance; this is obviously connected to the maximal mode of the minimal possibility for woman.

5. As for Hinduism, it is appropriate to take note of the fact that a concern for purity and the protection of sacred things is extreme in this environment, with priestly pedantry accomplishing the rest; this is true for women as well as for various categories of men deemed impure. Nonetheless—and this proves the prodigious "pluralism" of the Hindu spirit—"A mother is more venerable than a thousand fathers" (*Mānava Dharma Shāstra*, 2:145); and similarly in Tantrism: "Whoever sees the sole of a woman's foot, let him consider it as that of the spiritual master (*guru*)" (*Kubjika Tantra*).

It is one of the paradoxes of Buddhism that even the Amidist way, although it is founded on Mercy and the "power of the Other" and not on metaphysical meditation and the "power of oneself," has accepted the idea that woman must be reborn as man—through pure conventionalism and without insisting on it; this is all the more perplexing in that the *Mahāyāna*—in its Tibetan forms above all—has peopled its pantheon with feminine Divinities. The same paradox exists in Hinduism *mutatis mutandis*, where one of the greatest personalities of Shivaism is a woman, Lalla Yogishwari; it is unthinkable that a masculine body would add anything whatsoever to her from the point of view of spiritual wholeness.[6]

What we have just said results moreover from the bodily form: The female body is far too perfect and spiritually eloquent to be nothing more than a kind of transitory accident, and because it is human it communicates in its own way the same message as the masculine body, namely—to repeat ourselves—the absolutely Real and thereby the victory over the "round of births and deaths," hence the possibility of leaving the world of illusion and suffering. The animal, which can manifest perfections but not the Absolute, is like a closed door, enclosed as it were within its own perfection, whereas man is like an open door—a door that allows him to escape his limits, which are those of the world rather than his own.

*

* *

In an old book of legends the chronicler who tells of an appearance of the Blessed Virgin with the Child Jesus observes that the Virgin was sublimely beautiful but that the Child was "far more beautiful," which is absurd in more than one respect. There is no reason for the Child to be more beautiful than the Mother;[7] the divine nature of the Child certainly requires that he possess perfect physical beauty, but the incomparability of the Virgin requires it just as much; whatever Christ may possess that the Virgin does not could never result in a superior degree of beauty, given precisely that the beauty of the Virgin must be perfect; physical beauty belongs to the formal domain, and form is by definition the manifestation of an archetype, the intention of which necessarily excludes an indefinite gradation.

---

6. Let us also mention Maitreyi, wife of the *rishi* Yajnavalkya, who according to the *Brihadāranyaka Upanishad* "knew how to speak of *Brahma*," whereas the other wife of the sage "had scarcely more than the mind of a woman"; and similarly the female *rishis* Apala and Visvavara, both of whom revealed Vedic hymns; or the queen Chudala, wife and *guru* of the king Shikhidhwaja, who—according to the *Yoga Vasishtha*—had "realized *Ātmā*."

7. This would imply that Mary is "less beautiful" than Jesus, something that is inconceivable because it is meaningless.

In other words form coincides with an "idea," which cannot be something other than it is; the human body has its characteristic form, and this cannot be transcended without its ceasing to be itself; a beauty that can be indefinitely increased is meaningless and empties the very notion of beauty of all its content. It is true that the mode or degree of divine Presence can add an expressive quality to the body and above all to the face, but this is independent of beauty itself, which is a perfect theophany on its own plane; this means that the theophanic quality of the human body is to be found exclusively in its form and not in the sanctity of the soul inhabiting it, nor—at the purely natural level—in the psychological beauty of an added expression, whether that of youth or some noble sentiment.

It is therefore necessary to distinguish between the theophanic quality possessed by the human body as such—beauty coinciding in this case with the wholeness and intelligibility of the message—and the additional theophanic quality possessed by the bodies of *Avatāras*, such as Christ and the Virgin. As we have said, bodily beauty must in this second case be perfect, and it may also be distinguished by an originality emphasizing its majesty; but beauty of spiritual expression is of an altogether different order, and though it presupposes physical perfection and enhances it, it cannot create it.

The body of the *Avatāra* is therefore sacred in a particular sense, a sense that is super-eminent and so to speak sacramental by virtue of its quasi-divine content, but the ordinary body is also sacred—though in an altogether different respect—simply because it is human; in both cases physical beauty is sacred because it coincides with the divine Intention for the body, which is fully itself in proportion to its regularity and nobility.[8]

*

* *

There is not only the beauty of the adult but also that of the child, as our reference to the Child Jesus suggests. First of all it should be said that since a child is human it necessarily participates in the same symbolism and aesthetic expressivity as its parents—we are speaking always of man as such and not of particular individuals—and second that childhood is nevertheless a provisional state and does not in general have the definitive and representative value of maturity.[9] In metaphysical symbolism, this

8. Let it be said in passing that this is totally independent of questions of race: Every race, except more or less degenerate groups—though even a collective degeneration does not necessarily exclude cases of individual beauty—includes modes of perfect beauty, each expressing a fundamental aspect of the human theophany itself.

9. Although it can when the individual worth of a child visibly takes precedence over his state of immaturity, and this is notwithstanding the fact that childhood is in itself an incomplete state pointing toward its own completion.

provisional character expresses relativity: The child is what "comes after" its parents; it is the reflection of *Ātmā* in *Māyā*, at least to some extent and according to the ontological or cosmological level being considered; or it is even *Māyā* as such insofar as the adult is *Ātmā*.[10] But from an altogether different standpoint—and according to an application of inverse analogy, for which the seal of Solomon gives us the key[11]—the child represents what "came before," namely, what is simple, pure, innocent, primordial, and close to the Essence, and this is what its beauty expresses,[12] a beauty that has all the charm of promise, hope, and blossoming, and at the same time that of a Paradise not yet lost; this beauty combines the proximity of the Origin with a striving toward the Goal. And for this reason, childhood constitutes a necessary aspect of the complete human being, who is thus conformed to the divine Intention; the man who is fully mature always maintains—in perfect balance with his wisdom—the qualities of simplicity and freshness, of gratitude and trust, which he possessed in the springtime of his life.[13]

As we have just mentioned the principle of inverse analogy, we should take note of its application to femininity. Even though *a priori* femininity is subordinate to virility, it can be regarded from another point of view as superior to a given aspect of the masculine pole, for the divine Principle possesses an aspect of limitlessness, virginal mystery, and maternal mercy, and this takes precedence over a certain more relative aspect of determination, logical precision, and implacable justice.[14] Considered in this way, feminine beauty seems like an initiatic wine when compared to the rationality represented in certain respects by the masculine body.[15]

---

10. Polarized into "Necessary Being" and "All-Possibility."

11. When a tree is mirrored in a lake, its top is at the bottom, but the image is always that of a tree; the analogy is inverse in the first relationship and parallel in the second. Analogies between the divine order and the cosmic order always contain one or the other of these relationships.

12. We are not saying that every human individual is beautiful when he is a child, but we start with the idea that a human being, whether child or not, is beautiful to the extent that he is physically what he ought to be.

13. "Verily I say unto you, Except ye be converted, and become as little children, ye shall not enter into the kingdom of Heaven" (Matt. 18:3).

14. According to Tacitus the Germans discerned something sacred and visionary in women. The fact that in German the sun (*die Sonne*) is feminine whereas the moon (*der Mond*) is masculine bears witness to the same perspective.

15. Mahayanic art represents *Prajnāpāramitā*, the "Perfection of *Gnosis*," in feminine form; likewise *Prajnā*, which is liberating Knowledge, appears as a woman in relation to *Upāya*, the doctrinal system or art of convincing, which is represented as masculine. Buddhists readily point out that the *Bodhisattvas*, who in themselves are asexual, have the power to take a feminine form just as they do any other form; one would like to know for what reason they do so, for if the feminine form can produce so great a good, it is because it is intrinsically good; otherwise there would be no reason for a *Bodhisattva* to assume it.

A priori virility refers to the Principle and femininity to manifestation; but in an altogether different respect—that of complementarity *in divinis*—the masculine body expresses Transcendence and the feminine body Immanence, Immanence being closely related to Love and Transcendence to Knowledge.

Much could be said about the abstract and concrete symbolism of the different regions or parts of the body. A symbol is abstract insofar as it signifies a principial reality; it is concrete insofar as it communicates the nature of this reality, making it present within our experience. One of the most striking characteristics of the human body is the breast, which is a solar symbol and which expresses an accentuation differing according to sex: noble and glorious radiation in both the male and female but manifesting power in the first case and generosity in the second—the power and generosity of pure Being.[16] The heart is the center of man, and the breast is as it were the face of the heart; since the heart-Intellect contains both Knowledge and Love, one may say that this polarization is expressed in the human body by the complementary nature of the masculine and feminine breasts.

The human body includes three fundamental regions: the body properly so called, the head, and the sexual parts; these are practically three different subjectivities. The head represents a subjectivity that is at once intellectual and individual; the body, a collective and archetypal subjectivity, that of masculinity or femininity or that of race or caste; and the sexual parts, quite paradoxically, a dynamic subjectivity that is at once animal and divine, if one may put it this way. In other words the face expresses a thought, a becoming aware of something, a truth; the body expresses a being, an existential synthesis; and the sexual parts express a love that is both creative and liberating: the mystery of the generous substance that unfolds in the accidents and of the blessed accidents that flow back toward the substance—glory of self-giving and glory of delivering. Considered as a whole, the human body is intelligence, existence, love; certainty, serenity, faith.

One of the functions of dress is no doubt to isolate the mental subjectivity—the subjectivity that thinks and speaks—from the two existential subjectivities, which risk disturbing the message of thought with their own distinct messages; nonetheless this is a question of temperament and custom, for a more or less primordial man has different reflexes in this regard from those of a man overly marked by the fall—a man who has become at

16. The ritual dance of the dervishes—setting aside the variety of its forms—is often designated by the term *dhikr al-sadr*, "remembrance (of God) by the breast," which evokes this verse of the Koran: "Have We (God) not expanded thy breast?" (*Sūrah* "Solace" [94]:1). Moreover, Koranic language establishes a relationship between the acceptance of Islam—inasmuch as it is a "resignation" or "abandonment" (*islām*) to the divine Will—and dilation of the breast, calm and deep respiration expressing truth, peace, happiness.

once too cerebral and too passional and who has lost much of his beauty as well as his innocence.

The gait of a human being is as evocative as his vertical posture; an animal is horizontal and moves toward itself alone—since it is enclosed in its own form—but a man transcends himself in advancing; even his forward movement seems vertical and denotes a pilgrimage toward his Archetype, the celestial Kingdom, God. The beauty of the body's anterior indicates the nobility of man's vocational goal on the one hand and his manner of approaching it on the other; it expresses the fact that man directs himself toward God and that he does so in a manner that is "humanly divine," if one may put it this way. But the back of the body also has a meaning: It indicates the noble innocence of man's origin on the one hand and his noble manner of leaving behind what has been transcended on the other; it expresses in a positive way where we have come from while negatively it indicates the way in which we renounce what is no longer ourselves. Man comes from God, and he goes toward God; but at the same time he draws away from an imperfection that no longer belongs to him while approaching a perfection that is not yet his. His "becoming" bears the imprint of a "being"; he is what he becomes, and he becomes what he is.

*

* *

We alluded above to the evolutionist error; this was inevitable when considering the deiformity of man, and it permits us to insert a small digression here. Not only do the animal, vegetable, and mineral species manifest qualities or combinations of qualities; they also manifest defects or combinations of defects, for this is required by All-Possibility, which must express "possible impossibilities," or let us say negative and paradoxical possibilities, if it is not to be limited and thus not what it is; this entails excess as well as privation, and in this way norms are emphasized by means of contrasts. For example, the ape shows both what man is and what he is not, but certainly not what he has been; far from being the virtual form of a man, the ape incarnates an animal desire to be human, hence a desire for imitation and usurpation; but it finds itself as if before a closed door, and it falls back all the more heavily into its animal nature, the perfect innocence of which it can no longer recapture, if one may use such a metaphor; it is as if this animal, prior to the creation of man and in protest against it, had wished to anticipate this creation, a possibility that reminds one of the refusal of Lucifer to prostrate himself before Adam.[17] This does not prevent the ape

17. According to the Talmud and the Koran.

from being sacred in India, perhaps because of its human-like form but more likely because of certain ideas associated with an extrinsic symbolism;[18] this would also help to explain the role played by the apes in the *Rāmāyana*, unless in this case it is a question of subtle creatures—the *jinn* of Islam—of whom the ape would be only a likeness.[19]

One may ask whether the intrinsically noble animals—those possessing an immediately positive symbolism—are not themselves theophanies as well; indeed they are, and the same holds true for particular plants, minerals, and other cosmic or terrestrial phenomena, though in these cases the theomorphism is partial and not complete as in man. The splendor of the stag excludes that of the lion; the eagle cannot be the swan, nor the water lily the rose, nor the emerald the sapphire; from a somewhat different point of view we could say that the sun manifests the divine Majesty in a direct and simple manner, but it has neither life nor spirit;[20] man alone is the image-synthesis of the Creator,[21] and this is because he possesses the Intellect—hence also reason and language—and because he manifests it in his very form.

*
* *

Let us return to the question of traditional misogynist viewpoints. As we already noted, Buddhism is essentially a masculine, abstract, negative, ascetic, and heroic spirituality, at least *a priori* and in its broad outlines; the feminine body must therefore appear to it as the very embodiment of seduction and thus of *samsāra*, the round of births and deaths. But here we encounter another application of the inverse analogy we referred to above: What leads downward is in this case to be found above; femininity, to the extent that it seduces and binds, possesses this aspect precisely because it

18. As is the case for the boar, which represents priestly authority for the Nordic peoples, or as the rhinoceros symbolizes the *sannyāsin*.

19. The story recounted in the *Rāmāyana* is situated at the end of the "silver age" (*Treta Yuga*) and thus within a climate of possibilities entirely different from that of the "iron age" (*Kali Yuga*); the partition between the material and animic states was not yet "hardened" or "congealed," as is especially the case in our own era.

20. It can nonetheless have a sacramental function for men who are sensitive to cosmic *barakah*.

21. In spite of the loss of the earthly Paradise. One of the effects of what monotheistic symbolism calls the "fall of Adam" was a separation between the soul and the body, together with a separation between heaven and earth and between the spirit and the soul. The "resurrection of the flesh" is none other than the restoration of the primordial state; since the body is an immanent virtuality of the soul, it can be remanifested as soon as the separative "curse" has reached its term, which coincides with the end of a great cycle of humanity.

offers an image of liberating Bliss—in itself but also in the intention of the Creator; now a reflection is always "something" of what it reflects, which means that it "is" this reality in an indirect mode and on the plane of contingency. This is what Buddhists grasped within the framework of Mahayanic esotericism—the Tibetans and Mongols above all—and it is what permitted them to introduce nude *Tārās* and *Dākinīs* in gilded bronze into their sanctuaries; a bodily theophany of the feminine is here intended to actualize in the faithful a remembrance of the merciful and beatific dimension of *Bodhi* and *Nirvāna*.

What is true for a certain kind of Buddhism is true *a priori* for Hinduism, where sacred art expresses and accentuates the message of the two human bodies, the masculine and the feminine: a message of ascending and unitive verticality in both cases but in a rigorous, transcendent, objective, abstract, rational, and mathematical mode in the first case and in a gentle, immanent, concrete, emotional, and musical mode in the second. What we have on the one hand is a path based on the metaphysical Idea and Rigor, and on the other hand a path based on the sacramental Symbol and Gentleness; and let us not forget that there can also be combinations of these two perspectives, temperaments, or methods, for there is no such thing as an absolute male any more than an absolute female since there is only one *anthropos*. Thus, there are spiritualities and even entire religions that can be described as "feminine" without this implying that their followers lose anything of their virility;[22] and the converse is just as true, for women have sometimes followed paths that are foreign to their mentality; the two possibilities seem sufficiently obvious to excuse us from having to explore all the twists and turns of this paradox.

One may ask why Hindus, and even more Buddhists, are not concerned that their sacred art may occasion a fall, for it is a fact that beauty—sexual beauty above all—invites one to "mistake the shadow for the prey," that is, to become so attached to the earthly husk as to forget the transcendent content. Now it is not for nothing that Buddhist art has expressed the fearful aspects of cosmic manifestation more than any other form of art; at the very least this constitutes a "re-establishment of equilibrium," for the spectator is thereby warned never to lose sight of the ubiquitous menace of ruthless *samsāra* nor of the Guardians of the Sanctuary. *Darshana*—contemplation of the Divine in nature or art—clearly presupposes a contemplative temperament; it is this very temperament that includes a sufficient guarantee against the spirit of complacency and profanation.

22. In Krishnaism, the masculine adepts consider themselves to be *gopīs*, lovers of Krishna, which is altogether plausible since in relation to the Divinity every creature has something feminine about it.

The morality and mysticism of the West associate carnal sin with concupiscence alone, but this is a one-sided and insufficient perspective; in reality there is just as much sin in the profanation of a theophanic mystery, which consists in taking something that points by its very nature toward the lofty and the sacred and reducing it to the base, the frivolous, and the trivial. But sin or deviation can also be found—though in this case on a plane not entirely deprived of nobility—in a purely aesthetic and individualistic cult of the body; this was the situation in classical Greece, where the sense of clarity, measure, and finite perfection had completely obliterated an awareness of the transcendent, of mystery, and of the infinite. Sensible beauty became an end in itself; it was no longer man who resembled God but God who resembled man, whereas in Egyptian and Hindu art, which express the substantial and not the accidental, one senses that the human form is nothing apart from a mystery that at once fashions and transcends it and that calls us to Love and Deliverance.

Archetypal Man

The ground of existence: There is a human archetype
That floats unmoved within God's Spirit
Wholly untouched by everything our bodies
And souls experience in the earthly dream.

This is man: a Platonic idea
Enclosed within the Spirit and Goodness of God—
And then recast into a thousand beings;
Our life: first spring flowers, then snow—

An all and a nothing. An all inasmuch
As we are stars in God's Wisdom;
A nothing inasmuch as we stand in the world
Before God, whose Might contains the being of things.

Archetypal man: The meaning is not merely exclusive:
The One and Only is all that I am.
See how the enigma of things unfolds—

The Word must be.
        Truth pierces through Silence.

11

MAN AND CERTAINTY

Human intelligence is distinguished above all by its centrality and totality—its capacity to conceive of the Absolute—and from this arises a further capacity, that of objectification, which coincides with a sense of the relative. Without the contemplation of the Absolute and an intellective penetration of contingencies in relation to this Absolute, a man lives beneath the level of his intelligence and therefore beneath his humanity. To say man is to say intelligence capable of the Absolute and of objectification or relativization; an animal has neither the sense of the Absolute nor therefore a sense of contingency.

An intelligence capable of the Absolute necessarily implies free will; the will is free insofar as the intelligence is complete, and the intelligence is complete in man as such, regardless of its accidental obscurations; in other words every man of sound mind possesses enough sense of the Absolute to be able to use his will for the sake of the "one thing needful." If the normal and ultimate object of the intelligence is the Principle, the Absolute, the Infinite, then the normal object of the will must be what conforms to this supreme Reality, which means that the fundamental or quintessential function of the spirit is discernment between the Real and the illusory and contemplative concentration on the Real—in other words, truth and union.

Like container, like content, and conversely: In nature a container is made for a corresponding content, and it proves the reality of this content, which in turn serves to show that such proof, though not necessary for every understanding, has a secondary and provisional usefulness. A human womb proves the existence of human seed just as a feline womb proves the existence of feline seed; similarly the human Intellect proves its essential and total content: an absolute and therefore transcendent Reality and—together with it—the reverberations of this Absolute within the contingent. The nature of our complete or integral intelligence proves the existence of everything intelligible.

Whatever knows matter, and knowing it defines it as such, cannot itself be matter, nor can it be subject to the laws of matter; our immortality is therefore evident to "those who have ears to hear." The conscious subject is too vast and profound, or too real, to be at the mercy of a fact as contingent and accidental as death.

Man, we have said, is able to conceive of the Absolute and to will freely; as a result he is likewise capable of a love that surpasses phenomena and opens onto the Infinite and of an activity whose motive or object is beyond earthly interests. The specifically human abilities—or those that are noblest and most completely human—prove in their own way what their objective is, just as the wings of a bird prove the possibility of flight and thus the existence of a space in which the bird can fly.

Free will entails the possibility of a mistaken choice and therefore of a passional obscuration of the intelligence, for whoever chooses illusion has an interest in finding his happiness there, and man becomes what he chooses. To say complete intelligence is to say freedom, and to say freedom is to say possibility of error, whence the fall and the necessity of Revelation, which restores the "lost Word." And Revelation, which amounts to a "reminder" for humanity—or a given humanity—proves in its particular way the innateness of total Truth and therefore of all decisive truths.

*

* *

We could also express ourselves in the following manner: An animal gives proof of intelligence by the complexity of its adaptation to its environment and, in a higher sense, by its distinctive type of contemplativity, which is passive of course but nonetheless connected to the universal Intellect; but man proves his intelligence—or the complete character of human intelligence—by his consciousness of total Reality and of his situation within that Reality as well as by his contemplativity, by being centered on *esse* and not on *facere*, whatever the nature of his outward activity. There are four distinct aspects here: comprehension, concentration, discernment, and contemplation; in the last of these, "knowing" becomes "being." Conceptual understanding is the doorway to discernment, and concentration, combined with discernment, is the doorway to contemplation.

Man is surrounded by a bewildering multitude of phenomena; perfect intelligence consists in perceiving their homogeneity and outwardness in reference to a transcendent unity and a unified inwardness. The world then appears not as an incoherent mass of quasi-absolute phenomena but as a single veil into which the phenomena are woven; in this veil they are joined but not confused, distinct but not separated. In the center resides the discerning and unifying intelligence—an intelligence conscious of the Principle; it is thanks to this consciousness alone that the phenomenal world can appear both in its substantial homogeneity and in its contingency, outwardness, nothingness.

From a somewhat different point of view, which is connected with the experience of time—hence with the perspective of our life—the phenomenal world seems like a stream, in the midst of which intelligence abides as a motionless center; intelligence then becomes identical with the permanent present, with the sacred moment that belongs to God. It is consciousness of eternity.

These two spiritual dimensions also have a purely inward application insofar as the soul itself is the world and life, the "veil of *Māyā*" and the "stream of phenomena"; it expands and at the same time unfolds itself before the impersonal and inviolable gaze of the Intellect, which itself resides at the center and in the present and which becomes fully actual by means of the "remembrance of God" and on the basis of a metaphysical discernment between total Reality and its contingent reverberations, illusory as these are in the sight of the Absolute. For the Intellect, or for the spiritual act conforming to it, there is no difference between the outward and the inward: The outward is also within since the soul is everywhere the soul, on a macrocosmic scale as well as in the microcosm, and the inward in turn has an aspect of outwardness since phenomena are everywhere phenomena, whether inside or around us. Practically—and "alchemically"—it is therefore impossible to speak of the world and life without considering the soul and the flux of thought; the world is the soul, and the soul is the world.

From this it follows—and here is the whole point of a distinction that may seem tautological—that in acting on the inward we act on the outward; we hold both the world and our life within our own soul. Nevertheless, when we speak about the "world," the question of knowing whether we are thinking of the outward or the inward does not arise, for outward things come before inward things; our earthly environment existed before we were born, and a tree exists prior to our looking at it. The world is always *a priori* the realm of existence surrounding us; unless expressly specified, it is never our inward cosmos alone. The argument that the objective world is virtually identical to the sensations of the subject is invalid here, for these sensations—and the intelligence governing them—convey to us precisely the phenomenon of objectivity, in keeping with the real relationship; to deny this is to call into question any possibility of knowledge.

*

* *

Human life is studded with uncertainties; man loses himself in what is uncertain instead of holding onto what is absolutely certain in his destiny:

death, Judgment, Eternity. But besides these there is a fourth certainty, which is immediately accessible to human experience, and this is the present moment, in which a man is free to choose either the Real or the illusory and thus to ascertain for himself the value of the three great eschatological certainties. The consciousness of a sage is founded on these three points of reference, whether directly or indirectly and implicitly, through the "remembrance of God."

Besides the dimension of sequence, however, one must also consider the dimension of simultaneity, which is based on spatial symbolism. The world around us is full of possibilities presented to our choice, whether we wish it or not; it is thus full of uncertainties, not successive as in the flux of life but simultaneous like the things offered us by space. Now whoever wishes to resolve these uncertainties must once again lay hold of what is absolutely certain, and this is what stands above us: God and our immortality in God. But even when we are confronted with the multitudinous and bewildering possibilities of the world here below, there is something absolutely certain—something of which sacred forms represent so many exteriorizations—and this is metaphysical truth and the "remembrance of God": the center that is within us and that places us, insofar as we participate in it, beneath the "vertical" axis of Heaven, of God, of the Self.

Man finds himself in space and in time, in the world and in life, and these two situations contain two eschatological and spiritual axes, one static and "vertical" and the other dynamic and "horizontal"—or more or less temporal; this is how a contemplative man conceives of contingency in its relation to the Absolute, in its attachment to it, and in the manner in which it leads back to it. But these various points of reference are considered only insofar as a sage is necessarily conscious of contingent situations; they characterize his manner of taking account of his own relativity. Within this whole context—though entirely independent of it and not in any "localized" sense—resides the mystery in which knowing is being and being is knowing; what we mean is that these certainties of "succession" and "simultaneity," of "life" and "world," form the necessary framework of contemplation; they are like points of reference that serve to free us from the world and life or that facilitate this liberation. In the final analysis exotericism, which is the necessary basis of esotericism, considers nothing except those elements pertaining to our final ends, namely, Heaven and God, or death, Judgment, and Eternity, as well as our own earthly attitudes insofar as they bear on these realities.

The important thing to grasp here is that the actualization of consciousness of the Absolute—"remembrance of God" or "prayer" insofar as it brings about a fundamental confrontation of creature and Creator—anticipates every station along the two axes. It is already a death and a meeting with God, and it places us already in Eternity; it is something of Paradise and even—in its mysterious and "uncreated" quintessence—something of God. Quintessential prayer brings us out of the world and life, and in this way it bestows a new and divine life on the veil of appearances and the current of forms and gives a fresh meaning to our presence amid the play of phenomena.

Whatever is not here is nowhere, and whatever is not now will never be. What this moment is in which I am free to choose God, so will be death, Judgment, Eternity. And in this center, this divine point that I am free to choose when confronted by an immeasurable and multiple world, I am already in invisible Reality.

*

* *

We have seen that the world, life, and human existence show themselves in practice to be a complex hierarchy of certainties and uncertainties. If someone asks us what are the most important things a man should do, placed as he is in this world of enigmas and fluctuations, we would reply that there are four things to be done or four jewels that should never be lost from sight: first, to accept the Truth; second, to keep it in mind continually; third, to avoid whatever is contrary to Truth and the permanent consciousness of Truth; and fourth, to accomplish whatever is in conformity with Truth and this consciousness. All religion and all wisdom are reducible—extrinsically and humanly—to these four laws: In every tradition we see indeed an immutable truth; then a law of "attachment to the Real," of "remembrance" or "love" of God; and finally prohibitions and injunctions. Here we have a fabric of elementary certainties that encompasses and resolves every human uncertainty and in this way reduces the whole problem of earthly existence to a geometry at once simple and primordial.

Life

Thou art deceived in thinking that there is one life;
Think rather that in fact our lives are many.
Time transforms: Wast thou not a child?
Soon thou wilt be old, and the tavern of life will close.

Then the door to the next world will open.
Was there ever a life on earth?
Of all dream-deceit thou art suddenly cured:
The True shines forth and illusion shatters.

Thy kernel holds more than life's short term;
May God lead thee—till thou art eternal.

12

UNIVERSAL ESCHATOLOGY

Eschatology is part of cosmology, and cosmology is a prolongation of metaphysics, which in turn is essentially the same as the *sophia perennis*. It may be asked by what right eschatology is part of this *sophia* since, epistemologically speaking, pure intellection does not seem to reveal our destinies beyond the grave, whereas it does reveal universal principles; in reality, however, the knowledge of these destinies is accessible thanks to the knowledge of principles or their correct application. In fact it is by comprehending the profound nature of subjectivity and not solely by the outward way of Revelation[1] that we can know the immortality of the soul, for to speak of total or central subjectivity—not partial and peripheral like that of animals—is to speak thereby of a capacity for objectivity, an intuition of the Absolute, and immortality.[2] And to say that we are immortal not only means that we existed before our human birth—for what has no end cannot have a beginning—but that we are subject to cycles; life is a cycle, and our former existence must also have been a cycle within a chain of cycles. Our future existence may also proceed by cycles; at least it is condemned to do so if we have not been able to realize the purpose of the human state, which—precisely because it is central—allows us to escape from the "round of existences."

The human condition is the door to Paradise, to the cosmic Center, which—though forming a part of the manifested Universe—is nonetheless situated, thanks to the magnetic proximity of the divine Sun, beyond the rotation of the worlds and of destinies and thus beyond "transmigration." It is for this reason that "human birth is difficult to attain," according to a Hindu text; to be convinced of this, it is enough to consider the incommensurability between a center point and the innumerable points of the periphery.

1. Revelation, however, constitutes the occasional cause or initial condition of the corresponding intellection.

2. As we have demonstrated on other occasions, above all in the chapter "Consequences Flowing from the Mystery of Subjectivity."

*

* *

Some souls are fully or sufficiently conformed to the human vocation, and they therefore enter directly into Paradise; these are either the saints or the sanctified. In the first case are great souls illumined by the divine Sun, who are themselves dispensers of beneficent rays; in the second case are souls who have neither faults of character nor worldly tendencies and who are therefore free—or freed—from mortal sins and sanctified by the supernatural action of the means of grace that they have made their viaticum. Between the saints and the sanctified there are doubtless intermediary possibilities, but God alone is the judge of their position and rank.

Nevertheless, among the sanctified—those saved by a sanctification at once natural and supernatural[3]—some are not perfect enough to enter Paradise directly; hence they must await their maturity in a place that the theologians have termed an "honorable prison" but that in the opinion of Amidists is more than that, for according to them this place is located within Paradise itself; they compare it to a golden lotus bud, which opens when the soul is ripe. This state corresponds to the "limbo of the fathers" (*limbus* = "border") of Catholic doctrine; according to this very specific perspective, the righteous of the "Old Covenant" found themselves in this limbo before the Christ-Savior's "descent into hell"[4]—a conception above all symbolic and very simplistic, and yet perfectly adequate to the relevant principle and even literally true in cases which, given the complexity of the problem, we need not define here.

After the "lotus" we must consider "purgatory" properly so called. The soul that is faithful to its human vocation and that is sincere and persevering in its moral and spiritual duties cannot fall into hell, but before entering Paradise it may have to pass through that intermediary and painful state that the Catholic doctrine calls "purgatory"; this it does if it has faults of character or worldly tendencies or if it is weighed down by a sin for which it has not been able to compensate by its moral and spiritual attitude or by the grace of a sacramental means. According to Islamic doctrine "purgatory" is a temporary abode in hell: God saves from the fire "whomsoever He wills," which is to say that He alone is judge of the imponderables of our nature, He alone knowing what our fundamental possibility or substance is. If there are Christian

3. This is not a contradiction, for the specific nature of man includes by definition certain elements that are receptive to the supernatural.

4. All things considered, it is here that Dante places *de facto* the sages and heroes of antiquity, even though he makes them a part of his *Inferno* for theological reasons since they were "pagans."

denominations that deny purgatory, it is for the same basic reason—because the souls of those who are not damned and who *ipso facto* are destined for salvation are in the hands of God and are His concern alone.

Regarding Paradise, it is necessary to take into account its "horizontal" regions as well as its "vertical" degrees; the first correspond to circular sections and the second to concentric circles. The first separate the various religious or confessional worlds from one another, and the second distinguish the various degrees within each of these worlds. On the one hand there is the *Brahmaloka* of the Hindus, for example, which is a place of salvation like the Heaven of Christians, although it does not coincide with it;[5] but on the other hand, within one and the same Paradise, the place of Beatitude reserved for simple saints or the "sanctified" is not the same as that of great saints. "In my Father's house are many mansions,"[6] and yet there are no impenetrable barriers between the various degrees, for the "communion of saints" is a part of Beatitude;[7] there is no reason to think that communication is impossible between the various religious sectors, at least on the esoteric plane where it can have a meaning.[8]

Before going further we would like to make the following remark regarding eschatology in general: It has often been argued that neither Confucianism nor Shintoism explicitly accepts the ideas of the Hereafter and immortality, but this means very little since they do in fact have the cult of ancestors; if there were no afterlife, this cult would make no sense, and there would be no reason for an emperor of Japan to go to the tombs of departed emperors and solemnly inform their souls of this or that event. It is well known in any case that one of the characteristics of shamanistic traditions is the parsimony—though not the total absence—of eschatological information.

*

* *

5. The Hindu Paradises from which one is expelled after the exhaustion of "good *karma*" are not places of salvation but of transient reward; they are "peripheral" not "central" and are located outside the human state since they pertain to transmigration.

6. This saying contains implicitly an esoteric reference to the celestial sectors of the different religions.

7. And let us specify that if there are degrees in Paradise, there are also rhythms, which the Koran expresses by saying that the blessed will have their nourishment "morning and evening." In any case there is no such thing as a world without hierarchic levels or cycles, that is, without "space" or "time."

8. The possibility of inter-religious communication is borne out by the fact that one and the same personage, at once historical and celestial, can appear in different religions; this is the case with the Biblical Prophets, even though their functions differ according to the religion in which they are found.

We must now consider the infernal possibility, which maintains the soul in the human state, as well as the possibilities of "transmigration," which on the contrary cause the soul to leave this state. In the final analysis, hell is also a phase of transmigration, but before releasing the soul into other phases or states it imprisons it "perpetually," though not "eternally"; eternity belongs primarily to God alone, though also in a certain manner to Paradise because of the mystery of participation in the divine Immutability. Hell crystallizes a vertical fall; it is "invincible" because it lasts until the exhaustion of a certain cycle, whose duration is known only by God. Those who enter hell are not those who have sinned accidentally, "on the surface" so to speak, but those who have sinned substantially or with their "kernel," and this is a distinction that may not be perceptible from the outside; they are in any case the proud, the wicked, the hypocrites—hence all those who are the opposite of the saints and the sanctified.

Exoterically speaking, a man is damned because he does not accept a given Revelation, a given Truth, and does not obey a given Law; esoterically, he damns himself because he does not accept his own fundamental and primordial Nature, which dictates a given knowledge and a given comportment.[9] Revelation is none other than the objective and symbolic manifestation of the Light that man carries within himself in the depths of his being; it reminds him of what he is, and of what he should be since he has forgotten what he is. If before their creation all human souls must attest that God is their Lord—the Koran says so explicitly[10]—it is because they know "pre-existentially" what the Norm is; for the human creature, to exist is to know "viscerally" what Being, Truth, and Law consist in; fundamental sin is a suicide of the soul.

It remains for us to speak of another possibility of the afterlife, namely "transmigration,"[11] a possibility lying completely outside the "sphere of interest" of Semitic Monotheism, which is a kind of "nationalism of the human

9. "God wrongeth not mankind in aught; but mankind wrong themselves" (*Sūrah* "Jonah" [10]:44).

10. "And (remember) when thy Lord brought forth from the Children of Adam, from their reins, their seed, and made them testify of themselves (saying): Am I not your Lord? They said: Yea, verily. We testify. (That was) lest ye should say at the Day of Resurrection: Lo! of this we were unaware; or lest ye should say: (It is) only (that) our fathers ascribed partners to God of old and we were (their) seed after them" (*Sūrah* "The Heights" [7]:172–73). These pre-existential creatures are the individual possibilities necessarily contained within All-Possibility and called forth to Existence by existentiating Radiation, not produced by a moral Will.

11. Not to be confused with metempsychosis, in which the psychic elements of a dead person, which are perishable in principle, graft themselves onto the soul of a living person, giving the illusion of a "reincarnation." The phenomenon is benefic or malefic depending on whether the elements are good or bad, those of a saint or a sinner.

state" and which for this reason takes into consideration only what concerns the human being as such. Outside the human state—and setting aside angels and demons[12]—there is only a sort of nothingness for this perspective; according to Monotheism, to be excluded from the human condition amounts to damnation. Nevertheless, between this point of view and that of the transmigrationists—Hindus and Buddhists especially—there is a point of connection, namely, the Catholic notion of the "limbo of infants," where those who have died without baptism are said to abide without suffering; now this place or condition is none other than transmigration through worlds other than our own and consequently through nonhuman states, inferior or superior as the case may be.[13] "For wide is the gate, and broad is the way, that leadeth to destruction, and many there be which go in thereat": Since Christ could not have meant that most men go to hell and since "destruction" in monotheistic and Semitic language also means leaving the human state, one is obliged to conclude that this saying concerns in fact the mass of the lukewarm and worldly, including unbelievers who benefit from extenuating circumstances; these are souls that do not love God and that deserve, if not hell, then at least expulsion from that privileged state that is man—privileged because it provides immediate access to paradisiacal Immortality. As a matter of fact, the "paganisms" offered access to the Elysian Fields or the Isles of the Blessed only to initiates in the Mysteries, not to the mass of the profane, and the case of the "transmigrationist" religions is more or less similar. The fact that transmigration almost always begins—when setting out from the human state—with a kind of purgatory clearly reinforces the image of "destruction," that is, a definitive disgrace from the human point of view.

Aside from its intrinsic purpose, the baptism of newborns is intended to save them from this disgrace, and it has *de facto* the effect of keeping them within the human state if they die, which in their case will be a paradisiacal state; for all intents and purposes this outcome—which the

12. Islam also acknowledges the *jinn*, "spirits," such as the elementals—gnomes, water-spirits, sylphs, salamanders—and other immaterial creatures, which are sometimes attached to mountains, caves, trees, and sanctuaries; they intervene in white or black magic, that is, in either therapeutic shamanism or sorcery.

13. In other words, either "peripheral" or "central," like the state of animals in the first case or like that of men in the second; the fact that there is something absolute in the human state—just as there is something absolute in the geometric point—precludes the evolutionist and transformist hypothesis. Like earthly creatures, angels are also either "peripheral" or "central"; either they personify a divine Quality, which confers upon them both a given perfection and a given limitation, or they reflect the divine Being itself, in which case they are fundamentally one: This is the "Spirit of God," the celestial *Logos*, which is refracted among the Archangels and inspires the Prophets.

"nationalism of the human state" has in mind—coincides with the celestial end that the sacrament intends for adults; Muslims pronounce the Testimony of Faith in the ear of the newborn with precisely the same motive, a practice evoking the whole mystery of the sacramental power of the *Mantra*. The motivation is just the opposite in the very special case of the voluntary transmigration of *bodhisattvas*, which passes only through states that are "central" and thus analogous to the human state; for the *bodhisattva* does not desire to remain within the "golden prison" of the human Paradise but instead seeks to radiate in nonhuman worlds until the end of the great cosmic cycle. This is a possibility that Monotheism excludes and that is in fact confined to *Mahāyāna* Buddhism—though without being obligatory for all Mahayanists, even saints; Amidists in particular aspire only to the Paradise of Amitabha, which in practical terms is equivalent to the Hindu *Brahmaloka* and the Paradise of monotheistic religions and which is not considered a "celestial dead end," if one may put it this way, but on the contrary a virtuality of *Nirvāna*.

There is another aspect of the problem of destinies beyond the grave that cannot be passed over in silence. Theology—Islamic as well as Christian—teaches that animals are included in the "resurrection of the flesh,"[14] but whereas human beings are sent to either Paradise or hell, animals will be reduced to a state of dust, for they are not assumed to have an "immortal soul"; this opinion is based on the fact that the Intellect is not actualized in animals, hence the absence of the rational faculty and language. In reality the infra-human position of the animals does not mean that their subjectivity is unaffected by the law of *karma* and unconnected to the "wheel of births and deaths";[15] even the various vegetable species—though not a given isolated plant—are subject to this law, for each of them corresponds to an individuality, though it is not always possible to discern the limits of a species and what groups amount merely to modalities of it.

---

14. Bodily death and the subsequent separation of body and soul resulted from the fall of the first human couple, a provisional situation to be rectified only at the end of this cosmic cycle—except in the case of certain privileged beings such as Enoch, Elijah, Christ, and the Virgin, who mounted up to Heaven with their bodies "transfigured."

15. In Sufism it is "unofficially" agreed that particularly blessed animals were able to enter Paradise by following their masters, who were full of a *barakah* of exceptional power; all things considered this is not at all implausible. As for the question of knowing whether there are animals in Heaven, we cannot deny that there are, and this is because the animal world—like the vegetable world that constitutes the Heavenly "Garden" (*Jannah*)—is part of the natural human environment; but neither the paradisiacal animals nor the plants of the "Garden" need to come from the terrestrial world. According to Muslim theologians, the plants and animals of Heaven have been created then and there for the elect, which amounts to saying that they are of a quasi-angelic substance; "and God knoweth best."

*

* *

We have distinguished five posthumous outcomes of human life on earth: Paradise, limbo-lotus, purgatory, limbo-transmigration, hell. The first three outcomes maintain the human state; the fourth brings one out of it; and the fifth maintains it only to bring one out of it ultimately. Paradise and the lotus are beyond suffering; purgatory and hell are states of suffering in varying degrees; transmigration does not necessarily involve suffering for the *bodhisattvas*, but it is a mixture of pleasure and pain in other cases. Or again: There are two places of waiting for Paradise, one gentle and one rigorous, namely, the lotus and purgatory; and there are two exclusions from Paradise, also one gentle and the other rigorous, namely, transmigration and hell; in both of these latter cases the human condition is lost, either all at once as in the case of transmigration or ultimately as in that of hell. As for Paradise, it is the blessed summit of the human state, and strictly speaking it has no symmetrical opposite, notwithstanding certain simplifying schematizations that have a moral purpose;[16] for the Absolute—to which the celestial world pertains "by adoption"—has no opposite, except in appearance.

Eternity belongs to God alone, as we have said; but we have also alluded to the fact that what is called "eternity" in the case of hell is not the same as in the case of Paradise, for there is no symmetry between these two domains, the one feeding on cosmic illusion and the other being nourished by divine Proximity. Paradisiacal perpetuity is nonetheless relative by the very nature of things in the sense that it opens onto the *Apocatastasis*, through which all positive phenomena return to their Archetypes *in divinis*; but in this there is neither loss nor privation, first because God never gives less than He promises or never promises more than He intends to give, and second—or rather above all—because of the divine Plenitude, which can lack nothing.

Considered in this light, Paradise is really eternal;[17] the end of the "manifested" and "extra-principial" world is a cessation only from the point of view of the limiting agency of manifestation, but not from the standpoint of intrinsic and total Reality, which on the contrary allows beings to

---

16. The cosmic "opposite" of Paradise is not only hell but also transmigration, a fact that illustrates the transcendence and independence of Paradise. Let us add that there are *ahādīth* testifying to the disappearance—or the final emptiness—of hell; "watercress will spring up therein," the Prophet is supposed to have said, and also that God will pardon even the worst of sinners.

17. Which is indicated in Sufism by the expression "Garden of the Essence," *Jannat al-Dhāt*; this Garden divinely transcends the "Gardens of the Qualities," *Jannāt al-Sifāt*.

become again "infinitely" what they are in their Archetypes and in their single Essence.

*

* *

All of our preceding observations may seem arbitrary and imaginative in the highest degree to anyone still clinging to that immense simplification that is the scientistic perspective; but they become quite plausible when one acknowledges the authority of various traditional data—and we need not return here to the validity of this authority, which coincides with the very nature of the "naturally supernatural" phenomenon that Tradition constitutes in all its forms—and when one knows how to draw from human subjectivity all the immediate and far-reaching consequences it implies. It is precisely this subjectivity—this mystery of dazzling self-evidence—that modern philosophers, including the most pretentious psychologists, have never been able to grasp nor wished to grasp, which is not at all surprising since it offers the key to metaphysical truths as well as mystical experiences, both of which demand from us all that we are.

"Know thyself," said the inscription on the temple at Delphi;[18] the same is expressed by this *hadīth*: "Whoso knoweth his soul knoweth his Lord"; and similarly the *Veda*: "Thou art That," namely *Ātmā*, the Self at once transcendent and immanent, which projects itself into a myriad of relative subjectivities, themselves subject to cycles as well as localizations and extending from the least flower to that direct Manifestation of the Divine which is the *Avatāra*.

18. Recorded by Thales, then commented upon by Socrates.

Sketches from the Far East to the Far West

Sketches from the Far East to the Far West

IV

SACRED ART AND SYMBOLISM

Things are in God and God is in things with a kind of discontinuous continuity.

—*Logic and Transcendence*

Dawn

Morning shivers over the cypresses;
A last dream-image is scattered by the wind.
The lark arises and sings its song of love,
While the early star still stands in the sky.

Understand, O soul, what gentle beauty says:
God's Goodness is the substance of creation.
Let thy deepest heart remember this—
From dawn to the final hour.

13

THE QUESTION OF FORMS IN ART

It may be surprising that we would treat a subject having what seems a merely secondary importance, but in fact the question of forms in art is by no means insignificant.

Before proceeding, a few words of explanation are called for concerning our terminology. In speaking of "forms in art" and not merely "forms" in general, our purpose is to make it clear that we are not dealing with something "abstract" but on the contrary with things that are physically sensible; if on the other hand we avoid speaking of "artistic forms," it is because in current usage the adjective connotes the idea of luxury and thus superfluity, and this is diametrically opposed to what we have in mind. In the sense we intend, the expression "forms in art" is actually pleonastic, for it is impossible—traditionally speaking—to dissociate form from art since art is the very principle of the manifestation of form; we have nonetheless been obliged to make use of this pleonasm for the reasons just given.

If the importance of forms is to be grasped, the first thing one must understand is that at the level of symbolism a sensible form corresponds most directly to the Intellect,[1] and this is because of the inverse analogy connecting the principial and manifested orders: The highest realities are manifested most clearly in their most distant reflections, that is, in the sensible or material order; here can be found the deepest meaning of the saying "extremes meet." And it is for the same reason, let us add, that Revelation descends into the bodies and not only the souls of the Prophets, a fact presupposing the physical perfection of those bodies.[2] Sensible forms

1. According to Saint Thomas Aquinas, "Art is associated with knowledge."

2. Speaking of the *laylat al-qadr*—the night of the "descent" (*tanzīl*) of the Koran—René Guénon observes, "This night, according to Muhyi al-Din Ibn Arabi's commentary, is identified with the actual body of the Prophet. What is particularly important to note is the fact that the revelation is received not in the mind but in the body of the being who is commissioned to express the Principle: 'And the Word was made flesh,' says the Gospel ('flesh' and not 'mind'), and this is a very precise mode of expression—in the form proper to the Christian tradition—for the reality represented by the *laylat al-qadr* in the Islamic tradition" ("The Two Nights," *Études traditionnelles*, April–May, 1939). This truth is closely bound up with the relationship already mentioned between forms and intellections.

thus correspond more exactly to intellections; this is why traditional art has specific rules, rules that are meant to apply cosmic laws and universal principles to the domain of forms and that, beneath their more general outward aspect, reveal the style of the civilization in question, a style that in turn makes the form of intellectuality of this civilization explicit. When art ceases to be traditional and becomes merely human, individual, and therefore arbitrary, this is infallibly the sign—and secondarily the cause—of an intellectual decline; from the point of view of those who are skilled in the "discernment of spirits" and who can look on such phenomena with an unprejudiced eye, this decline can be seen in the more or less incoherent and spiritually insignificant—we would go even as far as to say unintelligible—character of the forms in question.[3]

In order to forestall a possible objection, we readily acknowledge the fact that in civilizations that are intellectually sound—the Christian civilization of the Middle Ages, to take just one example—spirituality is often expressed by an indifference to forms and sometimes even by a tendency to turn away from them, as is shown by the example of Saint Bernard, who proscribed images in the monasteries; it is important to emphasize, however, that this indifference no more signifies an acceptance of ugliness and barbarism than does poverty imply the possession of many things that are base. Be that as it may, in a world such as our own where traditional art is dead—where form itself has been invaded by everything contrary to spirituality and where nearly every formal expression seems corrupted at its very roots—the traditional regularity of forms assumes a very special spiritual importance that it could not have possessed in the beginning, for the absence of the spirit in forms of art was at that point something nonexistent and inconceivable.

---

3. We have in mind the decadence of certain branches of religious art during the Gothic period, especially toward its end, and of Western art as a whole from the Renaissance onward. Formerly sacred, symbolical, and spiritual, Christian art—including architecture, sculpture, painting, and liturgical goldsmithery—gave way before the invasion of a neo-antique and naturalistic, individualistic, and sentimental art; this art, which contained absolutely nothing "miraculous"—whatever those who believe in the "Greek miracle" may care to think—is quite unsuited for the transmission of intellectual intuitions, answering instead only to collective psychic aspirations; it is thus completely opposed to intellectual contemplation and takes into consideration sentimentality alone, which itself becomes degraded insofar as it reflects nothing more than the needs of the masses and ends up in a sickly sweet and pathetic vulgarity. It is strange that no one seems to have understood to what a degree this barbarism of forms, which reached a zenith of empty and miserable boastfulness in the period of Louis XV, contributed, and still contributes, toward driving many souls—and by no means the least—from the Church; they feel suffocated in surroundings that do not allow their intelligence room to breathe. Let us note in passing that the historical connection between the new Saint Peter's in Rome—in a Renaissance style and therefore anti-spiritual and ostentatious, or simply "human" if one prefers—and the beginning of the Reformation is unfortunately very far from fortuitous.

What we have said concerning the intellectual quality of sensible forms must not cause us to overlook the fact that the further back one goes toward the origins of a given religious tradition, the less those forms appear in a state of full development; as already noted, the pseudo-form—that is, the arbitrary form—is always ruled out, but it is possible for form as such to be lacking, or at least nearly so and in certain more or less peripheral domains. On the other hand, the nearer one draws toward the end of the traditional cycle in question, the greater the importance of formalism[4]—even from what is called an "artistic" standpoint—for by then the forms have become virtually indispensable channels for actualizing the spiritual deposit of the tradition. In any case, the absence of a formal element is in no way equivalent to the presence of the unformed, nor conversely; the unformed and barbarous can never attain to the majestic beauty of the void, whatever those with an interest in passing off a deficiency as a superiority may wish to believe.[5] This law of compensation, by virtue of which certain relationships become gradually inverted during the course of a traditional cycle, can be applied in all spheres. We may quote, for example, the following *hadīth* of the Prophet Muhammad: "In the beginning of Islam he who omits a tenth of the Law is damned, but in the latter days he who shall accomplish a tenth thereof will be saved."

The analogical relationship between intellections and material forms explains how it was possible for esotericism to be grafted onto the practice of the crafts, especially architecture; the cathedrals left behind by Christian initiates offer the most explicit as well as the most dazzling proof of the spiritual exaltation of the Middle Ages.[6] It should be noted that we are touching here on a most important aspect of the question before us: the effect that esotericism can have on exotericism through the medium of sensible forms, whose production is the prerogative of an artisanal initiation. Such forms can serve as true vehicles of an integral traditional doctrine, translating this doctrine—because of their symbolism—into a language that

4. This is ignored by certain pseudo-Hindu movements, whether of Indian origin or not, which abandon the sacred forms of Hinduism while believing themselves to represent its purest essence; in reality it is useless to give a man a spiritual method without having first of all forged in him a mentality in harmony with this method, a prerequisite quite apart from an obligatory attachment to an initiatic line; spiritual realization is inconceivable outside the appropriate psychic climate, one which conforms to the traditional surroundings of the method in question.

5. It has sometimes been claimed that Christianity, since it stands above forms, cannot be identified with any particular civilization; we understand completely why one would seek consolation for the loss of Christian civilization—including its art—but this opinion is nonetheless inexcusable.

6. When standing before a medieval cathedral, a person truly feels that he is located at the center of the world; standing before a church of the Renaissance, Baroque, or Rococo periods, he merely feels himself to be in Europe.

is at once immediate and universal. By making use of these forms esotericism is able to infuse an intellectual quality into the properly exoteric part of a religious tradition and in this way to ensure equilibrium; without this equilibrium, the whole civilization will eventually dissolve, which is precisely what happened in the Christian world. The abandonment of sacred art deprived esotericism of its most direct means of action while the outward tradition insisted more and more on its own particularity, hence its own limitation; in the end, the absence of the current of universality, which had previously quickened and stabilized the religious civilization through the language of forms, brought about reactions of a contrary sort. Formal limitations, instead of being compensated and thereby stabilized by means of the supra-formal interventions of esotericism, gave rise through their very opacity or massiveness to infra-formal negations, these negations resulting in turn from an individual arbitrariness, which—far from being a form of the truth—is merely a formless chaos of opinions and whims.

Returning to our initial idea, we would add that the Beauty of God corresponds to a deeper reality than His Goodness; at first glance this may seem surprising, but all one needs to do is to recall once again the metaphysical law by virtue of which the analogy between the principial and manifested orders is reversed. The principially great is small in the manifested order, and what is inward in the Principle appears as outward in manifestation; it is because of this reversal that beauty is outward in man while his goodness is inward—at least in the ordinary sense of these words—whereas the opposite prevails in the principial order, where Goodness is as an expression of Beauty.

*
* *

One is often struck by the fact that Oriental peoples, including those reputed to be the most artistic, prove to be almost entirely lacking in aesthetic discernment with regard to what comes to them from the West; all the ugliness born of a world more and more devoid of spirituality spreads over the East with unbelievable ease, not only under the influence of politico-economic forces, which would not be so surprising, but above all with the free consent of those who by all appearances had created a world of beauty—a civilization in which every expression, including the most modest, bore the imprint of the same genius. Since the very beginning of Western infiltration, it has been astonishing to see the most perfect works of art set side by side with the worst trivialities of industrial production, and these disconcerting contradictions have come about not only in the realm of art as such—of course in a normal civilization everything accomplished by man is related to the domain of art at least in some way—but in nearly every sphere.

The resolution of this paradox is actually quite simple, however, and it has already been suggested in the preceding pages. Forms, even the most unimportant, are the work of human hands only in a secondary manner, for they are derived above all from the same supra-human source from which all tradition originates, which is another way of saying that the artist who lives in a traditional world still devoid of fissures works under the discipline or inspiration of a genius that surpasses him; fundamentally he is but the instrument of this genius, if only because of his craftsman's qualification.[7] As a result individual taste plays only a relatively subordinate part in the production of the forms of such art, and this taste is in fact reduced to nothing as soon as the individual finds himself face to face with a form that is foreign to the spirit of his own tradition; this is what happens when people unfamiliar with European civilization encounter forms imported from the West. For this to occur, however, the people accepting such confusion must no longer be fully conscious of their own spiritual genius and no longer be living at the level of the forms with which they are still surrounded, and this proves that they were already suffering from a certain decadence; this being so they accept modern ugliness all the more easily because it reflects certain inferior possibilities that they were already spontaneously seeking to realize, in whatever fashion and perhaps quite unconsciously; the unreasoning readiness with which too many Eastern people—in fact

---

7. "A thing is not only what it is visibly, but also what it represents. Natural or artificial objects are not . . . arbitrary symbols of some other, higher reality but actual manifestations of this reality: The eagle or the lion, for example, is not so much a symbol or image *of* the Sun as it *is* the Sun in a likeness (the form being more important than the nature in which it may be manifested); and in the same way every house *is* the world in a likeness, and every altar situated at the center of the earth" (Ananda K. Coomaraswamy, "The Primitive Mentality," *Études traditionnelles*, August–September–October, 1939). It is solely and exclusively traditional art—in the widest sense of the word and implying everything that is of an outwardly formal order and therefore *a fortiori* everything belonging in some way or another to the ritual domain, transmitted with tradition and by tradition—which can guarantee an adequate analogical correspondence between the divine and cosmic orders on the one hand and the human or artistic order on the other. Therefore the traditional artist does not limit himself simply to imitating nature but "imitates nature in her manner of operation" (Saint Thomas Aquinas, *Summa Theologica*, Part I, Question 117, Article 1), and it goes without saying that the artist cannot with his own individual means improvise an operation that is so specifically cosmological. The full conformity of the artist to this "manner of operation," a conformity subordinated to the rules of tradition, is what makes the masterpiece; this conformity presupposes a knowledge that may be either personal, direct, and active or inherited, indirect, and passive; the latter is the case with those craftsmen who, unconscious as individuals of the metaphysical content of the forms they have learned to fashion, do not know how to resist the corrosive influence of the modern West.

the great majority—accept things that are utterly incompatible with the spirit of their tradition is best explained by the fascination exercised over an ordinary man by something corresponding to an as yet unexhausted possibility, the possibility in this case simply being that of arbitrariness or the absence of principles. Although one should be cautious about making sweeping generalizations as to what appears to be a total lack of taste among Easterners, one fact is absolutely certain: Too many of them no longer grasp the meaning of the forms, or indeed of the whole tradition, which they inherited from their ancestors.

Of course, everything that we have just said applies above all and indeed *a fortiori* to Westerners, who after having created—we do not say "invented"—a perfect traditional art proceeded to disown it in favor of the residues of the individualistic and empty art of the Greco-Romans; this is what has finally led to the artistic chaos of the modern world. We realize that some people will refuse at any price to admit the unintelligibility or ugliness of the modern world and will readily employ the term "aesthetic" with a derogatory nuance—like that of the words "picturesque" and "Romantic"—in order to discredit in advance a concern for forms and thus make themselves more comfortable in the self-sustaining system of their own barbarism; there is nothing surprising about such an attitude when it concerns avowed modernists, but it is rather illogical—indeed quite despicable—coming from those who still claim to be Christian. To reduce the spontaneous and normal language of Christian art, a language whose beauty can hardly be deserving of criticism, to a worldly matter of "taste"—as if medieval art could have been the product of whim—amounts to admitting that the imprint given by the genius of Christianity to all its expressions, both direct and indirect, was only a contingency unrelated to this genius and devoid of serious importance, or even due to a mental inferiority; "only the spirit matters," according to certain ignorant people, who are imbued with a hypocritical, iconoclastic, blasphemous, and impotent Puritanism and who pronounce the word "spirit" all the more readily because they are the last to know what it means.

In order to have a better grasp of the causes of the decadence of art in the West, it is important to note that there is a certain dangerous idealism in the European mentality, which is not without relevance to this decadence nor thus above all to the decay of Western civilization as a whole. This idealism has found its most dazzling—one might say its most "intelligent"—expression in certain forms of Gothic art, where a kind of dynamism that seems to want to remove the heaviness from stone is predominant.[8] Except in the case of sculpture and painting, which were already well on the way

8. Byzantine and Romanesque art, as well as a certain form of Gothic art in which the static power is preserved, are essentially intellectual and therefore realistic.

to decadence, this flamboyant form of Gothic art, however passionate it became, was nevertheless still a traditional art; or rather, to be more exact, it was the swan song of that art, for from the time of the Renaissance, which was truly the posthumous revenge of classical antiquity, European idealism began pouring itself more and more into the exhumed sarcophagi of Greco-Roman civilization, suicidally placing itself at the service of an individualism in which it believed it had discovered its own genius, only to end—after a number of intermediate stages—in the most vulgar and wildly fanciful affirmations of this individualism. This was really a double suicide: first the abandonment of medieval art, or simply Christian art, and second the adoption of Greco-Roman forms, which intoxicated the Christian world with the poison of their decadence.

But it is necessary to consider a possible objection here: Was the art of the first Christians not in fact Roman art? The answer is that the real beginnings of Christian art are to be found in the symbols inscribed in the catacombs and not in the forms which early Christians, themselves belonging in part to the Roman civilization, temporarily borrowed in a purely outward manner from the classical decadence; indeed Christianity was called on to replace this decadence with an art springing spontaneously from an original spiritual genius, and if in fact certain Roman influences have always persisted in Christian art, this applies only to more or less superficial details.

We said that European idealism succumbed to individualism and ended up stooping to the crudest expressions of this individualism; as for those things which the West finds to be crude in other civilizations, they are nearly always the more or less peripheral aspects of a realism that has no delusive and hypocritical veils. Of course it is important not to lose sight of the fact that idealism is not something bad in itself, for it finds its place in the outlook of heroes, who are rightly inclined toward the sublime and majestic; what is bad, and at the same time specifically Western, is the introduction of this mentality into all domains, including those in which it has no place. Islam, with its desire for equilibrium and stability, or simply realism, wished to avoid at all costs this errant—and therefore all the more fragile and dangerous—idealism, and it did so by taking into account the restricted possibilities of the present cyclic period, already far removed from man's origin; this is the source of that "down-to-earth" aspect for which Christians believe they must reproach Muslim civilization.

*
* *

In order to provide some idea of the principles of traditional art, let us call attention to a few of the most general and elementary. In the first place a work of art must conform to the use to which it will be put and must express this conformity, and if there is an added symbolism it must be consistent with the symbolism inherent in the object; second, there must be no conflict between the essential and the accessory but instead a hierarchical harmony, which results moreover from the purity of the symbolism; third, the treatment of the material used must be in keeping with the nature of this material even as the material must be in keeping with the use of the object; finally, the object must not give an illusion of being other than what it really is, for such an illusion always leaves a disagreeable impression of uselessness, and when illusion is the goal of the finished work—as is the case with all classicist art—it is the mark of a uselessness that is only too obvious. The great innovations of naturalistic art can be reduced to so many violations of these principles. With respect to sculpture this involves a violation of the inert material, whether stone, metal, or wood, and with painting there is a violation of the plane surface: In the first case the material is treated as if it were endowed with life even though it is basically static and therefore suited only for the representation of motionless bodies or essential or schematic phases of movement instead of arbitrary, accidental, or quasi-instantaneous movements; in the second case—that of painting—the plane surface is treated as if it had three dimensions by means of foreshortening and the use of shadows.

It should be understood that the traditional rules are not dictated by merely aesthetic considerations but represent on the contrary the application of cosmic and divine laws, beauty being their necessary result. Such beauty as may be found in naturalistic art does not reside in the work as such but solely in the object it copies, whereas in symbolic and traditional art it is the work itself that is beautiful, whether it is abstract or borrows its beauty to a greater or lesser extent from a natural model. There is no better illustration of this distinction than that afforded by a comparison between so-called classical Greek art and Egyptian art; the beauty of Egyptian art is not solely in the object represented but simultaneously and *a fortiori* in the work as such—in the inward reality that the work expresses. It is true that naturalistic art has sometimes succeeded in expressing nobility of feeling or vigorous intelligence, but this can be explained by cosmological considerations, the absence of which would be inconceivable; nevertheless its occasional successes have no connection with the art as such, and no individual value could ever make up for the falsification involved in this art.

The majority of moderns who claim to understand art are convinced that Byzantine or Romanesque art is in no way superior to modern art and that a Byzantine or Romanesque Virgin resembles Mary no more than do her naturalistic images, indeed just the opposite. The response is quite simple, however: A Byzantine Virgin—which traditionally goes back to

Saint Luke and the Angels—is infinitely closer to the truth of Mary than a naturalistic image, which of necessity is always that of another woman. For there are only two possibilities: Either an artist presents an absolutely correct portrait of the Virgin from the physical point of view, in which case it will be necessary for the artist to have seen her, a condition that obviously cannot be fulfilled—leaving aside the fact that naturalistic painting is ruled out by tradition—or else the artist presents a perfectly adequate symbol of the Virgin, but in this case physical resemblance, without being absolutely excluded, is no longer in question. It is this second solution—the only one that makes sense—that is realized in icons. What they do not express by means of a physical resemblance they express by the abstract but immediate language of symbolism, a language composed of both precisions and imponderables; the icon thus transmits not only the beatific power that it contains by virtue of its sacramental character but also the holiness of the Virgin herself—her inner reality—and thereby the universal reality of which she is an expression; in contributing to a state of contemplation as well as to a metaphysical reality, the icon becomes a support for intellection, whereas a naturalistic image transmits only the fact—apart from its obvious and inevitable falsehood—that Mary was a woman. It is true that in the case of a given icon the proportions and features may well be those of the living Virgin, but if such a likeness really came to pass, it would be independent of the symbolism of the image and could result only from a special inspiration, no doubt unconscious on the part of the artist himself. Naturalistic art could be legitimate up to a certain point if it were simply used to record the features of the saints, for the contemplation of saints—Hindu *darshana*—can be a precious help on the spiritual path since their outward appearance conveys the perfume as it were of their spirituality; but the use in this limited manner of a partial and at the same time disciplined naturalism is a most precarious possibility.

But let us return to the icon's symbolic and spiritual quality, the perception of which depends on a contemplative intelligence as well as "sacred science." It is false to claim as a justification for naturalism that people need an art that is accessible, which is to say platitudinous, for it is not the "people" who gave birth to the Renaissance; on the contrary, the art of the Renaissance—like all the "great art" derived from it—is an offence to the piety of the simple man. The artistic ideals of the Renaissance and of all modern art are thus very far from what people truly need, and this is proven moreover by the fact that nearly all the miraculous Virgins to which they flock are Byzantine or Romanesque; and who would dare claim that the black color of some of them agrees with the "taste" of most Europeans or is particularly "accessible" to it? Besides, the Virgins made by the hands of the people, when they have not been spoiled by the influence of academic art, are very much more real—if only in a subjective fashion—than those of such art. Be that as it may, even if one were to agree that the masses need empty or unintelligent images, are the spiritual needs of an elite never to be taken into consideration?

In the preceding paragraphs we have already implicitly answered the question as to whether sacred art is meant for an exclusively intellectual elite alone or whether it has something to offer the man of average intelligence; the question in fact answers itself when one takes into account the universality of all symbolism, for this universality enables sacred art to transmit—apart from metaphysical truths and facts derived from sacred history—not only spiritual states but also psychological attitudes that are accessible to everyone. In modern parlance one might say that such art is at once profound and naive; indeed the simultaneity of profundity and naiveté is precisely one of the most prominent characteristics of sacred art. The ingenuousness or candor of this art, far from being a spontaneous or affected inferiority, reveals on the contrary the normal state of the human soul, whether that of the average or the superior man; on the other hand the apparent intelligence of naturalism—its quasi-satanic skill in copying nature and thus in transmitting nothing more than appearances or emotions—corresponds only to a deformed mentality, one that has deviated from primordial simplicity or innocence; it should go without saying that such a deformation, resulting as it does from intellectual superficiality and mental virtuosity, is incompatible with the traditional spirit and therefore finds no place in a civilization that has remained faithful to this spirit. If sacred art speaks to contemplative intelligence, it likewise speaks to normal human sensibility, and this means that such art alone possesses a universal language and that no other art is better suited to appeal not only to an elite but to people at large. As for the apparently childish aspect of the traditional mentality, let us remember Christ's injunction to be "as little children" and "harmless as doves," words that quite plainly refer to psychological realities, whatever their spiritual meaning.

The Fathers of the eighth century, unlike those religious authorities of the fifteenth and sixteenth centuries who betrayed Christian art by abandoning it to the impure passions of worldly men and the ignorant imagination of the profane, were fully conscious of the holiness of all the means by which tradition expresses itself; therefore they stipulated at the Second Council of Nicea that "art [the integral perfection of the work] alone belongs to the painter, whereas the arrangement [the choice of the subject] and disposition [the treatment of the subject from the symbolic as well as the technical or material points of view] belong to the Fathers." *Non est pictoris—ejus enim sola ars est—rerum ordinatio et dispositio Patrum nostrorum.* This amounts to placing all artistic initiative under the direct and active authority of the spiritual leaders of Christianity.

But if this is the case, how can one explain the fact that during recent centuries religious circles have for the most part shown such a regrettable lack of understanding with regard to all those things that, having an artistic character, are in their opinion only "external" matters? First of all, besides the *a priori* elimination of every esoteric influence, there is the fact that a religious perspective as such tends to identify itself with the moral point of view, which appreciates merit alone and believes it necessary to ignore the sanctifying quality of intellectual knowledge and hence the value of the supports of such knowledge; now the perfection of a sensible form is no more "meritorious" in the moral sense than the intellection that the form reflects and transmits, and it is therefore only logical that when a symbolic form is no longer understood it will be relegated to the background—and even forsaken—in order to be replaced by a form that no longer speaks to the intelligence but only to a sentimental imagination capable of inspiring meritorious action; or so believes the narrow-minded man.

But speculating in this way about the likely reactions of people and resorting to means that are superficial and crude prove to be mistakes in the final analysis, for in reality nothing is better suited to influence the deeper dispositions of the soul than sacred art; profane art on the contrary, even if it has some psychological value for less intelligent people, exhausts its resources by the very fact of their superficiality and crudeness and ends up provoking reactions of contempt, which are only too well known and may be considered a backlash against the contempt in which sacred art was held by profane art, especially in its earlier stages.[9] Present experience makes it clear that nothing is able to offer a more immediately tangible nourishment to irreligion than the insipid hypocrisy of religious imagery, for what was meant to stimulate piety in believers merely confirms unbelievers in their impiety; sacred art does not possess this character of a "two-edged sword," for being itself more abstract it offers less hold to hostile psychological reactions.

In any case, regardless of speculations that attribute to the masses a need for images that are unintelligent and warped in their essence, elites do

9. In the same way the hostility of the representatives of exotericism toward all that surpasses their comprehension results in an increasingly massive exotericism, which cannot but suffer from fissures; once the "spiritual porosity" of tradition was lost—that is, the immanence of a transcendent dimension existing within the substance of exotericism and compensating for its heaviness—these fissures could be produced only from below; hence the replacement of the masters of medieval esotericism by the protagonists of modern unbelief.

exist and certainly require something different; what they need is a language that evokes divine profundities and not human platitudes—a language that cannot spring simply from profane taste nor even from genius but that must proceed essentially from tradition, which implies that a work of art must be executed by an artist who is saintly or "in a state of grace."[10] Far from serving merely for the more-or-less superficial instruction and edification of the masses, the icon—like the Hindu *yantra* and every other visible symbol—establishes a bridge from the sensible to the spiritual: "By the visible aspect," says Saint John Damascene, "our thoughts must be drawn up in a spiritual flight and rise to the invisible majesty of God."

But let us return to the errors of naturalism. As soon as art is no longer determined, illumined, and guided by spirituality, it is at the mercy of the artist's individual and purely psychic resources, and these must exhaust themselves in much the same way as the platitude of the naturalistic principle, which calls for nothing more than a copy of visible nature; reaching the end point of this platitude, naturalism inevitably engendered the monstrosities of "surrealism," which is nothing but a decomposing cadaver of art and which in any case should instead be called "infra-realism," for properly speaking it is the Satanic consequence of naturalistic Luciferianism. Naturalism is clearly Luciferian in its wish to imitate the creations of God, not to mention its emphasis on the psychic to the detriment of the spiritual, the individual to the detriment of the universal, and above all the bare fact to the detriment of the symbol. Normally, man must imitate the creative act, not the thing created; this is what all symbolic art accomplishes, and the results are "creations" that, far from being duplicates of the creatures of God, are rather reflections of them according to an analogy revealing the transcendent aspects of things; in this lies the sufficient reason for art, apart from any practical use of such objects.

What one finds here is the same metaphysical inversion of relationship we have already discussed. For God the creature is a reflection or exteriorized aspect of Himself, whereas for the artist the work reflects on the contrary an "inward" reality, of which he himself is only an outward aspect; God creates His own image whereas man fashions so to speak his own essence, at least symbolically. On the principial plane the inward shows itself forth in the outward, but on the manifested plane the outward fashions the inward;

10. Traditional iconographers, many of them monks, prepare themselves for their work by fasting, prayer, confession, and communion; sometimes the colors are mixed with holy water and the dust from relics, which would not be possible if the icon were not meant to possess a truly sacramental character.

a sufficient reason for all traditional art—of no matter what kind—is the fact that in a certain sense the work is greater than the artist himself and brings him back, through the mystery of artistic creation, to the proximity of his own divine Essence.[11]

11. This explains the danger, as far as the Semitic peoples are concerned, in the painting and especially in the carving of living things; Hindus and Far Easterners worship divine Reality through a symbol—a symbol truly being what it symbolizes as far as its essential reality is concerned—but Semitic peoples have a tendency to deify the symbol itself. One of the reasons for the prohibition of plastic and pictorial arts among the latter was undoubtedly the wish to prevent a naturalistic deviation, a very real danger for men whose mentality is predominantly individualistic and sentimental.

Woman

Why does Rumi say she whom we love
Is uncreated: the created woman?
Why does he say she is a divine ray
And through her golden body she manifests the Divine?

Woman's form and gaze reveal
Not only beauty, bliss of soul,
And motherly goodness;
The Infinite is here conjoined with form.

She is not limit, not a closed door,
For all creation rests and lives in her.
And that which to the fool appears mere pleasure—
Has united many noble hearts with God.

14

THE LIBERATING PASSAGE

From the standpoint of transcendence, there is obviously a discontinuity between the divine Principle and its manifestation, but from the point of view of immanence, there is continuity. According to the first relationship we say "manifestation and not Principle"; according to the second, "manifested Principle, hence still the Principle." When there is discontinuity we distinguish between Essence and form; when there is continuity we distinguish between Substance and accident. In both cases there is Reality and veil, Absoluteness and relativity.

In order to be less abstract let us specify that the accident is to the Substance what ice or steam is to water and that the form is to the Essence what a reflection is to the sun; or again, on quite a different plane: The relationship between the participle and the verb is the same as that between the accident and the Substance, and the relationship between the word and the thing signified is the same as that between the form and the Essence. And similarly on the spiritual plane: When we distinguish between a symbol and its principial archetype—the "Idea" (*eidos*)[1]—we are referring to the discontinuous and static relationship "form-Essence," but when we distinguish between a rite and its effect we are referring to the relationship "accident-Substance," which is continuous and dynamic. In other words the accident is a "mode" of the Substance whereas the form is a "sign" of the Essence.[2]

Every sacred symbol is an "enlightening form" that invites to a "liberating rite"; the form reveals the Essence to us whereas the rite leads us back to the Substance—to the Substance we are, the only one that is. All this concerns sacred art or "liturgy" on the one hand and the beauties of nature on the other; it is also related—and with all the more reason—to the symbolism of concepts and the rites of assimilation: vision of the Essence through the form and return to the Substance by means of the rite.

1. Or the "Paradigm," which is the Idea viewed as initial Norm or celestial Ideal. We employ capital letters when it is a question of the divine Order, even though we fear overusing them.

2. Nonetheless the terms "substance" and "essence" are synonymous insofar as they designate the archetypal content of a phenomenon.

There are visual and auditory symbols, and there are enacted symbols; all of these bring about a passage from outward to Inward, from accident to Substance, and thus from form to Essence.[3] A noble and profoundly contemplative man tends to see the Substance in the accidents, but an inferior man sees only the accidents and tends to reduce substantial manifestations to a trivializing accidentality. A sense of the sacred and the celestial is the measure of human worth.[4]

*

* *

When confronting the notions of "form" and "essence," one speaks of discontinuity; when confronting the notions of "accident" and "substance," one speaks on the contrary of continuity. But when one considers the conformation of form to essence and the manifestation of essence in form, or when one considers—and practically speaking this amounts to the same thing—the conformation of the accident to the substance and the manifestation of the substance in the accident, the question of discontinuity or continuity does not arise. For a conformation that is "ascending" and a manifestation that is "descending" are completely independent of the *distinguo* in question.

The divine symbol is paradoxically ambiguous by its very nature. On the one hand it "is God"—this is its reason for being—and on the other it "is not God"—this is its earthly materiality; it is "image" because it is manifestation and not Principle, and it is participating emanation and liberating sacrament because it is *Ātmā* in *Māyā*. The human body as such—but not in a given diminished form—is a symbol-sacrament because it is "made in the image of God"; this is why it is the object of love *par excellence*—not to the exclusion of the soul that dwells within it but together with this soul, for the human body has the form it does only because of the content for which it is made. The body invites us to adore it by its theomorphic form, and this is why it can be the vehicle of a celestial—and in principle salvific—presence; but as Plato teaches this presence is accessible only to a contemplative soul in which the passions do not dominate, and this is true whether the person is an ascetic or married. Sexuality does not mean animality except in perverted, hence subhuman, man; in the being who is

3. In an especially direct way music and dance are supports for a passage—at whatever stage—from the accident to the Substance, and this is the principal meaning of rhythm. The same thing can be said about sacred nudity and every contemplative appeal to virgin nature, the primordial sanctuary.

4. This cuts short the hasty and barbarous distinction between "savage" and "civilized."

properly human, sexuality is determined by what constitutes the prerogative of man, and this is attested to precisely by the theomorphic form of his body.

This leads us back to our *distinguo* between Essence and Substance: The masculine pole refers to essentiality and transcendence and the feminine pole to substantiality and immanence. The trajectory toward the Sovereign Good—which is at once the Absolute and the Infinite—necessarily includes modes that are masculine as well as feminine; *a priori* and *grosso modo* Truth pertains to Rigor and Justice whereas the Path pertains to Gentleness and Mercy. In loving woman, man essentially loves Infinitude and Goodness; in loving man, woman essentially loves Absoluteness and Strength; for the Universe is woven of geometry and musicality, of strength and beauty.

We said above that Transcendence means discontinuity between the Principle and its manifestation, hence separation, and that Immanence means continuity, hence union; thus divine Virility, possessing the implacability of the nature of things, imposes upon us principles derived from the Immutable, while divine Femininity, possessing on the contrary all the freedom that Love has in its power, grants us imponderable graces capable of bringing about the miracle of Salvation.

Flowers

What are you saying, silent flowers,
Joyfully adorning my meadow?
Who raised you out of the green grass
To give my eyes and heart delight?

Here are red stars, and there are blue,
The meadow's spring or summer dress;
And here are numberless white pearls,
Gleaming like snow and strewn across the grass.

It seems the earth too wished to sing;
She wished to be a love song and a lute,
Like birds, high-soaring on their wings—
And, highest of all, like little angels from Heaven.

15

AN ELEMENTARY CRITERIOLOGY OF CELESTIAL APPARITIONS

According to a *hadīth* the devil cannot assume the physical appearance of the Prophet; this incapacity is entirely plausible, and yet one may still ask what use this information is, for after the Companions disappeared there was no longer—and there is no longer—any witness to the Prophet's appearance. The practical significance of the *hadīth* is as follows: If the devil adopted the appearance of a deified man or angel, he would inevitably betray himself by some discordant detail; this discordance will doubtless go unnoticed by those whose intentions are not disinterested and are lacking in virtue and who, placing their desires above the truth, basically want to be deceived, but not by those whose intelligence is serene and whose intention is pure. A demon cannot assume the likeness of an "angel of light" objectively and in an entirely adequate way, but he can do so subjectively by flattering—and hence corrupting—a spectator who has laid himself open to illusion; this explains why celestial apparitions are sometimes uniformly dismissed in a climate of individualistic and passional mysticism, a precaution that would make no sense outside such a climate and that is in itself exaggerated and problematic, to say the least.

The proper attitude toward an apparition—or some other grace—that God does not impose with an irresistible certainty is one of deferential neutrality or perhaps pious expectancy, but even when a grace is accompanied by a sense of certainty it is important not to base oneself on this sense alone; otherwise one risks making the same mistake that many false mystics do at the beginning of their careers. The decisive basis of the spiritual path is always an objective value, without which there could be no question of a "path" in the proper sense of the term. What this means is that one must be neither discourteous nor credulous toward graces or visions and that it suffices to take one's stand on the unshakable elements of the path, namely

Doctrine and Method, the certainty of which is absolute *a priori* and which no authentic grace will ever disavow.[1]

Those who are in the grip of illusion do not know—and do not wish to know—that the devil can provide them with sound inspirations with the sole aim of gaining their trust in order finally to make them fall into error; that he can tell them the truth nine times in order to deceive them all the more easily on the tenth occasion; and that he deceives above all those who are seeking a confirmation or fulfillment of the illusions to which they are already attached.[2] This applies to visions as well as auditions or other messages.

*

* *

One particular type of grace is ecstasy; here too one must distinguish between the true and the false or between the supernatural and the merely morbid—indeed the demonic. A very rare and at the same time most paradoxical case, which should not go unmentioned, is the fortuitous ecstasy, in which a thoroughly secular person undergoes a real ecstatic experience without understanding how or why; such an experience is unforgettable and can have a more or less profound effect on the character of the person concerned. This is a matter of cosmic accident, the cause of which is remote; in other words it lies in the destiny or *karma* of the individual, as Hindus and Buddhists would say—in merits that were acquired in the past and before his birth; but it would be a serious mistake to suppose that such an experience necessarily entails a spiritual acquisition of a conscious and active nature, for the significance of the event is simply to serve as a call to an authentic path, in following which one must start from nothing: *Quaerite et invenietis.*

Even though ecstasy has no direct connection with celestial apparitions, it is nonetheless a way of "seeing God" through a veil that is woven of symbols or fashioned from ineffable light; it may in any case coincide with a vision, and if so it serves—just as sleep sometimes does—as the subjective condi-

1. In the same connection there is the problem of the Muslim *istikhārah*, which involves a question posed to God by means of a traditional ritual. For this procedure to be valid it is necessary for the intention to be pure and the interpretation correct, and this depends upon a variety of conditions, subjective as well as objective. For example, one cannot ask Heaven whether a particular dogma is true or whether one's spiritual master is right, for this would betray an attitude of unbelief or insubordination, contradicting the principle *credo ut intelligam*, which necessarily applies in such cases.

2. The satanic origin of a message is a matter of indifference when it is beneficent, but the devil gives such a message only to those whom he expects to deceive afterward; otherwise he would have no interest in doing so, to say the least. In this general context let us also recall that—according to the well-known ancient maxims—"heresy resides in the will and not in the intelligence" and that "to err is human but to persevere in error is diabolical."

tion for a supernaturally objective mode of perception; in other words it is the already celestial meeting point for a contact between earth and Heaven.

*
* *

Real or apparent graces include various "powers," such as healing, prediction of the future, hypnotic suggestion, telepathy, divination, and the ability to perform minor miracles; these powers may indeed be direct gifts from Heaven, but in this case they are related to some degree of sanctity; otherwise they are merely natural, though doubtless quite rare and unusual. Now in the opinion of all spiritual authorities one should distrust such powers and pay no attention to them, particularly since the devil may be involved and even has an interest in involving himself. Special powers may indicate *a priori* an election on the part of Heaven, but they can also cause the downfall of those who become attached to them and who neglect the purgative asceticism required by all spirituality; many heretics and false spiritual masters started out by becoming the dupes of some power with which they had been endowed by nature. For the truly spiritual man powers such as these are regarded in the first place as a temptation rather than a favor; he does not dwell on them, if only for the simple reason that no saint will ever take his own sanctity as axiomatic. God's measures are not at man's disposal—except in abstract terms or through a grace that is connected to a dignity already prophetic by nature—and no man can be both judge and party in his own cause.

It therefore goes without saying that powers may be just as hazardous as visions, though they may also be just as authentic, depending on the predisposition of a given man and according to the will of God. The criterion of a supernatural power is in a man's character, and the nobility of this character is at the same time—and essentially—one of the criteria of sanctity, which means that powers cannot serve as proofs of spiritual election on their own.[3]

*
* *

According to a well-known principle, angels always speak in the doctrinal or mythical language of those whom they are addressing, provided this language is intrinsically orthodox; now there are two elements of possible contradiction: differences of religion and differences of level. It follows that a celestial being may manifest itself not only in relation to a particular religion

3. The twin pillars of a virtuous character are humility and charity; one could also say patience and generosity or detachment and goodness. According to a saint, the devil would claim that he can do everything—except humble himself; what this means essentially is that he can do everything outward, for what is inward is precisely humility or sincerity.

or "denomination" but also in relation to a given degree of universality; and just as esotericism on the one hand extends and on the other hand contradicts exotericism—the first standpoint referring to the saving truth of exotericism and the second to its restrictive formalism—so celestial manifestations may in principle contradict one another within the framework of the same religion, depending on whether they take account of this particular cosmos alone or express on the contrary the single and universal Truth.

Having said this, we must underscore the fact that the spokesmen of Heaven never give lessons in universalist scholarship; they do not speak of *Vedānta* or Zen in a Semitic climate any more than they speak of Spanish mysticism or Hesychasm when addressing Hindus or Buddhists. Nevertheless there is nothing abnormal in the fact that Heaven may favor a given spiritual perspective by supernatural signs while favoring in the same manner another that surpasses it, as long as both perspectives are themselves intrinsically legitimate and even though they co-exist in the same religious cosmos.

*

* *

The question of the apparition of a deified man—or an *Avatāra*—raises another problem, that of the distinction between a visionary dream and an ordinary dream. Celestial beings appear only in visionary dreams and not in ordinary ones, but this does not mean that all celestial manifestations within the context of the ordinary are diabolical, for they may be merely natural; just as we can dream of something with which we are preoccupied, so we can dream innocently of a saint without the absence of any spiritual cause implying the presence of a malefic one. The situation is completely different when the apparition is self-contradictory or when the context is discordant, for then a satanic element has mingled with the purely natural cause—unless the satanic is, strictly speaking, the real cause of the mirage; if this is the case, the dream may even be taken for a vision, but it is precisely its content that betrays its origin.

Contrary to what occurs in ordinary dreams, visionary dreams are absolutely homogeneous and of a crystalline precision; when one awakens, they leave behind them an impression of freshness, luminosity, and happiness—unless they contain a threat from Heaven, and not a consolation or encouragement as is more often the case. In keeping with their supernatural character, visionary dreams are more or less rare, for Heaven is not prolix, and there is no reason a man should receive frequent celestial messages.[4]

4. An exception must be made in the case of a "message-stream," which takes the form of a habitual dialogue between a celestial personality and a privileged soul, as was the case with Sister Consolata; but in a situation like this there is only an interior discourse and no visible apparition.

Some observations concerning the relationship between the dreaming and waking states are appropriate here, for there are those who deny that the experience of a visionary dream affects the waking ego; certain modern Vedantists claim in fact that the two states are entirely unrelated, that the dreaming ego is not in any way the same as the waking one, that the two states are closed systems, and that it is a mistake to take waking consciousness as the point of reference for dreaming consciousness[5] since the things we dream of are in no way inferior to the things we perceive when awake, nor any less real.[6]

This extravagant and pseudo-metaphysical opinion is contradicted first by the fact that on awakening we remember our own dream and not that of someone else; second by the fact that the inconsistent and fluid character of dreams on the one hand and their reference to our objective experiences on the other prove their subjectivity, their passivity, and their accidentality; and third by the fact that while we are dreaming we can be perfectly aware that we are dreaming and that it is we who are dreaming and not someone else. The proof of this last point is that we may awaken of our own free will when the development of a dream takes a disturbing turn. By contrast no one ever tries to emerge from the waking state—however disagreeable the situation—in hopes of awakening into some paradisiacal state where he can then persuade himself that what he left behind was an accident of his own imagination, for he knows that the terrestrial world would remain precisely what it is. It is certainly true that the universe is a sort of illusion in relation to the Principle, but on the plane of relativity the objective world is not an illusion in relation to a particular subjectivity.[7]

"Behold, the angel of the Lord appeared unto him in a dream, saying, Joseph, thou son of David, fear not to take unto thee Mary thy wife. . . . Then Joseph being raised from sleep did as the angel of the Lord had bidden him." And again: "Behold, the angel of the Lord appeareth

5. Like Kant, Siddheswarananda seems to think that his own experiences limit those of others.

6. Some have even dared to claim that dreaming is superior to waking since it includes possibilities excluded by the physical world—as though these possibilities were anything but purely passive and as though the objective and decisive reality of the waking state did not infinitely compensate for such dream possibilities as rising into the air; after all one could just as well dream of being deprived of motion.

7. Shankaracharya, so misunderstood by some of his interpreters, takes the same view when he specifies in his commentaries on the *Vedānta Sūtras* that "the world of the intermediate state (the dream) is not real in the same way that the world woven of ether and the other elements is real"; he also says that "visions in a dream are acts of memory whereas visions in the waking state are acts of immediate consciousness (perception); and the distinction between memory and immediate consciousness is recognized by everyone as determined by the absence or presence of the object." And finally: "The mutability [experienced in dreams] comes solely from mental impressions (*vāsanā*) and is not real." All this obviously concerns ordinary and not visionary dreams; given their supernatural cause, the objective reality of the latter is self-evident.

to Joseph in a dream, saying, Arise, and take the young child and his mother, and flee into Egypt. . . . When he arose, he took the young child and his mother by night, and departed into Egypt." These passages from the Gospel show as clearly as one could wish the continuity—obvious in itself—between the dreaming and waking states or between the ego of the sleeper and that of the man who is awake; the fact that it is here a question of a visionary dream, hence an intrinsically objective phenomenon, rather than an ordinary dream in no way detracts from the force of this argument since the framework of the phenomenon is the dreaming not the waking consciousness. The angel, instead of making himself physically visible, has mirrored himself as it were in the psychic substance of the dreamer; this is precisely what characterizes visionary dreams, which thus combine an objective phenomenon with an eminently subjective state of consciousness—a state withdrawn from the external world;[8] here objective reality enters the dream-world, either unveiled or clothed in symbolism.

*

* *

The question of knowing which detail is inconsistent with the authenticity of a celestial apparition depends either on the nature of things or on a particular religious perspective, or else a particular level of this perspective. In other words certain elements are in themselves incompatible with celestial apparitions—whatever the religious or spiritual point of view—while the inconsistency in other cases results from the framework of a given perspective or spiritual standpoint; for example, according to Catholic criteriology total nudity is ruled out for the messengers of Heaven,[9] whereas in Hinduism it has either a neutral or a positive character. The reason for the Catholic attitude is that Heaven would never wish to excite concupiscence or offend against modesty—though even in a Christian climate there exists a certain margin—whereas the Hindu attitude is explained by the sacred character of nudity, which is based on the theomorphism of the body, hence in a sense on its "human divinity"; metaphysical transparency compensates in this case for fleshly ambiguity.[10] As for elements that are intrinsically incompatible

8. It is true that all knowledge, consciousness, or perception is subjective by definition, but when it comes to distinguishing a real from an imaginary experience what counts is the objective cause rather than the subjective phenomenon as such.

9. In the case of women probably even partial nudity, except in the case of *lactatio*, as indicated by Saint Bernard's vision and by certain icons.

10. Both Hindus and Muslims regard the body as something natural, not sinful. It will no doubt be objected that the same can be said for Christians, but while this is true in theory it is not so in practice, for the collective sentiment is not always at the same level as the theological *distinguo*. As for the opinions of modernists, these have nothing to do with authentic Christian sensibility.

with any celestial manifestation, these obviously include ugly or misshapen features—whether in the form of the apparition or in its movements, or even simply in its surroundings—as well as the mode of its speech as considered from the standpoint of both content and style; Heaven does not deceive nor does it speak excessively.[11] "God is beautiful, and He loveth beauty," the Prophet said; loving beauty, God also loves dignity—He who combines beauty (*jamāl*) with majesty (*jalāl*). "God is love," and though love need not exclude holy wrath, it most certainly excludes ugliness and pettiness.

A decisive criterion of authenticity, based on indispensable extrinsic criteria, is the spiritual or miraculous efficacy of the apparition; if nothing spiritually positive results from the vision, it should be regarded as doubtful—the measure of its doubtfulness being precisely the continuing imperfection of the visionary—though without necessarily being false even in a case such as this, for the motives of Heaven may escape us; if on the contrary the visionary draws a permanent grace[12] from the vision to the point of becoming a better man or if the vision proves to be the source of miracles without being accompanied by anything discordant, there can be no doubt that it is a true celestial apparition. *A fructibus eorum cognoscetis eos.*

*

* *

All things considered, our attitude regarding celestial manifestations depends on our understanding of the relationships between transcendence and immanence and between necessity and contingency, which reminds us of the mystery of the Veil. When we perceive a celestial sign we must not overlook the fact that it is a veil, though of course a luminous veil; nevertheless, knowing that it is a veil we must not forget *a fortiori* that its reason for being is the transmission of truth and presence and that in this respect the sign is so to speak transubstantiated, and thus itself becomes truth and presence. On the one hand the Virgin personifies and manifests the Mercy of God; on the other hand the divine Mercy is personified in the Virgin and manifested by her—not simply in the same way that every positive phenomenon necessarily manifests God, for in reality there is nothing but He, but insofar as God makes Himself manifest in an eminently direct way in the midst of His indirect and ordinary manifestations, which pertain to the natural and not the supernatural.

When perceiving the symbol or support, one can see God either after the form or before the form: after because the form evokes God; before because God has made Himself form. The mystery of the Veil contains the whole mystery of *hypostasis* and therefore of theophany.

---

11. This rules out a whole series of apparitions or "messages" that have been widely discussed in the second half of the twentieth century.

12. Which either modifies his habitual behavior or leads to a change in his character; the first result is extrinsic and the second intrinsic, though neither is entirely independent of the other.

The Fan

The opening of a fan tells how the world
Unfolds to show the marvels of creation;
Or how the goddess manifests herself,
Amaterasu, rising from the sea.

Just as in us the Spirit, self-unfolding,
Shapes its light anew in golden pictures.
The fan closes upon itself like a song fading away,
Like the sun sinking late into the sea.

So may the Spirit, after its unfolding,
Blissfully return to the Great One.

16

THE SYMBOLISM OF THE HOURGLASS

The hourglass is usually a symbol of time and death: In measuring duration, the flowing sand suggests time in its fatal and irreversible aspect—a slipping away that nothing can restrain and whose finalities no one has the power to annul. Moreover, the sterility of sand evokes the nothingness of things as mere earthly accidents, and the cessation of movement reminds us that the heart will stop and life will end.

From another point of view, the symbolism of the hourglass is drawn mainly from its form: The two compartments represent the high and the low, heaven and earth,[1] and the movement of the sand indicates a pole of attraction, that of the lower, which is the only pole the physical plane can offer us; but in reality there are two poles, one earthly and one heavenly, so that heavenly attraction should be represented by an ascending movement of the sand toward the upper compartment; since this is physically impossible, what symbolizes it in fact is the act of turning the hourglass upside down, an action that expresses this object's very reason for being. Spiritually, a movement toward the higher is always a sort of turning upside down, for the soul turns away from the world, which imprisons and disperses it, and reverses the movement of its will or love.[2]

The expression "pole of attraction" calls to mind the image of two magnetic centers, one above and one below, though this may lead to the objection that heaven and earth are not "points" but "spaces"; the response,

1. In Muslim countries there are drums having the same shape as an hourglass, one side called "earth" and the other "heaven"; in the Far East there are similar drums, which are marked on their two skins with a sign derived from the *Yin–Yang*, a visual symbol composed of two compartments with different colors, each of which contains a point of the opposite color.

2. The conical tent of the nomadic Indians of North America contains the same symbolism. In the Indian tipi the poles are placed in such a way that the ends extend considerably beyond their point of junction or crossing, and this represents the heavenly dimension; the point where the poles cross is not unlike the Gordian knot or the labyrinth, and it is considered by the Indians to be the passage along which souls escape to the Beyond.

however, is that above and below—and by extension inward and outward—each possesses two aspects, one reductive and one expansive: The world attracts like a magnetic center, but at the same time it is diverse and disperses; the "Kingdom of Heaven" also attracts like a magnet, but at the same time it is infinite and it expands. What is opposed to the space "world"—or what this space opposes—is the point "spirit": the "strait gate"; and what is opposed to the space "spirit," to the "Kingdom of Heaven" that is "within you," is the point "world": sin, Luciferian and passional contraction.[3] There is no point of contact between the world as such and Heaven as such; each will always appear as a bottleneck or prison to the other. At least this is so on the plane of moral alternatives, though beyond this plane, an immediate encounter—or a sort of coincidence—does come about between the two opposed points or spaces by virtue of the metaphysical transparency of things, as for example in contemplative alchemy; but in this case there is precisely no longer an opposition but simply a difference of degree, mode, manifestation. Clearly, earthly beauty cannot be identified with sin; it manifests heavenly Beauty and may for this reason serve as a spiritual leaven, as sacred art and the innocent harmony of nature both prove.

The compressive force of sin is the inverted shadow of the beatific attraction of the "strait gate," just as passional dispersion is the inverted shadow of inward dilation toward the Infinite. The "lower compartment" is made of either inertia or weight, either agitation or volatilization; inverting the hourglass—that is, choosing the other pole of attraction or changing direction—is pacification for the agitated soul and expansion for the languid soul.

Spiritual reality implies both the calm of the "motionless mover" and the life of the "central fire"; this is what the Song of Solomon expresses when it says: "I sleep, but my heart waketh."

*

* *

There is an analogical relationship between the "high" and the "inward" on the one hand and between the "low" and the "outward" on the other. What is inward is manifested by height, and conversely, depending on the planes or circumstances; the same is true *mutatis mutandis* for outwardness and lowliness, taking these words in their cosmic sense. When Christ or the

3. "Scripture, Faith, and Truth bear witness that sin is nothing else on the part of the creature than the fact of turning away from the unchangeable Good and toward the changeable good; the creature turns away from the Perfect in order to turn toward 'what is partial' and imperfect, and most often toward itself" (*Theologia Germanica*, 2).

Virgin depart from the visible world, they begin by "ascending"; on the other hand the angels "descend," and Christ will come again by "descending"; one also speaks of the "descent" of a Revelation and an "ascension" into Heaven. Height suggests the abyss between man and God, for the servant is below and the Lord above; inwardness for its part refers more to Selfhood or the Self: The outward is the shell or form; the inward is the Kernel or Essence.

To tend toward the higher thus also means to live toward the inward; now the unfolding of the inward begins with a certain abolition of the outward or on the basis of a mental or moral "concentration." The "strait gate" is *a priori* a sacrificial annihilation, but it also signifies—and more profoundly—a beatific annihilation. One recalls the analogy between death and love, *mors* and *amor*; like love death is a giving up of self, and like death love is generous; each is the model or mirror of the other. Man must "die to the world," but the world may also "die to man" when he has found the beatific mystery of the "strait gate" and has seized it; the "strait gate" is then the seed of Heaven, an opening toward Plenitude.[4]

The "strait gate" reveals its beatific quality when it appears not as a dark passageway but as the Center or Present—as the point of contact between the world or life and the "divine Dimension"; the Center is the blessed point beneath the divine Axis, and the Present is the blessed instant that leads us back to the divine Origin. As the neck of the hourglass shows, this apparent contraction in space and time, which seems to desire our annihilation, opens in reality onto a "new space" and a "new time" and thus transmutes both space, which surrounds and limits us, and time, which sweeps us along and eats away at us. Space is then situated as if within us, and time becomes a circular or spiral river flowing round a motionless center.

*

* *

4. "Verily with hardship goeth ease," says the Koran (*Sūrah* "Have We Not Expanded" [94]:5, 6), and this is a further allusion to the mystery of the "strait gate," especially since the same passage begins with the words: "Did We not expand thy breast?"—that is, the "inward" precisely. Other Koranic passages refer to the same symbolism: "He produced the two seas that meet. Between them is an isthmus they cannot cross" (*Sūrah* "The Most Merciful" [55]:19–20). "And it is He who produced the two seas, one sweet and palatable, the other salt and bitter; and He put between them an isthmus and a closed barrier" (*Sūrah* "The Discernment" [25]:53). According to the non-canonical Book of Esdras, "The sea is set in a wide place, that it might be deep and great. But put the case the entrance were narrow, and like a river; who then could go into the sea to look upon it, and to rule it? if he went not through the narrow, how could he come into the broad? . . . Then [after the fall of Adam] were the entrances of this world made narrow, full of sorrow and travail . . . for the entrances of the elder world were wide and sure, and brought immortal fruit" (2 Esdras 7:3–5, 12–13).

In the hourglass one compartment empties, and the other fills; this is the very picture of spiritual choice, a choice that is inescapable because "no man can serve two masters." It is in the nature of things that a superficially heterogeneous element may sometimes be combined with a spiritual attitude—for a man outwardly rich can be "poor in spirit"—but with regard to the very center of our being it is never possible to place ourselves simultaneously on two incompatible levels.

Another aspect of the symbolism of the hourglass—in this case cosmological—is the following: The flow of the grains of sand can be compared to the unfolding of all the possibilities included in a cycle of manifestation; when these possibilities are exhausted, the movement stops, and the cycle is closed.[5] This is true not only for cosmic cycles but also—and in fact above all—for the divine Cycle, which comes to an end in the *Apocatastasis* after the passing of myriad subordinate cycles; from this point of view the shower of sand indicates the exhaustion of possibilities and, conversely, their final and total integration in the divine or nirvanic Dimension.

The key doctrine of the hourglass is briefly this: God is One; now the number 1 is quantitatively the smallest of all, appearing in fact as the exclusion of quantity, hence as the extreme of poverty; but beyond number and at the level of principles, which number reflects in an inverted sense, Unity coincides with the Absolute and therefore with the Infinite, and it is precisely numerical indefiniteness that reflects in its way divine Infinitude. All the positive qualities that we notice in the world are limited; they are like the extreme and in a certain sense inverted points of essences, which unfold beyond our sense experience and even beyond all earthly consciousness. The "strait gate" is inversion and analogy, darkness and light, death and birth.

*

* *

The hourglass also suggests a division of universal realities—or the phenomenal orders representing these realities—into two compartments, if one may express it this way; in other words the fundamental distinction between the relative and the Absolute, the outward and the Inward, the earthly and the Celestial may assume the following forms:

One may distinguish between the material or visible world and the immaterial and invisible world; *grosso modo* this is the perspective of shamanists, in which the animic powers are considered prolongations of Divinity.

5. At the beginning of the flow the movement of sand is imperceptible, but toward the end it becomes quicker and quicker; this phenomenon is strictly analogous to what occurs in the unfolding of a cycle.

A second distinction places the line of demarcation between the world and God beyond the animic domain and at the threshold of the angelic domain; in this perspective the angels are essentially divine aspects.[6]

A third way of distinguishing between the two great dimensions of the Universe is to draw the line of demarcation in such a way as to separate the material, animic, and angelic domains from the archangelic and divine domains.[7] In this case the divine Spirit, which appears at the center of the cosmos and which represents as it were the heart-intellect of the world, encompasses the Archangels, who are its essential functions, and this Spirit is the Face of God turned toward the world; this perspective is to some extent adopted by Semitic monotheists, whose points of view vary in different cosmic or theophanic contexts. The Spirit of God is the great mystery the Koran refuses to define.[8] This Spirit is either uncreated or created; it is the *Logos* or Word or Book, the archetype of every Revealer and every Revelation, containing the *Dhyāni-Buddha*s and their prolongations or functions as embodied in the great *Bodhisattva*s.

According to a fourth perspective, which is metaphysical and represents the essential and invariable perspective of Semitic and Vishnuite monotheists, it is necessary to distinguish between manifestation and Principle, the existent cosmos and existentiating Being, creation and Creator—in short, between the world and God; a distinction is then drawn within God between the Qualities and the Essence.

A fifth perspective, which is that of Shaivite Vedantists, distinguishes between *Māyā* and *Paramātmā*; God the Creator is also included in *Māyā*, for *Paramātmā* alone is purely the Absolute, whereas *Ātmā* encompasses at one and the same time the pure Absolute and the Absolute clothed in relativity: *Para-Brahma*, the "Supreme," and *Apara-Brahma*, the "Non-Supreme."

To summarize, the human mind is capable of making an essential distinction between the material or visible and the Immaterial or Invisible; or between the formal—matter, soul, spirits—and the angelic Non-formal, rooted in the Divine; or between the peripheral—extending from the physical cosmos to the angelic cosmos—and the Central, the manifested Spirit of God with its archangelic functions and metacosmic Root; or between existence and Being, the created and the Creator, together with its Essence,

6. When the Essence has been forgotten in practice, the result is angelolatry or a form of polytheism in the ordinary meaning of the word; otherwise this is not the case.

7. Polytheism may come about in this case as well, and in fact it usually has its origin in the distinction in question; it must not be forgotten, however, that the Archangels have their roots in the divine Qualities or "Names," hence in Being itself; it is therefore impossible to assign a clearly determined metaphysical plane to the polytheistic deviation properly so called.

8. *Al-Rūh*, the Angel who is greater than all the others put together; in Hebrew, *Ruah Elohīm*.

which is Beyond-Being; or finally between Relativity—metacosmic as well as cosmic—and the Absolute as such.

But there are also two non-distinctions, one from below and the other from above. According to the first everything is God, and we are therefore parts of God; this amounts to pantheism unless one compensates for this perspective by emphasizing its transcendent complement, as does shamanism but not philosophical pantheism. According to the second non-distinction nothing is except *Ātmā*; this is the Vedantic thesis, which never excludes distinctions wherever they can and should apply; it is also the Sufic thesis, according to which the world is *Allāh* as *al-Zāhir*, the Outward.[9] The same teaching is found in *Mahāyāna* Buddhism: *Samsāra* is *Nirvāna*, and *Nirvāna* is *Samsāra*; Existence is an aspect of Beyond-Existence, the supreme "Void," and it is for this reason that every consciousness contains in its substance a point of access to the "Void" or the Infinite, which is pure Beatitude. The interpenetration of the two Realities is depicted by the movement of the sand in the hourglass; but Reality is one just as the grains of sand are identical, and it is only differences of situation, if one may put it this way, that give rise to a disparity whose terms are incommensurable, a disparity that is unilateral since one of the terms, even though it appears as "inward" in relation to the outwardness of the related term, is simply That which is.

9. It is this doctrine that allows Christ to identify "one of these little ones" with himself, hence with Divinity.

A. Maghreb

B. Celestial Virgin and Child

C. The Christ

D. The River

E. Sioux Chief

F. The Descent of the Sacred Pipe

G. The Thunderstorm

H. The Terrace

V

SPIRITUALITY

It is not we who know God;
it is God who knows Himself in us.

—*Esoterism as Principle and as Way*

Here and Now

Center and Now: these are the remedies
That give delight to all wise hearts—
And whose images Nature shows to us.

Here is the safety of the mountain cave:
Its deep, warm, and motherly inwardness;
There is the total freedom of the summit:
With the pure air of snow-clad peaks.

Such is the soul, standing before God:
Both root and crown—
        Yet one sole prayer.

17

MODES OF SPIRITUAL REALIZATION

According to an Islamic saying there are as many paths to God as there are human souls. But since there is no complexity that cannot finally be reduced to syntheses and thus to simple formulas—provided these result from the nature of things and not from philosophical artifice—the diversity of souls and paths can in the last analysis be reduced to three fundamental positions, which may be designated by the terms "knowledge," "love," and "action."

We shall speak first of action, the most outward of the three. Unlike love—and all the more knowledge—action does not have its sufficient reason within itself; if the path of action is not to be restricted to exotericism, it must therefore be related to one of the two higher paths, which give it its full meaning. This eminently dependent character of the way of action becomes clear when one makes use of analogies drawn from the sensible order—when for example one considers the pair "light–heat": Light represents knowledge, and heat represents love, but action is not represented by anything, unless in the form of an extrinsic quality, such as the devouring power of fire, the manifestation of which depends on the presence of a combustible material; action, therefore, is not equivalent to either love or knowledge. These two paths transcend and abolish the narrow determinism of works; faith saves whereas knowledge sets free.

The path of action (the Hindu *karma-mārga*) refers to the Divinity's aspect of Rigor, hence, the connection between this path and "fear" (the *makhāfah* of Sufism); this aspect is manifested for us by the indeterminacy and ineluctability of cosmic vicissitudes, and the goal of the path of action is liberation from these vicissitudes, not from Existence itself as is the case for the path of knowledge. Liberation through action is nonetheless a genuine deliverance, a deliverance from the cosmos of suffering;[1] and if it

1. It would be wrong to conclude that Buddhism contains only a cosmic path simply because it is founded on the premise of suffering. Since suffering is a subjective aspect of relativity, it can serve perfectly well as the negative starting point for liberation by knowledge, whereas the positive starting point is the idea of *Nirvāna*; in keeping with its initiatic subjectivism, Buddhist doctrine envisages the Supreme Reality not in its aspect of "Principle" but in its aspect of "State."

is action that here plays the role of support, this is because it is by means of action that we place ourselves in time, which as the destroyer of beings and things is precisely a manifestation of Rigor. The connection between Kali, the Hindu Divinity of destruction or transformation, and *kāla* or time and the connection in turn between *kāla* and *karma*—time and action—can help us understand in what sense "fear" is related to *karma-mārga*. What gives action its liberating quality is its sacrificial character;[2] action is to be viewed as the fulfillment of *dharma*, "duty of state," which results from the very nature of the individual, and it must therefore be accomplished not only to perfection but without attachment to its fruits (*nishkāma karma*).

The most direct form of disinterested action is the form that most visibly entails forgetfulness of self and that for this reason abolishes the barrier between "self" and "others"; in the work of charity the neighbor serves as a quasi-methodic transposition of Divinity, for "inasmuch as ye have done it unto one of the least of these my brethren, ye have done it unto me." The ego is as it were absorbed by the "other," who in turn becomes "God," so that disinterestedness here lies in the very nature of things; nevertheless the purely cosmic finality of this path is easily discernible in the fact that everything occurs at the creaturely level, hence in the outward and objective world. It is important to note that the path of action is inevitable inasmuch as action itself is inevitable. Because action is rooted in the very nature of things, even the person who follows a purely contemplative path must act in keeping with *karma-mārga*; in other words he must act in careful conformity with the constituent elements of action[3]—hence with its symbolism—and always without attachment to the fruits of his work. Thus we can see why the great spiritual methods, even those most expressly insisting on the excellence of an eremitical life, have never rejected the possibility of a path that is followed in the midst of worldly occupations. The question we now propose to address is how it is possible to combine an intense spiritual life with material and social obligations, and even to integrate these obligations to a certain extent into the inward life; for if everyday work is not an obstacle to the path, it must in some way play a

---

2. This path of liberation through sacrificial action served as the basis of the warrior civilizations; we put this in the past tense because, with the exception of Shintoism and the nearly extinct religion of the American Indians, no such civilizations seem to survive in our day.

3. It is well known that great saints, far from disdaining the humblest aspects of daily life, insisted that everything should be done in the most logical and practical way possible—that nothing should be done halfway; a thing must either be done perfectly or not at all. If the path of action is of fundamental importance from the exoteric point of view, this is because it is sufficient for reaching the end proposed by the common religion—namely, an escape from the cosmic periphery and its sufferings—and because action alone is accessible to all men without distinction and is even strictly necessary for them.

positive role in that path, or rather—more precisely—it must be a secondary support of spiritual realization.

The integration of work in spirituality depends on three fundamental conditions, which we shall call "necessity," "sanctification," and "perfection." First, the activity to be spiritualized should correspond to a necessity and not a caprice. One can sanctify—that is, offer to God—every normal activity required by the demands of life itself but not an occupation lacking in sufficient reason and certainly nothing of a reprehensible nature; this implies that every necessary activity is predisposed to being a support for the spiritual life and that such an activity possesses a certain universality, which makes it eminently symbolic. Second, the activity thus defined should be effectively offered to God, which means that it must be accomplished out of love for God and without rebelling against destiny; this is the point of the prayers that are used in most if not all religions to consecrate and ritualize work; in this way the work becomes a "natural sacrament"—a shadow as it were of the "supernatural sacrament" of a rite properly so called and a secondary counterpart to it. Finally, the work must be logically perfect, for it is obvious that one cannot offer God something imperfect or consecrate an unworthy object to Him; the perfection of the act, like the perfection of existence itself, is in any case self-evident insofar as every act necessarily retraces the divine Act and is a modality of it. The perfection of action includes three aspects, which concern first the activity as such, then the means, and finally the end or aim. The activity as such must be objectively and subjectively perfect, which implies that it must be consistent with or proportionate to the goal to be achieved; the means must also be consistent with the goal, and this implies that the instrument of the work must be well chosen and then wielded with skill, hence in perfect conformity with the nature of the work; and the result or end of the work must be perfect, corresponding precisely to the need that gave rise to it.

These conditions constitute what one might call the internal and external logic of the activity, and if they are fully met the work in question will not only cease to be an obstacle to the inward path but will even be a help to it. Conversely, a badly accomplished piece of work, one not corresponding to any divine Possibility, will always be an impediment to the path; God is Perfection, and to approach Him man must be perfect in action as well as in non-active contemplation.

*

* *

In the path of love (the Hindu *bhakti-mārga*, the *mahabbah* of Sufism), speculative activity—which by definition is of the intellectual order—does not play the predominant role it does in the way of knowledge (*jnāna-mārga*, *maʿrifah*); the "lover"—the *bhakta*—obtains everything by means of love and divine Grace;[4] paradoxical as it may seem, given the initiatic character of *bhakti*, doctrinal considerations do not possess the crucial importance in this path which they have in *jnāna*,[5] and this explains why *bhakta*s were able to reject Shankarian advaitism with impunity. One might say that bhaktic doctrine, as exemplified by Ramanuja, represents far more a sort of background for spiritual work than a disinterested and perfectly adequate expression of Truth; in order to love one must limit, and this means that attention must be given to a single aspect of Reality, for considering the whole Truth is more or less incompatible with the subjectivism of an exclusive love. The way of love is comparable to a rhythm or melody, not an act of reasoning; it is a path of "beauty" not "wisdom"—if one may risk seeming to say that beauty is without wisdom and wisdom without beauty; in short the perspective of the *bhakta* contains inevitable limitations because of the subjective and emotional character of "bhaktic" method.

In matters of doctrine the *bhakta* has nothing to resolve by intelligence alone, for the entire religion "thinks" for him by means of all the symbols it possesses, scriptural and otherwise. This explains why the normal flowering of *bhakti* depends on a homogeneous religious framework; this framework constitutes what one might call an external skeleton, a protection against foreign and unassimilable influences; deviations of *bhakti* have in fact often been caused by contact with a foreign civilization.[6]

A comparison of the "bhaktic" doctrine of someone like Ramanuja with the "jnanic" doctrine of a figure like Shankara shows what the essential limitations of doctrinal *bhakti* consist of; to recognize these limitations,

---

4. For example, in order to understand that gold is merely clay—as the Hindu Scriptures teach—Ramakrishna, who was having difficulty understanding this fully, prayed to the Divinity to reveal it to him; finally, "I heard, like the trumpeting of more than ten thousand elephants clamoring in my ears, Clay and gold are but one for you!"

5. According to Ramakrishna, "It is unimportant whether we believe that Radha and Krishna are *Avatāras*. . . . But we must all have intense devotion (*anurāga*); this is the only thing that is necessary."

6. The case of Vivekananda is particularly eloquent in this connection. To those who would criticize his master, Ramakrishna, for lacking the "discernment of spirits," we would reply with the Buddhist monk who converted King Menander (Milinda)—the king having asked him whether a perfect man, such as the Buddha, could be deceived and make mistakes—that "a perfect man may be uninformed in secondary things of which he has no experience, but he cannot be deceived regarding things that his insight has already revealed to him. He is perfect here and now. He understands the entire mystery, the Essence of the Universe, but he may not know the purely outward variations by which this Essence is manifested in time and space. He knows clay, but he has not acquired knowledge of all the forms it can be given. The perfect man knows the soul, but he does not know all the forms and combinations in which it can be manifested."

however, does not mean that *bhakti* is merely lacking in relation to *jnāna*—this would be as absurd as seeking to reduce femininity to a mere lack of virility—for it goes without saying that it is not enough to be lacking in *jnāna* in order to be a *bhakta*; *bhakti*, while being a less direct mode of knowledge than *jnāna*, nonetheless represents in itself a positive reality. It is incontestable that the doctrine of Ramanuja is providential in the highest sense of the term and that it is thus directly "willed by God"—that it represents, in short, a fundamental mode of spirituality; but at the same time it is no less true that its negative attitude toward Shankarian doctrine betokens a shortcoming that cannot be ignored.

It is important to note that the Islamic term *mahabbah* is not in every respect synonymous with the Hindu *bhakti*; it does not point exclusively to a way of love but also has a significance pertaining to the way of knowledge, and this is why all Muslim initiates use it, whatever their personal path. Let us also add that in Islam "love" and "knowledge" do not appear as two clearly separate paths as is the case in Hinduism; depending on the individuals involved, there is instead a predominance of one over the other, as seems to be the case in Christianity as well. The use of the term "love" in various esotericisms to designate an intellectual reality can be explained by the fact that sentiment, while being inferior to reason because of its emotional subjectivity, is nevertheless symbolically comparable to something that is superior to reason, namely, the Intellect; this is because sentiment—like the Intellect at its antipodes—is direct, simple, spontaneous, and limitless rather than discursive; compared with reason, sentiment appears free from form and fallibility, and this is why the divine Intelligence can be called "Love" and why it really is so—in a transposed sense—in relation to the paltry human intelligence; here one finds a simultaneous application of the "parallel" and "inverse" analogies that at once link and separate the divine and cosmic orders.

One could define *bhakti* as a "path of beauty"; on this subject it is worth pointing out that beauty—like knowledge—is misunderstood and neglected in the perspective of merit, which ends up conferring an essentially moral structure on spirituality; such a perspective cannot but be unaware of the fact that beauty is eminently a support for intellection, and with its characteristically methodical and blind mistrust the path of merit therefore sees beauty as a temptation and thus a road toward sin, all the more so in that this perspective is *a priori* ignorant of the nature, value, and role of pure intelligence. When beauty is associated with a contemplative attitude, it is as pleasing to God as a sacrifice. Christ—the Wisdom of God—was borne by Beauty: the Virgin.

*

* *

The third and last mode of spirituality—in ascending order—is the path of knowledge (the Hindu *jnāna-mārga*, the *maʿrifah* of Sufism); its dependence on doctrine is the greatest possible, for doctrine is an integral and immediate part of this path, whereas in *bhakti* doctrinal considerations can be reduced to very simple syntheses and are in practice situated as it were outside the path. On the other hand *jnāna* as such is completely independent of any doctrinal formulation precisely insofar as it realizes the "spirit," which—although necessarily expressing itself by means of the "letter"—always remains transcendent and incommensurable in relation to its symbols. A maxim from Meister Eckhart expresses admirably the general attitude of a *jnānin*: "Truth is so noble that, if God wished to turn away from it, I would remain with Truth and leave God; but God Himself is Truth."

The speculative faculty, which constitutes an essential qualification and a *sine qua non* for *jnāna-mārga*, is the "natural" ability to contemplate transcendent Realities; we call this ability "natural" because the one who possesses it makes use of it more or less like any other faculty—in other words without the intervention of a "supernatural" state. Thus the knowledge that a *bhakta* attains in a "state of grace" a *jnānin* possesses in his state of ordinary consciousness. It may be objected that intellectual intuition is no more natural than ecstasy and that ecstasy is no more supernatural than intuition, to which we reply that we are using these words in an entirely provisional manner—and moreover in an easily understandable sense—unless one prefers that we speak of the "naturally supernatural" or the "supernaturally natural," which, though offering certain advantages, would complicate our terminology. We could also describe the speculative faculty here in question in the following terms: He alone is really an intellectual who possesses the truth in an active manner, not he who accepts it passively; the first case is that of a man who, having learned a metaphysical truth, recognizes himself in a certain fashion within it and is able to formulate it spontaneously—hence in an original and inspired manner—while projecting the light of his knowledge upon the most diverse contingencies, thanks to a direct vision of the realities concerned and not by means of reasoning; the second case is that of a man who, having heard the same truth, has a presentiment of its self-evidence but is incapable of expressing it otherwise than by repeating the doctrinal statement that first brought it to his attention.

Intensity in the way of love corresponds to certainty in the way of knowledge. In *bhakti* the mental process consists in the ideal projection—using "ideal" in the Platonic sense of the word—of the limited beatitudes of this world, such as beauty or goodness, into the limitless Beatitude of Being; the appearances of the world are accepted as a foretaste of this Beatitude, but they are at the same time rejected because of their limitations—because of what illusorily separates them from divine Beatitude or Beauty. By contrast *jnāna*, instead of finding its starting point in the experience of earthly things, proceeds so to speak by abstraction, and this is because the knowledge that is its means—together with the self-evidence implied by this knowledge—is by definition "not of this world"; seemingly external things—including the soul, which needless to say is also conceived here as outward—appear as illustrations or traces of intellectual, hence "paracletic," knowledge.[7] This exteriorization of the microcosm is accompanied by an interiorization of the macrocosm, which is why, according to Shankaracharya, "the *yogin*, whose intellect is perfect, contemplates everything as dwelling within himself, and thus by the eye of knowledge he sees that everything is *Ātmā*."

*
* *

Certain highly secular moralists who prefer man to God, if indeed they do not replace God with man, are often astonished or indignant over the indifference that saints—both Western and Eastern—have sometimes seemed to show toward the human miseries of the world where they lived. There is a twofold reason for this indifference. In the first place many of the miseries in the body of a traditional world must be regarded as "lesser evils"—as necessary channels for calamities that are themselves inevitable but that can be reduced to a minimum; this is a point of view modern people have never understood, for they fail to realize that there are things in the cosmos that cannot at any price be avoided, the apparent and artificial suppression of which only causes even more "massive" cosmic reactions;[8] second, the indifference of spiritual people with regard to these contingencies is explained by their desire to deal with evil at its root and to help the world, not by dissipating energies in fragmentary and indeed illusory efforts, but by returning directly to the very source of the Good. The abuses one finds in all ancient civilizations are more or less inevitable, for suffering—since it is implied by Existence itself—is inherent in everything and cannot but express itself in one way or another; it might be possible to eliminate some of these abuses—those for example that have taken root in the Hindu caste system, and action to this end has been undertaken already—but only if

7. It is thus false to maintain that *nihil est in intellectu quod non prius fuerit in sensu*. From the point of view of *jnāna*, which is that of total Truth, the exact opposite is true.

8. Nothing has meaning outside the truth; there is an idealism that is stupid and criminal. As for "altruism" we may recall that Christ said, "Love thy neighbor as thyself"; he did not say "more than thyself" or "do not love thyself"; and yet his words have been interpreted in this way by a certain hypocritical and impotent moralism.

one proceeds from within the civilization in question and on the basis of its spiritual content. In the majority of cases, however, this would require a return of the collectivity itself to this living spring; in the present cyclical circumstances this would mean returning to the golden age pure and simple, which is unfortunately not possible.

Another point we wish to mention is the following: In metaphysical knowledge reasoning can play no other role than that of an occasional cause of intellection, which intervenes in a sudden—not a continuous or progressive—fashion as soon as the mental operation, conditioned in turn by an intellectual intuition, possesses the quality or perfection that makes it an effective symbol. When the heat produced by rubbing two pieces of wood together—or by a lens capturing a ray of sunshine—reaches the precise degree that is its culminating point, a flame suddenly bursts forth; in just the same way intellection, as soon as the mental operation is capable of supplying an adequate support, instantly grafts itself onto this support. It is thus that human intelligence assimilates its own universal Essence, thanks to a sort of reciprocity between thought and Reality. As for rationalism, it instead seeks the culminating point of the cognitive process on its own plane; it looks for Truth in the realm of mental formulations and rejects *a priori* the possibility of a knowledge that is accessible only beyond these formulations and that thus eludes the resources of human language, at least to a certain extent; one might as well go in search of a word that is entirely what it designates.

From this fundamental contradiction two things follow: first an inability to discover mental forms that can properly serve as vehicles for intellectual intuition and hence for Truth, for badly posed questions are no more conducive to light than they are derived from it; second an inability to perceive the intellectual dimensions adumbrated by a particular formulation, however defective. Rationalism proceeds like a man who tries to draw a geometric point by making it as small as possible or who wishes to reach an absolute perfection on a given plane of relativity by denying either the necessary imperfection of the plane or the transcendence of pure Perfection. It is impossible to assert too strongly that a doctrinal formulation is not perfect because it exhausts infinite Truth on the plane of logic, for this is impossible, but because it realizes a mental form that is able to communicate a ray of that Truth—and thereby a virtuality of the total Truth—to whoever is intellectually qualified to receive it; this explains why traditional doctrines always appear naive, at least from the point of view of philosophers who do not understand that the aim and sufficient reason of wisdom do not lie on the plane of its formal affirmation and that there is by definition no common measure and no continuity between thought, the developments of which have no more than a symbolic value, and pure Truth, which is identical with That which "is" and thereby includes the one who thinks.

In conclusion let us briefly mention the qualities that are indispensable for spirituality in general. First is a mental attitude that—for want of a better term—could be designated by the word "objectivity"; this is a perfectly disinterested attitude of the intelligence, free from ambition and prejudice and thus accompanied by serenity. Second is a quality pertaining to the psychic life of the individual, and this is nobility, which consists in the elevation of the soul above everything petty or mean; fundamentally this amounts to a discrimination in psychic mode between the essential and accidental or between the real and unreal. Last comes the virtue of simplicity, in which a man is freed from all unconscious tension rooted in self-love; such a person has a perfectly original and spontaneous attitude toward creatures and things, which means that he is without artifice and is free from all pretension, ostentation, or dissimulation, being in a word without pride. This simplicity is never an affected humility, however, but an absence of innate prejudices, hence a natural effacement of the "self" or of the "hardened heart" of the Scriptures—a "naive" effacement, through which a man symbolically returns to childhood. Every spiritual method demands above all an attitude of poverty, humility, simplicity, or effacement, which is like an anticipation of Extinction in God.

Veritas

First the Truth, which clarifies all things;
Then our becoming what the Truth proclaims.
And then the Name, which nourishes with Light;
Then Beauty, flowing back into the One.

Be thou with God, and God will be with thee;
Turn not thy gaze from Him who is the One.
The living Truth will act in thy heart's shrine—

All else lies in the Hands of God.

18

THE ANONYMITY OF THE VIRTUES

According to Saint Augustine, "All the other vices attach themselves to evil that it may be accomplished; pride alone attaches itself to good that it may perish." And likewise the Curé d'Ars: "Humility is to the virtues what the string is to the rosary; remove the string and all the beads escape; remove humility and all the virtues disappear." Pride consists in glorying in one's virtues, either before others or before oneself alone, and this destroys the virtues for two reasons: first because one takes them away from God to whom they belong in reality, thus putting oneself—like Lucifer—in place of the divine Source; and second because one attributes *de facto* a disproportionate value to a phenomenon that is necessarily relative. "When thou doest alms, let not thy left hand know what thy right hand doeth."

It would however be a mistake to conclude that a virtuous man has no awareness of his virtues and that to be aware of them is pride; the fact that someone who is proud readily attributes all the virtues he can think of to himself in no way implies that every man who is aware of his virtues is proud, for people are not all alike, and one awareness is not the same as another. Man, being "made in the image of God," has the gift of intelligence; to speak of intelligence is to speak of objectivity, which means that the thesis—whether philosophical or moralistic—of the fundamental subjectivity of man is a contradiction pure and simple; for whoever is deprived of objectivity can ascertain nothing whatsoever, not even that he is subjective.[1] Endowed with objectivity, a man possesses by that very fact the ability to look at himself as if he were another person; but if we must admit that other people have qualities—and humility demands we do so—we cannot deny the possibility of having them ourselves; if on the contrary we must piously believe ourselves incapable of any good, we must also believe this of others. In any case a humble man does not wish for virtue to be attributed to himself; he is attached to virtue for its own sake, to virtue as such—not

1. The thesis of the insuperable subjectivity of the human spirit destroys the very definition of man.

because it may be his but because it is beautiful. And being beautiful it necessarily belongs to the Sovereign Good.

It may be asked what the basis is for the equation "intelligence is pride"; if one means that a purely mental—not "cardiac" or "intellective"—intelligence runs the risk of succumbing to the profane and worldly temptation of an autocratic Luciferianism, then the equation is justified; but it is a mistake not to specify this point and to give the impression that intelligence is prideful in itself, which is a contradiction in terms. No doubt the equation at issue serves the purpose of waging a preventive war against a rationalism that is hostile to faith; this is an excuse but not a justification.

But returning to the question of moral qualities: Since every virtue by definition contains a beatitude, even the humblest of men cannot help enjoying a good conscience—unless they deprive themselves of it because of some unrealistic, though possibly efficacious, mystical zeal; nor can they help knowing *a priori* that we necessarily possess in a relative manner what God has bestowed on us and what He possesses—He alone—in an absolute fashion. For even if a value belongs to us because God has given it to us, so that we truly possess it on our own level, it nevertheless belongs to Him entirely since no value can be situated outside the Sovereign Good. One could say that a man enters into virtue as he would enter into a sanctuary and that virtue expels the ambitious who claim it for themselves.

Furthermore, a man who is both humble and intelligent can be thoroughly convinced he has virtues, but at the same time he knows that God's measures are not at his disposal; he knows that our situation as earthly men does not allow us to rest on the all too precarious awareness of our qualities. For there is always the distinction between the Absolute and the relative and thus a sense of proportion; no intelligent man can escape these responsibilities of the spirit.

*
* *

Strictly speaking, a man should not wish to "acquire" a particular virtue but to eliminate a particular vice; to realize a quality is to destroy the fault that is contrary to it, for what is normal is the primordial state, and the primordial precedes the fall and decadence. This truth leads us to the following observation: There are men with the vain ambition to be exceptionally intelligent, and this makes them all the more stupid; their case would not be hopeless if they had the good sense and humility to recognize their limitations—for which Heaven could not reproach them—and if they modestly took their stand upon wholesome, hence intelligent, principles. A mirror has no need for ornaments but instead needs purity; an ornament in this case means an "ideal" that is at once individualistic and perfectionistic, whereas purity refers to the demands of the real; now our intention, like a mirror, should be true to its object, and it should be so in essence and effectiveness, not merely in form. It is true that intelligence—since we mention it—is not a virtue but an extra-moral quality or more precisely a faculty, though this makes no difference from the point of view that interests us here, for intelligence is in any case closely combined with virtue; insofar as it is faithful to its innermost nature, it is "objectivity," hence detachment and impartiality; to be entirely objective is to die a little.

In a certain metaphysical sense, only our faults belong to us; our qualities belong to God, to the Good as such. By eliminating the vices, we allow the qualities of God to penetrate our soul; from another point of view—as we noted above—it is we who enter into virtue. Obviously the merit of virtue eludes someone who believes, "I am virtue"; to be conscious of a virtue is one thing, but to be self-satisfied with this consciousness is quite another.

We could also express ourselves as follows: Every man likes to be out in the light and fresh air—no one wants to be shut up in a dark and airless tower—and this is how one should love the virtues and detest the vices. No man who enjoys sunshine and air would think of proclaiming, "I am the sun" or "I am the sky"; one loves an atmosphere of light and air, and this is why one enters it. It is in just the same way that one should enter the virtues: because of their self-evident nature and because one loves their atmosphere.

A proud man either denies a fault for which he is criticized or else he minimizes it, while perhaps assuming responsibility by saying with a cynical individualism, "But that is the way I am made"; this attitude is fundamentally diabolical, for God alone has the right to say: "I am that I am." A proud man either denies his faults or is proud of them; the corollary of this attitude is that he exaggerates the faults of other people or even projects his own faults—without minimizing them this time—onto others, including those who have not the slightest trace of them; indeed he does this all the more with such people out of a kind of vengeance.

A humble man on the contrary does not believe he has a right to a fault, and he certainly does not believe that he has faults that are interesting and lovable. A humble man would rather be a beggar in the light and fresh air than a king in a dark and airless tower, and he would not dream of saying either that darkness is light or that he is the light. Of course a proud man may have certain natural qualities, but pride should never be excused on account of them; for a man has no right to love what is unacceptable to God.

*

* *

In order to vanquish a fault, it is necessary to use everything one has and everything one is: intelligence, will, and sentiment. By this last word we mean the capacity to love, which also implies the capacity to hate; the sense of the beautiful necessarily implies the sense of the ugly, for we live in a world of contrasts or contrasting manifestation. Likewise no one can venerate if he does not have the capacity to despise;[2] there is of course a metaphysical or mystical standpoint transcending all differences and considering phenomena only with respect to their mere existence—their character of divine manifestation or *Māyā*—but this point of view cannot be legitimately applied in all situations; one must know how to put each thing in its place.

Intelligence informs us of the cosmic significance of the virtues and their human necessity, both individual and social; it shows us their obvious value and at the same time the absurdity of the vices. Sentiment—the feeling soul—convinces us through beauty. As for the will, it puts into practice both our comprehension of the true and our sense of the beautiful. To vanquish a fault it is therefore necessary first to understand its nature, second to detest it, and third to put this understanding and disposition into practice; now to understand the nature of a fault is above all to understand the nature of the virtue it denies; in the same way hatred of evil is conceivable only in relation to the good it denies and in relation to the love of this good. It is knowledge and love that give wings to the will; it is not so difficult to want something when we understand its self-evidence and necessity and when moreover we love it and therefore detest its absence or opposite.

If in fact we are saints, this is of interest to Heaven, for Heaven is concerned with our spiritual welfare; but our individualistic and perfectionistic desire for sanctity is of no interest to it. We may pray and ask God to free us from a fault—provided we neglect nothing that will help to free us from it—but we may not ask God to make us perfect; one must overcome a fault in order to rid the world of an evil rather than with the intention of adorning oneself with a quality. The desire to be perfect is certainly not lacking in logic, but the desire not to be imperfect is more realistic and more concrete, and also more modest.

---

2. If one were to love and admire everything, as for example certain dreamers of a more or less Buddhist inclination would have it, the fulminations of the *Magnificat* or Sermon on the Mount would be inexplicable. Charity or "compassion" is not weakness, to say nothing of the fact that charity may require hardness.

Nothing can be accomplished without the aid of Heaven; now Heaven has given us the capacity to think, to will, to act, and to love. Spirit became flesh that flesh might become Spirit.

Ad Astra

Ad astra—to the stars—is the Path;
Adastra is the name I choose.
Mine is the star-path, and I belong to it—
Crystal of Truth and music of the soul.

Islands of light in cold and boundless night:
I think I see my heart a thousand times.
Far and yet near is our way to the Self—
To ultimate beatitude in God's Heights.

19

THE NATURE AND FUNCTION OF THE SPIRITUAL MASTER

The Vedantic ternary *Sat*, *Chit*, and *Ānanda* can serve as a key when considering a wide variety of topics; here it will be applied to the spiritual master, not because there is no other way of approaching this subject, but because it provides in this connection an especially appropriate means of access. For the master represents and transmits a reality of being (*Sat*); a reality of intelligence or truth (*Chit*); and a reality of love, union, and happiness (*Ānanda*).

The element "being," without which the master would be as if deprived of reality or existence, is the religion to which he belongs and by which he is mandated or else a spiritual organization within the framework of this religion; the religion, or the esoteric cell that sums it up and offers us its essence, confers on man the "being" without which there can be no concrete and effective path. The function of the founders of religion is to restore to fallen man his primordial being; hence the first condition of spirituality is to be virtually "reborn" and thus to realize the quasi-ontological basis of the two constituent elements of the path, namely, discernment or doctrine on the one hand and concentration or method on the other.

Representing *a priori* a "substance" or "being," *Sat*, the spiritual master is *a posteriori* and on this very basis the vehicle of an "intellection" or "consciousness," *Chit*, by which is to be understood a providential doctrine determining the tone or style of every subsequent formulation. It needs to be stressed that this doctrine depends on Revelation—in the direct and plenary sense of the word—and that its orthodox ramifications therefore have a quality of absoluteness and infinitude, which makes all recourse to extraneous sources unnecessary, even though it is certainly possible for formulations originating in such a source to be extrinsically adopted by a given master and integrated into the perspective he incarnates insofar as they are mentally compatible with the dogmatic or mythological system in question. Noteworthy examples are provided by the Neo-Platonic concepts adopted by Sufis and by Christianized Aristotelianism; it would be wrong to see a form of syncretism in such cases, for the foreign concepts are accepted only because they can be assimilated, and they can be assimilated only because of their inward concordance with the tradition in question, and because Truth is one. Another aspect of this issue of intellectuality is infallibility: The master is in principle infallible with regard to the revealed doctrine which he represents and which he even personifies by virtue of his "being" or "substance," but this infallibility, which is not unconnected with grace, is conditioned by the equilibrium between spiritual science and virtue or between intelligence and humility.

Thus the master must realize the ternary "being," "discernment," "concentration." By "being" we mean "new substance,"[1] "consecration," or "initiation"; by "discernment," the truth that distinguishes between the Real and the illusory or between *Ātmā* and *Māyā*;[2] and by "concentration," the method that allows the "consecrated" contemplative to fasten himself—at first mentally and then with the center of his being—upon the Real, the self-evidence of which we carry within ourselves. As a reality of union and thus of "love" and "bliss," this fastening corresponds analogically and by participation to the element *Ānanda* in the Vedantic ternary.

The importance in spirituality of what may be called the existential element results from the fact that it is impossible to approach God or the Absolute or the Self without the blessing and aid of Heaven: "No man cometh unto the Father, but by me" (Christianity), and "no one will meet Allah who has not met His Messenger" (Islam); "he that gathereth not with me scattereth abroad" and "without me ye can do nothing" (Christianity); and "ye will not, unless Allah willeth" (Islam). This *conditio sine qua non*, whose mainstays are first and foremost "consecration" and "orthodoxy"—which we have connected respectively to *Sat* and *Chit*—explains why a spirituality deprived of these bases can only end up as a psychological game without any relation to the unfolding of our higher states.

Because the profane man is "nonexistent" from the point of view at issue here, the master gives him "spiritual existence" by affiliation or consecration; next he gives him doctrine, or "intelligence" if one prefers; and finally he gives him "life," that is, a spiritual means pertaining to the element "concentration." Now this means, which is an engagement "unto death"—for in order to "live" inwardly one must "die" outwardly—is essentially a gift from the master and Heaven, for otherwise it would be lacking in the indispensable Grace; doubtless there have been very exceptional cases in which other modalities came into play, but these have always involved

1. "Put on the new man," says Saint Paul.

2. Or between *Nirvāna* and *samsāra* in Buddhist terms.

persons whose sanctity guaranteed purity of intention and protected the spiritual means from any profanation.[3]

In a word, we can make use of a spiritual means only if we enter into a concrete and solemn engagement, thereby accepting the fact that Heaven disposes of us according to its good pleasure; and this engagement is irreversible: The way is one of no return.

*

* *

As a guide for the disciple's personal path—which is always inscribed within the general path traced out by divine authority through tradition—the spiritual master becomes in a sense a continuation of the disciple's ego. Every spiritual alchemy involves an anticipated death and therefore losses of equilibrium or periods of obscuration in which the disciple is no longer fully master of his "self"; he is no longer completely of this world nor yet of the other, and his experience seems to call into question all the existential categories of which we are as if woven. In these "trials" and the "temptations" accompanying them—for lower *māyā* or the downward quality (*tamas*) takes advantage of the slightest fissure—the spiritual master plays the role of "motionless center"; he brings objective, immutable, and incorruptible truth to bear in opposing the temptation of giving rational form to irrational troubles. The same is true with regard to temptations of the opposite kind, when the disciple, overcome by some contemplative state beyond his usual reach—and such a state may be only accidental and is not a proof of any realization—may think that he has become superhuman to some degree; in this case lower *māyā*—or the devil, which here amounts to the same thing—will not fail to suggest to the disciple that he should declare himself master or give way to some other pretension of this kind. The case is rather like that of a drunken man, who no longer perceives the true proportion of things; the master for his part has realized "sober drunkenness," his human substance being adapted to his spiritual state, for mastery is precisely "keeping a cool head"—but without the least pretension—within the beatific experience. All that has just been said shows clearly that faith is an indispensable quality in a disciple; without faith there is no spiritual continuity and thus no traversing of "hells," nor any possible victory over the ego.

---

3. The seeds of sanctity are fear of God and a sense of the sacred, at the very least. It must be recognized that these qualities are totally absent from the general mentality of our time, all criticism of which is taboo.

In a certain sense *gnosis* transcends and abolishes faith, but only when faith is understood as a quasi-moral acceptance of revealed truths and not as a concrete presentiment of the Inexpressible; certainly *gnosis* is a "vision" and not a "thinking," but it is so only in a certain respect, for it never completely does away with the veil separating the earthly creature from pure Being.[4] Understood in this way, faith—the *shraddhā* of the Hindu *chelā*—is a necessary element of spiritual development; faith in the master is of the same order insofar as he incarnates the knowledge to be attained.[5] The master, being a living man and not a logical demonstration, corresponds to the element of non-fixation and limitlessness, which is present everywhere in the cosmos and which is indispensable for the subjective actualization of theoretical data.

What we have said clearly shows that spiritual mastership is a very special function and that it is therefore false to describe every teaching authority as a "spiritual master." The functions of "doctor" and "master" often coincide, but they need not do so in one and the same person; the master does not necessarily write treatises, but he always possesses a sufficient doctrinal authority.[6]

*
* *

The spiritual master is not obliged to reveal all his knowledge or all the graces he has received; here is the whole problem of secrecy and asymmetry[7] or of inward limitlessness and the laws of life. On the one hand a plant needs an invisible element, its roots, and on the other hand it manifests the potentialities of this element in a way combining strictness with play or the determinate with the indeterminate; a spiritual teaching should not aim to fully unveil or expend the truth that inspires it or to give it the implacable and exhaustive form of a mathematical equation. One must not seek to introduce a quasi-absolute element of conclusiveness, hence of

---

4. To think otherwise is to misinterpret certain ellipses in sacred teaching.

5. Shri Shankara: "My refuge is neither my mother nor my father, nor my children nor my brothers, nor anyone else. . . . May my supreme refuge be the foot my *guru* has placed on my head" (*Svātmanirūpana*, 146, 148).

6. The case of a saint with the quality of a *Pratyeka*-Buddha (Buddhism) or a *Fard* (Islam) should be remembered here; he has no spiritual posterity properly so called but nonetheless acts by his presence.

7. According to an old adage, presumably Chinese, "He who knows ten must teach only nine." But this law of the secret also concerns the disciple: as a contemporary Hindu master has observed, "The *sādhaka* must not reveal his spiritual experiences except to his *guru* or a saint."

petrifaction and sterility, into the very expression of truth; strictly speaking, this is no doubt an impossibility, but it is certainly possible to express a doctrinal teaching concerning the most intimate aspects of the spiritual life—as distinct from generalities or concomitances—with a prolixity having no relation to the recipient's power of concrete assimilation; this is condemned traditionally as creating a disequilibrium between doctrine and method. In other words theoretical teaching must not exhaust in advance the capacities for awareness it aims to awaken in the disciple; the disciple needs light, but he also needs an element of obscurity, which will act as a leaven in connection with the light received and which will help him release the element of light he carries within his own substance; instead of "obscurity" we might also say "generative disequilibrium," for which the *kōans* of Zen Buddhism doubtless provide the best example.

Verbal demonstrations are certainly indispensable, but the symbol—with its power of direct, total, and unlimited suggestion and its double function of unveiling (re-velation) and veiling—retains all its rights in the subsequent phase of contemplative realization. We should also mention teaching by sign or gesture: Where the spoken word is insufficient, the master makes a "gash" in the soul of the disciple, marking it with the red-hot iron of the pure symbol; this sign, which may well coincide with a humiliation, is meant to release the necessary awareness in the disciple and at the same time to actualize the corresponding virtue. One must take care not to fall into either extreme: One must neither despise words, which are venerable when they are what they ought to be—otherwise man would not possess the gift of speech—nor imagine that one can do everything with them; here as always wisdom consists in putting everything in its proper place. God instructs the collectivity *a priori* by the revealed Word, but He instructs the individual *a posteriori* by destiny; this principle is reflected in a particular way in every spiritual method.

*
* *

A question arises that has often been debated: Can the function of a spiritual master extend beyond the boundaries of a given religion? This cannot be ruled out categorically, but it is nevertheless a very precarious possibility because of the high degree of spirituality it demands on the part of the master as well as because of the difficulty with which he may be faced in assessing facts situated in a traditional world other than his own; moreover, in such a case he must act as the vehicle of a foreign *barakah*, and this presupposes a spirituality concretely transcending the world of forms; it is necessary to add the word "concretely" because universalist verbiage is one thing and realization of the Essence quite another. In a case of this kind there must also be a sufficient reason of overriding significance; such reasons do exist accidentally, as is shown for example in the relationship between the young Ibrahim ibn Adham and the monk Symeon, a master of *gnosis*, and as indicated in a passage in "The Life of the Russian Pilgrim," which acknowledges that in the absence of a *starets* a seeker may receive instruction "even from a Saracen," with the help of Heaven. Such an encounter is conceivable only if the two parties are in full conformity with their respective traditions, for the Christian must be really Christian and the Muslim really Muslim, however paradoxical this may seem in view of the spiritual communion to be established between them;[8] since it is necessary for their mutual understanding to be based on more than a philosophical abstraction, it must incorporate points of departure that are extrinsically and provisionally separative, not because they are separative or exclusive but because they guarantee a true intuition of unity by their intrinsic veracity.

This seeming paradox is comparable to the paradox involved in our relationship with the Infinite. This relationship cannot be unitive without first having been separative or, to be more exact, without being separative at its base and in our individual consciousness, for there is at once an order of succession and a parallelism; the most accomplished gnostic or the perfect *jnānin* "prostrates himself at the feet of Govinda," which implies a separation. From a more contingent point of view the station of unity means that a sage has transcended the level of forms and hence also of doctrinal formulations; though these formulations are sacred and always remain valid in their own sphere, it must be noted that this station is not dependent on a master's being informed about a given religion other than his own; in this particular connection the state of union does not imply a *de facto* attitude but a capacity in principle.[9] This means that the spiritual master must manifest both the particularity of the form and the unity of the spirit while at the same time taking into account the nature of their different levels; he must conform to holy separation at the base so as to be able to realize holy union at the summit,[10] a summit that can be reached

8. The situation may appear in a somewhat different light in the case of Hindus and Muslims in India. In our day, however, modernist influences seriously compromise the advantages of the spiritual climate of India.

9. For example, the inward and essential knowledge of a theologically exclusive Muslim may be infinitely closer to the Christic mysteries than is the mental and sentimental universalism of a profane despiser of "separatist dogmas."

10. "When one has attained (perfect) Love, one must not despise social rules (institutions and rites), but rather conform to them (without attachment to their fruits)" (*Nārada Sūtra*, 62).

only by first perceiving the element of unity in the revealed form itself and by loving this form as a quality of the Non-formal. For every sacred form is *Shūnyamūrti*, "Manifestation of the Void."

*
* *

Since the very term "spiritual master" often gives rise to disproportionate and ill-sounding associations, it may be useful to say a few words on the question of hierarchical differences; all told, the misconceptions—whether serious or slight—are simply another form of the very common error that, analogically speaking, assimilates the circle to the sphere on the pretext that both figures are round; this is a type of error found in the most diverse domains but above all in history and psychology. One of two things: Either we apply the term "spiritual master" to the founders of religion, in which case the term can no longer be applied to the sages who succeed them and who are not prophets in the proper sense of the word, or else it is the sages whom we call "masters," in which case it would be improper to use the term "spiritual master" to refer to such beings as the founders of religion—or the *Avatāras* of Vishnu—for this would be a tautology, undermining their super-eminent dignity by comparing them with their representatives. For a similar reason it might also be asked whether *mutatis mutandis* the title "master" is appropriate for the greatest of these representatives, such as Christ's Apostles, since their greatness is proven by the fact that they alone were the direct disciples of the "Word made flesh" and participated instrumentally in the Revelation;[11] this scruple is entirely legitimate in the present context, but in certain cases there are considerations that permit one to disregard it, as we shall see.

In comparing a Benedictine master or abbot—of the fifteenth century, for example—with Saint Benedict, and then comparing the latter with Saint John, we obtain a sufficiently clear picture of the principal degrees, not of spiritual mastery in itself, but of its manifestation in breadth, for it is important not to confuse what might be called the cosmic function with inward knowledge; certainly the most eminent saint or sage is always in possession of the "greater" or the "whole" by virtue of his traditional position, but a less eminent sage does not necessarily represent something "less" with regard to his inward reality, although even on this level certain

11. On the one hand Saint John is not Christ, and on the other hand no Christian mystic could equate himself with the author of the Fourth Gospel and the Apocalypse; the relationship between the Prophet, his son-in-law Ali, and the Sufis is similar.

relationships of dimension or breadth must be taken into account when considering the most glorious figures of the traditional "iconostasis." This factor is of special importance when the figure concerned incarnates a non-supreme mode of spirituality, as is the case for someone like Ramanuja or Confucius—the function of Confucius, incidentally, being greater than that of Ramanuja—since one might be tempted to place these eminent figures below a *jnānin* of lesser breadth; this would be an optical illusion, especially in the case of the Chinese revealer, whose inward reality necessarily and immensely transcended the role assigned him by Providence.

Be that as it may, in comparison with the worldly and profane—and from their standpoint—every true master is quite close not only to the great teachers of "apostolic" rank but even to the founding *Avatāra*, and this is a compensatory truth that allows us to appreciate more fully the cult of the master in India and elsewhere. The cosmic breadth of the *Avatāra* and his direct extensions obviously presupposes spiritual perfection, but conversely this perfection does not imply the cosmic rank of the very greatest, whence the disparities we have mentioned.

It is doubtless not always possible or even necessary to avoid every ambiguity—to settle the question, for example, of whether there is a real difference between the "apostolic" degree of someone like Nagarjuna and certain later but particularly eminent manifestations, such as Padma Sambhava in Tibet and Kobo Daishi in Japan, who may be said to represent central reverberations of the spiritual Sun in a new world;[12] but it is always possible—and even necessary in certain cases—to take factual evidence and traditional opinion into account in order to show respect for the irreplaceable majesty of divine manifestations.[13]

But these considerations must not cause us to lose sight of the compensatory truth just mentioned: namely, that every spiritual master—by his knowledge and function and by the graces attached to them—is mysteriously identified with his prototypes and, both through them and independently of them, with the primordial Prototype, the founding *Avatāra*. At

12. Saint Francis of Assisi and Saint Bernard are similar cases, for the first was "adopted" directly by Christ and the second by the Virgin.

13. One of the worst abuses is the presumption involved in "psychologically" analyzing an *Avatāra* on the basis of his deeds and gestures, when in fact one is in the presence of an order of greatness that completely eludes profane investigation. It may be noted that Ramakrishna often used the term *Avatāra* in a wide sense, including all the avataric modes—"total," "partial," "major," and "minor"—and in this he is hardly to be blamed, not only because he clearly defined the transcendent nature of the "God-Man" in his teaching, but also because he himself was effectively situated within the "divine Ray."

the level of this synthesis, it could even be added that there is but one sole Master and that the various human supports are like emanations from Him, comparable to the rays of the sun, which communicate one and the same light and are nothing without it.

A Song

There is no greatness that begets not beauty
        In its striving;

There is no beauty without greatness;
        Such is love.

Perhaps love wounds thy heart
        In silent pain;

But beauty dwells in thy heart's depth
        In profound joy.

Be happy, heart, with noble wisdom's wine;
        For light inebriates.

The wise man with his whole being
        Is drowned in God.

Let, O my soul, this world fade away
        In God's infinity;

The heart will melt in ultimate love—
        For all eternity.

20

THE STATIONS OF WISDOM

Human nature comprises three planes: the plane of the will, the plane of love, and the plane of knowledge; each is polarized into two complementary modes, which appear respectively as renunciation and act, peace and fervor, discernment and union.

The will is divided in a certain sense into an affirmative mode and a negative mode, for it can only accomplish or abstain; it must either do "good" or avoid "evil." In the spiritual life the negative attitude comes in principle before the positive or affirmative act because the will is *a priori* entrenched in its state—natural since the fall—of passional and blind affirmation; every path must begin with a "conversion," an apparently negative turning around of the will, which consists in an indirect movement toward God in the form of an inward separation from the false plenitude of the world. This withdrawal corresponds to the station of renunciation or of detachment, sobriety, fear of God: What must be overcome is desire, passional attachment, idolatry of ephemeral things; the error of passion is proven by its connection with impurity, corruption, suffering, and death.[1] The divine prototype of the virtue of detachment is Purity, Impassibility, Immortality; this quality—whether we envisage it *in divinis*, in ourselves, or in the world around us—is like crystal or snow, or the cold serenity of high mountains; in the soul it is a spiritual anticipation of death and thereby a victory over it. It is fixation in instantaneity, spiritual immobility, fear of God.

The will, as we have said, must both deny and affirm: If it must deny because of the falsity of its habitual objects, which are impermanent, it must on the other hand affirm by reason of its positive character, which is freedom of choice. Since the spiritual act must assert itself forcefully against

1. *Gnosis* objectifies sin—enacted error—by reducing it to its impersonal causes but subjectifies the definition of sin by making the quality of an action depend on personal intention; by contrast the moral perspective subjectifies the act by identifying it as it were with the agent but objectifies the definition of sin by making the quality of an action depend on its form, hence on an external standard.

the lures of the world or the soul, which seek to capture and corrupt the will, it involves the combative virtues: decisiveness, vigilance, perseverance; and it is in turn conditioned by them, not in its unique actuality but in its relationship with duration, which demands repetition, rhythm, the transmutation of time into instantaneity. On its own plane the spiritual act is a participation in Omnipotence, divine Liberty, pure and eternal Act. What must be actively conquered is natural and habitual passivity toward the world and the images and impulses of the soul; spiritual laziness, inadvertence, dreaming must all be overcome; what gives victory is the divine Presence, which is "incarnate" as it were in the sacred act—prayer in all its forms—and which thus regenerates the individual substance. The symbols of this spiritual station—the station of combat, victory, pure act—are lightning and the sword; *in divinis* it is fulgurating and invincible Perfection, and in man, holy anger or holy warfare, but above all the inward act as affirmation of the Self.

*

* *

On the plane of love, the affective life of the soul, we can distinguish an active mode and a passive mode, as we can in everything that lives. Passive virtue is made of contemplative contentment, hence also of patience: It is the calm of what rests in itself, in its own virtue; it is generous relaxation, harmony; it is repose in pure Being, equilibrium of all possibilities. This attitude loosens the knots of the soul; it removes agitation, dissipation, then the tension that is the static counterpart of agitation; there is within it neither curiosity nor disquiet. The quality of calm is derived from the divine Peace, which is made of Beatitude, infinite Beauty; beauty everywhere and always has at its root an aspect of calm, existential repose, equilibrium of possibilities;[2] this means that it has an aspect of limitlessness and happiness. The essence of the soul is beatitude; what makes us strangers to ourselves is dissipation, which casts us into destitution and ugliness, into a state of barren wastefulness similar to a trembling palsy, a disordered movement that has become a state, whereas normally the static is the basis of the dynamic and not conversely. Beauty bears within itself every element of happiness, hence its character of peace, plenitude, satisfaction; now beauty is in our very being, and we live by its substance. It is the calm, simple,

2. According to the *Philokalia*, "the natural state of the soul" is virtue; this teaching enables us to grasp what the Asian traditions mean when they speak of "going beyond the virtues": A virtue is a limit insofar as it is an expression of ourselves, and it is transcended—or realized to the full, which amounts to the same thing—when it no longer belongs to us in any way as our own.

and generous perfection of the pool, which mirrors the depth of the sky with its serenity; it is the beauty of the water lily, of the lotus opening to the light of the sun.[3] It is repose in the center, resignation to Providence, quietude in God. We can distinguish in this station a gentle aspect and a stern aspect: a happy quietude founded on the certainty that all we love is to be found infinitely in God and an ascetic contentment based on the idea that God suffices us.

But besides this repose in our initial equilibrium or existential perfection, there is a positive tendency that is its opposite, a "going out of oneself" in active mode: This is fervor, trusting and charitable faith; it is the melting of the heart in the divine warmth, its opening to Mercy, essential Life, infinite Love. Man in his fallen state is closed to the Mercy that would save him; this is "hardness of heart," indifference toward God and the neighbor, egoism, avarice, mortal triviality; such triviality is as it were the inverse counterpart of hardness, the frittering of the soul among sterile facts, among their insignificant and empty multiplicity, their desiccating drab monotony; it is the feckless to and fro of "ordinary life" where ugliness and boredom pose as "reality." In this state the soul is as hard as stone and as pulverized as sand; it lives on the dead husks of things and not in the Essence, which is Life and Love; it is at once hardness and dissolution. The spiritual liquefaction of the ego is entirely different from this dissolution; it is fervor, intense unification of the movements of the soul in an upward flow of faith in divine Mercy; it is also the warm and gentle quality of spring or of fire melting ice and restoring life to frozen limbs. Charitable acceptance of the neighbor is a necessary manifestation of this alchemical liquefaction of the heart; it is as it were the criterion of that tendency—or state—of the intelligence and the will that we may call "love of God": first because egoism, which is a form of petrifaction, is compensated and overcome whenever we "go outside" ourselves, and second because God appears in our neighbor; in other words one must love God not only in losing oneself but also in recognizing Him in others. This spiritual quality is like fire, which burns and liquefies, or like blood, which gives life to bodies from within; or again it is like love or wine, which produce intoxication and seem to bring everything back to the essences, or like the red rose, whose color burns and whose perfume is inebriating. In addition to its active aspect, which is founded on the conviction that God surely responds to our fervor,[4] this

3. It will be remembered here that Buddhist iconography represents the Buddha seated on a lotus and that the Buddha is called the "Jewel in the lotus" (*Mani padme*). The Buddhas bring salvation not only by their teaching but also by their super-human beauty.

4. "Knock, and it shall be opened unto you," says the Gospel. Fervor is in fact affirmed by tirelessly repeated appeals, as several passages of the New Testament bear witness.

station includes a passive aspect, which is founded on the melting of the heart in the divine Warmth; there is in this second attitude a kind of noble sadness, something related to the gift of tears and mystical love; it is like nostalgia for the Beauty of the Beloved. Joy and melancholy meet in fervor, as beatitude and sobriety—or hope and resignation—meet in peace.

*

* *

The plane of knowledge, which by definition goes beyond the realm of the ego as such, contains a separative mode and a unitive mode as the very nature of *gnosis* requires; we could also say an objective mode and a subjective mode in the deepest sense of these terms. Knowledge in fact operates either by discernment or by identification; it is "perceiving" or "conceiving" or else it is "being." Discriminative knowledge separates the unreal from the Real: The mind must be conscious of the nothingness of the ego and the world; it must surmount the congenital confusion that attributes to the unreal the quality of the Real; it must empty the ego and empty itself of the ego, for the unique Reality can be known only in the void. To see the unicity of the Real is to see at the same time our own nothingness; to see our nothingness, however, is not to see Reality in a direct and total manner, for only unitive knowledge can realize wholeness. Discriminative knowledge is like a night when the moon is shining; we easily distinguish the moon from the night, but we are not in broad daylight even though moonlight is the light of the sun. In this perspective of metaphysical discrimination the subject is false, the Object alone being real; the subject is individuation, illusion, limitation; the Object—that which is "outside us"—is the Principle, the Absolute.

But if the intelligence can "know Reality," it can also "realize the Knower," in principle if not in fact; in this realization—unitive knowledge—the Subject is true and the object is false; the Subject is the infinite Self, and the object is that which veils it, namely, limited or objectified consciousness. In this ultimate knowledge there is no longer discernment, only pure Light;[5]

---

5. Once this viewpoint of unitive knowledge is stated in a doctrinal and thus mental form, however, it in turn needs discernment, for neither the mind nor the world in which it operates is in the state of union. This is why the *Vedānta* distinguishes between the pure Subject and objectification or illusion; its central truth is not this discernment, however, but the Self and identity with the Self. Let us recall once again that pure metaphysics is essentially symbolic and descriptive, not literal and conjectural; to describe what one sees is quite a different thing from trying to construct what one does not see. Put differently, the depth of a statement and its fecundity in no way depend on its formal complexity; the value of an expression lies in the profundity of the truth it actualizes for those to whom it is by its very nature addressed.

it is identity, not confrontation. The "I" is otherness; it is separative illusion, the error of believing that I am identified with the empirical "I," which is composed of outward and inward experiences, mental images and volitions; it is introducing a division into Reality. The truth is "to become What we are," hence to identify ourselves with our own Essence; but our thought is incapable of passing ontologically beyond objectification and fundamental dualism, for it is by definition separative in its very substance; compared to Reality it is like the color white in relation to light: White is distinct from black, but it is invisible without light and can illuminate nothing. Now if our "being" must become "knowing"—and this is the point of view of discernment—our "knowing" must become "being"; if on the one hand it is necessary to "discern" instead of "exist," it is necessary on the other hand to "be" instead of to "think," for thought indicates a direction but does not attain the goal; it does not embrace our entire being, nor *a fortiori* total Reality.

The two stations or degrees of knowledge could be respectively characterized by the following formulas: "To know only That which is: God"; "To be only That which knows: the Self." Or again: "extinction of the subject by virtue of the unicity of the Object, which is without associate"; "extinction of objects by virtue of the unity of the Subject, which is without scission." If we represent Truth—or Reality—by a circle, we could say that the first point of view eliminates an error comparable to a duplication of the circle, whereas the second eliminates an error comparable to the division of this figure; as we have seen, the first error adds the world, including the ego, to the Reality of God, whereas the second error cuts off the knowing "I"—the intellectual and sensory subject—from its divine Source; the world and the ego are indeed separated from God when considered as contents, whether subjective or objective, but they are "identified" with Him—the world with Being and the ego with the Self—in the respective relationships of Existence and Intelligence.[6] God—in the total sense, which transcends "Person" and "Being"—is "pure Object" and "unique"; the Self is "pure Subject," the one and indivisible "Witness"; and God is the Self.

There is thus an inversion of the subject and its complement in passing from one of these metaphysical perspectives to the other: The first perspective is "to know Being," the exclusive Reality; the second is "to be Knowledge," undifferentiated Consciousness. It is necessary to know That which alone is

6. The relationship "Existence" includes symbolism, which is its intellectual aspect and which connects the contents to the Prototypes; symbolism is in a way the intelligence of things. Conversely, the relationship "Intelligence" has an existential aspect: What symbolism is for things, the "person" is for consciousness; symbols are things "qualified" by Intelligence, and the person is consciousness "fixed" or "coagulated" by Existence.

and to be That which alone knows; in the first of these stations the subject is "empty" since it is determined by the Object, which is the unique Reality; it is reduced to its content,[7] or rather it is excluded or annihilated by objective Reality; in the second station the subject is "identified" with its Essence, that is, it is absorbed and integrated by infinite Consciousness, in relation to which the relative subject is an "objectification," as is the entire cosmos.

I am; therefore I am everything, principially and virtually; my being as such is all the Being there is. Likewise I know; therefore I know all; my knowledge as such is all the Knowledge there is. Nonetheless my knowledge, insofar as it is individual, must become being; and likewise my being, insofar as it is individual, must become knowledge, consciousness, ipseity.[8]

*
* *

The plane of the will, which comprises the stations of renunciation and act, and the plane of love, which comprises the stations of contentment and fervor, belong either to exotericism or esotericism, depending on the levels of understanding and application; because of its "liquid" nature, however, the plane of love is nearer to esotericism than is the plane of the will. As for the plane of knowledge, it belongs exclusively to esotericism; as we have seen it includes both doctrinal understanding and unitive wisdom. All these stations concern God, the Metacosm, on the one hand, and the soul, the microcosm, on the other; but they are thereby also keys for the "alchemical" comprehension of the world, the macrocosm. From another standpoint, if these positions—by the very fact that they are contemplative—presuppose the fundamental virtues, still more do they imply these virtues and sublimate them.

The perspective of metaphysical discernment, of the unique and exclusive Reality, is like a synthesis—though on the plane of the intellect and in transcendent mode—of the two perspectives of the will, namely, detachment and action; in a similar way the perspective of identity, of the Self, is like a synthesis—though on the plane of unitive knowledge and beyond the human—of the perspectives of peace and fervor. The viewpoint of fervor or life can be placed in harmonious opposition to that of detachment or death just as the viewpoint of contentment or peace can be opposed without antinomy to that of action or combat.

7. "The soul is all that it knows," says Aristotle.

8. For the gnostic—always in the etymological and not sectarian sense of the term—or *jñānin*, there can be no question of "egoism" since the ego is not "himself." The "I" is for him the "other," objectification—the vital, tangible center of the world.

These fundamental stations of wisdom can be combined in different ways, and each can serve as a point of departure. Christian mysticism is closely akin to the perspective of renunciation and purity as well as to that of love and mercy; Christianity thus compensates for its aspect of renunciation with the passion of love. Buddhism also takes renunciation as its starting point but is akin to the perspective of peace and beatitude; it compensates for its renunciation with nirvanic peace. As for Islam, it is like a combination between the perspective of combat and that of peace; it compensates for its combative aspect by its aspect of equilibrium, resignation, generosity. *Vedānta*—like all *gnosis*—is based on discernment between the Real and the unreal, and it compensates for the specifically intellectual—non-volitive—content of this perspective by an "existential," or rather supra-existential, concretization, which is identification with the Self. All these indications are no doubt very schematic; there are things that cannot be said without risk but that one must nonetheless risk saying. Be that as it may, it is important not to lose sight of the fact that each tradition includes in one way or another—and necessarily—all six stations of wisdom, even if the stations of *gnosis* must sometimes withdraw behind veils of esoteric symbolism.

In addition to these considerations, we would like to suggest the following relationships. The world is division, movement, becoming, disquiet, and thus we are divided, restless, changeable, anxious; it is to this cosmic spectacle that the truth of Unity (Islam) responds: unity of God, the soul, society, metaphysical Reality;[9] likewise the truth of "God made man" (Christianity) is the response to the spectacle of sinful nature, human impotence, the downfall of our will; or again the truth of renunciation and extinction (Buddhism) responds to the spectacle of universal suffering and instability.[10]

*

* *

Some people see a kind of incompatibility between metaphysics—which they confuse with the more or less logical constructions of the mind—and the love of God, of which they seem to see only the most human side. Let us recall that "love of God" is something universal. The term "love" designates

---

9. The emphasis is placed on Unity because Unity is obvious; to speak of Unity is to speak of self-evidence, truth, reality, absoluteness, and in turn of a reason for being and living.

10. *Nirvāna* is the "motionless center" of the "cosmic wheel"; the Buddha is the manifestation of the "Void" in the sense that nirvanic Reality appears as void in relation to the world; Buddhahood (*bodhi*, "enlightenment") is realizing that the wheel is none other than the "Void" in both the negative and the transcendent sense of the term.

not only a path pertaining to the will and feeling but also—and this is its broadest meaning—every path insofar as it links us to the Divine; "love" is everything that makes us prefer God to the world and contemplation to earthly activity, wherever such alternatives have a meaning. The highest form of love will not be that which most resembles what the word "love" can evoke in us *a priori* but that which will attach us most steadfastly or most profoundly to Reality; to love God is to keep oneself near Him in the midst of the world and beyond the world; God wants our souls, whatever our attitudes or methods.

And likewise: "God is Love" not only toward creation and because He loves the world but also in Himself and because He is profoundly steeped in His own infinitude; in the first sense God is Love because He "wills" the world and is therefore "merciful," and in the second sense He is Love because He wills Himself or because He wills nothing outside the Self.

All great spiritual experiences agree in this: There is no proportion between the means put into operation and the result. "With men this is impossible; but with God all things are possible," says the Gospel. What actually separates man from divine Reality is but a thin partition: God is infinitely close to man, but man is infinitely far from God. This partition for man is a mountain; man stands in front of a mountain that he must remove with his own hands. He digs away the earth, but in vain, for the mountain remains; man however goes on digging in the name of God. And the mountain vanishes. It was never there.

The One

O man, consider that which thou canst not avoid:
Thou wilt, O soul, arrive before the One—
It waits for thee; sooner or later
Thou wilt see not the many but the One.

Yet this One is neither poverty nor want;
It is the All, the gate of Paradise—
The fullness of God, which begets existence
And gives it life anew.
In the beginning was the Word.

CONCLUSION

RELIGIO PERENNIS

One of the keys to understanding our true nature and ultimate destiny is the fact that the things of this world are never proportionate to the actual range of our intelligence. Our intelligence is made for the Absolute, or else it is nothing; among all the forms of intelligence in this world the human spirit alone is capable of objectivity, and this implies—or proves—that the Absolute alone confers on our intelligence the power to accomplish to the full what it can accomplish and to be wholly what it is.[1] If it were necessary or useful to prove the Absolute, the objective and transpersonal character of the human Intellect would be a sufficient testimony, for this Intellect is the indisputable sign of a purely spiritual first Cause, a Unity infinitely central but containing all things, an Essence at once immanent and transcendent. It has been said more than once that total Truth is inscribed in an eternal script in the very substance of our spirit; the different Revelations do nothing other than "crystallize" and "actualize"—in varying degrees as the case may be—a nucleus of certainties that not only abides forever in the divine Omniscience but also sleeps by refraction in the "naturally supernatural" kernel of the individual, as well as in that of each ethnic or historical collectivity and of the human species as a whole.

Much the same thing can be said in the case of the will, which is no more than a prolongation or complement of the intelligence. The objects it commonly sets out to achieve or those that life imposes on it do not measure up to the fullness of its range; only the "divine dimension" can satisfy the thirst for plenitude in our willing or love. What makes our will human and therefore free is the fact that it is proportioned to God; in God alone is it

1. "Heaven and earth cannot contain Me (*Allāh*), but the heart of My faithful servant containeth Me" (*hadīth qudsī*). Similarly Dante: "I perceive that our intellect is never satisfied if the True does not enlighten it, outside which no truth is possible" (*Paradiso* 4:124–26).

liberated from all constraint, hence from everything that limits its nature.

The essential function of human intelligence is discernment between the Real and the illusory or between the Permanent and the impermanent, and the essential function of the will is attachment to the Permanent or the Real. This discernment and this attachment are the quintessence of all spirituality; carried to their highest level or reduced to their purest substance, they constitute the underlying universality in every great spiritual patrimony of humanity, or what may be called the *religio perennis*;[2] this is the religion to which the sages adhere, one that is always and necessarily founded on formal elements of divine institution.[3]

*

* *

Metaphysical discernment is a "separation" between *Ātmā* and *Māyā*; contemplative concentration, or unifying consciousness, is a "union" of *Māyā* with *Ātmā*. "Doctrine" refers to discernment, which separates,[4] and "method" refers to concentration, which unifies; "faith" is connected to the first element and "love of God" to the second.

To paraphrase the well-known saying of Saint Irenaeus, the *religio perennis* is fundamentally this: The Real entered into the illusory so that the illusory might be able to return into the Real. From the point of view of *gnosis*, this mystery—together with the metaphysical discernment and contemplative concentration that are its complement—is the only important thing in an absolute sense; for the gnostic—in the etymological and rightful sense of this word—there is finally no other "religion." It is what Ibn Arabi called the "religion of Love," placing the accent on the element "realization."

The twofold definition of the *religio perennis*—discernment between the Real and the illusory and a unifying and permanent concentration on the Real—contains the criteria of intrinsic orthodoxy for every religion and all

---

2. These words recall the *philosophia perennis* of Steuchus Eugubinus (sixteenth century) and the neo-scholastics; but the word *philosophia* suggests rightly or wrongly a mental elaboration rather than wisdom and therefore does not convey exactly the sense we intend. *Religio* is what "binds" man to Heaven and engages his whole being; as for the word *traditio*, it is related to a more outward and sometimes fragmentary reality, besides suggesting a retrospective outlook; a new-born religion "binds" men to Heaven from the moment of its first revelation, but it does not become a "tradition"—or have "traditions"—until two or three generations later.

3. This is true even in the case of the pre-Islamic Arab sages, who lived spiritually on the heritage of Abraham and Ishmael.

4. This is what the Arabic word *furqān* signifies, namely "qualitative differentiation," from *faraqa*, to separate, discern, bifurcate; it is well known that *Furqān* is one of the names of the Koran.

spirituality; in order to be orthodox a religion must possess a mythological or doctrinal symbolism establishing the essential distinction in question, and it must provide a path that guarantees both the perfection of concentration and its continuity; in other words a religion is orthodox if it provides a sufficient, if not always exhaustive, idea of the Absolute and the relative—and thus of their reciprocal relationships—and a spiritual activity that is contemplative in its nature and effectual with regard to our ultimate destiny. For it is an acknowledged fact that heterodoxies always tend to adulterate either the idea of the divine Principle or the manner of our attachment to it; they offer a worldly, profane, or—if one prefers—"humanist" counterfeit of religion or else a mysticism containing nothing but the ego and its illusions.

*

* *

It may seem disproportionate to treat a subject as complex as that of spiritual perspectives in simple and as it were schematic terms, but since the very nature of things allows us to take into consideration an aspect of simplicity, the truth would be no better served by following the twists and turns of a complexity not called for in this case. Analysis is one function of the intelligence, and synthesis is another; the common association of intelligence with difficulty and of facility with presumption obviously has no relation to the true nature of the Intellect. It is the same with intellectual vision as it is with optical vision: Some things must be examined in detail if they are to be understood, while other things are better seen from a certain distance and convey their real nature all the more clearly in appearing simple. Truth can expand and be divided indefinitely, but it is also contained in a "geometrical point"; grasping this fact is everything, no matter what symbol—or symbolism—brings about intellection.

Truth is one, and it would be vain to want to look for it in a single place, for the Intellect contains in its substance everything that is true, and therefore truth cannot but be manifested wherever the Intellect is deployed in the atmosphere of a Revelation. Space can be represented by a circle as well as by a cross, a spiral, a star, or a square, and just as it is impossible for there to be only one figure representing the nature of space or extension, so it is impossible for there to be only one doctrine reflecting the Absolute or describing the relationship between it and contingency; in other words believing that there can be only one true doctrine is like denying the plurality of geometrical figures used to indicate the characteristics of space or—to choose a very different example—the plurality of individual consciousnesses and visual points of view. In each Revelation, God says "I" while placing Himself extrinsically at a point of view other than that of earlier Revelations, whence the appearance of contradiction on the plane of formal crystallization.

The objection might be raised that the various geometrical figures are not strictly equivalent in their capacity to represent spatial extension and thus that this very comparison could be used as an argument against the equivalence of traditional perspectives; to this we reply that the traditions are not meant to be absolute adequations—or not at least *a priori*—but rather paths of salvation and means of deliverance. And in any case, although we readily acknowledge that a circle—not to mention a point—is a more direct adequation of form and space than is a cross or any other differentiated figure, since it reflects more perfectly the true nature of extension, we must nonetheless take into account the fact that a cross, a square, or a spiral expresses explicitly a spatial reality that a circle or point expresses only implicitly; the differentiated figures are thus irreplaceable—otherwise they would not exist—and they are in no sense various kinds of imperfect circles; the cross is infinitely nearer the perfection of a point or a circle than is an oval or trapezoid, for example. Similar considerations apply to traditional doctrines when one examines their differences of form and their merits as adequations.

*

* *

Let us return to the *religio perennis*, considered either as metaphysical discernment and unifying concentration or as the descent of the divine Principle, which becomes manifestation in order that manifestation may return to the Principle.

In Christianity—according to Saint Irenaeus and others—God "became man" that man might "become God"; in Hindu terms one would say that *Ātmā* became *Māyā* in order that *Māyā* might become *Ātmā*. In Christianity contemplative and unifying concentration is to dwell in the manifested Real—the "Word made flesh"—so that this Real might dwell in us, who are illusory, according to what Christ said in a vision granted to Saint Catherine of Siena: "I am He who is; thou art she who is not." The soul dwells in the Real—in the kingdom of God that is "within us"—by means of permanent prayer of the heart, as is taught by the parable of the unjust judge and the injunction of Saint Paul.

In Islam the same fundamental—because universal—theme is crystallized according to a very different perspective. Discernment between the Real and the non-real is affirmed by the Testimony of Unity (the *Shahādah*); the correlative concentration on the Symbol or permanent consciousness of the Real is effected by this same Testimony or by the divine Name that synthesizes it and that is thus the quintessential crystallization of the Koranic Revelation. This Testimony or Name is also the quintessence of the Abrahamic Revelation—through the lineage of Ishmael—and it goes back to the primordial Revelation of the Semitic branch. The Real "descended" (*nazzala, unzila*); it entered into the non-real or illusory, the "perishable" (*fānin*),[5] in becoming the Koran—or the *Shahādah* that summarizes it, or the *Ism* (the "Name") that is its sonorous and visible essence, or the *Dhikr* (the "Remembrance") that is its operative synthesis—in order that the illusory might return by means of this divine barque to the Real, to the "Face (*Wajh*) of the Lord that alone abides" (*wa yabqā Wajhu Rabbika*),[6] whatever metaphysical import may be attributed to the ideas of "illusion" and "Reality." In this reciprocity lies all the mystery of the "Night of Destiny" (*Laylat al-Qadr*), which is a "descent," and of the "Night of Ascension" (*Laylat al-Miʿrāj*), which is the complementary phase; contemplative realization—or "unification" (*tawhīd*)—partakes of the ascension of the Prophet through the degrees of Paradise. "Verily"—says the Koran—"prayer guards against the major (*fahshā*) and minor (*munkar*) sins, but the remembrance (*dhikr*) of God is greater."[7]

Nearer to the Christian perspective in one way but much more remote in another is the Buddhist perspective, which on the one hand is based on a "Word made flesh" but on the other hand knows nothing of the anthropomorphic notion of a creator God. In Buddhism the two terms of the alternative—or of discernment—are *Nirvāna*, the Real, and *Samsāra*, the illusory; and the path is the permanent consciousness of *Nirvāna* as *Shūnya*, the "Void," or else it is concentration on the saving manifestation of *Nirvāna*, the Buddha, who is *Shūnyamūrti*, "Manifestation of the Void." In the Buddha—notably in the form of Amitabha—*Nirvāna* became *Samsāra* in order that *Samsāra* might become *Nirvāna*; and if *Nirvāna* is the Real and *Samsāra* is illusion, the Buddha is the Real in the illusory, and the *Bodhisattva* is the illusory in the Real,[8] which suggests the symbolism of the *Yin-Yang*. The passage from the illusory to the Real is described in the *Prajnāpāramitā Hridaya Sūtra* in these terms: "Gone, gone—gone for the other shore, attained the other shore, O Enlightenment, be blessed!"

---

5. The word *fanāʾ*, sometimes translated as "extinction" by analogy with the Sanskrit *nirvāna*, has the same root and literally means "perishable nature."

6. *Sūrah* "The Merciful" [55]:27.

7. *Sūrah* "The Spider" [29]:45.

8. See "Le mystère du Bodhisattva" (*Études traditionnelles*, May–June, July–August, September–October, 1962).

*

* *

It is in the nature of things that every spiritual outlook must place a conception of man in contrast with a corresponding conception of God; hence arise three ideas or definitions: first, of man as such; second, of God as He reveals Himself to man thus defined; and third, of man as determined and transformed by God as a result of the outlook in question.

From the point of view of human subjectivity, man is the container and God the contained; from the divine point of view—if one may express it this way—the relationship is reversed, for all things are contained in God and nothing is able to contain Him. To say that man is made in the image of God means at the same time that God assumes something of that image *a posteriori* in connection with man. God is pure Spirit, and man is consequently intelligence or consciousness; conversely, if man is defined as intelligence, God will be "Truth." In other words God, desiring to affirm Himself under the aspect of "Truth," addresses Himself to man insofar as man is endowed with intelligence, just as He addresses Himself to man in distress to affirm His Mercy or to man endowed with free will to affirm Himself as the saving Law.

The "proofs" of God and religion are in man himself: "Knowing his own nature, he also knows Heaven," says Mencius, in agreement with other similar and well-known maxims. We must extract from the givens of our own nature the key-certainty that opens up the way to certainty of the Divine and Revelation; to speak of "man" is to speak implicitly of "God"; to speak of the "relative" is to speak of the "Absolute." Human nature in general and human intelligence in particular cannot be understood apart from the religious phenomenon, for it is this which characterizes them in the most direct and most complete way possible. Grasping the transcendent—not the "psychological"—nature of the human being, we thereby grasp the nature of revelation, religion, tradition; we understand their possibility, their necessity, their truth. And in understanding religion, not only in a particular form or in a literal way but in its non-formal essence, we also understand the religions—that is, the meaning of their plurality and diversity; this is the plane of *gnosis*, of the *religio perennis*, where the extrinsic antinomies of dogma are explained and resolved.

*

* *

On the outward and therefore contingent plane, which nonetheless clearly has its importance in the human order, there is a concordance between the *religio perennis* and virgin nature on the one hand and between this *religio* and primordial nudity on the other—the nudity of creation, birth, resurrection, or of the high priest in the Holy of Holies, a hermit in the desert,[9] a Hindu *sādhu* or *sannyāsin*, an American Indian in silent prayer on a mountain.[10] Nature inviolate is at once a vestige of the earthly Paradise and a prefiguration of the heavenly Paradise; sanctuaries and garments differ, but virgin nature and the human body remain faithful to the initial unity. Sacred art, which seems to move away from this unity, in fact simply serves to restore to natural phenomena their divine messages—messages to which men have become insensitive; in art the perspective of love tends toward overflowing and profusion whereas the perspective of *gnosis* tends toward nature, simplicity, silence; such is the contrast between Gothic richness and Zen sobriety.[11] But this must not lead us to lose sight of the fact that outward frameworks or modes are always contingent and that all combinations and compensations are possible, especially since in spirituality every possibility can be reflected in every other according to the appropriate modalities.

A civilization is integral and healthy to the extent that it is founded on the "invisible" or "underlying" religion, the *religio perennis*, that is, to the extent that its expressions or forms are transparent to the Non-Formal and tend toward the Origin, thus conveying not only the recollection of a Lost Paradise but also—and with all the more reason—the presentiment of a timeless Beatitude. For the Origin is at once within us and before us; time is but the movement of a spiral around a motionless Center.

---

9. Such as Mary of Egypt, in whose case the non-formal and wholly inward character of a love effected by God so fully partook of the qualities of *gnosis* that one could call it a "*gnosis* of love" in the sense of *parabhakti*.

10. The simplicity and color of clothing, white in particular, sometimes replace the symbolism of nudity within the framework of vestimentary art; on every plane the laying bare inspired by the naked Truth counterbalances a worldly "culturism." In other connections, however, a sacred robe symbolizes the victory of the Spirit over the flesh, and its hieratic richness—which we are far from criticizing—expresses the inexhaustible profusion of Mystery and Glory.

11. It is quite apparent, however, that the most sumptuous sacred art is infinitely nearer to *gnosis* than the ignorant and affected "sobriety" of those of our contemporaries who profess to be "making a clean sweep." Only a simplicity that is qualitative, noble, and conformable to the essence of things reflects and transmits the perfume of non-formal wisdom.

APPENDIX

SELECTIONS FROM LETTERS, SPIRITUAL TEXTS, AND MEMOIRS

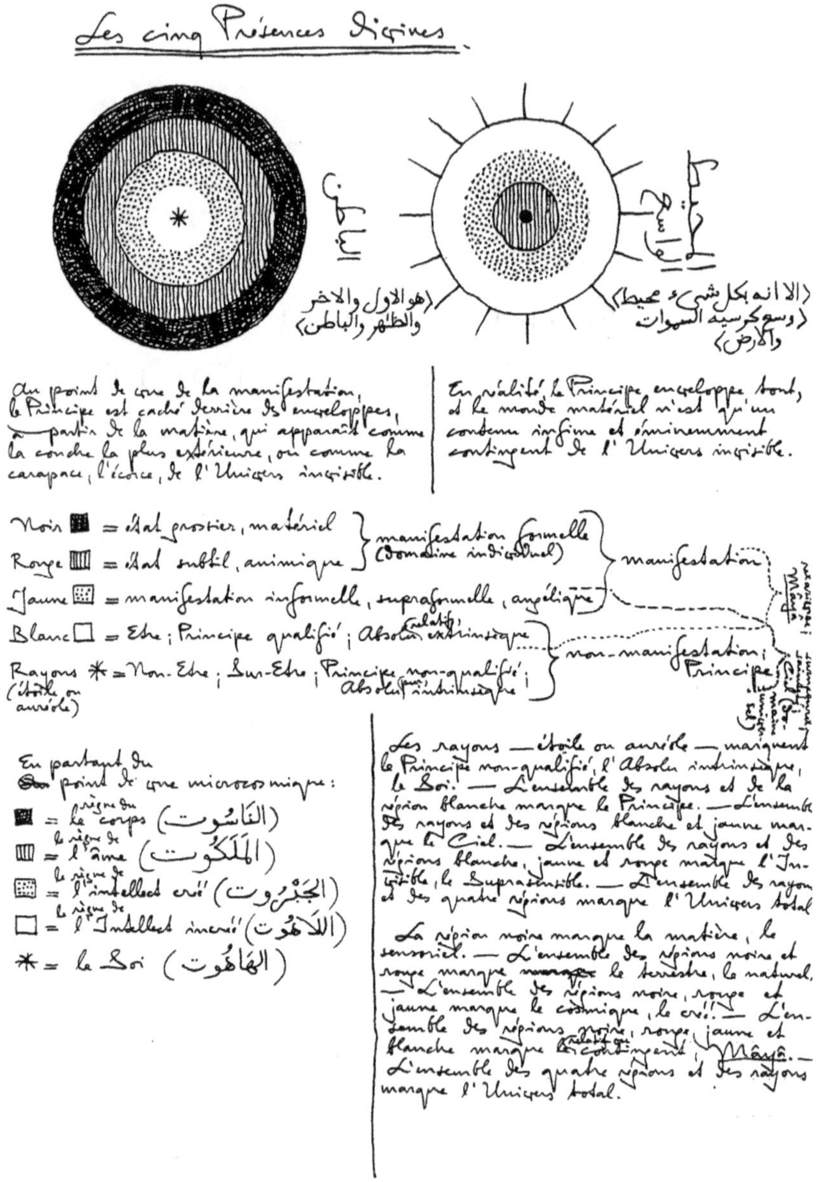

The Book of Keys, No. 74, The Five Divine Presences (Original French Manuscript)

The Five Divine Presences

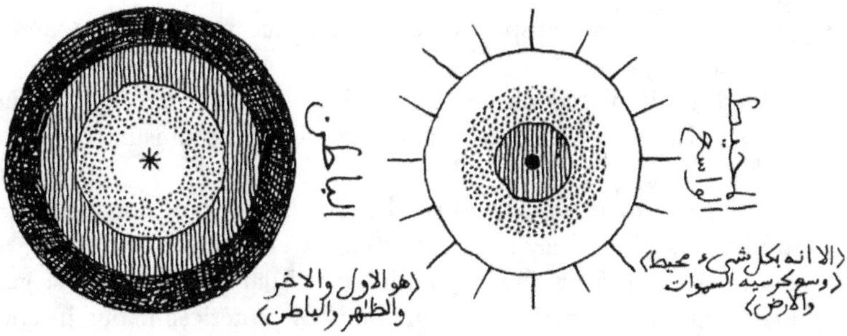

From the viewpoint of manifestation, the Principle is hidden behind envelopes, beginning with matter, which appears as the most exterior layer, or like the carapace, the shell, of the invisible Universe.

In reality, the Principle envelops everything, and the material world is only the lowest and eminently contingent content of the invisible Universe.

Black ■ = gross, material state }
Red ▥ = subtle, animic state } formal manifestation (individual domain) } manifestation } relativity, Māyā
Yellow ▩ = non-formal, supra-formal, angelic manifestation } manifestation

White □ = Being; qualified Principle; relative, extrinsic Absolute } non-manifestation; Principle
Rays ✱ (star or aureole) = Non-Being; Beyond-Being; non-qualified Principle; pure, intrinsic Absolute } non-manifestation; Principle

supernatural; holiness; Heaven (universal domain)

Starting from the microcosmic viewpoint:

■ = the realm of the body (النَّاسُوت)

▥ = the realm of the soul (المَلَكُوت)

▩ = the realm of the created intellect (الجَبَرُوت)

□ = the realm of the uncreated Intellect (اللَّاهُوت)

✱ = the Self (الهَاهُوت)

The rays — star or aureole — denote the non-qualified Principle, the intrinsic Absolute, the Self. — Taken together, the rays and the white region denote the Principle. — Taken together, the rays and the white and yellow regions denote Heaven. — Taken together, the rays and the white, yellow and red regions denote the Invisible, the Supra-sensible. — Taken together, the rays and the four regions denote the total Universe.

The black region denotes matter, the sensorial. — Taken together, the black and red regions denote the earthly, the natural. — Taken together, the black, red and yellow regions denote the cosmic, the created. — Taken together, the black, red, yellow and white regions denote the relative or contingent, Māyā. — Taken together, the four regions and the rays denote the total Universe.

The Book of Keys, No. 74, The Five Divine Presences (English Translation)

1

The foundation of our perspective is pure, hence universal and non-confessional, Metaphysics.

All accent is placed on the Invocation, which contains in principle all other practices and which in certain exceptional circumstances may even replace them.

This being so, the practices of the general religion are reduced to a legal minimum, which may vary according to circumstances.

In a certain respect the dogmatic and ritual symbols of the general religion support the doctrines and methods of esotericism, but in another respect there is opposition between form and essence, hence between exoteric formalism and esoteric truth; no one is truly an esotericist unless he is conscious of both these relationships.

It is necessary to recognize in principle the legitimacy of every intrinsically orthodox religion. It is impossible for divine Truth to assume only one form, just as it is impossible for God to permit a religion that is worldwide and centuries old to be false.

Since beauty is the expression of Truth, it is necessary to be attentive to beauty on all planes; outward or formal beauty must correspond to inward moral beauty. "God is beautiful, and He loves beauty," says a *hadīth*. This question scarcely arises in traditional civilizations, which practice beauty by vocation and are beautiful by definition, but it does arise in the modern world, which denies beauty on all planes precisely because it expresses the Truth.

It is necessary to reject the modern world—its errors, tendencies, trivialities; on the plane of the unavoidable one does what one can, for there is almost everywhere a margin permitting a choice.

2

Very early in my life I saw the falseness of modern civilization—the "White Man's way"—and I saw it for two reasons: First, I saw with my eyes and my heart the beauty, grandeur, and spirituality of the other civilizations and the ugliness and selfishness, the slave-minded materialism, of the modern civilization in which I grew up; second, I could never believe that one religion alone in the whole world was the true one and that all other religions were false. As a boy, when I read about non-Western peoples in books my father gave me, I could not believe that so many noble and wise men could have been abandoned by God and that so many bad Western whites could have received the truth; how could God, wishing to save every human soul, have given the saving truth to only one people and thus condemned so many others, who are no worse than these, to remain forever in deadly darkness?

I soon came to feel that this must be false and that the holy Truth must have many forms, just as a light may have many colors; God—the Great Spirit—gave the indispensable Truth to every race in a form that suited its corresponding mentality. Of course, there have been people who forgot this Truth, such as the ancient Europeans to whom God sent Christianity, but He did not send Christianity to all the people in the world, for most had not forgotten the meaning of their religion. A heathen is a man who worships idols and ignores or rejects God; as for the American Indians, they never worshiped idols nor did they ignore or reject God, the Great Spirit. Consequently, the Indians are not heathens, and their religion, though not fully understood by every individual Indian, is a true one, and God is working in it and gives His Grace through it. This you know best, of course.

When I was older I saw that the spiritual and contemplative way I was seeking could not be realized on the basis of the very superficial culture of Europe. I wished to live in God. I wished not only to love God but to know Him as well, and the Christianity of our time tends to teach only the love of God, not the knowledge. Moreover I knew from an early age that God would charge me with a mission. As for the knowledge of God I was seeking—because it is a need of my nature, and God wishes to be worshiped by every man according to the nature He gave him—I found this sacred knowledge through a holy man of the Arab people, whose name was Ahmad al-Alawi. He was a spiritual Master and had many disciples. There I found what I was searching for: the knowledge of God and the means to realize God. This Master told me: "When a man is not like snow in the hands of Truth and does not vanish away in Truth, then Truth is like snow in the man's hand and vanishes away." I was then a young man, and I had left Europe for North Africa, where I found this Master. He is dead now, but he is always present in me; he is above life and death and is one with God.

The Great Spirit gave the indispensable Truth to every race: He gave the Indians their manner of praying just as He gave Christians and Muslims and Hindus and Yellow peoples theirs. Every old and true religion is a necessary form of the eternal Truth and a gift from God, the most-high *Wakan-Tanka*. Therefore, nothing in the Indian creed is a mere human invention or a senseless thing; every symbol or rite known and practiced by the Indians finds a similar form and explanation in the traditions of other peoples—perhaps most directly in the Hindu tradition, for it is as old as that of the Native Americans, whereas younger traditions are in a certain sense more simplified expressions of the same eternal Truth. All the "spirits" or "gods" known and invoked by the Indians—the Sun, the Sky, the Earth, the Rock, the Moon, the Winged-One, the Wind, the Mediator, the Four Winds, and the other cosmic Powers—are universal Principles known to every tradition, whatever may be the form of the symbols; the Angels of the Christian, Muslim, and Jewish religions are the same celestial beings as the Indian Powers or Spirits; the Indian "Thunderbird" is none other than the Muslim "Jibrail" and "Israfil" or the Hindu "Shiva." All Indian rites, such as smoking the most Holy Pipe, or the Sweat Lodge, or fasting and calling to the Great Spirit in search of a vision or a power or an illumination, or the Sun Dance and other rites—all this has without doubt its deep metaphysical meaning and therefore its spiritual efficacy. Of course, not every rite has the same central importance, and the fact that the Sun Dance is no longer held in its old form by no means implies that "the tree is withered"; for the essential part of every religion, besides the ritual transmission of a spiritual influence preserved and given by the priests, is prayer or Invocation of God's Name. When bestowed under the proper ritual conditions by a traditional priest, a "medicine man" possessing the corresponding authority, function, or power, and when accomplished in a proper manner—pronounced in a holy language with serious concentration of the mind, at first with fasting and above all with the confident hope, indeed the faith and the certainty, that one will be accepted by God and attain Him after death or even during this life—the Invocation of God, the Great Spirit, is the very essence of every religion.

At the beginning of my spiritual way, I was ordered to enter a small, dark room and to remain there, fasting every day until sunset and invoking God's Name in Arabic, for this is a sacred language; I remained there ten days. From that time on I invoked the Most High every day, in the morning, at midday, and in the evening or at night. I do not tell these things to anyone except my disciples, but I tell them to you because you are Black Elk's son. I invoked in this way for many years. Only after about ten years of Invocation and suffering did the great illumination come to me. It came over me like the ocean and swept me away: I saw everything in myself and myself in everything. At that time six holy truths were given to me from Heaven; I shall tell you about them in another letter when God allows me to do so. From that time on I was quite another man: It was not I who invoked the Holy Name; it was the Holy Name that invoked me.

Before my Master gave me the Holy Name, he gave me the initiation. This same initiation—or transmission of a spiritual seed—was bestowed one thousand three hundred years ago on the Prophet Muhammad. He received this spiritual seed from the highest Angel sent by God, and this seed he put into the hearts of his immediate disciples, not all his followers. When this spiritual seed, with the help of which the divine Name purifies and transforms man's heart over time, is bestowed on a new disciple of our order, the Master grasps his hand in the same manner that the Angel grasped the Arabian Prophet's hand one thousand three hundred years ago; and in the same moment the Master pronounces a sacred formula, also revealed to the Prophet by the Angel, so that the spiritual seed or power may enter the disciple's heart. Every tradition possesses such an initiation, whether through gestures, speech, looks, or other means, and in certain exceptional cases even through dreams.

God is really present in His Name, and therefore when invoking Him our heart must be present too. Then He purifies us by the grace of His Name; He gives us perfections we did not have before, and finally He leads us back to Himself.

3

The "doctrine of Awakening" briefly presented at the beginning of your book is correct in principle; this is obvious. But it becomes totally false and therefore spiritually inoperative—to say the least—once it becomes "agnostic," "iconoclastic," and "anti-religious," for in this case any religious dogmatism is more real or less false than it.

The orthodox religions alone provide an adequate basis for the "doctrine of Awakening," and they do this in their esotericisms. As messages of salvation, they are of course situated within the dream world, but this does not mean that they are just anything, for distinctions must be made even here; within the dream these messages realize in a symbolic and horizontal way what "Awakening" is totally and vertically, and thus they represent an indispensable point of departure for "Awakening." It is impossible to escape the dream without the Will of Him who dreams—*Brahma saguna*—and without the Grace of Him who, within the dream, reflects Him who dreams. This reflection is the *Avatāra*, and it is only through the *Avatāra*—and therefore through God—that we can escape the dream; otherwise our "doctrine of Awakening" is nothing more than inoperative philosophy and spiritual suicide.

"Without me ye can do nothing," and also "He that gathereth not with me scattereth abroad." The *Avatāra*—whether Christ or Muhammad or the Buddha—is *Shūnyamūrti*, "Manifestation of the Void," hence of "Awakening"; following the Buddha, for example, does not mean imitating some model as it appears in books; it means entering the Buddhist *Sangha* in one of its traditional forms—hence the "Triple Refuge"—and integration into the *Theravāda* or, on the Mahayanic side, into *Jōdo-Shinshū* or Zen, with all the liturgical consequences this implies. An "Awakening" without the *Avatāra*, hence without religion, will turn into Satanism; the dream itself will play the "Awakening," and this leads nowhere.

Furthermore, I absolutely do not see what harm there could be in salvation simply because it is still part of the dream—but it is the summit of the dream!—for this dream, all things considered, is not an unintelligible chaos; if it were, there would be no qualitative differentiations, and the notion of "Awakening" itself would not exist. Before one can leave the dream, one must prostrate oneself before the Lord of the dream, who is God, and before His central reflection and spokesman in the dream: the Revealer, the *Avatāra*.

4

A certain number of those who claim to subscribe to an esoteric science believe that human virtues can be neglected or even scorned when in fact they form a part of initiatic qualification and of the way itself, as Sufi treatises tirelessly reiterate; my point of view may strike some people as strange, but it is no more moralistic than that of the *Yoga-Shāstras*, for example, which also place a high value on virtue. If it is true that every perfection has above all a symbolic meaning, this hardly means that perfection itself is superfluous; on the contrary the symbol is the necessary support for the reality symbolized; in fact it is a mode of this reality. Every virtue is an eye that sees God.

When I receive a jumble of a letter, for example, full of petty, sterile, vain, and futile concerns, written hastily and in a worried tone, I do not see in it the reflection of a soul that is the receptacle of the Real Presence; the structure, the style, or the rhythm of the soul must correspond to the object of its aspirations, and this object is the divine Reality, free from all infirmity. The Divine is Beauty, Grandeur, Solitude; thus the soul must realize these qualities not by imaginative improvisation—which would be fatal—but in conformity with divine truths; greatness of soul must not be sought by means of a hollow and sentimental attitude, as the wretched Vivekanandists would do, but by hierarchizing the psychic or mental contents and suppressing what opposes the "one thing needful." Abu al-Mawahib al-Shadhili says: "Purify thyself of thy vulgar and contemptible traits and adopt His qualities, worthy of praise and full of glory."

5

It often surprises me how deeply most men are sunk in phenomena, how much they identify themselves with their own everyday world of appearances, and how little strength of imagination they have; this surprised me even as a child insofar as I was capable of noticing it; I did notice it without any doubt, for otherwise I would not so often have felt myself to be as one standing outside, disinterested, an onlooker as it were. For the contemplative man the experience of vastly different worlds—the West, Islam, the American Indians—can and must have a particular spiritual significance. The forms become transparent; they act as supports, yes, but they are no longer confining. What is distraction for one can for another be soaring flight.

6

In principle the universal authority of the metaphysical and initiatic traditions of Asia, which reflect the nature of things more or less directly, takes precedence—when such an alternative presents itself—over the generally more "theological" authority of the monotheistic religions; I say "when such an alternative presents itself" because there are obviously cases where there is no such alternative, whether in esotericism or in essential symbolism; no one can deny, however, that in Semitic doctrines the formulations and precepts are usually determined by what is thought to be dogmatically, morally, and socially appropriate. But this does not apply to pure Islam—to the authority of its essential doctrine and fundamental symbolism: The *Shahādah* cannot but mean that "the world is false and *Brahma* is true" and "Thou are That" (*tat tvam asi*) or "I am *Brahma*" (*aham Brahmāsmi*); it is a pure expression of both the unreality of the world and the Supreme Identity. In the same way the other "pillars of Islam" (*arqān al-Dīn*), as well as such fundamental rules as dietary and artistic prohibitions, obviously constitute supports of intellection and realization, which universal metaphysics—or the "Unanimous Tradition"—can illuminate but not abolish.

When universal wisdom affirms that the Invocation contains and may replace all other rites, this is of decisive authority against those who would make the *sharīʿah* or *sunnah* into a kind of exclusive *karma-yoga*, and it even permits us to draw conclusions by analogy (*qiyās*, *ijtihād*) that most shariites would find illicit; if a given Muslim master required us to introduce every *dhikr* with an ablution and two *rakʿāt*, the universal—and "antiformalist"—authority of *japa-yoga* would take precedence over his authority, at least in our case. On the other hand, if a Hindu or Buddhist master advised us to practice *japa* in front of an image or gave an order for such a practice, it goes without saying that the authority of Islamic symbolism would take precedence for us, independently of any question of universality, for forms are forms, and some of them are essential and rejoin thereby the universality of the spirit.

7

Your difficulties stem from the fact that you are not aware of the full gravity of the human condition, and you are not aware of this because nothing in your habitual surroundings—the world you live in—suggests it, to say the least. It is finally a question of imagination; I am not saying you are directly responsible for this, but you are in any case its victim, and you are not alone in being so. The articles I am presently writing—"The Cross of Space and Time in Koranic Onomatology" and "Man in the Universe"—can give you many answers.

Most people believe that a person goes to Paradise because he follows the rites of a religion and has neither killed nor stolen; but in fact only the saints and sages go straight to Paradise, and even they do so only because Mercy dissolves their imperfections, not because they are perfect. When you are walking along the street, you believe that "I"—Miss H.—"am here," "on this street," "now"; you do not see, I can only assume, the metaphysical and eschatological abysses surrounding you. In the Middle Ages the whole civilization was structured in such a way as to give a person at least some sense of his cosmic situation; today we live in a kind of misleading "extraterritoriality," in opaque back rooms that hide reality. Nonetheless God touches us everywhere, for there is no empty space and no respite. He is "the First" and "the Last," "the Outward" and "the Inward" (*al-Awwalu wa'l-Ākhiru wa'l-Zāhiru wa'l-Bātin*); man is like the point of intersection of the "divine dimensions."

You must detach your life from an awareness of the multiple and reduce it to a geometrical point before God. You have but one life, and it is not just anything; this life is everything for you, and it owes its greatness to its divine origin and goal. The human condition is something great because its foundation is God; the modern error is to believe we are small, that we are biological accidents, that we are entitled to be lukewarm—that we are free to be small, apathetic, mediocre. In reality we are condemned to greatness, if I may express it this way, and we find this greatness in spiritual smallness before the divine Greatness. It is God who is great, but we must open ourselves up to this Greatness, knowing that there is only He, that we are bound to Him, that we cannot escape Him; knowing this we must resign ourselves to our human and personal condition—to the fact that the sacred is everywhere—and we must repose in trust.

8

Starting with the idea that the spiritual Way consists essentially in discernment between the Real and the illusory and in concentration on the Real, the question must be answered: How can we perpetuate our concentration on the Real?

To be able to do this, what we need essentially are two things: effort, which is of the will and proceeds from without, and comprehension, which is of the intelligence and proceeds from within. The result of persevering effort is the mental art or technique of concentration; one must subdue the soul, break its natural resistance, acquire salutary mental habits. The result of the persevering practice of comprehension—by meditation—is the inward transformation of the imagination or subconscious, the acquisition of reflexes that conform to spiritual reality. It is all very well for the intelligence to affirm metaphysical or eschatological truths; the imagination or subconscious nonetheless continues to believe firmly in this world, not in God or the next world, for every man is *a priori* hypocritical. The Way is precisely the passage from natural hypocrisy to spiritual sincerity.

One must replace the soul's habitual and involuntary dreaming with the remembrance of God; one must repose in this remembrance and not in dreams. It is thus that a bird in flight reposes in limitlessness and not in heaviness; it is a heavenly not an earthly repose. One must replace natural and passional repose with a repose that is supernatural and contemplative. But establishing concentration in duration—attaining the mental art and transforming the imagination—is possible only with the help of grace; the intelligence and will alone and unaided are not enough. Now the conditions *sine qua non* for grace are the rites, which must be performed as perfectly as possible, and the virtues, which are essentially spiritual poverty, generosity, intrinsic sincerity; or humility, charity, veracity—hence logic and impartiality.

The rites refer to man as such and to the collectivity, whereas the virtues refer to each particular man, hence the individual as such. There must be a collective and normative religion, but there must likewise be what might be called a personal religion; this is the spiritual manifestation not of man or humanity as such but of a particular man, with his helplessness and his seeds of immortality.

9

You allude in your letter to the painful invectives of Shankara against the Buddha. What is at stake in this case is not the intrinsic reality of the Buddha but an extrinsic aspect, that of the destroyer of Brahmanism; in fact Buddhism threatened to overrun the world of the *Veda* and the castes completely. Hindus readily grasped the *distinguo* I have just mentioned well before our time, and I have reason to believe that in our day all Hindus venerate the Buddha without thereby disavowing Shankara, who was in his time the medium of a reviving Hinduism; it is as if the Brahmanic gods had armed him with a sword.

As for a spiritually positive reality becoming the symbol of a negative and hostile reality in another spiritual and traditional perspective, there is more than one instance of this phenomenon, but it does not concern intrinsic truth. Such a phenomenon can be repeated even within one and the same tradition; Shiism is an extreme example of this. In our Western world I could mention the demonization of the gods of antiquity by Christianity and within Christianity itself the antagonistic interpretations of Saint Thomas Aquinas and Saint Gregory Palamas, each of whom is regarded as orthodox or heretical, good or bad, depending on denominational prejudice.

10

Regarding primordial man, I do not think he either laughed or wept, for his psyche was not as developed or therefore as exteriorized as that of fallen man; primordial man was much closer to the state of *prajnā*, or rather *samādhi*, which means that everything in him was reabsorbed into a state of beatific indifferentiation; laughter is only a kind of fallen and vulgar fragment of this beatitude, intensified as a result of outwardness; the physical manifestation of laughter stems from the same source.

What I mean is that there is no such thing as primordial laughter, at least not in the sense in which you seem to understand it. It goes without saying that insofar as a thing is positive it has a primordial prototype, but this prototype can be markedly different from what issues from it. Abd al-Qadir al-Jilani says that the Name of Allah dispels all sadness from the heart of man, but he does not say that this Name makes one laugh. I willingly gave up my sadness when Allah removed it from me. But let no one speak to me of gaiety!

I believe I mentioned to you in my last letter that I have always noticed that vulgar people love above all what makes them laugh, and they flee from what is serious; outside their work they seek lighthearted things, abhorring everything that represents gravity and dignity and that evokes pain or death. I am surprised I am writing this to you, for it seems to me obvious. In your article you mentioned several saints who spent the better part of their life laughing and jesting. This is plausible only if their attitude was paradoxical and intentional, as with the *malāmatiyah*; but we are dealing then with an example of asceticism, and this contradicts your interpretation.

I would never think of criticizing spontaneous and unassuming gaiety, provided it is not incompatible with dignity; such gaiety is a question of temperament and thus in itself something neutral. But once gaiety is established as a matter of principle, I do condemn it because it then ceases to be unassuming; it loses its spontaneity and becomes pretentious; it opens the door to stupidity while including a kind of self-sufficiency, which is paralyzing with regard to spirituality even when it is more or less unconscious. Far be it from me to criticize your gaiety as long as it does not harm your path.

11

As for the question "Why invoke?" the most profound response would no doubt be, "Because I exist," for in a certain manner Existence is the Word of God, by which He names Himself. God pronounces His Name in order to manifest Himself—to "create"—in the direction of "nothingness," and the relative being pronounces this same Name in order to "be," in other words to "become once again what he is" in the direction of Reality. Humanly speaking, the idea of duty is very useful in this regard, for the world needs the Invocation. What matters is neither our personal worth nor the graces God makes apparent to us but the manifestation of the Name. Indeed we have no worth except thanks to this Name. We are incapable of doing any good by ourselves; everything we do is conjectural except invoking the Name, the agent of which is God precisely; in this way we put ourselves at the disposal of the divine act.

Japanese Buddhists have rightly stressed that the Invocation is not meant to produce joy; lack of joy is ourselves. If grace pierces this wall, so much the better, but that is something independent of the immediate efficacy and final validity of our prayer. You are right to say that the ego wishes to seize everything for itself, even grace. I think that books on Japanese *Jōdo-Shinshū* would provide you with insights on this subject.

As for possibly eliminating outward expressions of the *dhikr*, I would say this question has no importance; everything here is a matter of interpretation and temperament. Personally, I like all the means of Invocation, from the quietest to the loudest, although the voice should not exceed its natural and average strength; but there is also the collective *dhikr* pronounced aloud.

12

The errors of the Mahesh Yogi movement are patently obvious. In reality the goal of meditation is not to have access to "limitless energy, heightened efficiency of thought and action, and release from tensions and anxiety [leading] to peace of mind and happiness"! None of these advantages has any spiritual value, for it is not happiness that matters; it is the motive and nature of happiness. The Sadhu says nothing of this, the sole important question, and this is what condemns him.

But there are also extrinsic criteria: the complete lack of intelligence and *barakah*, the propagandistic triviality, the modernist and pseudo-yogic style, the quasi-religious pretension. For instance, the Sadhu preaches in the West; how could he believe that Christ failed to bring men everything they need? After all he cannot replace Christianity and the other orthodox religions, and yet this is what he pretends to do in declaring that he brings "the *summum bonum* of all that Christ and Krishna, Buddha and Muhammad taught."

Heresies always arise from a terrible lack of any sense of proportion. Add to this the passional and sentimental element and then propaganda, and we have the irreversible infernal circle. I suppose the Sadhu in question is not a very intelligent man, but perhaps he is endowed with some psychic power; he may also be ambitious. None of this is necessarily malicious *a priori*, but it easily becomes so, and in this sense the Sadhu himself is a victim. False masters are dangerous because they are a mixture of good and evil, and they seduce with the good. I am inclined to believe the Sadhu is largely unconscious of the role that the modern situation is making him play.

But this question of knowing what kind of man the Sadhu is has no importance, and it is perfectly fruitless to discuss it further. This is an appalling case of deviation from a real *barakah*, which stems from an incapacity to discern the true nature of the modern world and to resist the temptations resulting from it. A typical error is to believe that the rapid expansion of a modern sect thanks to mechanical means is comparable to the miraculous expansion of the traditional religions. Everything is "confusion," "belittling," and "falsification."

It must be said that India is a very dangerous terrain for most Westerners; they become imbued there with irremediable prejudices and pretensions. It goes without saying that I prefer the most narrow-minded of Catholics—if they are pious—to these pseudo-Hinduists, arrogant and permanently damaged as they are. The latter scorn the religious point of view, which they do not understand in the least and which alone could save them. One sometimes hates what one needs the most.

And what can one say about the infinite naiveté of believing that a method of meditation could change the whole of humanity, hence even politics? If this "Regeneration Movement" really came from Heaven, its first concern would be to defend the religions, to show their validity and unanimity, as Ramakrishna did; it would be to show their absolute necessity, to indict the modern outlook, to explain that this outlook is the culmination of the *Kali Yuga*, and perhaps to teach *japa*, with all the mandatory precautions.

13

Existential limitations should never be expressed in individual terms, for example by speaking of the ego "which sat so heavily on my shoulders." Every metaphysician ought to know that transcending the ego does not and cannot require the ego's destruction, contrary to a certain literalist interpretation—based on ignorance—of the elliptical dialectic of the East; there is no common measure between Deliverance and individuality, which means that the second could never be opposed to the first. The difference between the non-delivered person and the delivered person is not that the second has no more individuality, which would be a contradiction in terms since he is still a man; the difference consists simply in the fact that someone who is non-delivered is locked within his individuality whereas a delivered person is detached from it; he "possesses" individuality but "is" not that individuality. Without question *Avatāra*s are real people, not only on earth but also in Heaven, and this in no way conflicts with the fact of their Supreme Identity, for once again there is no common measure; this is what the *Mahāyāna* teaches by means of the doctrine of the "simultaneous bodies" of the Buddhas: *nirmāna-kāya*, *sambhoga-kāya*, and *Dharma-kāya*, the third of which is nirvanic or divine.

Were they not real people, the delivered ones could not appear after their death in visions or beatific dreams, for Heaven never deceives anyone.

14

The heliocentric system is not exclusively modern; I will not be telling you anything new in recalling here that Aristarchus of Samos and Hipparcus—and later al-Battani—taught it. Nonetheless it is clear why the ancients finally preferred the geocentric system; this system corresponds to immediate experience, hence to sacred symbolism, whereas the opposite system is beyond most men's capacity for assimilation and entails serious dangers—it "troubles the repose of the Gods," as the opponents of Aristarchus said—which does not of course mean that it is astronomically incorrect. In any case, pushing scientific curiosity too far—to the detriment of contemplation and the inward knowledge of appearances—is imprudence and Luciferianism, and it is partly for this reason that the ancients instinctively retained the geocentric doctrine. Needless to say, the knowledge of realities that are normally unknown and contrary to current experience is a matter of indifference from the point of view of pure intellectuality and esotericism.

15

According to some of the Greek Fathers and Orthodox theologians, the Incarnation brought about a kind of universal blessing, an effusion of Christic grace even outside the visible Church. In order to give this remarkable doctrine its full scope and complete universality, it is necessary to understand that the Incarnation can touch non-Christians only if it is situated outside of history.

The Self is "incarnated" in separativity or illusion; *Ātmā* is "incarnated" in *Māyā*; it is the entry of the Self into *Māyā*, giving rise to *Īshvara*, that constitutes the "Incarnation" *in divinis*, the eternal Incarnation, and it is this Incarnation that has saved beings—first as possibilities—from nothingness, if one may put it this way. On a more reduced scale—or at a lower degree of reality—the Incarnation is *Buddhi*, that is, the "sacrificial" entry of *Purusha* into Existence; it is the existential *fiat lux*, the illumination of darkness or chaos. Understood in a more particular way, which concerns man, *Buddhi* saves in its capacity as Vishnu or Shiva, that is, through *bhakti* or *jnāna*, for it has both an existential function and an intellectual function, and it is the second that can be referred to as "Christic."

Christ manifests these prototypes of the "Incarnation" and "Redemption" historically and directly through his very person; but every other Revelation manifests them too, each in its fashion, depending on the aspects of the Real and possible perspectives. *Ātmā*, by entering *Māyā* as *Īshvara*, has "saved" possibilities from nothingness; *Īshvara* has saved potentialities from Non-Being and virtualities from non-manifestation; *Buddhi* saves beings—in an inverse and ascending manner—from negative manifestation, then manifestation as such; it does so objectively through the *Avatāra* and subjectively through the Intellect.

None of this in any way excludes the fact that the birth and death of Christ had the effect of bringing about a universal effusion of graces, but the same thing is true for every Revelation; in this case it is not a matter of decisive and salvific graces—which are already bestowed by the respective Revelation—but of vivifying graces. Thus the "Descent" (*tanzīl*) of the Koran can be said to have mysteriously touched other spiritualities, including the Christian, and the "Enlightenment" (*Bodhi*) of the Buddha illuminated Hindu spirituality; one can even say, paradoxically, that Christ vivified the esotericism of the Greco-Roman tradition even though it was perishing through the mere fact of his advent.

Some might object that Christ alone directly manifests the eternal "Incarnation"; this is true, but in just the same way only the Buddha directly manifests the eternal *Bodhi* whereas it appears in an indirect manner in Christ. We speak of "Incarnation" because of Christ and of "Enlightenment" because of the Buddha; but the possible designations of the prototype of Revelation and Deliverance are indefinite in number. There is in manifestation an unfolding of symbols, and each symbol refers to a real aspect of the divine Model or the universal models derived from it; but since it is a question here of the same principial and primordial reality—namely, the entry of the Absolute into relativity, whatever the degree considered—the modes or symbols are not mutually exclusive; the entry of the Koranic Revelation into the body of the Prophet can be termed an "incarnation" of the Word, just as the entry of the Holy Spirit—bearer of the Word—into the body of the Virgin is a "descent" of the divine Book; and likewise these two modes are within *Bodhi* just as *Bodhi* is within them.

16

If matrimonial fidelity for the ordinary woman is the equivalent of Mary's virginity, this is because unlike Mary she is not the "Immaculate Conception"; hence an ordinary woman need not imitate the Virgin except by an appropriate transposition of Mary's virginal state into the normal condition of womanhood; the same is true for a man, who is chaste through fidelity to his spouse and who loses his chastity through adultery. It should go without saying that this interpretation—which is self-evident within its own domain—in no way excludes spiritual paths involving an outward imitation of virginity or chastity, provided one is aware of the profound meaning of this exceptional state; and let us note that an exceptional state—one which is contrary to natural law—can never be more than a voluntary means and not a necessary condition for spiritual realization. This is what is expressed by the phrase "apostolic counsel."

As for Christ's chastity, it is an expression of his Divinity not his humanity; having no human father, it was not possible for him to have a human wife, and he could therefore be an example in this respect only for someone who likewise had no human father, namely Adam; indeed Adam did not have a human wife in the ordinary sense of the word, for Eve was taken from his own substance and was therefore an exteriorization of the femininity contained within the Adamic androgyne. Likewise, or rather conversely, Christ carried his wife within himself by virtue of his divine and human soul: masculine by his divinity, emanating from the divine "Father," and feminine by his humanity, emanating from the human Mother.

17

To conquer avidity (exteriorizing, passional expansion) we must realize its opposite, Abstention (crystallizing, ascetic contraction), as well as its positive analogue, Life (interiorizing, fervent expansion).

To conquer indifference (petrifying, prideful contraction) we must realize its opposite, Life, as well as its positive analogue, Abstention.

To conquer sloth (corrupting solution) we must realize its opposite, the Act (victorious fixation that unites), as well as its positive analogue, Repose (stabilizing, peace-giving solution).

To conquer dissipation (agitated fixation that separates) we must realize its opposite, Repose, as well as its positive analogue, the Act.

To conquer outwardness (scattering separation that deprives) we must realize its opposite, Immanence (liberating union), as well as its positive analogue, Transcendence (discerning, illuminative separation).

To conquer egoism (compressive union) we must realize its opposite, Transcendence, as well as its positive analogue, Immanence.

18

Eastern masters almost never understand the situation of the Westerners they initiate; they nearly always lose sight of two factors, fundamental though these are: on the one hand psychological conditions and on the other hand conditions of ambiance. One might call these the moral and aesthetic conditions of the path, both of which are difficult to fulfill in an abnormal world like ours, whereas in the traditional East the question never really arose. When the practices of Zen—to take one example—are grafted onto the mental trivialities engendered by modern life, this is why they are generally more harmful than useful; for one must be deeply imbued with a sense of the sacred and a kind of holy childlikeness to be able to benefit from initiatic or spiritual graces as such. This obviously concerns Christians as well, who in general live on the margin and not within their religion; to be a true Christian one must become medieval again, psychologically and aesthetically speaking—though of course without sacrificing any real and spiritually useful knowledge. The *Golden Legend* does not prevent us from understanding the *Bhagavad Gītā*.

Be that as it may, here is what I would tell a Christian who is seeking an esoteric path—a path going beyond basic belief and conventional mediocrity:

Every religion is first of all a doctrine; now the fundamental content of this doctrine is discernment between the Absolute and the contingent or between the Real and the illusory; then comes the method, namely—and essentially—continuous, or at least frequent, concentration on the Absolute or the Real. To doctrinal discernment and methodical concentration one must add intrinsic virtue as a condition *sine qua non*, and this means beauty of soul; for truth requires beauty. The Christian seeker should know that the quintessence of his religion is to be found in these elements, for they are the quintessence of all possible religion and all spirituality; the rest is *upāya*, "mythology," formal clothing. Discernment (doctrine); Concentration (method); Virtue (moral beauty).

The question you must ask yourself is whether you are Christian or Buddhist in the eyes of God; assuming that your sense of the sacred and your intuition of spiritual forms have enabled you to assimilate the specific atmosphere of the *Mahāyāna* to a sufficient degree, the situation is strictly analogous to what it is in Christianity, for the central spiritual means is the *mantra*—the ejaculatory orison—and this is all the more true in your case since you have received an initiation based on the grace of Amitabha Buddha, who corresponds metaphysically to Christ. I would not advise a Western Buddhist to follow any other path than that of the Invocation of Amitabha—whether in its Japanese or Tibetan form—assuming of course that one has a valid reason in the eyes of God for being a Buddhist and for entering upon a path so foreign to our traditional climate in the West.

If I understand you correctly, you sometimes receive what you call "metaphysical" communion in the Church; but if you are validly affiliated with Buddhism and practice a Buddhist method, every Christian rite is forbidden you. Moreover, one does not receive communion "metaphysically"; one concentrates on God, the Absolute, the Real, or on the radiation of His Mercy, and one lets God act as He will. What you are doing, according to your letter, is doubly dangerous: first because it is a heterogeneous mixture of sacred forms and second because we have no right to impose a doctrinal program on grace; grace acts as it wills. Tibetans, not knowing Western religions, confuse them with secondary cults and are not competent in these matters. And you most certainly have not "passed beyond both infidelity and religion"!

19

I have made a painting depicting the White Buffalo Woman bringing the Sacred Pipe to the Indians. Someone might ask why I made this painting, or others, and why I take such an interest in the American Indians. In a related vein it appears that many readers of *Études traditionnelles* have been critical of me, given my function within Sufism, for having written a long article on Shinto; it would be more normal, they say, if I restricted myself to writing on Islam; such opinions obviously do not preoccupy me.

But to return to my paintings or their content, what accounts for them is my position at the crossroads of traditional worlds, and this position is explained in turn by the cyclical moment in which we live; as for the Indians, they present a "neutral" possibility in the traditional universe, and at the same time they also exhibit something relatively "primordial." Moreover it is worth noting that there is a relationship between them and the Japanese. In the last century the Japanese were the only non-"decadent" Oriental people, whereas the Indians seem to be the only true "primitives" among all the "savages"; this amounts to two "miracles," one might say. Both peoples have something fascinating about them, for the *kshatriya* spirit, which is very pure in each case, is at the same time penetrated with a *brāhmana* spirit: The warrior spirit is "complete" but it is not "worldly," allowing Heaven to shine through.

20

What distinguishes us above all—"psychologically" one could say—from people who were born into Muslim families or who converted to Islam is that our mind is *a priori* centered on universal metaphysics (*Advaita Vedānta*, *Shahādah*, *Risālat al-Ahadīyah*) and the universal path of the divine Name (*japa-yoga*, *nembutsu*, *dhikr*, prayer of the heart); it is because of these two factors that we are within a traditional form, which in fact—but not in principle—is Islam. The universal orthodoxy emanating from these two sources of authority determines our interpretation of the *sharīʿah* and Islam in general, somewhat as the moon influences the oceans without being situated on the terrestrial globe; in the absence of the moon the motions of the sea would be inconceivable and "illegitimate." Universal metaphysics and the "onomatological" science connected to it have decisive authority for us, a fact which once earned us the reproach of "de-islamicizing Islam"; but it is less a matter of the conscious application of principles formulated outside of Islam and by metaphysical traditions from Asia than of inspirations that are in conformity with those principles. In a situation such as ours the spiritual authority—or the soul that is its vehicle—becomes like a point of intersection for all the rays of truth, whatever their origin.

21

When experiencing spiritual difficulties, it is important not to forget that there are three principal ways of confronting them, according to the ternaries *makhāfah*, *mahabbah*, *maʿrifah*, and *karma*, *bhakti*, *jnāna*: One always needs a measure of constraint, discipline, practicality, and action; then a measure of joy—for joy lies within us, so that it suffices to extract it from our substance and project it into the *mantra*; and finally a measure of consciousness of the nature of things, hence discernment, analysis, a searching for the causes. Priority is granted to one or another of these three means depending on our state.

Thus when the mind is agitated we must ask ourselves why this is so in order to be aware of the illusory character of what agitates it or the disproportion between the object agitating us and the infinite Essence of our nature or between the relative and the Absolute, for agitation cannot help but cease when its cause is perfectly understood and reduced to its correct proportions; whatever the causes, we have no choice since we are made for Eternity. Next—or first, depending on which sequence is more effective—we must throw ourselves into the *mantra* with perfect insouciance; let *samsāra* be what it may, we will not change it, for the only essential thing is that the Infinite should welcome us; this is the point of view of faith and trust, of joy and also beauty, and it is connected to the beauty of the sacred Image, the language of which is direct and somehow musical; we are mere husks, but Reality is music. In either case one must act, and this means above all practicing *japa*; the real question is knowing which of the other two supports—intellectual or affective—we should give our preference to, depending on circumstances or on our character.

Sometimes it is useful to change our surroundings, to isolate ourselves somewhere in nature, to go where we do not have the temptation of reading or writing. Too habitual an environment—one's own house for example—sometimes has something crushing about it.

22

When I am conscious of the sovereign Good with wholehearted faith and without any pretension—knowing full well that I cannot save myself by my own means—then it is a matter of indifference where I am, when I am, who I am, what I have experienced, and what I have done or failed to do.

For then I am in a state which has God the Transcendent for its object and whose subject in the final analysis is God the Immanent, a state which corresponds to my very reason for being and whose fruits cannot be taken away from me by any power in the world.

"The Lord is my shepherd; I shall not want."

23

Poetry is the "language of the gods," and *noblesse oblige*! What I mean is that the poet has certain responsibilities; in poetry the musicality of things or their cosmic essentiality erupts onto the plane of language, and this process requires the grandeur, hence the authenticity, of both image and feeling.

The poet spontaneously intuits the underlying musicality of phenomena; under the pressure of an image or emotion—the emotion being naturally combined with concordant images—he expresses an archetypal beauty; without this pressure there is no poetry, which means that true poetry always has an aspect of inward necessity, whence its irreplaceable perfume. The grandeur of language must be drawn from its own resources, and this is the whole formal art of poetry. Dante not only had grandeur; he also knew how to infuse this grandeur into language, wielding words in such a way as to make them adequate to his inward vision. Similarly when Shakespeare describes something, he almost always succeeds in presenting its quintessence, and in this way he brings appearances back to their cosmic musicality, whence the liberating feeling characteristic of all true poetry.

I am actually rather hostile to the writing of poetry because hardly anyone knows how to do it—spiritual motives notwithstanding—and because most true poets are the dupes of their talent and get lost in prolixity instead of letting the muse take over, for the muse is sometimes very parsimonious!

24

I am completely against ecumenism as it is practiced today—with its ineffective "dialogues" and gratuitous and sentimental gestures amounting to nothing. Certainly an understanding between religions is possible and even necessary, though solely on the basis of common ideas and common interests and not on the dogmatic plane. The common ideas are a transcendent, perfect, all-powerful, merciful Absolute, then a hereafter that is either good or bad depending on our merits or demerits; all the religions, including Buddhism—Buddhist "atheism" is simply a misunderstanding—are in agreement on these points. The common interests are a defense against materialism, atheism, perversion, subversion, and modernism in all its guises. I believe Pius XII once said that the wars between Christians and Muslims were but domestic quarrels compared to the present opposition between the world of the religions and that of militant materialism-atheism; he also said it was a consolation to know that there are millions of people who prostrate themselves five times a day before God.

25

The *philosophia perennis* is founded essentially and intrinsically on the nature of things as perceived by intellectual intuition; only formally and extrinsically is it founded upon a particular revealed Text, and it could never be dependent on it.

It is altogether erroneous to believe that religion in the ordinary sense of the term—including an esotericizing exotericism—is the indispensable condition and sole guarantee of intellectual intuition and the practical consequences deriving from it. The fact that all spirituality extrinsically depends on a Tradition in no way signifies that the human Intellect is inoperative outside the framework of a traditional symbolism or a sacramental means.

As Meister Eckhart said: "There is something in the soul that is uncreated and uncreatable; if the entire soul were such, it would be uncreated and uncreatable; and this is the Intellect." Similarly, the Islamic formula: "The Sufi is not created."

According to the *Brahma Sūtra*, "Man can acquire true divine Knowledge even without observing the prescribed rites; and indeed in the *Veda* there are to be found many examples of people who failed to perform such rites or were prevented from doing so and who nonetheless acquired true Knowledge because their attention was perpetually concentrated and focused on the supreme *Brahma*."

In principle man—"made in the image of God"—contains everything within himself; in fact, however, he needs elements of actualization coming from outside, hence from Tradition; this does not mean that a man needs every possible support, but he does need the supports his particular nature requires. Necessity is not the only issue; there is also what is appropriate in a given case; the useful is not always the indispensable.

According to Guénon, "True esotericism is something quite different from the outward religion, and if it has some connections with it, this can be only insofar as it finds in the religious forms a mode of symbolic expression; moreover it matters little whether these forms are those of this religion or that since what is in question is the essential unity of doctrine that lies hidden beneath their apparent diversity. This is why the initiates of old participated in all the outward forms of worship without distinction, following the established customs of the various countries wherein they found themselves. Pure metaphysics is neither pagan nor Christian but rather universal; the mysteries of antiquity were not paganism, but they were superimposed upon it."

The pure pneumatic will sometimes act in a manner that is foreign to a particular religious perspective and particular prescriptions, but he never acts in a manner contrary to the nature of things, for he bears the essential, universal, and primordial Law in the depths of his own heart. For this reason deviation or corruption is in his case impossible, whatever the appearances from a particular limited perspective.

26

To return to your article on chess, it is noteworthy that this game was invented by a *brāhmana* for the benefit of *kshatriyas*, the *brāhmana* Sissa having made a gift of it to a rajah; no doubt he did this to neutralize the ardor of the *kshatriyas*' activity while at the same time giving them an instrument for the education of the mind and even a means of speculative intuition.

From a speculative point of view, chess pieces are principial possibilities, that is, possibilities as such; the rules of their motion are the potentialities of their manifestation, hence these possibilities seen in connection with their respective expressions; and their actual motions as played out on the chessboard are the manifestations of these possibilities. This is the relationship between cause and effect with an intermediary aspect; there are thus three realities: the pieces, their principial motions or modes, and their contingent motions, which are the various applications of the principial motions. But there are also compensations between the different possibilities; for example, the bishop realizes a possibility not allowed the rook since it can march diagonally, but it cannot change state like the rook, which for its part dominates the white and black squares simultaneously; the squares are obviously the alternations of states. As for the fact that the queen is the most powerful figure in manifestation whereas the king is merely present and dominates in a non-acting way, one finds in this an application of the motionless center and of the relationship between Non-Being and Being.

27

If only it were easier for a man to do what most people are incapable of doing, namely, to step outside himself and see himself from outside—an outside that is in reality the inside! Then he would be standing in a vast, silver silence, and he would see his ego as something quite small, as something strangled, seething, and noisy.

What makes spiritual realization so difficult is that the ego is inverted, as if turned inside out, a stranger to Reality. Within this inversion it is not so difficult to chase after mirror-reflections of Reality, if the corresponding gifts are there; but to step out of this invertedness into the open—that is difficult, humanly speaking.

28

What makes your correspondent's position so fragile is precisely its theoretical insufficiency, for if it is easy to understand—easy, that is, for someone who possesses the necessary metaphysical notions—that the goal of man is simply to return to the "Absolute Subject," *Chit*, it is nonetheless far from easy to know how to do it; to believe that it is enough to close one's eyes and think of nothing or to concentrate on what one feels in one's depths, as certain modern "Vedantists" do, is truly the height of naiveté. Only the tradition of the spiritual Masters, with all the complexity and subtlety of its doctrine and method, can address this "how."

It is not a question of grasping the Ungraspable but of removing the obstacles that take us away from our own infinite Essence; one cannot simply desert the ego, not even to arrive at this Essence, for if we were to attempt in this way to leave the "self" by our own means, the "self" would nevertheless not leave us. This is why it must be transmuted; it must realize the Prophet as it were—the purified and consecrated "place" where "theogenesis" may occur—for "none shall meet God who hath not first met His Prophet." To transmute the "self" into a seat of the "Real Presence" is a science, a science as complex as it is indispensable. If one does not follow a legitimate spiritual way—in conformity with realities that are individual as well as universal—one will never encounter the real *Chit*; the gross or "unformed" mentality of the profane man can never do so.

Japa (*dhikr*) is the symbolic, but also "supernatural," seat of the Real Presence of *Chit*; *japa*, together with the conditions that are indissolubly bound to it, guarantees the rectitude of the *deva-yana* (*al-sirāt al-mustaqīm*); our spiritual concentration on the "Absolute Subject" is accomplished in parallel with *japa* and does not stop at *manolaya*, which in itself has nothing transcendent about it. Outward traditional affiliation (*samskāra*), initiatic affiliation (*dīkshā*), spiritual means (such as *tapas*, *yantra*, *mantra*, *japa*), and finally—at the center of all—permanent concentration on "what I as Self am." Such is the way.

Some modern theorists of the "direct way" do not seem to ask themselves whether it is psychologically possible to persevere a whole lifetime by one's own means in mere concentration on the "Absolute Subject," nor whether such efforts—assuming they were feasible—could lead to a positive result. They forget that Christ said, "No man cometh to the Father, but by me" and "Without me ye can do nothing"; this means that the doctrine and grace of the Word can alone render possible what is humanly impossible, hence that only revealed and orthodox doctrine can give spiritual concentration the required "quality" and that only initiatic means can enable this concentration to attain its supreme Goal.

29

This exotericist passion is a very strange thing in a man like your friend; there is a tremendous lack of imagination here, a total inability to put himself in the place of a Christian or Buddhist. He refers to the authority of Muslim saints; very well, but what becomes of the hundreds of non-Muslim saints? What does the wisdom of a Shankara or Kobo Daishi signify in the eyes of God? I have always been surprised at the lack of imagination, spiritual sensitivity, and rational perspicacity among those who lock themselves fanatically within a single religion in an age such as ours where civilizations touch and where—for those with a minimum of culture—foreign religions are more than simplistic abstractions.

All told one would like to ask your friend: Why do you think your religion is truer than another or alone is true? Because your religion says so? But other religions do the same. Because you were born into it? But other men are born into other religions. Because the arguments of your religion are better than those of other religious systems? This is an error; the arguments of any religion are acceptable and irrefutable from its own point of view without being convincing outside it. The intrinsic truth of Islam is something we acknowledge from the vantage point of metaphysics, hence on the basis of the *religio perennis*, and not by virtue of Muslim argumentation; what enables us to accept Islam—otherwise we would have remained Christians—is precisely what enables us to accept other religions as well, or rather what obliges us to do so.

All this is self-evident for you and me; I repeat it here simply because of the stubbornness of your friend. He was born into Islam, so his imagination, sensibility, and way of reasoning are derived from this perspective; he ignores the fact that others were born into Christianity and that their imagination, sensibility, and way of thinking were molded by it, so that their conviction of being born into the truth is also total, which makes them impervious to Muslim arguments without being stupid or perverse men.

30

The Imam Shadhili had a vision in which God showed him a list of all the Shadhiliyyah *fuqarā*ʾ, promising him that none of them would fall into hell. This is a "conditionally absolute" promise, which means that its fulfillment depends on the authenticity of the *faqīr*; before asking, What is the import of this promise? it is fitting to ask, What is a *faqīr* who is truly worthy of the name? We reply that in order for someone to be an authentic *faqīr* he must be sincere, humble, generous; on the basis of the invocatory way, he must accomplish what brings him closer to God and abstain from what separates him from God, with gratitude and confidence.

But there are no rigorous lines of demarcation between human perfections and imperfections; between the ideal and the minimum there is necessarily a margin, and this permits us to distinguish degrees in the application of the divine promise made to Imam Shadhili; there are in fact three degrees in the eschatological promise.

First, it means that the man who is fully a *faqīr* will go directly to Paradise. Second, it means that the man who is a *faqīr* without being so fully—but who is so honorably, if one may put it this way—will also go to Paradise but not immediately: He will be purified in a paradisiacal *khalwah*, which is free from suffering since it is contained within Paradise, but nonetheless without enjoying plenary beatitude since the *khalwah* in question is nonetheless distinct from Paradise; this place or state has been compared to a lotus bud enclosing the soul, which will open when it has sufficiently ripened. Third, the eschatological promise means—and this is its minimal but still merciful significance—that a *faqīr* who is a sinner but possessed of good will will not be damned but must nevertheless expiate his faults in a region above hell, in "purgatory," even if only for a moment. This third meaning, far from being deceiving, is absolutely plausible and necessary; otherwise self-satisfied mediocrity, impenitent unconstraint, and lack of discipline without shame and without fear of God would triumph. Now the fear of God is an aspect of our sense of the divine Majesty or sense of the Sacred, without which there is no *faqr* precisely.

Another eschatological question: The idea that the soul of the *faqīr* evaporates after death into the "supreme Principle" is completely false; this is an error that comes from misunderstanding the *yogin* or the *apocatastasis*. If we admit that the human form on earth is not an obstacle to union with God, or to supreme realization if one prefers—and the infinite sanctity of the Prophets and Sayyidatna Maryam proves it—we must also admit that this union in Heaven does not prevent the persistence of the human form, as is demonstrated by the apparitions of the Prophets and saints.

31

Some object that a temporal fact cannot lead to a timeless outcome, but if a given sin corresponds to the fundamental tendency of a given person—a tendency which will either be in conformity with or contrary to the pure Essence of divine Reality—then this tendency cannot be limited to the temporal order; if the soul is immortal, so too is its fundamental tendency, and sin will simply be its signature. In contrast to animals and spirits—that is, angels or demons—it is nonetheless difficult to determine the fundamental tendency of an individual in the human state as long as this tendency has not been disclosed by means of a spiritual touchstone. The person's contact with the Divine always provides such a touchstone, and it is his response that betrays his fundamental tendency—though even then it is usually difficult, if not impossible, to determine the precise nature of this tendency as long as the person is still alive. All that can be said for sure is that if a given individual dies without repenting in a way that is accepted by God he is damned; that he will die without repenting and without grace remains uncertain, but that he will be damned if he does die without repenting and without grace is absolutely certain.

Another objection formulated against hell is based on divine Goodness and human misery—that is, irresponsibility. This is a very feeble objection and hardly deserves to be taken into account since divine Goodness, though unconditional in itself, is conditional in its manifestation and since there really is such a thing as human responsibility. Man is metaphysically and necessarily free by virtue of his ontological participation in divine Freedom; this is the fundamental character of the human species, and the existence of heaven and hell prove it precisely. People like to repudiate hell because of its "atrocious" and "definitive" aspects, but what they forget is that the atrocious and the definitive are cosmic possibilities. A secondary cycle always reflects a total cycle; earthly life is a secondary cycle, and the existence of the soul is a total cycle. Atrocities can certainly be definitive for a given earthly life; this suggests that they can be so for a total cycle as well. Imagine a child who, while playing, has an accident resulting in the loss of his sight or one of his hands; no supplication can restore life to his blinded eyes or make a missing hand grow back. The accident is therefore definitive in spite of divine Goodness, which goes to show that there are things whose definitive character results from their own nature; the same applies to hell and paradise.

The "sin against the Spirit," which is never forgiven, is hatred of divine Reality; I am not talking about hatred of sacred literature or traditional art but of "divine Reality." Actual contact with this Reality is thus the criterion; most men have never had this contact, which does not mean that they cannot hate the divine Reality in forms accessible to them.

32

We may replace the Greek word *Sophia* with the Latin *Religio* in order to specify that Wisdom contains all religion and lacks nothing, hence to specify that Wisdom is our Religion.

The *Religio Perennis* has two origins: one non-temporal, vertical, and discontinuous, and one horizontal and continuous. The first is like rain, which can descend from Heaven at any moment and anywhere; the second is like a stream originating from a spring. Both modes of Revelation may be combined: Of the first Christ said, "The Spirit bloweth where it listeth"; the second has its starting point in a given Founder of Religion. The first mode is totally independent of the second whereas the second cannot be independent of the first. One may compare the first mode to mistletoe—celestial and sacred plant for the Celts—whose seed, falling from the sky, alights upon trees.

There are very old Christian and Muslim texts in which some Apostle or Companion says, in substance: "If I were to divulge all I know, you would stone me," which may—and more than likely does—refer to the vertical and totally independent Revelation of the *Religio Perennis*.

33

Some people talk about what they call the "method of the Maharshi," but such a method does not exist for the simple reason that the Maharshi himself never followed any method. He owes his realization to a sudden enlightenment and not to spiritual exercises, and since he never followed a method he cannot teach one; his teaching through the question "Who am I?" is much more the expression of his inner reality or a principial and symbolic expression of all spiritual Paths than a method that can be imitated in the absence of any other support.

This does not mean that the Maharshi has no radiance or does not transmit graces but simply that he cannot have the mission of forming disciples since he never had to follow a Path himself, and this in fact is the reason he refuses to accept disciples; to claim that *mauna-dīkshā* constitutes a complete Path in itself, instead of simply representing the essential aspect of every Path, amounts to saying that the descent of the Holy Spirit on the Apostles constitutes a spiritual method. Let no one object that the Apostles were therefore unable to form disciples since, like the Companions of the Prophet, they experienced a quasi-sudden realization; the case of the Apostles and Companions is altogether different, for they received not only an initiation but also a method to be transmitted; this method, which was "simple" and "synthetic" at the beginning, was "differentiated" and rendered more explicit by the Holy Spirit as the origin and its flood of spiritual graces receded and as it became necessary to adapt to increasingly precarious conditions; thus the position of a figure such as Saint John or Sayyidna Ali is in no way comparable to that of a later saint—that is, someone who is not the direct disciple of the founder of a traditional form.

As for the Maharshi, he is clearly one of those of whom Ramakrishna says that they obtain realization independently of their will and in a sudden and spontaneous manner; these are the men Sufism knows under the name of *afrād*, and the initiatic meaning of this saying of Christ applies to them: "They that be whole need not a physician." But the existence of such men does not imply that initiatic rites, which exist in Hinduism as in any other tradition, are merely meaningless contrivances or stupidities; the fact that these rites exist means that they must correspond to some kind of reality and necessity. There really should be no problem here: If someone is a *fard*, then the initiatic question does not apply to him, and discussions on this subject are pointless for him; if he is not a *fard*, then he has no choice but that of a normal way transmitted by tradition. With a proper intention and with the assistance of *barakah*, he needs to seek an orthodox *murshid* and receive from him what this *murshid* himself received from his *murshid*.

But returning to the Maharshi: To follow his "Path" is to imitate what he did or rather what made him what he is, and it is thus to have one's great-grandparents cursed or blessed by a *sannyāsin*, then to be surprised and unexpectedly overcome during adolescence by a spiritual force, then to remain in *samādhi* for weeks and months on end, and finally to enjoy a spiritual realization obtained as a gift without any inward work; to wish to emulate this "Path" would be as absurd as to wish to be crucified by Pontius Pilate and rise the third day.

34

You write: "The crucial question in his case as in my own is not the question of tradition, of *silsilah* or method, but of the Guru's realization." But how can you know what "the Guru's realization" is? For either you are not a perfect Sage, in which case you have no means of verifying whether the Guru is a "perfect Sage," or else you are yourself a "perfect Sage," in which case you have no need of a Guru. All the disciple can know is that the Guru is spiritually superior to him, and this he can know only thanks to the tradition to which he belongs and from which the Guru has issued. Once the disciple attains the degree of the Guru, he can then seek another Guru, but it is in any case impossible for the disciple to know the "realization" of the Guru, and besides this would be of no use at all.

Only tradition can make up for this impossibility facing the disciple, and it does so on the one hand by the *silsilah*, which constitutes a first guarantee, and on the other hand by the light of doctrine, which allows the disciple to recognize the spiritual superiority of the Master. You say, "The one thing indispensable is an immediate relation with the embodied Absolute"; but what proves to the disciple that he is really in the presence of this "Absolute"? You go on to say, "Whether he 'discusses' the point or not, a serious disciple must satisfy himself as best he can that his prospective master is fully realized." Now I would like to know what the disciple could do to verify whether the Master possesses a wisdom the disciple himself does not have. You say that once one admits the difference between the *Shaykh al-barakah* and the *muqaddam*—or rather in this case the *khalīfah*—"the emphasis now falls on inspiration rather than experience," to which I reply: By no means! For the experience of the Master, whatever his degree of realization, is always amply sufficient for the disciple.

"Apart from this," you write, "it seems to me self-evident that any kind of experience can be used by a Master to take a disciple to the Goal. The line followed need not be traditional at all, and its virtue as tradition—the virtue of its founder—is altogether secondary to the virtue of the Master who makes use of it." This is not at all "self-evident," and if there is anything that seems to me evident it is the exact opposite of what you are saying: namely, that the disciple could never be brought to the Goal by just any means whatsoever; on the contrary, no matter what the means may be, it must correspond to the Goal, and it is precisely tradition—with all the degrees it contains—that guarantees this correspondence by its very structure. This is why "the line followed" has to be traditional; in its most inward aspect, which is also its essential reality, tradition is nothing other than the prototype of the Way. The traditional virtue of a method is everything, for without it there would be no guarantee for the disciple of being rightly guided; likewise the spiritual virtue of the *Avatāra* or Prophet to which the tradition refers is everything, and the virtue of the Master would be inconceivable without that of the respective *Avatāra*; the "greater" can never come from the "lesser," and—for multiple reasons—tradition is never revealed by means of a man not possessing perfect Wisdom.

35

The *Mihrāb* is the Heart; Maryam is the inward soul that invokes and is thus withdrawn from the world. This separation is indicated by the veil behind which the Virgin was hidden, having withdrawn to "a place toward the East," which is precisely the *Mihrāb*. The *Mihrāb* is equivalent to the Holy of Holies in the Temple, which amounts to saying that the Virgin was the high priest and that her *Mihrāb* was the Holy of Holies during the time she was present in the Temple.

Zachariah is the outward soul, which thinks and exists in relation to the sensory world. Looking toward the inward soul, which is in a state of prayer, the outward soul—the temporal ego—recognizes that the inward is nourished by the infinite Center or the Self; the immortal soul is nourished by the divine Name, and this nourishment is unlimited—it is given "without reckoning"—and thus coincides with the "immense reward" referred to in the *Sūrah* of Victory.

Maryam was entrusted to Zachariah; it is thus that the inward soul or the Invocation, which is the same thing in practice, is entrusted to the outward man. Maryam's reason for existence is God, and Zachariah's reason for existence is Maryam. Zachariah is not the outward soul of just any man; he is the outward soul of the pious man, the initiate, which is indicated precisely by the fact that Maryam was entrusted to him. And if Zachariah asks: "O Maryam, whence hast thou this nourishment?" it is because nourishment comes from outside from the point of view of sensory experience and because the miraculous character of the inward nourishment must be pointed out.

36

The blessing and wisdom present in the Name of *Allāh* can be compared to a field of snow: an endless, white, pure, cool quietude. The Jesus Prayer corresponds instead to a glowing center—to a burning rose, we might say. When one has experienced the grace of a divine Name directly—that is, with one's whole being—it is no longer possible to feel any desire for another Name and another grace. A lifetime is not too long to assimilate the grace that lies in the Name of God. The Name must break something in us; hence a man may sometimes wish to flee from it as from an enemy. How much passion, faintheartedness, distraction, hardening, how much pettiness, narrowness, and ugliness must give way in a man before his soul, penetrated by the Name of God, becomes a white expanse like a snow-covered plain in which all is clear! Then time stands still; space lies within us.

In every life there are dangers seeking to entwine a man; he then grows fainthearted, melancholic, bitter, skeptical. But all this is nothing; the Name of God is a ship that cleaves through every danger. It is important to know this when weakness, bitterness, and doubt say, "Now you are ours"—to know that you are none of these.

Man has only one life; unfortunate is he who trusts his vacillating soul. How can that save which is itself in need of saving? How can that bless which is itself in need of blessing? Truth does not lie in our impotent thinking but in the medium of God's grace, which we cannot understand *a priori*. When man is reduced to nothing, when he thinks he can no longer see anything, then the Name of God sees in him and for him—until the two become one.

37

Esotericism resides as a permanent virtuality in the ideas and symbols of religion, of every religion.

On the one hand esotericism prolongs exotericism by deepening it, but on the other hand it is independent of it and can even be opposed to certain exoteric points of view, so that there can never be any question of reducing esotericism to theology or wishing to adapt every possible truth to theology.

Metaphysical truths are not specifically "Christian," "Muslim," and so forth in the usual sense of these terms; they are necessarily found within the framework of every religion for the simple reason that they are truths, and it is precisely this universality that confers upon them an "esoteric" character in relation to a given creed. From another point of view it can be said that an idea becomes "Christian" in being assimilated by a Christian; there is no need to seek for it in a Meister Eckhart or a forgotten or misunderstood passage of a Church Father or Scholastic, for the truth is "Christian" *a priori* and as a matter of principle.

Within the framework of a given religion the esoteric path consists essentially in assimilating the metaphysical and mystical truths and their resulting attitudes and virtues on the basis of an ejaculatory orison—in principle perpetual—while at the same time practicing the rites of the religion; these rites will be integrated into esotericism by the very fact of practicing meditative Invocation. In other words this practice actualizes the esoteric virtualities of the religion.

Entry into the path requires not only an initiation but also an initiatic promise—an intention conformable to the path, hence a vow.

The role of a spiritual master, or if necessary his representative, consists in defining the nature of the obstacles and pointing out the remedies; and this demands intuition as well as experience, inspiration as well as sanctity, to one degree or another. The function of the spiritual master is comprised in this saying of Christ: "Without me ye can do nothing."

38

There are three great crises in life: The first is when a child becomes an adult, the second when the adult enters into the second half of his life, around 50 years of age, and the third when he enters old age, at around 70 years. Just as at 50, this third transition requires a readjustment and demands a great deal of voluntary sacrifice, resignation, and serenity. By means of a deliberate spiritual act, one must accept all the risks and servitudes of the new condition; this is what is called detachment. One must free oneself absolutely from all regret, all sadness, all bitterness. There are many men who do not age well because they drag behind them the psychology of a bygone time. If one must bury oneself somewhat at 50, one must do so even more at 70. It is as if one were to conclude, on a personal basis, a new pact with God. What is absolutely imperative is to be pleased with one's condition.

Every age has its advantages: From a certain point of view, old people are to be envied; their state simplifies many things; all they need to do is live in God until the end; they can be sure God asks no more of them.

39

A hundred years ago some poet racked his brains over some worthless play; somewhere in the world someone is dreaming of success; a statesman is greedily absorbed in some petty project; yesterday a Zen monk swept the floor-boards in Kyoto; and today, quite near, a cricket chirps in the grass. The world is mad.

One might object that every being, every man, is thus completely locked into a narrow world of experience, in a picture book, in a dream. Yes and no, and in a certain sense absolutely not! I have seen venerable men in whom one could perceive no trace of being locked into a dream world nor any trace of aridity; they looked as if they had experienced everything that can be experienced and as if they were conscious of all possible limits and of the Unlimited.

40

The supreme Name is represented within us by the heart and also under certain conditions by the brain. When the brain contains Truth and not error, when it is silent for God and abides in holy emptiness, then it will be filled with God's silvern, cooling presence; then it sleeps a holy sleep. And likewise when the virtues and love of God are joined to the Truth, the heart awakens; it sings in God and abides in holy recollection and is filled with God's golden, warming nearness.

Thus man has two centers, one wholly inward and the other more outward, namely, heart and brain, and each of them is the divine Name: the heart in itself through its original nature and the brain by being filled with Truth and holy silence. And each of these centers—sun and moon—is in its own way the center of the body: the heart in the fullest sense and the brain more outwardly. Hence the body partakes at one and the same time of the brain's pure coolness and the heart's blessed warmth; the body is cool toward the senses and warm inwardly toward God.

Thus it is that in the holy Invocation first the brain and then the heart are the seat of the supreme Name; the body also contains or conveys this Name in its own way and through being deeply moved by the supernatural.

Now the body has its own center in relation to the heart and the brain, namely, the lungs: Even as the heart penetrates the body with blood and even as the brain penetrates the body with nerves, so the lungs penetrate the body with air. The brain as discriminating consciousness contains the Truth; the heart as spiritual kernel contains or conveys Reality and therefore also in a way Beauty and Love; the body—or in its place the breathing lungs—conveys joy in both, in cool Truth and warm Beauty. Thus the deep-breathing lungs are also the divine Name, not in themselves—except on a purely vital level—but through their joy or beatitude in the holy silence or holy singing, in the silence of the mind and the sound of the heart, in holy sleep and holy waking. Hence there is also a way to God in the breath, as in meditation and in remaining in the depths of the heart. The heart is sun, the brain is moon, the body is earth; and the breath is like the pure, liberating mountain heights and mountain solitude, like the space between earth and heaven. The lungs as center of the body are like a holy mountain, close to heaven in the midst of the outstretched earth.

In this way the supreme Name dwells at the same time in the head, heart, and breast, in true thinking and its quietness, in deep recollection and its primordial sound—for holiness is like a golden note in the heart—and also in deep, devout breathing for God. The head is Truth and Peace, the heart is Being, Reality, Love, and the breast is Joy; but nothing exists outside the heart that cannot also—and first of all—be found within the heart; and everything lies in the supreme Name. In the human form there are paths to God, but these paths are at the same time cause and effect; they point to the Divine and are determined and brought to fulfillment by God.

Thus one can distinguish three ways of remembering God: remembrance by thinking of the Truth and therefore by extinguishing all aimless thought; remembrance by concentration in the heart and—as a prerequisite—by beauty of soul, virtue, love of God; and remembrance through breathing, which conveys the divine Name by breathing in, breathing out, and holding the breath; this way of remembering God presupposes both the others.

It has been said that there is an Invocation through visualizing the written Name, another through uttering or hearing the Name in the heart, and a third through uttering the Name with one's whole body; this last takes place through God-dedicated breathing, which penetrates the whole body with the purifying and transforming presence of the supreme Name. Then truth and virtue are present, and the breath too can remember God.

Each breath is pure, for it names God. Even so are the heartbeats pure, for they also name God. But in our thoughts we are free, suspended between true and false, good and evil; so our thoughts must become like heartbeats and breaths, and this is brought about by the Invocation of the supreme Name. Not that the Invocation must exclude all other thoughts, for we live in the world; but our thoughts must be as it were embedded in the vibration of prayer, and this can take place only with true and noble thoughts.

The ego lives most directly in the brain and the senses, hence in the inward and outward consciousness; in the heart God lives as it were within us—or we live through God—whereas in our breathing we live from the outside; the outer world gives us life through the breath we breathe, and through this breath it lives in us. Yet in the pure, bright air, which fills us from outside and frees us from ourselves, we symbolically meet God and His bliss-giving Spaciousness once again. God is the Inward and the Outward.

The lungs breathe, the brain perceives and thinks, the heart knows and gives life from within, containing indeed the very secret of life; breath is joy in existing, consciousness is alternately accepting and shaping, the heart is outwardly life and inwardly knowing Being, and Being is outwardly the bestower of existence and the giver of life; it is Creator and Preserver. Or again the earth—the breathing breast—is as it were pure existence, existence with its dilating joy; the moon—reflective consciousness—is discriminating, indirect knowledge; the sun—the heart—is pure, direct knowledge: It is Being-Knowledge and therefore also Love, for where Knowledge is not mere separation and confrontation, it is Love or Beatitude. This is why earthly love has something of pure Knowledge in it, and this is why sages often call this Knowledge Love; and not without reason is it commonly said that love dwells in the heart.

The saint lives at once in the motionless Being of the heart and in the peaceful movement of the breath. The Invocation of God is both Being and Vibration; its vehicle is both heart and breath, and the two meet in the consciousness, for the Invocation is movement toward God and also motionlessness in God; it is an inexhaustible stream of light and yet—in its deepest essence—the unique, uncreated Word. The Name-Prayer is beginningless aspiration toward the Infinite and unconditioned, motionless Ipseity; it is ever-anew-resounding, radiant Spaciousness, and it is eternal Being, deeply immersed in itself.

TRANSLATOR'S NOTES

Numbers in **bold** indicate pages in the text to which the following notes refer.

PREFACE

xlix: René *Descartes* (1596–1650) propounded a method of philosophical inquiry based on a systematic doubting of everything except one's own self-consciousness, a method summed up in the phrase *cogito ergo sum* ("I think; therefore I am").

li: *Anselm* (c. 1033–1109), Archbishop of Canterbury, was the first to formulate an ontological argument for the existence of God (*Proslogion*, Ch. 2), whom he defined as "that than which nothing greater can be conceived."

Thomas Aquinas (c. 1225–1274), a giant among the medieval scholastics, offered "five ways" of proving the existence of God in his monumental *Summa Theologica* (Pt. 1, Quest. 2, Art. 3); see translator's notes for Ch. 3, p. 27; Ch. 7, p. 60; Ch. 8, p. 72; Ch. 13, p. 121, note 1; Ch. 15, p. 140, note 2.

lii: For the opposition between *Christianity* and *pagan rationalism*, see Schuon's essay "The Dialogue between Hellenists and Christians" in *Light on the Ancient Worlds*, ed. Deborah Casey (Bloomington, Indiana: World Wisdom, 2006).

CHAPTER 1: THE SENSE OF THE ABSOLUTE IN RELIGIONS

4: "And the *Word* was *made flesh*, and dwelt among us" (John 1:14).

The mystery of Sinai: "When the children of Israel were gone forth out of the land of Egypt, the same day came they into the wilderness of Sinai. . . . And Moses went up unto God, and the Lord called unto him out of the mountain, saying, Thus shalt thou say to the house of Jacob, and tell the children of Israel: Ye have seen what I did unto the Egyptians, and how I bare you on eagles' wings, and brought you unto myself. Now therefore, if ye will obey my voice indeed, and keep my covenant, then ye shall be a peculiar treasure unto me above all people: for all the earth is mine. And ye shall be unto me a kingdom of priests, and an holy nation" (Exod. 19:1–6).

5: "*Closer than your jugular vein*": "We verily created a man and We know what his soul whispereth to him, and We are nearer to him than his jugular vein" (*Sūrah* "*Qāf*" [50]:16).

6: In the author's original French, the term rendered *self-evidence* is *évidence*, which includes the idea of obviousness or indisputability, while at the same time suggesting corroboration or proof.

Note 3: "Jesus said unto them, Verily, verily, I say unto you, *Before Abraham was, I am*" (John 8:58).

The French Islamicist Louis *Massignon* (1883–1962), best known for his magisterial study of the Sufi saint Mansur al-Hallaj, published the article here cited by Schuon, "Christ in the Gospels according to al-Ghazzali," in 1932.

8: "*The soul is all that it knows*": According to *Aristotle* (384–322 B.C.), "The thinking part of the soul, while impassible, must be capable of receiving the form of an object; that is, it must be potentially identical in character with its object without being the object" (*On the Soul*, 3.4); see translator's note for Ch. 7, p. 59.

"Jesus saith unto him, *I am the way, the truth, and the life*: no man cometh unto the Father, but by me" (John 14:6).

9: Note 4: *Cabalists* are Jewish mystics and esotericists.

10: Note 5: *Indra* is the most important of the deities of Vedic Hinduism; in one of the best known of his mythic exploits, Indra entered into battle against the serpent-demon Vritra—in Sanskrit, a "storm-cloud" of ignorance and sloth—who held the rivers of the world in his coils, preventing them from flowing for the benefit of man; when the demon was destroyed, the benefic waters were released, along with the sun and the dawn.

Note 6: Charles *Péguy* (1873–1914) was a French poet and essayist, who sought to combine certain Christian ideas with a Utopian brand of socialism.

11: The *Golden Legend* is a medieval manual compiled by Jacob of Voragine (c. 1230-c. 1298); it features lives of saints and short meditations on the major Christian festivals, organized in accordance with the liturgical year.

Note 8: "*Three Mary Magdalenes*": Roman Catholic tradition associates Mary Magdalene with three distinct figures in the Scriptures: first, "a woman in the city, which was a sinner," who washed Jesus' feet "with tears, and did wipe them with the hairs of her head, and kissed his feet, and anointed them with ointment" (Luke 7:37–38); second, "Mary called Magdalene, out of whom went seven devils" (Luke 8:2); and third, the sister of Lazarus and Martha, who "sat at Jesus' feet, and heard his word," whom Christ commended, saying, "One thing is needful: and Mary hath chosen that good part, which shall not be taken from her" (Luke 10:39, 42; cf. John 11:1–2).

13: Note 11: *Valmiki* is the traditional author of the *Rāmāyana*, the epic story of the *avatāra Rama*; when the syllables of this name are reversed, "Rama" becomes "Mara," the name of a diabolical spirit of pestilence and mortal disease.

14: *The "faith that moves mountains"*: "If ye have faith as a grain of mustard seed, ye shall say unto this mountain, Remove hence to yonder place; and it shall remove; and nothing shall be impossible unto you" (Matt. 17:20).

Note 12: *Prologue to the Gospel of John*: John 1:1–18.

The talk by night with Nicodemus: "There was a man of the Pharisees, named Nicodemus, a ruler of the Jews; the same came to Jesus by night" (John 3:1–2).

"*In my Father's house are many mansions*: if it were not so, I would have told you. I go to prepare a place for you" (John 14:2).

CHAPTER 2: TWO ESOTERICISMS

17: "*God became man that man might become God*": The teaching expressed by this *Patristic formula* is common to a number of early Church Fathers, including Irenaeus (c. 130-c. 200), according to whom "the Son of God became the Son of man so that man, by entering into communion with the Word and thus receiving divine sonship, might become a son of God" (*Against Heresies*, 3:19), and Athanasius (c. 296–373), who wrote, "The Son of God became man in order that we might become God" (*On the Incarnation*, 54:3).

18: Mansur *al-Hallaj* (858–922), the first Sufi martyr, was flayed and crucified by the exoteric authorities as punishment for his mystical—and seemingly blasphemous—pronouncement, *anā 'l-Haqq*, "I am the Truth."

Meister Eckhart (c. 1260–1327), a German Dominican writer whom Schuon regarded as the greatest of Christian metaphysicians and esotericists, was charged by the Church with heresy for teaching that *aliquid est in anima quod est increatum et increabile*, that is, "there is something in the soul that is uncreated and uncreatable," adding that "this is the *Intellect*" (*hoc est Intellectus*) (as quoted in the papal Bull *In agro dominico* [1329]); elsewhere Eckhart writes, "Sometimes I have spoken of a light that is uncreated and not capable of creation and that is in the soul" (Sermon 48); and again, "I have often said that there is a power in the soul that touches neither time nor flesh. . . . If the spirit were always united with God in this power, a man could never grow old" (Sermon 2); see translator's notes for Ch. 5, p. 45; Ch. 15, p. 140, note 2; Ch. 17, p. 160.

"God created man in His own image, *in the image of God* created He him; male and female created He them" (Gen. 1:27).

According to *Meister Eckhart*, all food is Holy Communion for those who are pure in heart.

Clement of Alexandria (c. 150-c. 215), head of the famous Catechetical School of Alexandria and author of a treatise *On Spiritual Perfection*, taught that assimilation to God through *gnosis* is the chief aim of the Christian life and the key to human perfection.

Origen (185–252), a successor to Clement as head of the Catechetical School and the most prolific and influential of the early Church Fathers, is perhaps best known for his doctrine of *apocatastasis* or universal salvation, a doctrine esoterically linked with the recovery, through sleepless attention, of man's primordial unity in God.

According to tradition, *Dionysius the Areopagite* (dated c. 500 by most scholars) was a disciple of Saint Paul (see Acts 17:34) and the author of several important mystical works, including *The Divine Names*, *Mystical Theology*, and *The Celestial Hierarchy*.

Jakob *Boehme* (1575–1624) was a Lutheran spiritual writer and mystic, whose esoteric insights, often couched in Hermetic and alchemical language, can be found in such treatises as *Aurora*, *The Way to Christ*, and *Dialogue of the Supersensual Life*.

Note 1: The Jewish philosopher Baruch *Spinoza* (1632–1677), placed under a ban by his co-religionists because of his pantheism, taught that God is the universal substance of which all things are made.

19: Abu Hamid Muhammad *al-Ghazzali* (1058–1111), widely regarded as one of the greatest religious authorities in Islam, was a jurist and theologian before entering upon the Sufi path; see translator's note for Ch. 7, p. 60.

Muhyi al-Din *Ibn Arabi* (1165–1240), author of such works as *Meccan Revelations* and *Bezels of Wisdom*, was a prolific and profoundly influential Sufi mystic, known in tradition as the *Shaykh al-Akbar*, the "great master."

The Sefer ha-*Zohar*, that is, "The Book of Splendor," published in Spain c. 1285, is an esoteric commentary on the *Torah* and one of the most important texts of *Cabala* or Jewish mysticism.

Ramanuja (1017–c. 1157) was the classic exponent of *Vishishta Advaita*, the Hindu *darshana* or perspective of "qualified non-dualism," in which emphasis is placed on the personal nature of God.

20: *Plato* (427–347 B.C.), greatest of the ancient Greek philosophers, carefully distinguished between reason (*dianoia*) and intellection (*noesis*) in the *Republic*, Bk. 6 (509d–511e); see translator's notes for Ch. 6, p. 52; Ch. 7, p. 59 and p. 64, note 9; Ch. 14, p. 136.

"*It must needs be that offenses come*; but woe to that man by whom the offence cometh" (Matt. 18:7).

The "*unmoved mover*," or motionless mover, is the classic expression of Aristotle (see translator's note for Ch. 1, p. 8) for the divine Principle, as in the *Metaphysics*, 1072b.

21: *Vishnuite*, or Vaishnavite, *Vedānta* is an interpretation of the *Upanishads* by theistic Hindus who equate the personal God Vishnu with the Supreme Reality.

CHAPTER 3: CONCERNING NAIVETÉ

27: According to *Thomas Aquinas* (see translator's notes for Preface, p. li; Ch. 7, p. 60; Ch. 8, p. 72; Ch. 13, p. 121, note 1; Ch. 15, p. 140, note 2), "*An error concerning the creation*, by subjecting it to causes other than God, *engenders a false science of God*, and takes men's minds away from Him, to whom faith seeks to lead them" (*Summa contra Gentiles*, Bk. 2, Ch. 3, Sect. 1).

28: "And the *Word* was *made flesh*, and dwelt among us" (John 1:14).

Publius Cornelius *Tacitus* (c. 55-c. 117) was a Roman historian, whose *De origine et situ Germanorum* (The Origin and Location of the Germans) describes in great detail the German peoples at the end of the first century A.D., contrasting the simplicity of their lives with the sophistication of Rome.

29: The English poet and playwright William *Shakespeare* (1564–1616) places these words in the mouth of the King in *King Henry IV, Part 2* (Act 4, Scene 5, 126–27).

30: For *Plato*, see translator's notes for Ch. 2, p. 20; Ch. 6, p. 52; Ch. 7, p. 59 and p. 64, note 9.

CHAPTER 4: THE MYSTERY OF THE HYPOSTATIC FACE

34: For "*God became man that man might become God*," see translator's note for Ch. 2, p. 17.

Spiritus autem ubi vult spirat: "The wind [or Spirit] bloweth where it listeth" (from the Vulgate translation of the Gospel of John 3:8).

35: "*God alone is good*": "Why callest thou me good? There is none good but one, that is, God" (Matt. 19:17, Mark 10:18; cf. Luke 18:19).

"*My kingdom is not of this world*" (John 18:36).

36: Note 6: "In vain they do worship me, teaching for doctrines the *commandments of men*" (Matt. 15:9; Mark 7:7; cf. Isa. 29:13).

37: Note 8: "*God doeth what He will*" (*Sūrah* "The Family of Imran" [3]:40 passim).

Note 9: *Palamite theology* refers to the teaching of Gregory Palamas (c. 1296–1359), a monk of Mount Athos and archbishop of Thessaloniki, who is perhaps best known for his defense of the theology and spiritual practice of the Hesychast Fathers.

38: Note 11: "*God hath chosen thee (O Mary) and hath purified thee, and hath raised thee above all women*" (*Sūrah* "The Family of Imran" [3]:42).

39: Note 13: *Umar* ibn Abd al-Aziz (c. 682–720) was the second *caliph* of the *Umayyad* dynasty in Sunni Islam, ruling from 717 to 720.

Umar ibn al-Khattab (c. 581–684) was a *companion of the Prophet* Muhammad and the *second caliph* of Islam; when offered the keys to the city of Jerusalem by the Greek bishop Sophronius and invited to pray at the Church of the Holy Sepulcher, Umar declined so as not to endanger its status as a Christian temple.

CHAPTER 5: SUMMARY OF INTEGRAL METAPHYSICS

45: *Augustine* (354–430), Bishop of the North African city of Hippo and author of such classic works as *The City of God* and *Confessions*, was the most influential of the Western Church Fathers.

The *Eckhartian* "*Godhead*" alludes to the teaching of Meister Eckhart (see translator's note for Ch. 2, p. 18; Ch. 15, p. 140, note 2; Ch. 17, p. 160), who distinguished the personal God (*Gott*) from the transpersonal Godhead (*Gottheit*).

46: According to the Definition of Chalcedon, promulgated by the fourth of the Ecumenical Councils (451 A.D.), Christ the *Logos* is at once "*true man and true God.*"

47: Note 1: *The trinity which the Koran attributes to Christianity*: "They surely disbelieve who say: Lo! God is the third of three. . . . The Messiah, son of Mary, was no other than a messenger, messengers (the like of whom) had passed away before him. And his mother was a saintly woman. And they both used to eat (earthly) food" (*Sūrah* "The Table Spread" [5]:73, 75).

49: "For *where your treasure is, there will your heart be also*" (Luke 12:34).

CHAPTER 6: CONSEQUENCES FLOWING FROM THE MYSTERY OF SUBJECTIVITY

51: For *the Cartesian cogito ergo sum*, see translator's note for Preface, p. xlix.

"*In the beginning* God created the heaven and the earth. And the earth was without form, and void; and darkness was upon the face of the deep. And *the Spirit* of God moved upon the face of the waters" (Gen. 1:1–2).

52: According to *Plato* (see translator's notes for Ch. 2, p. 20; Ch. 7, p. 59 and p. 64, note 9; Ch. 14, p. 136), "seeking and learning are in fact nothing but recollection" (*Meno*, 81d), for all knowledge is the result of an *archetypal remembrance.*

53: "It must needs be that *offenses come*; but woe to that man by whom the offence cometh" (Matt. 18:7).

55: "*I am black, but beautiful*, O ye daughters of Jerusalem, as the tents of Kedar, as the curtains of Solomon" (Song of Sol. 1:5).

Note 5: The pronouncement "*Know thyself*," carved into the lintel of Apollo's Temple at Delphi, is the most famous of the *Delphic* oracles or *mysteries.*

CHAPTER 7: TRACING THE NOTION OF PHILOSOPHY

59: For Muhyi al-Din *Ibn Arabi*, see translator's note for Ch. 2, p. 19.

Abd al-Karim al-*Jili* (c. 1365–c. 1412) systematized the teachings of Ibn Arabi, notably in his most important work, *The Universal Man*, which is concerned with both cosmological and metaphysical questions.

Pythagoras of Samos (c. 569–c. 475 B.C.), often credited with coining the word "philosophy," was one of the greatest sages of ancient Greece, teaching a doctrine that is at once philosophical, mathematical, astronomical, and musical.

Heraclitus (fl. 500 B.C.), perhaps best known for his aphorism that "one cannot step twice into the same river," believed nonetheless that there is a single, underlying, and unchanging order in the cosmos, which he called the *Logos*; see translator's note for Ch. 9, p. 83.

Plato (see translator's notes for Ch. 2, p. 20; Ch. 6, p. 52; Ch. 14, p. 136) taught that the things of this physical and sensory world are subject to belief or opinion alone, whereas true *knowledge* pertains to the changeless world of the *Ideas* or Forms.

According to *Aristotle* (see translator's note for Ch. 1, p. 8), to know a thing is to understand it in light of its *causes*: material, efficient, formal, and final (*Physics*, 194b).

According to *Solomon*, wisdom "is a treasure unto men that never faileth: which they that use become the friends of God, being commended for the gifts that come from learning" (Wisd. of Sol. 7:14).

"*Fear of God*": "The fear of the Lord is the beginning of wisdom: a good understanding have all they that do his commandments" (Ps. 111:10; cf. Prov. 1:7, 9:10 passim).

60: *Thomas* Aquinas (see translator's notes for Preface, p. li; Ch. 3, p. 27; Ch. 8, p. 72; Ch. 13, p. 121, note 1; Ch. 15, p. 140, note 2) followed Aristotle in teaching that "the principle of knowledge is in the senses" (*Summa Theologica*, Pt. 1, Quest. 84, Art. 6).

Abu Hamid Muhammad *al-Ghazzali* (see translator's note for Ch. 2, p. 19) wrote the *Tahāfut al-Falāsifah*, "The Incoherence of the Philosophers," a work accentuating the inadequacies of reason and the necessity of revelation and mystical knowledge.

Note 2: Hermann *Türck* (1856–1933) was the author of *Der geniale Mensch*, "The Man of Genius" (1903).

61: *Ibn al-Arif* (1088–1141), an Andalusian Sufi master, is best known for his writings on the science of the virtues.

62: *Plotinus* (c. 205–270), founder of the Neo-Platonic school, endeavored to synthesize the teachings of *Plato* and *Aristotle* in his monumental *Enneads*, a collection of discourses compiled by his disciple Porphyry.

Note 4: Ibn Arabi's *Fusūs al-Hikam*, or "Bezels of Wisdom," is a study of the Koranic prophets from the point of view of the spiritual types they exemplify.

63: *One cannot testify to great truths except by the Holy Spirit*: "No man can say that Jesus is the Lord, but by the Holy Spirit" (1 Cor. 12:3).

64: In the cosmology of the pre-Socratic teacher *Empedocles* (c. 492–432 B.C.), the universe is a tapestry woven from four primary elements, fire, air, water, and earth (see Schuon's footnote 7), which are repeatedly brought together and then dispersed by two fundamental forces, love and strife.

Muhammad ibn Abd Allah *Ibn Masarrah* (883–931), an early Andalusian mystic and Neo-Platonic philosopher, taught that the visible world and its creatures result from the creative descent of the divine Will into primordial matter or "dust" (*al-habā'*).

Note 9: *Plato* wrote, "There does not exist, nor will there ever exist, any treatise of mine dealing therewith [i.e., with "the subject which I seriously study"]. For it does not at all admit of verbal expression like other studies, but as a result of continued application to the subject itself and communion therewith, it is brought to birth in the soul on a sudden, as light that is kindled by a leaping spark, and thereafter it nourishes itself" (*Letter VII*, 341d).

Synesius of Cyrene (c. 370–c. 414), who studied in Alexandria under the celebrated Neo-Platonic mathematician and philosopher Hypatia, was the Christian bishop of Ptolemais.

Note 10: In his introduction to *The Transcendent Unity of Religions* (first published in 1948 as *De l'unité transcendante des religions*), Schuon explained: "This book is founded on a doctrine that is metaphysical in the most precise meaning of the word and cannot by any means be described as philosophical. Such a distinction may appear unwarrantable to those who are accustomed to regarding metaphysics as a branch of philosophy, but the practice of linking the two together in this manner, although it can be traced back to Aristotle and the Scholastic writers who followed him, merely shows that all philosophy suffers from certain limitations which, even in the most favorable instances such as those just quoted, exclude a completely adequate appreciation of metaphysics. In reality the transcendent character of metaphysics makes it independent of any purely human mode of thought. In order to define clearly the difference between the two modes in question, it may be said that philosophy proceeds from reason, which is a purely individual faculty, whereas metaphysics proceeds exclusively from the Intellect" (trans. Peter Townsend [Wheaton, Illinois: The Theosophical Publishing House, 1993], p. xxix).

65: The term *Pyrrhonic* applies to the *logic* of Pyrrho (c. 360–c. 270 B.C.), a Greek skeptic, who maintained that all knowledge, including the evidence of the senses, is uncertain.

Koranic story of the initial pact between human souls and God: "And (remember) when thy Lord brought forth from the Children of Adam, from their reins, their seed, and made them testify of themselves, (saying): Am I not your Lord? They said:

Yea, verily. We testify. (That was) lest ye should say at the Day of Resurrection: Lo! of this we were unaware" (*Sūrah* "The Heights" [7]:172).

"*Whoso knoweth his soul knoweth his Lord*" (*hadīth*).

66: Note 11: *Ananda Coomaraswamy* (1877–1947), for many years the curator of Indian art in the Boston Museum of Fine Arts and one of the founding figures of the perennialist school, was the author of numerous books and articles on art, religion, and metaphysics.

"*Unto you your religion, and unto me mine*" (*Sūrah* "The Disbelievers" [109]:6).

67: "*Beauty is the splendor of the true*" is a fundamental axiom of Schuon's perspective, an axiom he attributes to *Plato*.

For *Descartes*, see translator's note for Preface, p. xlix.

For *Pyrrho*, see translator's note above, p. 65.

CHAPTER 8: UNDERSTANDING AND BELIEVING

72: "*Obscure merit*" *of faith*: According to Thomas Aquinas (see translator's notes for Preface, p. li; Ch. 3, p. 27; Ch. 7, p. 60; Ch. 13, p. 121, note 1; Ch. 15, p. 140, note 2), "The merit of faith consists in this, that man through obedience assents to things he does not see" (*Summa Theologica*, Pt. 3, Quest. 7, Art. 3).

Taqi al-Din *ibn Taimiyyah* (1263–1328) set himself in opposition to Sufis, Islamic philosophers, and other Muslims who did not agree with his literalistic interpretations of the Koran and the *sunnah*.

Note 3: *Abraham and Mary had the merit of great faith*: "By faith Abraham, when he was called to go out into a place which he should after receive for an inheritance, obeyed; and he went out, not knowing whither he went. . . . By faith Abraham, when he was tried, offered up Isaac; and he that had received the promises offered up his only begotten son" (Heb. 11:8, 17); "And Mary said, Behold the handmaid of the Lord; be it unto me according to thy word" (Luke 1:38).

73: Abu al-Hasan al-*Ashari* (873–935), one of the most important of the early Muslim theologians, insisted that Koranic descriptions of God are to be understood literally and not metaphorically, but that it is impossible to know in exactly what way they pertain to God, who is utterly beyond human understanding.

Note 5: *Al-samā᾿ al-dunyā* is a Koranic expression signifying the terrestrial firmament.

75: Note 8: "*There is no lustral water like unto knowledge*" (*Bhagavad Gītā*, 4:38).

76: *The famous Verse of Light*: "God is the Light of the heavens and the earth. The similitude of His light is a niche wherein is a lamp. The lamp is in a glass. The glass is as it were a shining star. (This lamp is) kindled from a blessed tree, an olive neither of the East nor of the West, whose oil *would almost glow forth* (*of itself*) *though no fire touched it.* Light upon light, God guideth unto His light whom He will. And God speaketh to mankind in allegories, for God is the Knower of all things" (*Sūrah* "Light" [24]:35).

Note 10: According to Hindu tradition, the sacred waters of *the pool Manikarnika,* which lies in close proximity to the river *Ganges* in the city of Benares, are the perspiration that flowed from Vishnu when he finished creating the world.

77: "And the third day there was a *marriage in Cana* of Galilee. . . . And when they wanted wine, the mother of Jesus saith unto him, They have no wine. . . . And there were set there six waterpots of stone. . . . Jesus saith unto them, Fill the waterpots with water. And they filled them up to the brim. And he saith unto them, Draw out now, and bear unto the governor of the feast. And they bare it. When the ruler of the feast had tasted the water that was made wine, and knew not whence it was (but the servants which drew the water knew), the governor of the feast called the bridegroom, and he saith unto him, Every man at the beginning doth set forth good wine; and when men have well drunk, then that which is worse: but thou hast kept the good wine until now" (John 2:1–10).

79: For *Ibn Arabi,* see translator's note for Ch. 2, p. 19.

CHAPTER 9: MAN IN THE UNIVERSE

83: Πάντα ῥεῖ (*panta rhei*), "all things flow," was the teaching of the Greek pre-Socratic philosopher *Heraclitus* (see translator's note for Ch. 7, p. 59).

84: In the author's original French, the term rendered "evidence" in the phrase *the evidence is in the Intellect* is *évidence,* which includes the idea of obviousness or self-evidence, while at the same time suggesting corroboration or proof.

86: The English poet and playwright William *Shakespeare* (1564–1616) places these words in the mouth of Prospero in *The Tempest* (Act 4, Scene 1, 156–57).

87: Note 5: The German writer Johann Wolfgang von *Goethe* (1749–1832) has Mephistopheles (the devil) say, "I am the spirit that negates. / And rightly so, for all that comes to be / Deserves to perish wretchedly; / 'Twere better nothing would begin. / Thus everything that your terms sin, / Destruction, evil represent— / That is my proper element" (*Faust,* Pt. 1).

Note 7: "*Mistaking a rope for a snake*": "One who is overpowered by ignorance mistakes a thing for what it is not: It is the absence of discrimination that causes one to mistake a rope for a snake. . . . It is the mistaking of transitory things as real that constitutes bondage" (Shankara, *Viveka-Cūdāmani* [The Crest Jewel of Discrimination], 138).

CHAPTER 10: THE MESSAGE OF THE HUMAN BODY

91: "*Made in the image of God*": "God created man in His own image, in the image of God created He him; male and female created He them" (Gen. 1:27).

92: Note 2: "There appeared a *chariot of fire*, and horses of fire, and parted them both asunder; and *Elijah* went up by a whirlwind into heaven" (2 Kings 2:11).

"And when he had spoken these things, while they beheld, he was taken up; and a *cloud* received him out of their sight" (Acts 1:9).

94: *Lalla Yogishwari* was a fourteenth-century Kashmiri poet and saint; Schuon often quoted the following lines from her poetry: "My guru spake to me but one precept. He said unto me, 'From without enter thou the inmost part.' That to me became a rule and a precept, and therefore naked began I to dance."

Note 6: According to the *Brihadāranyaka Upanishad* (2.4.1ff), *Maitreyi* became the wife of the sage *Yajnavalkya* because of her great desire for his spiritual teaching and with the consent of his *other wife*, Katyayani.

Apala and *Visvavara* are among the women sages honored by the Hindu tradition as ancient seers of the *Vedas*.

The *Yoga Vasishtha* tells the story of the prince *Shikhidhwaja*, who happened upon the maiden *Chudala* while he was hunting in the forest; overcome by her beauty and intelligence, he promptly asked her to be his wife. Not until many years later, having conquered the kingdom but unable to conquer his mind, did he discover that she was a fully realized *jīvan-mukta*, utterly indifferent to the wealth and worldly power he had so lavishly bestowed on her.

96: Note 14: For *Tacitus*, see translator's note for Ch. 3, p. 28.

98: *The refusal of Lucifer to prostrate before Adam*: "And when We said unto the angels: Prostrate yourselves before Adam, they fell prostrate, all save Iblis [the Koranic name for Lucifer]. He demurred through pride, and so became a disbeliever" (*Sūrah* "The Cow" [2]:34).

Note 17: The *Talmud* is a body of traditional Jewish writings and commentaries based on the oral law given to Moses on Sinai, second in authority only to the *Torah*.

99: The *Rāmāyana*, a Hindu epic attributed to the sage Valmiki, recounts the story of Rama, the seventh *avatāra* of Vishnu.

CHAPTER 11: MAN AND CERTAINTY

103: "*One thing* is *needful*: and Mary hath chosen that good part, which shall not be taken from her" (Luke 10:39, 42; cf. John 11:1–2).

104: "*Those who have ears to hear*": "Who hath ears to hear, let him hear" (Matt. 13:9 passim).

CHAPTER 12: UNIVERSAL ESCHATOLOGY

109: "*Human birth is difficult to attain*": According to the advaitic sage Shankara (788–820), whom Schuon regarded as the greatest of Hindu metaphysicians,

"Three things are difficult to achieve and are attained only by the grace of God: human birth, the desire for liberation, and finding refuge with a great master" (*Viveka-Cūdāmani* [The Crest Jewel of Discrimination], 3).

Note 2: "*Consequences Flowing from the Mystery of Subjectivity*": See Ch. 6 above.

110: Note 4: The Italian poet *Dante* Alighieri (1265–1321) places his encounter with *the sages and heroes of antiquity*, "who in that Limbo dwelt suspended" (*Inferno*, Canto IV:45), along the "border" (*limbum*) of the pit of hell; see translator's note for Appendix, p. 220.

111: "*In my Father's house are many mansions*: if it were not so, I would have told you. I go to prepare a place for you" (John 14:2).

"I believe in the Holy Spirit, the holy Catholic Church, the *communion of saints*, the forgiveness of sins, the resurrection of the body, and the life everlasting" (Apostles' Creed, Art. 3).

Note 7: "Gardens of Eden, which the Beneficent hath promised to His slaves in the Unseen. Lo! His promise is ever sure of fulfillment. They hear therein no idle talk, but only Peace; and therein they have *nourishment morning and evening*" (*Sūrah* "Mary" [19]:61–62).

113: "Enter ye in at the strait gate: *for wide is the gate, and broad is the way, that leadeth to destruction, and many there be which go in thereat*: because strait is the gate, and narrow is the way, which leadeth unto life, and few there be that find it" (Matt. 7:13–14).

114: Note 14: "All the days of *Enoch* were three hundred sixty and five years: And *Enoch* walked with God: and he was not; for God took him" (Gen. 5:23–24).

"Behold, there appeared a chariot of fire, and horses of fire, and parted them both asunder; and *Elijah* went up by a whirlwind into heaven" (2 Kings 2:11).

"When [*Christ*] had spoken these things, while they beheld, he was taken up; and a cloud received him out of their sight" (Acts 1:9).

It is a dogma of the Roman Catholic Church that "the Immaculate Mother of God, the ever *Virgin* Mary, having completed the course of her earthly life, was assumed body and soul into heaven" (Encyclical of Pope Pius XII, *Munificentissimus Deus*, 1 November 1950).

116: For *the inscription on the temple at Delphi*, see translator's note for Ch. 6, p. 55, note 5.

"An invisible and subtle essence is the Spirit of the whole universe. That is Reality. That is Truth. *Thou art That* [*Tat tvam asi*]" (*Chāndogya Upanishad*, 7.6).

Note 18: *Thales* of Miletus (c. 624–c. 547 B.C.) was one of the Seven Sages of ancient Greece.

According to *Socrates* (c. 470–399 B.C.), his friend Chaerephon once went to Delphi to ask the god Apollo "whether there was anyone wiser" than Socrates, and he received the answer that there was no one, an answer which set Socrates on his lifelong path of cross-examining all the purportedly wise men he met, and thence to the conclusion that "the wisest of men is he who has realized, like Socrates, that in respect of wisdom he is really worthless" (*Apology*, 21a, 23b).

CHAPTER 13: THE QUESTION OF FORMS IN ART

121: Note 1: "*Art is associated with knowledge*": According to *Thomas Aquinas* (see translator's notes for Preface, p. li; Ch. 3, p. 27; Ch. 7, p. 60; Ch. 8, p. 72; Ch. 15, p. 140, note 2), "The knowledge of the artist is the cause of the things made by his art inasmuch as the artist works by his intellect" (*Summa Theologica*, Pt. 1, Quest. 14, Art. 8).

Note 2: *René Guénon* (1886–1951), a French metaphysician and prolific scholar of religions, was one of the formative authorities of the perennialist school and a frequent contributor to the traditionalist journal *Études traditionnelles* ("Traditional Studies").

For *Muhyi al-Din ibn Arabi*, see translator's note for Ch. 2, p. 19.

"*And the Word* was *made flesh*, and dwelt among us" (John 1:14).

122: Like other medieval Cistercian authorities, *Bernard* of Clairvaux (1090–1153) insisted that the churches of his monastic order should be plain in character and that vestments and ornaments should not be made of precious materials; see translator's note for Ch. 15, p. 144, note 9.

Note 3: *Louis XV* (1710–1774), the king of France from 1743 until his death, led a scandalous and ostentatious personal life and contributed greatly to the decline of royal authority.

125: Note 7: For *Ananda K. Coomaraswamy*, see translator's note for Ch. 7, p. 66, note 11.

130: "Verily I say unto you, Except ye be converted, and become *as little children*, ye shall not enter into the kingdom of heaven" (Matt. 18:3).

"Behold, I send you forth as sheep in the midst of wolves: be ye therefore wise as serpents, and *harmless as doves*" (Matt. 10:16).

The *Second Council of Nicea* (787) defended the painting and veneration of icons of Christ, the Mother of God, and the saints, declaring "with all certitude and accuracy that the venerable and holy images, in painting and mosaic and other fit materials, should be set forth in the holy churches of God . . . and given due salutation and honorable reverence." Literally, the Latin phrase cited by the author means: "The ordering and arrangement of the things of our Fathers is not for the artist, for the art alone is his."

132: *John Damascene*, or John of Damascus (c. 675–c. 749), an important Church Father and the author of numerous commentaries, hymns, and apologetic writings, was a vigorous defender of the veneration of icons, composing three discourses on the subject during the height of the iconoclastic controversy.

CHAPTER 14: THE LIBERATING PASSAGE

136: "*Made in the image of God*": "God created man in His own image, in the image of God created He him; male and female created He them" (Gen. 1:27).

According to *Plato* (see translator's notes for Ch. 2, p. 20; Ch. 6, p. 52; Ch. 7, p. 59 and p. 64, note 9), "The candidate for initiation into the mysteries of Love must begin, when he is young, by applying himself to the contemplation of physical beauty, and if he is properly directed by his guide, he will first fall in love with one particular beautiful person. Later he will understand how nearly related the beauty of any one body is to the beauty of any other and will see that if he is to devote himself to loveliness of form it would be absurd to deny that the beauty of each and every body is in this sense the same. Having reached this point, he must set himself to be the lover of every lovely body, overcoming the intensity of his passion for one particular body, because he will realize that such a passion is beneath him and of small account" (*Symposium*, 210b).

CHAPTER 15: AN ELEMENTARY CRITERIOLOGY OF CELESTIAL APPARITIONS

140: The Latin phrase *quaerite et invenietis*, "seek, and ye shall find," appears in the Vulgate translation of the Gospel of Matthew: "Ask, and it shall be given you; seek, and ye shall find; knock, and it shall be opened unto you" (Matt. 7:7).

Note 1: The Latin phrase *credo ut intelligam*, "I believe so that I may understand," was used by Saint Anselm (see translator's note for Preface, p. li), who prefaced his ontological argument for the existence of God (in the *Proslogion*) with the words: "I do not seek to understand so that I may believe; but I believe so that I may understand."

Note 2: "*Heresy resides in the will and not in the intelligence*": According to Thomas Aquinas (see translator's notes for Preface, p. li; Ch. 3, p. 27; Ch. 7, p. 60; Ch. 8, p. 72; Ch. 13, p. 121, note 1), "Heresy is a species of unbelief," and "unbelief resides in the will and not in the intellect" (*Summa Theologica*, Pt. 2-2, Quest. 11, Art. 1; Quest. 10, Art. 2). In defending himself against charges of heresy, Meister Eckhart (see translator's notes for Ch. 2, p. 18; Ch. 5, p. 45; Ch. 17, p. 160) responded, "I can be in error, but I cannot be a heretic, for the first belongs to the intellect, the second to the will."

142: *Hesychasm* refers to the spiritual practices of Orthodox Christian monastics, notably those of Mount Athos, whose aim is to reach a state of *hesychia*—inner stillness—through the use of the Jesus Prayer or other "prayer of the heart."

Note 4: *Sister* Mary *Consolata* (1903–1946), an Italian Capuchin nun, is best known for her "act of love," which she is said to have received from Christ himself and which consists of the mantric formula, "Jesus, Mary, I love you! Save souls!"

143: "*Behold, the angel of the Lord appeared unto him in a dream, saying, Joseph, thou son of David, fear not to take unto thee Mary thy wife. . . . Then Joseph being raised from sleep did as the angel of the Lord had bidden him*" (Matt. 1:20, 24).

Note 5: Immanuel *Kant* (1724–1804), founder of the "critical" philosophy, insisted that man's knowledge is limited to the domain of sensible objects and that the idea of God is no more than a postulate of reason having no objective certainty.

Swami *Siddheswarananda* (1897–1957) was a monk of the Ramakrishna Order and a popularizing writer and lecturer on religious ecumenism.

Note 7: For *Shankara*, see translator's note for Ch. 12, p. 109.

143–44: "*Behold, the angel of the Lord appeareth to Joseph in a dream, saying, Arise, and take the young child and his mother, and flee into Egypt. . . . When he arose, he took the young child and his mother by night, and departed into Egypt*" (Matt. 2:13–14).

144: Note 9: Standing before a statue of the Blessed Virgin in which she was depicted nursing (*lactatio*) the Child Jesus, *Bernard* of Clairvaux (see translator's note for Ch. 13, p. 122) repeatedly prayed, "Show that you are a mother"; according to tradition the statue miraculously came alive, and milk came forth from the Virgin's breast.

145: "He that loveth not knoweth not God; for *God is love*" (1 John 4:8).

The Latin phrase *a fructibus eorum cognoscetis eos*, "by their fruits ye shall know them," appears in the Vulgate translation of the Gospel of Matthew: "Ye shall know them by their fruits. Do men gather grapes of thorns, or figs of thistles? Even so every good tree bringeth forth good fruit; but a corrupt tree bringeth forth evil fruit" (Matt. 7:16–17).

CHAPTER 16: THE SYMBOLISM OF THE HOURGLASS

148: "Enter ye in at the *strait gate*: for wide is the gate, and broad is the way, that leadeth to destruction, and many there be which go in thereat: Because strait is the gate, and narrow is the way, which leadeth unto life, and few there be that find it" (Matt. 7:13–14; cf. Luke 13:24).

"Behold, the *kingdom* of God is *within you*" (Luke 17:21).

The "*motionless mover*," or unmoved mover, is the classic expression of Aristotle (see translator's note for Ch. 1, p. 8) for the divine Principle, as in the *Metaphysics*, 1072b.

"*I sleep, but my heart waketh*" (Song of Sol. 5:2).

Note 3: The *Theologia Germanica* ("German Theology") is an anonymous mystical treatise of the late fourteenth century that follows in the tradition of Dionysius the Areopagite (see translator's note for Ch. 2, p. 18) as well as sharing the same essential vision as that of Meister Eckhart (see translator's notes for Ch. 2, p. 18; Ch. 45, p. 5; Ch. 15, p. 140, note 2).

150: "*No man can serve two masters*: for either he will hate the one, and love the other; or else he will hold to the one, and despise the other. Ye cannot serve God and mammon" (Matt. 6:24).

"Blessed are the *poor in spirit*: for theirs is the kingdom of heaven" (Matt. 5:3).

152: Note 9: "Take heed that ye despise not *one of these little ones*; for I say unto you, That in heaven their angels do always behold the face of my Father which is in heaven" (Matt. 18:10).

CHAPTER 17: MODES OF SPIRITUAL REALIZATION

155: *There are as many paths to God as there are human souls* (*Al-turūqu ila'Llāhi ka-nufusi bani Adam*) is a traditional saying often cited in Sufi circles.

156: "*Inasmuch as ye have done it unto one of the least of these my brethren, ye have done it unto me*" (Matt. 25:40; cf. Matt. 25:45).

158: *Shankarian advaitism* is the "non-dual" doctrine of Shankara (see translator's note for Ch. 12, p. 109).

For *Ramanuja*, see translator's note for Ch. 2, p. 19.

Note 4: *Ramakrishna* (1834–1886), a devotee of the Hindu Goddess Kali, was one of the best-known Hindu saints of modern times.

Note 5: In Hindu tradition, *Radha* was one of the *gopīs*, or cowherd girls, who loved *Krishna*, the eighth of the incarnations of Vishnu, and she was the one whom he especially loved in return; though not an *avatāra*, she is understood to be the *shakti*, or radiant power, of Krishna and an embodiment of *Ānanda*.

Note 6: Swami *Vivekananda* (1863–1902), a disciple of Ramakrishna, was greatly influenced by the ideas of such modern Western social theorists as John Stuart Mill, which led to his joining the *Brahmo Samāj*, a nineteenth-century Hindu reform movement. Concerning the relationship between Ramakrishna and Vivekananda, Schuon writes elsewhere, "The insufficiently doctrinal character of Ramakrishnian *jnāna* and his lack of discernment with regard to conceptual forms—which did not seem to exist for him—then his ill-defined and somewhat imprudent universalism, and finally the dynamic and sentimental tendencies of Vivekananda: All this would have been free from danger within the framework of a Hinduism that was whole, closed, free from fissures; the environment would have rectified, neutralized, and counterbalanced whatever there might have been that was 'subjective,' 'fragile,' or 'hazardous' in certain attitudes of [Ramakrishna]. Furthermore an integral or total Hinduism would not have allowed Vivekananda to open his mind to Western influences, which were unknown and incomprehensible to Ramakrishna but which stimulated in the disciple exactly those tendencies whose development had at times been feared by the master. . . . Quite against his inclination and moreover quite unsuspectingly [Ramakrishna] thus found himself at the crossroads of two worlds between which there was no common measure. His altogether primordial simplicity and candor, even his modesty, were not 'up to'—we ought to say 'down to'—dealing with these conditions; he grasped in them neither the principle nor the complexity" (*Spiritual Perspectives and Human Facts*, ed. James S. Cutsinger [Bloomington, Indiana: World Wisdom, 2007], 125–26).

Menander (*Milinda*) is thought to have been a second- or first-century B.C. king of the Eastern Punjab; he is known to Buddhist tradition because of his debate with *the Buddhist monk* Nagasena, who successfully countered each of the eighty-two problems the king had posed, thus converting him to Buddhism.

160: From the "Table Talk" of *Meister Eckhart* (see translator's notes for Ch. 2, p. 18; Ch. 5, p. 45; Ch. 15, p. 140, note 2); Eckhart adds elsewhere, "God speaks the truth and swears by himself, who is the Truth. If God were to fall short of His Word, His Truth, He would fall short of His divinity and would not be God, for He is His Word, His Truth" (*The Book of Divine Consolation*, Sect. 2).

161: "My kingdom is *not of this world*" (John 18:36).

For *Shankaracharya* (Shankara), see translator's note for Ch. 12, p. 109.

Note 7: The Latin phrase *nihil est in intellectu quod non prius fuerit in sensu*, "nothing is in the intellect that was not before in the senses," expresses the fundamental conviction of empiricists such as John Locke (1632–1704).

Note 8: "*Love thy neighbor as thyself*" (Matt. 19:19, Matt. 22:39, Mark 12:31; cf. Luke 10:27).

163: "*Hardened heart*": "He hath blinded their eyes, and hardened their heart; that they should not see with their eyes, nor understand with their heart, and be converted, and I should heal them" (John 12:40; cf. Exod. 7:13, Deut. 2:30, 2 Chron. 36:13, Isa. 63:17 passim); "For the hardness of your heart [Moses] wrote you this precept" (Mark 10:5).

CHAPTER 18: THE ANONYMITY OF THE VIRTUES

165: For *Augustine*, see translator's note for Ch. 5, p. 45.

The *Curé d'Ars* was Jean-Baptiste Marie Vianney (1786–1859), a parish priest and much sought after confessor and spiritual father from the French village of Ars, who was widely known for his gift of reading souls.

"But *when thou doest alms, let not thy left hand know what thy right hand doeth*" (Matt. 6:3).

"*Made in the image of God*": "God created man in His own image, in the image of God created He him; male and female created He them" (Gen. 1:27).

167: "And God said unto Moses, *I am that I am*: and He said, Thus shalt thou say unto the children of Israel, I AM hath sent me unto you" (Exod. 3:14).

168: Note 2: The *Magnificat,* a hymn of praise sung by the Blessed Virgin after she had been greeted by her cousin Elizabeth as the mother of Christ, is so named because of the first word of the hymn in the Vulgate text: "And Mary said, My soul doth magnify the Lord [*Magnificat anima mea Dominum*]. And my spirit hath rejoiced in God my Savior. For He hath regarded the low estate of His handmaiden: for, behold, from henceforth all generations shall call me blessed. For He that is mighty hath done to me great things; and holy is His name. And His mercy is on them that fear Him from generation to generation. He hath shown strength with His arm; He hath scattered the proud in the imagination of their hearts. He hath put down the mighty from their seats, and exalted them of low degree. He hath filled the hungry with good things; and the rich He hath sent empty away. He hath helped His servant Israel, in remembrance of His mercy. As he spake to our fathers, to Abraham, and to his seed for ever" (Luke 1:46–55).

Christ's *Sermon on the Mount* is recorded in the Gospel of Matthew (Chapters 5–7) and includes such *fulminations* as the following: "Whosoever is angry with his brother without a cause shall be in danger of the judgment . . . and whosoever shall say, Thou fool, shall be in danger of hell fire" (5:22); "If thy right eye offend thee, pluck it out, and cast it from thee: for it is profitable for thee that one of thy members should perish, and not that thy whole body should be cast into hell" (5:29); "And when thou prayest, thou shalt not be as the hypocrites are: for they love to pray standing in the synagogues and in the corners of the streets, that they may be seen of men. Verily I say unto you, They have their reward" (6:5); "The light of the body is the eye: if therefore thine eye be single, thy whole body shall be full of light. But if thine eye be evil, thy whole body shall be full of darkness. If therefore the light that is in thee be darkness, how great is that darkness!" (6:22–23); "Enter ye in at the strait gate: for wide is the gate, and broad is the way, that leadeth to destruction, and many there be which go in thereat" (7:13); "Every tree that bringeth not forth good fruit is hewn down, and cast into the fire" (7:19); "Many will say to me in that day, Lord, Lord, have we not prophesied in thy name? and in thy name have cast out devils? and in thy name done many wonderful works? And then will I profess unto them, I never knew you: depart from me, ye that work iniquity" (7:23).

CHAPTER 19: THE NATURE AND FUNCTION OF THE SPIRITUAL MASTER

172: "I am the way, the truth, and the life: *no man cometh unto the Father, but by me*" (John 14:6).

"*No one will meet Allah who has not met His Messenger*" (*hadīth*).

"He that is not with me is against me; and *he that gathereth not with me scattereth abroad*" (Matt. 12:30).

"I am the vine, ye are the branches: He that abideth in me, and I in him, the same bringeth forth much fruit: for *without me ye can do nothing*" (John 15:5).

"*Ye will not, unless Allah willeth*. Lo! Allah is All-Knowing, All-Wise" (*Sūrah* "Man" [76]:30).

Note 1: "*Put on the new man*, which after God is created in righteousness and true holiness" (Eph. 4:24); "Lie not one to another, seeing that ye have put off the old man with his deeds; and have *put on the new man*, which is renewed in knowledge after the image of Him that created him" (Col. 3:9–10).

174: Note 5: For *Shankara*, see translator's note for Ch. 12, p. 109.

176: *Ibrahim ibn Adham* (d. c. 790), born into a royal family at Balkh in Central Asia, renounced his life of worldly wealth and power; he is credited with having made the first Sufi classification of the stages of the ascetical life.

"*Even from a Saracen*": The *Russian pilgrim* is told by a hermit, "The holy Fathers assure us that if with faith and right intention one questions even a Saracen, he can speak words of value to us. If on the other hand one asks for instruction from a Prophet, without faith and a righteous purpose, then even he will not satisfy us" (*The Way of a Pilgrim: The Pilgrim Continues His Way*, Ch. 7).

"*Prostrates himself at the feet of Govinda*": In the Hindu tradition, Govinda, literally "cow-finder," is a devotional epithet for either the God Vishnu or the Lord Krishna, the eighth of Vishnu's *avatāras*.

177: "And the *Word* was *made flesh*, and dwelt among us" (John 1:14).

Benedict of Nursia (c. 480–c. 550), the father of Western monasticism, drew on the sayings of the Desert Fathers and the writings of John Cassian in composing a short *Rule* for the communities of monks in his charge, a rule that came in time to define the spiritual practices of the Order associated with his name.

According to tradition, *John*, the disciple "whom Jesus loved" (John 13:23) and whom he instructed to care for the Blessed Virgin (John 19:26), is the author of the Fourth Gospel, the Apocalypse, and the three Epistles that bear his name.

178: For *Ramanuja*, see translator's note for Ch. 2, p. 19.

Although the works of *Confucius* (c. 552–479 B.C.) are often said to be of a purely ethical nature, this *Chinese revealer* regarded his teachings as fully religious in character, emphasizing that "Heaven is the author of the virtue that is in me" (*Analects*, Bk. 7, Ch. 22).

Nagarjuna (c. 150–250), founder of the *Mādhyamaka* or "middle way" school of Buddhism, is regarded by the *Mahāyāna* tradition as a "second Buddha"; he is best known for his doctrine of *shūnyatā*, or "emptiness," and for teaching that *Nirvāna* and *Samsāra* are essentially identical.

Padma Sambhava (eighth century A.D.), invited to Tibet by King Trisong Detsen on the strength of his reputation for magical and dialectical prowess, is credited with subduing the demons of that land and establishing Buddhism as the dominant religion of Tibet.

Kobo Daishi—the "great teacher Kobo," the posthumous title of the Japanese monk and scholar Kukai (774–835)—brought the Shingon, or esoteric, school of Buddhism from China to Japan.

Note 12: *Francis of Assisi* (1181/2–1226), founder of the Order of Friars Minor, or Franciscans, interpreted the admonition of Christ to abandon all things for his sake (Matt. 10:7–19) as a personal call to poverty and holiness; Francis was noted for bearing the stigmata of Christ.

For *Bernard* of Clairvaux, see translator's notes for Ch. 13, p. 122 and Ch. 15, p. 144, note 9.

Note 13: For *Ramakrishna*, see translator's note for Ch. 17, p. 158, note 4.

CHAPTER 20: THE STATIONS OF WISDOM

182: Note 2: The *Philokalia* is a collection of ascetical and mystical writings by spiritual masters of the Christian East, compiled by Saint Nikodimos of the Holy Mountain (1748–1809) and Saint Makarios of Corinth (1731–1805).

183: Note 4: "Ask, and it shall be given you; seek, and ye shall find; *knock, and it shall be opened unto you*" (Matt. 7:7, Luke 11:9).

186: Note 7: For Aristotle's teaching that *the soul is all that it knows*, see translator's note for Ch. 1, p. 8.

188: "He that loveth not knoweth not God; for *God is love*" (1 John 4:8).

"*With men this is impossible; but with God all things are possible*" (Matt. 19:26).

CONCLUSION: *RELIGIO PERENNIS*

191: Note 1: For *Dante*, see translator's note for Ch. 12, p. 110, note 4.

192: For *the well-known saying of Saint Irenaeus*, see translator's note for Ch. 2, p. 17.

For *Ibn Arabi*, see translator's note for Ch. 2, p. 19.

Note 2: Augustinus *Steuchus* (1496–1549)—also known as *Eugubinus* and, in Italian, as Agostino Steuco—was a Renaissance theologian, antiquarian, linguist, and director of the Vatican Library; he was the first to use the phrase "perennial philosophy" to speak of a common teaching underlying and uniting a variety of religious and philosophical traditions.

Etymologically, the Latin word *religio* means "to bind" (*ligare*) something "back" (*re-*) to its source; the term *traditio* refers to the process of passing forward something received from the past.

194: "And the *Word* was *made flesh*, and dwelt among us" (John 1:14).

Catherine of Siena (1347–1380), a Roman Catholic visionary, ascetic, and "mystical spouse" of Christ, was the author of a *Dialogue*—also known as the *Treatise on Divine Providence*—consisting of a series of conversations between God and the human soul.

The kingdom of God that is "within us": "Behold, the kingdom of God is within you" (Luke 17:21).

The parable of the unjust judge: "And [Jesus] spake a parable unto them to this end, that men ought always to pray, and not to faint; saying, There was in a city a judge, which feared not God, neither regarded man: and there was a widow in that city; and she came unto him, saying, Avenge me of mine adversary. And he would not for a while: but afterward he said within himself, Though I fear not God, nor regard man; yet because this widow troubleth me, I will avenge her, lest by her continual coming she weary me. And the Lord said, Hear what the unjust judge saith. And shall not God avenge His own elect, which cry day and night unto Him, though He bear long with them?" (Luke 18:1–7).

The injunction of Saint Paul: "Pray without ceasing" (1 Thess. 5:17).

195: *Amitabha* (Sanskrit) or Amida (Japanese) is the name of the Buddha of "infinite light," who, as a *Bodhisattva* named Dharmakara, vowed not to enter *Nirvāna* until he had brought all who invoke his Name to the paradise of his Pure Land, also known as *Sukhāvatī* ("place of bliss") or the Western Paradise.

Note 8: For an English translation of this article by Schuon, see "The Mystery of the *Bodhisattva*" in *Treasures of Buddhism* (Bloomington, Indiana: World Wisdom Books, 1993), pp. 107–34.

196: *Mencius* (c. 391–c. 308 B.C.), known as the "Second Sage" after Confucius, was one of the most influential of early Confucian philosophers.

197: Note 9: *Mary of Egypt* (c. 344–c. 421) lived for forty-seven years in the desert, without clothing and surviving only on herbs.

APPENDIX: SELECTIONS FROM LETTERS, SPIRITUAL TEXTS, AND MEMOIRS

202: Selection 1: "The Book of Keys," No. 531, "The Perspective."

Selection 2: Letter of 7 October 1947.

203: *Ahmad al-Alawi* (1869–1934), a famous Algerian Sufi *shaykh*, was Schuon's spiritual master.

204: "*The tree is withered*": "The day-break star and the pipe, you have given from the east; and from the south, the nation's sacred hoop and the tree that was to bloom. To the center of the world you have taken me and showed the goodness and the beauty and the strangeness of the greening earth, the only mother—and there the spirit shapes of things, as they should be, you have shown to me and I have seen. At the center of this sacred hoop you have said that I should make the tree to bloom. With tears running, O Great Spirit, Great Spirit, my Grandfather—with running tears I must say now that the tree has never bloomed. A pitiful old man, you see me here, and I have fallen away and have done nothing. Here at the center of the world, where you took me when I was young and taught me; here, old, I stand, and *the tree is withered*, Grandfather, my Grandfather!" (*Black Elk Speaks: Being the Life Story of a Holy Man of the Oglala Sioux*, as told through John G. Neihardt [Lincoln, Nebraska: University of Nebraska Press, 1988], 273).

This letter was written to *Black Elk's son*, Benjamin (c. 1899–1973), whom Schuon met in 1959 and with whom he corresponded for a number of years. Black Elk (Hehaka Sapa, 1863–1950) was a famous Oglala Sioux medicine man.

The *six holy truths* are an important dimension of the spiritual method that Schuon practiced and taught, and they include as points of reference: Purity, Act, Peace, Love, Knowledge, and Being; see Ch. 20, "The Stations of Wisdom."

205: Selection 3: Letter of February 1971.

"I am the vine, ye are the branches: He that abideth in me, and I in him, the same bringeth forth much fruit: for *without me ye can do nothing*" (John 15:5).

"He that is not with me is against me; and *he that gathereth not with me scattereth abroad*" (Matt. 12:30).

In taking the "*Triple Refuge*," a Buddhist commits himself to three things: following the Buddha, practicing the *Dharma*, and becoming a member of the *Sangha*.

206: Selection 4: Letter of 11 September 1945.

The *Yoga-Shāstras* belong to a category of Hindu sacred texts dealing with law and morality.

Vivekanandists are followers of Swami Vivekananda (see translator's note for Ch. 17, p. 158, note 6).

"*One thing* is *needful*: and Mary hath chosen that good part, which shall not be taken from her" (Luke 10:39, 42; cf. John 11:1–2).

Abu al-Mawahib Muhammad ibn Ahmad *al-Shadhili* (c. 1407–c. 1477)—also known as Ibn Zaghdan—was the author of *Illumination in Islamic Mysticism.*

Selection 5: "Travel Meditations," 10 July 1963 (dated entry in "Memories and Meditations," Schuon's unpublished memoirs).

207: Selection 6: Letter of 28 January 1956.

"*The world is false, and* Brahma *is true*; the soul is not other than *Brahma*" is a summation of *Advaita Vedānta* traditionally ascribed to Shankara (see translator's note for Ch. 12, p. 109).

"An invisible and subtle essence is the Spirit that pervades the whole universe. That is Reality. That is Truth. *Thou art That* (*tat tvam asi*)" (*Chāndogya Upanishad*, 6.14.3).

"The Self was indeed *Brahma* in the beginning. It knew only that '*I am Brahma*' (*aham Brahmāsmi*). Therefore It became all. And whoever among the gods knew It also became That; and the same with sages and men. . . . And to this day whoever in like manner knows '*I am Brahma*' becomes all this universe. Even the gods cannot prevail against him, for he becomes their Self" (*Brihadāranyaka Upanishad*, 1.4.10).

208: Selection 7: Letter of 17 December 1960.

"*The Cross of Space and Time in Koranic Onomatology*" appeared in the French journal *Études traditionnelles* in 1961 and was later included in *Forme et substance dans les religions* (Paris: Derby-Livres, 1975; *Form and Substance in the Religions* [Bloomington, Indiana: World Wisdom, 2002]); "*Man in the Universe*," Ch. 9 of the present collection, was first published in *Études traditionnelles* in 1965 and was included in *Regards sur les mondes anciens* (Paris: Éditions Traditionnelles, 1968; *Light on the Ancient Worlds* [Bloomington, Indiana: World Wisdom, 2006]).

"*The First*," "*the Last*," "*the Outward*," and "*the Inward*" are among the ninety-nine Names of God in Islam.

Selection 8: "The Book of Keys," No. 61, "The Way."

209: Selection 9: Letter of 7 August 1979.

For *Shankara*, see translator's note for Ch. 12, p. 109.

210: *Thomas Aquinas* (see translator's notes for Preface, p. li; Ch. 3, p. 27; Ch. 7, p. 60; Ch. 8, p. 72; Ch. 13, p. 121, note 1; Ch. 15, p. 140, note 2) and *Gregory Palamas* (see translator's note for Ch. 4, p. 37, note 9) are often regarded as typifying the divergence between the Scholasticism of the Western Church and the Hesychasm of the Christian East.

Selection 10: Letter of 1 May 1940.

Abd al-Qadir al-Jilani (1077–1166) was a gifted preacher and teacher and the founder of the Qadiriyya Sufi order.

211: Selection 11: Letter of 5 January 1957.

Selection 12: Letter of 15 March 1961.

Mahesh Prasad Varma *Yogi* (1917–2008), founded the "Spiritual *Regeneration Movement*"—later renamed the Transcendental Meditation movement—in 1957; Schuon is quoting in English from a promotional pamphlet for the organization.

213: Selection 13: "Reflections concerning a Letter" (undated).

Selection 14: Letter of 22 June 1964.

Aristarchus of Samos (c. 310–c. 230 B.C.) and *Hipparcus* (c. 190–c. 120 B.C.) were Greek astronomers and mathematicians; Muhammad ibn Jabir al-Harrani *al-Battani* (c. 850–929)—known in the West as Albategnius—was a Muslim astronomer and mathematician.

214: Selection 15: Letter of 7 October 1960.

215: Selection 16: "On Love" (unpublished article, c. 1940).

Saint Bernadette Soubirous (1844–1879), to whom the Blessed Virgin is said to have appeared several times, asked "the beautiful Lady" who she was and received the reply, "I am the *Immaculate Conception*."

It was the "*apostolic counsel*" of Saint Paul, although not his commandment, that fellow Christians prefer celibacy to marriage: "I would that all men were even as I myself. But every man hath his proper gift of God, one after this manner, and another after that. I say therefore to the unmarried and widows, It is good for them if they abide even as I" (1 Cor. 7:7–8).

Selection 17: "The Book of Keys," No. 399, "*Al-Tawbah*."

216: Selection 18: Letter of 31 May 1975.

For the *Golden Legend*, see translator's note for Ch. 1, p. 11.

The *Bhagavad Gītā*, a dialogue between the prince Arjuna and the *avatāra* Krishna, is regarded by many Hindus as the most profound and important of all their sacred texts.

217: For *Amitabha Buddha*, see translator's note for the "Conclusion: *Religio Perennis*," p. 195.

Selection 19: Letter of 20 November 1958.

The *White Buffalo Woman* was a beautiful maiden who brought the Sioux people the *sacred pipe* and who, as she departed their camp, was transformed into a white buffalo calf; some of Schuon's paintings of this celestial messenger and other Indian figures may be found in *The Feathered Sun: Plains Indians in Art and Philosophy* (Bloomington, Indiana: World Wisdom Books, 1990); see also the sixth print in the color gallery of Schuon's art (following p. 152).

The author contributed articles to the French journal *Études traditionnelles* ("Traditional Studies") from 1936 to 1984.

218: Selection 20: Letter of 28 January 1956.

Selection 21: Letter of 31 January 1965.

219: Selection 22: "The Book of Keys," No. 1113, "Security."

Selection 23: Letter of January 1971.

220: *Dante* (see translator's note for Ch. 12, p. 110, note 4) was well aware of the *grandeur* of his poetry, boldly placing himself among the greatest poets of history, including Homer, Horace, Ovid, Lucan, and Virgil (see *The Inferno*, Canto IV:88–102).

For *Shakespeare*, see translator's notes for Ch. 3, p. 29 and Ch. 9, p. 86.

Selection 24: Letter of 22 February 1976.

Pius XII (1876–1958) was Pope of Rome from 1939.

Selection 25: "The Book of Keys," No. 1075, "Not To Be Lost from Sight."

221: For *Meister Eckhart*, see translator's notes for Ch. 2, p. 18; Ch. 5, p. 45; Ch. 15, p. 140, note 2; Ch. 17, p. 160.

The *Brahma Sūtra*, attributed to the sage Badarayana (first century B.C.), summarizes the teachings of the principal *Upanishads* concerning the Supreme Reality, *Brahma*.

"God created man in His own image, *in the image of God* created He him; male and female created He them" (Gen. 1:27).

For René *Guénon*, see translator's note for Ch. 13, p. 121, note 2.

222: Selection 26: Letter of 23 May 1940.

Tradition ascribes the origin of the game of chess to *Sissa*, a *brāhmana* in the court of the rajah Balhait; concerned about gambling and the playing of games of pure chance, Balhait had summoned the saint to create a game requiring mental skill and inculcating the virtues of prudence and circumspection.

Selection 27: "Travel Meditations," 14 August 1963 (dated entry in "Memories and Meditations," Schuon's unpublished memoirs).

Selection 28: Letter of 5 May 1945.

223: "*None shall meet God who hath not first met His Prophet*": *hadīth*.

"I am the way, the truth, and the life: *no man cometh unto the Father, but by me*" (John 14:6).

"I am the vine, ye are the branches: He that abideth in me, and I in him, the same bringeth forth much fruit: for *without me ye can do nothing*" (John 15:5).

Selection 29: Letter of 27 November 1970.

224: For *Kobo Daishi*, see translator's note for Ch. 19, p. 178.

Selection 30: "The Book of Keys," No. 720, "Two Eschatological Questions."

Imam Abu al-Hasan al-*Shadhili* (1196–1258) was the founder of the Shadhiliyya *tarīqah*, an initiatic lineage from which are derived a number of other Sufi orders, including the Darqawiyya and Alawiyya.

225: *Sayyidatna Maryam*, "Our Lady Mary," is a traditional Muslim form of address for the Blessed Virgin.

Selection 31: Letter of 8 May 1942.

226: "*The sin against the Spirit*": "All manner of sin and blasphemy shall be forgiven unto men: but the blasphemy against the Holy Spirit shall not be forgiven unto men" (Matt. 12:31; cf. Luke 12:10). Elsewhere Schuon writes: "Sins against the Holy Spirit exclude those dispositions of soul through which the remission of sins takes place. They are six in number: 1. Presumption (overestimating oneself, in principle or in fact); 2. Despair (doubting God's Mercy); 3. Attack against the known truth; 4. Envy of another's gifts of grace; 5. Obstinacy (in evil, intellectual or moral); 6. Final Impenitence (in the face of death)" (see *The Fullness of God: Frithjof Schuon on Christianity*, ed. James S. Cutsinger [Bloomington, Indiana: World Wisdom, 2004], 169).

Selection 32: "The Book of Keys," No. 1014, "Of the Origin of the *Sophia Perennis.*"

227: "*The Spirit bloweth where it listeth*": "The wind [Greek *pneuma* = spirit, wind, breath] bloweth where it listeth, and thou hearest the sound thereof, but canst not tell whence it cometh, and whither it goeth: so is every one that is born of the Spirit" (John 3:8).

"*If I were to divulge all I know, you would stone me*": "[Jesus] took [Thomas] and withdrew and told him three things. When Thomas returned to his companions, they asked him, What did Jesus say to you? Thomas said to them, If I were to tell you one of the things that he told me, you would pick up stones and throw them at me, and a fire would come out of the stones and burn you up" (*Gospel of Thomas*, 13).

Selection 33: Letter of 5 May 1945.

Ramana *Maharshi* (1879–1950), a widely respected and influential Hindu *jnānin*, experienced the identity of *Ātmā* and *Brahma* while still in his teens, and the fruit of this experience remained with him as a permanent spiritual station throughout his life.

The descent of the Holy Spirit on the Apostles: "And when the day of Pentecost was fully come, they were all with one accord in one place. And suddenly there came a sound from heaven as of a rushing mighty wind, and it filled all the house where they were sitting. And there appeared unto them cloven tongues like as of fire, and it sat upon each of them. And they were all filled with the Holy Spirit, and began to speak with other tongues, as the Spirit gave them utterance" (Acts 2:1–4).

Saint John was "the disciple whom Jesus loved" (John 21:20); *Sayyidna Ali*, one of the four Companions of Muhammad, was also the Prophet's nephew and son-in-law.

For *Ramakrishna*, see translator's note for Ch. 17, p. 158, note 4.

228: "*They that be whole need not a physician*, but they that are sick" (Matt. 9:12, Luke 5:31; cf. Mark 2:17).

Selection 34: Letter of December 1946.

229: Selection 35: "The Book of Keys," No. 328, "The Verse of the *Mihrāb*."

"And make mention of Mary in the Scriptures, when she had withdrawn from her people to *a place toward the East*, and had chosen seclusion from them. Then We sent unto her Our spirit" (*Sūrah* "Mary" [19]:16–17).

230: "And her Lord accepted her with full acceptance and vouchsafed to her a goodly growth; and made *Zachariah* her guardian. Whenever *Zachariah* went into the sanctuary where she was, he found that she had food. He said: *O Maryam, whence hast thou this nourishment?* She answered: It is from God. God giveth *without reckoning* to whom He will" (*Sūrah* "The Family of Imran" [3]:37).

"Whosoever keepeth his covenant with God, on him will He bestow *immense reward*" (*Sūrah* "Victory" [48]:10); "God hath promised, unto such of them as believe and do good works, forgiveness and *immense reward*" (*Sūrah* "Victory" [48]:29).

Selection 36: Letter of 28 March 1951.

The *Jesus Prayer* is the most common form of invocatory prayer among the Hesychast masters of the Christian East; it consists of the words, or some variation: "Lord Jesus Christ, Son of God, have mercy upon us."

231: Selection 37: Letter of September 1983.

"I am the vine, ye are the branches: He that abideth in me, and I in him, the same bringeth forth much fruit: for *without me ye can do nothing*" (John 15:5).

Selection 38: Letter of June 1958.

232: Selection 39: "Travel Meditations," 25 August 1963 (dated entry in "Memories and Meditations," Schuon's unpublished memoirs).

Selection 40: "The Book of Keys," No. 72, "*Oratio Cordis*."

GLOSSARY

Ab alio (Latin): "from another"; originating from an extrinsic source.

Ab extra (Latin): "from outside"; proceeding from something external.

Ab intra (Latin): "from inside"; proceeding from something internal.

A contrario (Latin): literally, "from the opposite"; a form of argument in which a certain position is established or strengthened by highlighting the deficiencies of what opposes it.

Ad majorem Dei gloriam (Latin): "to the greater glory of God."

Advaita (Sanskrit): "non-dualist" interpretation of the *Vedānta*; Hindu doctrine according to which the seeming multiplicity of things is regarded as the product of ignorance, the only true reality being *Brahma*, the One, the Absolute, the Infinite, which is the unchanging ground of appearance.

Afrād (Arabic): see *fard*.

Agathon (Greek): "the Good"; in Platonism, a name for the Supreme Reality.

Aham Brahmāsmi (Sanskrit): "I am Brahma."

Anā ʾl-Haqq (Arabic): "I am the Truth."

Anamnesis (Greek): literally, a "lifting up of the mind"; recollection or remembrance, as in the Platonic doctrine that all knowledge is a recalling of truths latent in the soul.

Ānanda (Sanskrit): "bliss, beatitude, joy"; one of the three essential aspects of *Apara-Brahma*, together with *sat*, "being," and *chit*, "consciousness."

Anthropos (Greek): the human being, male or female.

Apara-Brahma (Sanskrit): the "non-supreme" or penultimate *Brahma*, also called *Brahma saguna*; the "relative Absolute."

Apocatastasis (Greek): "restitution, restoration"; among certain Christian theologians, including Clement of Alexandria, Origen, and Gregory of Nyssa, the doctrine that all creatures will finally be saved.

A posteriori (Latin): literally, "from after"; proceeding from effect to cause or from experience to principle.

A priori (Latin): literally, "from before"; proceeding from cause to effect or from principle to experience.

A se (Latin): "from itself"; self-originated.

Ātmā or *Ātman* (Sanskrit): the real or true "Self," underlying the ego and its manifestations; in the perspective of *Advaita Vedānta*, identical with *Brahma*.

Avatāra (Sanskrit): the earthly "descent," incarnation, or manifestation of God, especially of Vishnu in the Hindu tradition.

Barakah (Arabic): "blessing," grace; in Islam, a spiritual influence or energy emanating originally from God, but often attached to sacred objects and spiritual persons.

Bhakta (Sanskrit): a follower of the spiritual path of *bhakti*; a person whose relationship with God is based primarily on adoration and love.

Bhakti, *bhakti-mārga* (Sanskrit): the spiritual "path" (*mārga*) of "love" (*bhakti*) and devotion; see *jnāna* and *karma*.

Bodhi (Sanskrit, Pali): "awakened, enlightened"; in Buddhism, the attainment of perfect clarity of mind, in which things are seen as they truly are.

Bodhisattva (Sanskrit, Pali): literally, "enlightenment-being"; in *Mahāyāna* Buddhism, one who postpones his own final enlightenment and entry into *Nirvāna* in order to aid all other sentient beings in their quest for Buddhahood.

Brahma or *Brahman* (Sanskrit): the Supreme Reality, the Absolute.

Brahmaloka (Sanskrit): "domain of Brahmā"; Hindu heaven in the company of God as creator (Brahmā as distinct from *Brahma*).

Brāhmana (Sanskrit): a member of the highest of the four Hindu castes; a priest or spiritual teacher.

Brahma saguna (Sanskrit): *Brahma* "qualified" by attributes and predicates; God insofar as He can be understood conceptually; also called *Apara-Brahma*.

Buddhi (Sanskrit): "Intellect"; in Hinduism, the mental faculty capable of intuitive discernment.

Chelā (Sanskrit): in Hinduism, the student or disciple of a *guru*.

Chit (Sanskrit): "consciousness"; one of the three essential aspects of *Apara-Brahma*, together with *sat*, "being," and *ānanda*, "bliss, beatitude, joy."

Civitas Dei (Latin): "city of God."

Corruptio optimi pessima (Latin): "the corruption of the best is the worst."

Creatio ex nihilo (Latin): "creation out of nothing"; the doctrine that God Himself is the sufficient cause of the universe, needing nothing else; often set in contrast to emanationist cosmogonies.

Credo ut intelligam (Latin): "I believe in order that I might understand."

Dākinī (Sanskrit): in Tibetan Buddhism, a female spirit who attends and inspires the *yogin*, transmitting to him secret teachings in dreams.

Darshana (Sanskrit): a spiritual "perspective," point of view, or school of thought; also the "viewing" of a holy person, object, or place, together with the resulting blessing or merit.

Deva-yana (Sanskrit): "way of the gods"; in Hinduism, the path followed after death by the truly faithful, leading to the realization of *Brahma*.

Dharma (Sanskrit): in Hinduism, the underlying "law" or "order" of the cosmos as expressed in sacred rites and in actions appropriate to various social relationships and human vocations; in Buddhism, the practice and realization of Truth.

Dharma-kāya (Sanskrit): literally, "*dharma* body"; the ultimate or non-manifest form of a Buddha; see *nirmāna-kāya, sambhoga-kāya.*

Dhikr (Arabic): "remembrance" of God, based upon the repeated invocation of His Name; central to Sufi practice, where the remembrance often consists of the single word *Allāh.*

Dhyāni-Buddha (Sanskrit): Buddha "of meditation"; a Buddha, such as Amitabha (Amida in Japanese), who appears to the eye of contemplative vision but is not accessible in a historical form.

Dīkshā (Sanskrit): "consecration," "initiation"; bestowed by the spiritual master when a disciple enters a spiritual path.

Distinguo (Latin): literally, "I mark or set off, differentiate," often used in the dialectic of the medieval scholastics; any philosophical distinction.

Esse (Latin): "to be"; being, existence.

Ex cathedra (Latin): literally, "from the throne"; in Roman Catholicism, authoritative teaching issued by the pope and regarded as infallible.

Ex nihilo (Latin): "out of nothing."

Facere (Latin): "to make, to do"; doing, action.

Fanā' (Arabic): "extinction, annihilation, evanescence"; in Sufism, the spiritual station or degree of realization in which all individual attributes and limitations are extinguished in union with God.

Faqīr (Arabic, plural *fuqarā'*): literally, the "poor one"; in Sufism, a follower of the spiritual path, whose "indigence" or "poverty" (*faqr*) testifies to complete dependence on God and a desire to be filled by Him alone.

Faqr (Arabic): "indigence, spiritual poverty"; see *faqīr.*

Fard (Arabic, plural *afrād*): "alone"; in Sufism, one who realizes the truth on his own and without membership in a *tarīqah*, or even without belonging to a revealed religion, receiving illumination directly from God.

Fātihah (Arabic): the "opening" *sūrah*, or chapter, of the Koran, recited in the daily prayers of all Muslims and consisting of the words: "In the Name of God, the Beneficent, the Merciful. Praise to God, Lord of the Worlds, the Beneficent, the Merciful. Owner of the Day of Judgment, Thee (alone) we worship; Thee (alone) we ask for help. Show us the straight path, the path of those whom Thou hast favored, not (the path) of those who earn Thine anger, nor of those who go astray."

Fiat lux (Latin): "Let there be light" (cf. Gen. 1:3).

Fitrah (Arabic): in Islam, the natural predisposition of man, as created by God, to act in accordance with the will of Heaven; the original uprightness of humanity; the primordial norm or "nature of things."

Fuqarā': see *faqīr*.

Geronda (Greek): literally, "old man, elder"; in the Christian East, a spiritual master or guide; equivalent of Russian *starets*.

Gnosis (Greek): "knowledge"; spiritual insight, principial comprehension, divine wisdom.

Gopī (Sanskrit): literally, "keeper of the cows"; in Hindu tradition, one of the cowherd girls involved with Krishna in the love affairs of his youth, symbolic of the soul's devotion to God.

Guna (Sanskrit): literally, "strand"; quality, characteristic, attribute; in Hinduism, the *guna*s are the three constituents of *Prakriti*: *sattva* (the ascending, luminous quality), *rajas* (the expansive, passional quality), and *tamas* (the descending, dark quality).

Guru (Sanskrit): literally, "weighty," grave, venerable; in Hinduism, a spiritual master; one who gives initiation and instruction in the spiritual path and in whom is embodied the supreme goal of realization or perfection.

Hadīth (Arabic, plural *ahādīth*): "saying, narrative"; an account of the words or deeds of the Prophet Muhammad, transmitted through a traditional chain of known intermediaries.

Hadīth qudsī (Arabic): "divine, holy narrative"; a saying in which God Himself speaks through the mouth of the Prophet.

Hypostasis (Greek, plural *hypostases*): literally, "substance"; in Eastern Christian theology, a technical term for one of the three "Persons" of the Trinity; the Father, the Son, and the Holy Spirit are distinct *hypostases* sharing a single *ousia*, or essence.

Ihsān (Arabic): "excellence, perfection"; in Islam, virtuous or beautiful action; spiritual excellence.

Ijtihād (Arabic): literally, "exertion"; in Islamic law, an independent judgment concerning a legal or theological question, arrived at through a reinterpretation of the Koran or *sunnah* by those possessing the necessary qualifications.

In divinis (Latin): literally, "in or among divine things"; within the divine Principle; the plural form is used insofar as the Principle comprises both *Para-Brahma*, Beyond-Being or the Absolute, and *Apara-Brahma*, Being or the relative Absolute.

Īshvara (Sanskrit): literally, "possessing power," hence master; God understood as a personal being, as Creator and Lord; manifest in the *Trimūrti* as Brahmā, Vishnu, and Shiva.

Islām (Arabic): "surrender, submission, peace"; the condition of peace resulting from faithful submission to God.

Ism (Arabic): "name"; in Sufism, a Name or the Name (*Allāh*) of God.

Istikhārah (Arabic): in Islam, a formal prayer for divine guidance in times of uncertainty.

Japa-Yoga (Sanskrit): method of "union" or "unification" (*yoga*) based upon the "repetition" (*japa*) of a *mantra* or sacred formula, often containing one of the Names of God.

Jinn (Arabic, singular *jinnī*): in Islam, creatures of "fire" belonging to the subtle order; capable of changing size and shape and of helping or harming human beings.

Jīvan-mukta (Sanskrit): one who is "liberated" while still in this "life"; a person who has attained a state of spiritual perfection or self-realization before death; in contrast to *videha-mukta*, one who is liberated at the moment of death.

Jnāna or *jnāna-mārga* (Sanskrit): the spiritual "path" (*mārga*) of "knowledge" (*jnāna*) and intellection; see *bhakti* and *karma*.

Jnānin (Sanskrit): a follower of the path of *jnāna*; a person whose relationship with God is based primarily on sapiential knowledge or *gnosis*.

Jōdo or *Jōdo-Shinshū* (Japanese): "pure land" or "true pure land school"; a sect of Japanese Buddhism founded by Shinran, based on faith in the power of the Buddha Amida to bring devotees to his celestial realm; characterized by use of the *nembutsu*.

Kalām (Arabic): literally, "speech, discourse"; Muslim science of theology that brings reason to bear on Koranic interpretation.

Kali Yuga (Sanskrit): in Hinduism, the fourth and final *yuga* in a given cycle of time, corresponding to the Iron Age of Western tradition and culminating in a *pralaya* or the *mahāpralaya*; the present age of mankind, distinguished by its increasing disorder, violence, and forgetfulness of God.

Karma (Sanskrit): "action, work"; in Hinduism and Buddhism, the law of consequence, in which the present is explained by reference to the nature and quality of past actions; one of the principal *mārga*s or spiritual "paths" of Hinduism, characterized by its stress on righteous deeds; see *bhakti* and *jnāna*.

Khalīfah (Arabic): literally, "successor"; in Islam, a representative, used in reference to man as such as the vicar of God on earth and also in reference to the successors of the Prophet Muhammad; in Sufism, the deputy of a *shaykh*, normally having an administrative rather than strictly spiritual authority.

Khalwah (Arabic): "seclusion, retreat"; in Sufism, the practice of withdrawing from the world, often during a night vigil, for the purpose of a more intense spiritual practice.

Kōan (Japanese): literally, "precedent for public use," case study; in Zen Buddhism, a question or anecdote often based on the experience or sayings of a notable master and involving a paradox or puzzle that cannot be solved in conventional terms or with ordinary thinking.

Kshatriya (Sanskrit): a member of the second highest of the four Hindu castes; a warrior or prince.

Lā ilāha illā ʾLlāh (Arabic): "There is no god but God"; see *shahādah*.

Logos (Greek): "word, reason"; in Christian theology, the divine, uncreated Word of God (cf. John 1:1); the transcendent Principle of creation and revelation.

Mahabbah (Arabic): "love"; in Sufism, the spiritual path based on love and devotion, analogous to the Hindu *bhakti-mārga*; see *makhāfah* and *maʿrifah*.

Mahāpralaya (Sanskrit): in Hinduism, the "great" or final "dissolving" of the universe at the end of a *kalpa*, or "day in the life of Brahmā," understood as lasting one thousand *yugas*.

Mahāyāna (Sanskrit): "great vehicle"; the form of Buddhism, including such traditions as Zen and *Jōdo-Shinshū*, which regards itself as the fullest or most adequate expression of the Buddha's teaching; distinguished by the idea that *nirvāna* is nothing other than *samsāra* seen as it truly is.

Makhāfah (Arabic): "fear"; in Sufism, the spiritual path based upon the fear of God, analogous to the Hindu *karma-mārga*; see *mahabbah* and *maʿrifah*.

Malāmatiyah (Arabic): literally, "the blameworthy"; a Sufi sect that accentuated self-reproach and endeavored to conceal virtue behind a façade of ignoble action.

Manolaya (Sanskrit): in *yoga*, the temporary cessation of thoughts through the absorption of the mind in an object of meditation.

Mantra (Sanskrit): "instrument of thought"; a word or phrase of divine origin, often including a Name of God, repeated by those initiated into its proper use as a means of salvation or liberation; see *japa-yoga*.

Maʿrifah (Arabic): "knowledge"; in Sufism, the spiritual path based upon knowledge or *gnosis*, analogous to the Hindu *jnāna-mārga*; see *mahabbah* and *makhāfah*.

Materia (Latin): "matter"; in Platonic cosmology, the undifferentiated and primordial substance that serves as a "receptacle" for the shaping force of divine forms or ideas; universal potentiality.

Mauna-dīkshā (Sanskrit): "silent initiation, initiation by silence"; the wordless transmission of initiatic grace simply through the presence of a spiritual teacher.

Māyā (Sanskrit): "artifice, illusion"; in *Advaita Vedānta*, the beguiling concealment of *Brahma* in the form or under the appearance of a lower reality.

Māyā in divinis (Sanskrit and Latin): literally, "illusion within or among divine things"; an expression of the metaphysical teaching that relativity, and thus a certain degree of illusion, can be found even within the divine Principle, beginning with the personal God or "relative Absolute"; only *Brahma*, the Absolute as such, is fully real.

Mihrāb (Arabic): the "niche" in a mosque indicating the direction of Mecca, toward which the faithful pray.

Muqaddam (Arabic): literally, "one who brings forth"; the representative of a *shaykh*, having the authority to instruct and initiate postulants, offer spiritual advice, and oversee the proper order of a *tarīqah*.

Murshid (Arabic): "one who leads straight"; in Sufism, a spiritual guide.

Nembutsu (Japanese): "remembrance or mindfulness of the Buddha [Amitabha]," based upon the repeated invocation of his Name.

Nirmāna-kāya (Sanskrit): literally, "transformation body"; the human or physical form of a Buddha; see *sambhoga-kāya, dharma-kāya.*

Nirvāna (Sanskrit): "blowing out, extinction"; in Indian traditions, especially Buddhism, the extinction of the fires of passion and the resulting, supremely blissful state of liberation from egoism and attachment; analogous to the Sufi idea of *fanā'*.

Parabhakti (Sanskrit): "supreme love."

Paramātmā or *Paramātman* (Sanskrit): the "supreme Self."

Para-Brahma (Sanskrit): the "supreme" or ultimate *Brahma*, also called *Brahma nirguna*; the Absolute as such.

Philosophia perennis (Latin): "perennial philosophy."

Pontifex (Latin): "bridge-maker"; man as the link between heaven and earth.

Prajnā (Sanskrit): "wisdom, intelligence, understanding"; in Hinduism, the self-awareness of *Ātmā*; knowledge of things as they truly are.

Prakriti (Sanskrit): literally, "making first"; the fundamental, "feminine" substance or material cause of all things; see *purusha.*

Pralaya (Sanskrit): "dissolution"; Hindu teaching that all appearance is subject to a periodic process of destruction and recreation; see *mahāpralaya.*

Pratyeka-Buddha (Sanskrit): "independent Buddha"; one who attains enlightenment without a teacher and who makes no attempt to instruct disciples.

Pro domo (Latin): literally, "for (one's own) home or house"; serving the interests of a given perspective or for the benefit of a given group.

Purusha (Sanskrit): "man"; the informing or shaping principle of creation; the "masculine" demiurge or fashioner of the universe, whose primordial sacrifice gives rise to all creation; see *prakriti.*

Qalb (Arabic): "heart"; in Sufism, the physical and spiritual center of man and seat of the uncreated Intellect; the place of intersection within the microcosm between the Divine and the human.

Qiyās (Arabic): literally, "measure, analogy"; analogical reasoning in Islamic logic and law; a method for applying the teachings of the Koran and *sunnah* to issues and circumstances not explicitly dealt with in the traditional sources.

Quod absit (Latin): literally, "which thing, let it be absent"; a phrase commonly used by the medieval scholastics to call attention to an idea that is absurdly inconsistent with accepted principles.

Rajas (Sanskrit): in Hinduism, one of the three *guna*s or qualities of *prakriti*, of which all things are woven; the quality of expansiveness, manifest in the material world as force or movement and in the soul as ambition, initiative, and restlessness; see *sattva* and *tamas*.

Rakʿah (Arabic, plural *rakʿāt*): literally, "bowing"; in Islamic prayer, one complete set of movements and postures, comprising an upright stance, bowing at the waist, two prostrations, and sitting on the heels.

Religio caeli (Latin): "religion of heaven."

Religio cordis (Latin): "religion of the heart."

Religio perennis (Latin): "perennial religion."

Risālat al-Ahadīyah (Arabic): "message of unity."

Rishi (Sanskrit): "seer"; in Hinduism, one of the ancient sages whose visions and auditions of truth are transcribed in the *Veda*s.

Roshi (Japanese): "venerable teacher"; in Zen Buddhism, a spiritual master.

Ruah Elohīm (Hebrew): "spirit of God" (cf. Gen. 1:2 passim).

Rūh (Arabic): "spirit"; in Islam, the Spirit of God (*Rūh Allāh*), also used as a name of Jesus in the Koran (4:171); the spirit of a man, breathed into him by God at his creation (15:29) and distinguished from his soul or lower self (*nafs*).

Sādhaka (Sanskrit): in Hinduism, one who follows a *sādhana* or spiritual path, especially a path involving the use of a *mantra* and visualization of the chosen deity.

Sādhu (Sanskrit): literally, "accomplished"; one who has mastered, or is seeking to master, his senses; an ascetic.

Samādhi (Sanskrit): literally, "putting together, union"; in Hinduism, a state of consciousness in which the concentration of the *yogin* becomes so intense and complete that the distinction between subject and object is eliminated.

Sambhoga-kāya (Sanskrit): literally, "enjoyment body"; the celestial or magical form of a Buddha; see *nirmāna-kāya*, *dharma-kāya*.

Samsāra (Sanskrit): literally, "wandering"; in Hinduism and Buddhism, transmigration or the cycle of birth, death, and rebirth; also the world of apparent flux and change.

Sanātana Dharma (Sanskrit): "eternal law"; in Hinduism, the universal or absolute law or truth underlying specific and relative laws and truths.

Sangha (Sanskrit): "gathering, community"; the community of those who follow the teachings of the Buddha.

Sannyāsin (Sanskrit): "renunciate"; in Hindu tradition, one who has renounced all formal ties to social life.

Sat (Sanskrit): "being"; one of the three essential aspects of *Apara-Brahma*, together with *chit*, "consciousness," and *ānanda*, "bliss, beatitude, joy."

Sattva (Sanskrit): in Hinduism, one of the three *guna*s or qualities of *prakriti*, of which all things are woven; the quality of luminosity, manifest in the material world as buoyancy or lightness and in the soul as intelligence and virtue; see *rajas* and *tamas*.

Shahādah (Arabic): the fundamental "profession" or "testimony" of faith in Islam, consisting of the words *Lā ilāha illā 'Llāh, Muhammadan rasūlu 'Llāh*: "There is no god but God; Muhammad is the messenger of God."

Shakti (Sanskrit): creative "power," expressed in Hinduism in the form of divine femininity.

Sharī'ah (Arabic): "path"; in Islam, the proper mode and norm of life, the path or way willed and marked out by God for man's return to Him; Muslim law or exotericism.

Shāstra (Sanskrit): "command, rule"; traditional Hindu book of law.

Shaykh (Arabic): literally, "old man, elder"; in Sufism, one who has attained spiritual mastery through submission to the discipline and instruction of another master in a lineage (see *silsilah*) that can be traced to the founder of a given *tarīqah*, and thence to the Prophet Muhammad.

Shaykh al-Barakah (Arabic): a *shaykh* in the strictest sense of the term, whose authority is absolute and who benefits from a spiritual inspiration (cf. *barakah*) of the first magnitude.

Shraddhā (Sanskrit): literally, "application of faith"; in Hinduism, an offering to the sages, the gods, or the ancestors; the trustful obedience of the Hindu *bhakta*.

Shūnyamūrti (Sanskrit): "the form or manifestation of the void"; traditional epithet of the Buddha, in whom *shūnyatā* or ultimate "emptiness," the final absence of all being or selfhood, becomes incarnate.

Silsilah (Arabic): in Sufism, the initiatic "chain" of transmission running in succession from the Prophet Muhammad down to the *shaykh* of a given *tarīqah*.

Sirāt al-mustaqīm (Arabic): "the straight path"; in Islam, the path to God; see *fātihah*.

Sophia (Greek): "wisdom"; in Jewish and Christian tradition, the Wisdom of God, often conceived as feminine (cf. Prov. 8).

Sophia Perennis (Greek): "perennial wisdom"; the eternal, non-formal Truth at the heart of all orthodox religious traditions.

Starets (Russian): literally, "old man, elder"; in the Christian East, a spiritual master or guide; equivalent of Greek *geronda*.

Sub omni caelo (Latin): literally, "under all the heaven," that is, everywhere.

Sub specie aeternitatis (Latin): literally, "under the gaze of eternity," that is, from an eternal perspective.

Sunnah (Arabic): "custom, way of acting"; in Islam, the norm established by the Prophet Muhammad, including his actions and sayings (see *hadīth*) and serving as a precedent and standard for the behavior of Muslims.

Sūtra (Sanskrit): literally, "thread"; a Hindu or Buddhist sacred text; in Hinduism, any short, aphoristic verse or collection of verses, often elliptical in style; in Buddhism, a collection of the discourses of the Buddha.

Tamas (Sanskrit): in Hinduism, one of the three *guna*s or qualities of *prakriti*, of which all things are woven; the quality of darkness or heaviness, manifest in the material world as inertia or rigidity and in the soul as sloth, stupidity, and vice; see *rajas* and *sattva*.

Tapas (Sanskrit): literally, "heat"; in *yoga*, ascetical practice, austerity.

Tārā (Sanskrit): literally, "she who saves"; the title of a number of Tibetan female *Bodhisattva*s and Hindu goddesses.

Tarīqah (Arabic): "path"; in exoteric Islam, a virtual synonym for *sharīʿah*, equivalent to the "straight path" mentioned in the *fātihah*; in Sufism, the mystical path leading from observance of the *sharīʿah* to self-realization in God; also a Sufi brotherhood.

Tasawwuf (Arabic): a term of disputed etymology, although perhaps from *sūf* for "wool," after the garment worn by many early Sufis; traditional Muslim word for Sufism.

Theravāda (Pali): "teaching of the elders"; early form of Buddhism based on the sacred texts of the Pali canon and stressing the importance of individual liberation from *samsāra*; see *Mahāyāna*.

Torah (Hebrew): "instruction, teaching"; in Judaism, the written law of God, as revealed to Moses on Sinai and embodied in the Pentateuch (Genesis, Exodus, Leviticus, Numbers, Deuteronomy).

Trimūrti (Sanskrit): literally, "having three forms"; in Hindu tradition, a triadic expression of the Divine, especially in the form of Brahmā, the creator, Vishnu, the preserver, and Shiva, the transformer.

ʿUlamāʾ (Arabic, singular *ʿalīm*): "those who know, scholars"; in Islam, those who are learned in matters of law and theology; traditional authorities for all aspects of Muslim life.

Upanishad (Sanskrit): literally, "to sit close by"; any esoteric doctrine requiring direct transmission from master to disciple; in Hinduism, the genre of sacred texts that appear at the end of the *Veda*s; see *vedānta*.

Upāya (Sanskrit): "means, expedient, method"; in Buddhist tradition, an adaptation of spiritual teaching to a form suited to the spiritual or intellectual level of one's audience.

Veda (Sanskrit): "knowledge"; in Hinduism, the body of sacred knowledge held to be the basis of orthodoxy and right practice; transmitted in four classic *Vedas*, sacred texts composed of hymns, ritual formulas, and metaphysical doctrines.

Vedānta (Sanskrit): "end or culmination of the *Vedas*"; one of the major schools of traditional Hindu philosophy, based in part on the *Upanishads*, esoteric treatises found at the conclusion of the Vedic scriptures; see *advaita*.

Wakan-Tanka (Lakota): "Great Spirit"; among the Oglala Sioux, a name for God.

Yantra (Sanskrit): literally, "instrument of support"; a geometrical design, often representing the cosmos, used in Tantric Hinduism and Tibetan Buddhism as a visual support or focus for meditation.

Yin–Yang (Chinese): in Chinese tradition, two opposite but complementary forces or qualities, from whose interpenetration the universe and all its diverse forms emerge; *yin* corresponds to the feminine, the yielding, the moon, and liquidity; *yang* corresponds to the masculine, the resisting, the sun, and solidity.

Yoga (Sanskrit): literally, "yoking, union"; in Indian traditions, any meditative and ascetic technique designed to bring the soul and body into a state of concentration.

Yogin (Sanskrit): one who is "yoked or joined"; a practitioner of *yoga*.

Zāwiyah (Arabic): literally, "corner, nook"; in Sufism, the regular meeting place, whether a single room or a building or complex of buildings, of a *ṭarīqah*.

SOURCES

The chapters included in this anthology have been selected and translated from the following sources; see the Bibliography of Works by Frithjof Schuon for a complete listing of the author's books and articles.

"Preface": "Préface," *Les Stations de la sagesse* (Paris: L'Harmattan, 2011), 7–12.

1. "The Sense of the Absolute in Religions": "Le sentiment d'absolu dans les religions," *Sentiers de gnose* (Gaillac: La Place Royale, 1996), 9–28.

2. "Two Esotericisms": "Deux ésotérismes," *Résumé de métaphysique intégrale* (Paris: Le Courrier du Livre, 1985), 73–80.

3. "Concerning Naiveté": "Propos sur la naiveté," *Regards sur les mondes anciens* (Paris: Éditions Traditionnelles, 1980), 123–35.

4. "The Mystery of the Hypostatic Face": "Le mystère du Visage hypostatique," *Résumé de métaphysique intégrale* (Paris: Le Courrier du Livre, 1985), 55–65.

5. "Summary of Integral Metaphysics": "Résumé de métaphysique intégrale," *Résumé de métaphysique intégrale* (Paris: Le Courrier du Livre, 1985), 13–22.

6. "Consequences Flowing from the Mystery of Subjectivity": "Conséquences découlant du mystère de la subjectivité," *Du Divin à l'humain: Tour d'horizon de métaphysique et d'epistémologie* (Paris: Le Courrier du Livre, 1981), 11–18.

7. "Tracing the Notion of Philosophy": "Sur les traces de la notion de philosophie," *Le Soufisme: voile et quintessence* (Paris: Éditions Dervy, 2007), 97–107.

8. "Understanding and Believing": "Comprendre et croire," *Logique et transcendance* (Paris: Éditions Traditionnelles, 1972), 219–30.

9. "Man in the Universe": "L'homme dans l'univers," *Regards sur les mondes anciens* (Paris: Éditions Traditionnelles, 1980), 137–46.

10. "The Message of the Human Body": "Le message du corps humain," *Du Divin à l'humain: Tour d'horizon de métaphysique et d'epistémologie* (Paris: Le Courrier du Livre, 1981), 91–105.

11. "Man and Certainty": "L'homme et la certitude," *Logique et transcendance* (Paris: Éditions Traditionnelles, 1972), 287–93.

12. "Universal Eschatology": "Eschatologie universelle," *Sur les traces de la religion pérenne* (Paris: Le Courrier du Livre, 1982), 97–109.

13. "The Question of Forms in Art": "La question des formes d'art," *De l'Unité transcendante des religions* (Paris: Éditions du Seuil, 1979), 81–98.

14. "The Liberating Passage": "Le passage libérateur," *Le Jeu des masques* (Lausanne: L'Âge d'Homme, 1992), 117–21.

15. "An Elementary Criteriology of Celestial Apparitions": "Critériologie élémentaire des apparitions célestes," *L'Ésotérisme comme principe et comme voie* (Paris: Dervy-Livres, 1978), 207–14.

16. "The Symbolism of the Hourglass": "Le symbolisme du sablier," *Logique et transcendance* (Paris: Éditions Traditionnelles, 1972), 185–92.

17. "Modes of Spiritual Realization": "Des modes de la realisation spirituelle," *L'Œil du cœur* (Paris: Dervy-Livres, 1974), 101–10.

18. "The Anonymity of the Virtues": "Anonymat des vertus," *Résumé de métaphysique intégrale* (Paris: Le Courrier du Livre, 1985), 109–15.

19. "The Nature and Function of the Spiritual Master": "Nature et fonction du maître spirituel," *Logique et transcendance* (Paris: Éditions Traditionnelles, 1972), 241–52.

20. "Stations of Wisdom": "Les stations de la sagesse," *Les Stations de la sagesse* (Paris: L'Harmattan, 2011), 147–57.

Conclusion: "*Religio Perennis*": "*Religio Perennis,*" *Regards sur les mondes anciens* (Paris: Éditions Traditionnelles, 1980), 173–83.

The poems have been chosen from *Songs for a Spiritual Traveler: Selected Poems* (Bloomington, Indiana: World Wisdom, 2002) and *Adastra & Stella Maris: Poems by Frithjof Schuon* (Bloomington, Indiana: World Wisdom, 2003). Titles and pages from these volumes are as follows:

"The Gift," *Adastra*, 139
"Sanctuaries," *Adastra*, 181
"*Gnosis*," *Adastra*, 69
"Creation's Play," *Adastra*, 163
"Winter," *Adastra*, 175
"*Sophia Perennis*," *Songs*, 81
"I-ness," *Adastra*, 31
"*Māyā*," *Adastra*, 83
"*Bodhi*," *Adastra*, 109
"*Samsāra*," *Adastra*, 65
"Lalla," *Adastra*, 149
"Archetypal Man," *Songs*, 109
"Life," *Adastra*, 45
"Dawn," *Adastra*, 187
"Woman," *Adastra*, 161
"Flowers," *Adastra*, 25
"The Fan," *Songs*, 145
"Here and Now," *Adastra*, 117
"*Veritas*," *Adastra*, 7
"*Ad Astra*," *Adastra*, 245
"A Song," *Adastra*, 153
"The One," *Adastra*, 63

BIBLIOGRAPHY OF WORKS BY FRITHJOF SCHUON

PROSE

Leitgedanken zur Urbesinnung [Guiding Thoughts for Primordial Meditation]. Zürich: Orell Füssli Verlag, 1935. Revised edition: *Urbesinnung: Das Denken des Eigentlichen.* Freiburg im Breisgau: Aurum Verlag, 1989; Frankfurt: H. J. Maurer, 2009.

> *Primordial Meditation: Contemplating the Real.* Trans. Gillian Harris and Angela Schwartz. *Sacred Web: A Journal of Tradition and Modernity*, No. 20 (November 2007), "Special Tenth Anniversary of *Sacred Web*, Dedicated to Frithjof Schuon (1907–1998) on the Occasion of His Birth Centenary," 19–120.
>
> Four sets of meditations based on notebook entries for the period 1928–34: "First Collection: Besançon, 1928–29; Paris, 1930–32"; "Second Collection: Monastery of Notre Dame de Scourmont, Forges-lez-Chimay, 1932"; "Third Collection: Basle, Lausanne, Marseilles, 1932"; "Fourth Collection: Mostaghanem, 1932–33."

De l'Unité transcendante des religions. Paris: Gallimard, 1948, 1958. Revised editions: Paris: Éditions du Seuil, 1979; Paris: Éditions Maisonneuve & Larose, 1989; Paris: Sulliver, 2000.

> *Von der inneren Einheit der Religionen.* Trans. the author. Interlaken: Ansata-Verlag, 1979; Frankfurt: H. J. Maurer, 2007.
>
> *The Transcendent Unity of Religions.* Trans. Peter N. Townsend. London: Faber and Faber, 1953; New York: Pantheon, 1953. Revised edition: New York: Harper and Row, 1975, 1984; Wheaton: Theosophical Publishing House, 1984, 1993.
>
> "Conceptual Dimensions," "The Limitations of Exotericism," "Transcendence and Universality of Esotericism," "The Question of Forms in Art," "Limits of Religious Expansion," "The Ternary Aspect of Monotheism," "Christianity and Islam," "The Particular Nature and Universality of the Christian Religion," "To Be Man Is To Know."

L'Oeil du cœur. Paris: Gallimard, 1950; Paris: Dervy-Livres, 1974; Lausanne: L'Âge d'Homme, 1995.

The Eye of the Heart. Bloomington, Indiana: World Wisdom Books, 1997.

"The Eye of the Heart," "On Knowledge," "*Al-Nūr*," "*Nirvāna*," "Concerning the Posthumous States," "Christianity and Buddhism," "The Mystery of the *Bodhisattva*," "Elementary Observations concerning the Enigma of the *Kōan*," "*Īmān, Islām, Ihsān*," "Intellectuality and Civilization," "Modes of Spiritual Realization," "Microcosm and Symbol," "Prayer and the Integration of the Psychic Elements," "Transgression and Purification," "On Sacrifice," "The Twofold Stumbling Block," "On Meditation."

Perspectives spirituelles et faits humains. Paris: Cahiers du Sud, 1953; Maisonneuve & Larose, 1989; Lausanne: L'Âge d'Homme, 2001.

Spiritual Perspectives and Human Facts. Trans. Macleod Matheson. London: Faber and Faber, 1954. Revised edition, trans. Peter N. Townsend: London: Perennial Books, 1969, 1970, 1987. New translation with selected letters, ed. James S. Cutsinger (trans. Mark Perry, Jean-Pierre Lafouge, and James S. Cutsinger): Bloomington, Indiana: World Wisdom, 2007.

"Thought and Civilization," "Aesthetics and Symbolism in Art and Nature," "Contours of the Spirit," "*Vedānta*," "Knowledge and Love," "The Spiritual Virtues."

Sentiers de gnose. Paris: La Colombe, 1957; Gaillac: La Place Royale, 1987, 1996.

Gnosis: Divine Wisdom. Trans. G. E. H. Palmer. London: John Murray, 1959; London: Perennial Books, 1978, 1988, 1990. New translation with selected letters, ed. James S. Cutsinger (trans. Mark Perry, Jean-Pierre Lafouge, and James S. Cutsinger): Bloomington, Indiana: World Wisdom, 2006.

"The Sense of the Absolute in Religions," "Diversity of Revelation," "Is There a Natural Mysticism?," "Vicissitudes of Spiritual Temperaments," "The Doctrine of Illusion," "*Gnosis*: Language of the Self," "The Ternary Aspect of the Human Microcosm," "Love of God, Consciousness of the Real," "Seeing God Everywhere," "Some Observations [on Christianity]," "Christic and Virginal Mysteries," "The Cross."

Castes et races. Lyon: Derain, 1957; Paris: Dervy-Livres, 1979.

Castes and Races. Trans. Marco Pallis and Macleod Matheson. London: Perennial Books, 1959, 1982.

"The Meaning of Caste," "The Meaning of Race," "Principles and Criteria of Art."

Les Stations de la sagesse. Paris: Buchet/Chastel-Corrêa, 1958; Maisonneuve & Larose, 1992; Paris: L'Harmattan, 2011.

Stations of Wisdom. Trans. G. E. H. Palmer. London: John Murray, 1961; London: Perennial Books, 1980. Revised translation: Bloomington, Indiana: World Wisdom Books, 1995.

"Orthodoxy and Intellectuality," "The Nature and Arguments of Faith," "Manifestations of the Divine Principle," "The Complexity of the Idea of Charity," "Modes of Prayer," "The Stations of Wisdom."

Images de l'Esprit: Shintō, Bouddhisme, Yoga [Images of the Spirit: Shintoism, Buddhism, Yoga]. Paris: Flammarion, 1961; Paris: Le Courrier du Livre, 1982.

Revised chapters anthologized in *Language of the Self*, *In the Tracks of Buddhism/Treasures of Buddhism*, and *The Feathered Sun* (see below).

"The Symbolist Mind," "The Mythology of *Shintō*," "Treasures of Buddhism," "A View of *Yoga*."

Comprendre l'Islam. Paris: Gallimard, 1961; Éditions du Seuil, 1976.

Understanding Islam. Trans. Macleod Matheson. London: Allen & Unwin, 1963, 1972, 1976, 1989; New York: Roy Publishers, 1963, 1964; Baltimore: Penguin Books, 1972. London: Unwin and Hyman, 1986. Bloomington, Indiana: World Wisdom Books, 1994, 1998. New translation with selected letters, ed. Patrick Laude (trans. Mark Perry and Jean-Pierre Lafouge): Bloomington, Indiana: World Wisdom, 2011.

"Islam," "The Koran and the *Sunnah*," "The Prophet," "The Path."

Regards sur les mondes anciens. Paris: Éditions Traditionnelles, 1965, 1980; Falicon: Nataraj, 1997.

Light on the Ancient Worlds. Trans. Lord Northbourne. London: Perennial Books, 1965; Bloomington, Indiana: World Wisdom Books, 1984. New translation with selected letters, ed. Deborah Casey (trans. Deborah Casey, Mark Perry, Jean-Pierre Lafouge, and James S. Cutsinger): Bloomington, Indiana: World Wisdom, 2006.

"Light on the Ancient Worlds," "Fall and Forfeiture," "The Dialogue between Hellenists and Christians," "American Indian Shamanism," "Tracing *Māyā*," "Concerning Naiveté," "Man in the Universe," "The Universality and Timeliness of Monasticism," "Keys to the Bible," "*Religio Perennis*."

Logique et transcendance. Paris: Éditions Traditionnelles, 1970, 1972; Paris: Sulliver, 2007.

Logic and Transcendence. Trans. Peter N. Townsend. New York: Harper and Row, 1975; London: Perennial Books, 1975, 1984. New translation with selected letters, ed. James S. Cutsinger (trans. Mark Perry,

Jean-Pierre Lafouge, and James S. Cutsinger): Bloomington, Indiana: World Wisdom, 2009.

"The Contradiction of Relativism," "Abuse of the Ideas of the Concrete and the Abstract," "Rationalism Real and Apparent," "Concerning Proofs of God," "The Argument from Substance," "Evidence and Mystery," "Oriental Dialectic and Its Roots in Faith," "The Demiurge in North American Mythology," "The Alchemy of the Sentiments," "The Symbolism of the Hourglass," "The Problem of Qualifications," "Implications of the Love of God," "Understanding and Believing," "The Servant and Union," "The Nature and Function of the Spiritual Master," "The Delivered One and the Divine Image," "Truths and Errors Concerning Beauty," "The Vow of Dharmakara," "Man and Certainty."

Forme et substance dans les religions. Paris: Dervy-Livres, 1975; Paris: L'Harmattan, 2012.

Form and Substance in the Religions. Trans. Mark Perry and Jean-Pierre Lafouge. Bloomington, Indiana: World Wisdom, 2002.

"Truth and Presence," "Form and Substance in the Religions," "*Ātmā-Māyā*," "Substance: Subject and Object," "The Five Divine Presences," "The Cross of Space and Time in Koranic Onomatology," "Insights into the Muhammadan Phenomenon," "The Koranic Message of Sayyidna Isa," "The Virginal Doctrine," "Synthesis of the *Pāramitās*," "A Note on the Feminine Element in *Mahāyāna*," "The Mystery of the Two Natures," "The Question of Theodicies," "Some Difficulties Found in Sacred Scriptures," "Paradoxes of Spiritual Expression," "The Human Margin," "Comments on an Eschatological Problem," "The Two Paradises."

L'Ésotérisme comme principe et comme voie. Paris: Dervy-Livres, 1978, 1997.

Esoterism as Principle and as Way. Trans. William Stoddart. London: Perennial Books, 1981, 1990. New translation with selected letters, ed. James S. Cutsinger (trans. Mark Perry, Jean-Pierre Lafouge, and James S. Cutsinger): Bloomington, Indiana: World Wisdom, forthcoming.

"Understanding Esotericism," "The Mystery of the Veil," "Hypostatic and Cosmic Numbers," "The Primordial Tree," "The Triple Nature of Man," "Virtues in the Path," "The Nature and Role of Sentiment," "What Sincerity Is and Is Not," "The Problem of Sexuality," "Dimensions of the Human Vocation," "The Supreme Commandment," "The True Remedy," "Criteria of Worth," "Foundations of an Integral Aesthetics," "The Degrees of Art," "The Role of Appearances," "The Function of Relics," "An Elementary Criteriology of Celestial Apparitions," "The Sun Dance," "The Religion of the Heart," "The Way of Oneness."

Le Soufisme: voile et quintessence. Paris: Dervy-Livres, 1980; Paris: Éditions Dervy, 2007.

Sufism: Veil and Quintessence. Trans. William Stoddart. Bloomington, Indiana: World Wisdom Books, 1981. New translation with selected letters, ed. James S. Cutsinger (trans. Mark Perry, Jean-Pierre Lafouge, and James S. Cutsinger): Bloomington, Indiana: World Wisdom, 2006.

"Ellipsis and Hyperbolism in Arab Rhetoric," "The Exo-Esoteric Symbiosis," "Paradoxes of an Esoterism," "Human Premises of a Religious Dilemma," "Tracing the Notion of Philosophy," "The Quintessential Esoterism of Islam," "Hypostatic Dimensions of Unity."

Christianisme/Islam: visions d'oecuménisme ésotérique. Milan: Arché, 1981; Paris: Dervy-Livres, 1981.

Christianity/Islam: Essays on Esoteric Ecumenicism. Trans. Gustavo Polit. Bloomington, Indiana: World Wisdom Books, 1985.

Christianity/Islam: Perspectives on Esoteric Ecumenism. New Translation with selected letters, ed. James S. Cutsinger (trans. Mark Perry, Jean-Pierre Lafouge, and James S. Cutsinger): Bloomington, Indiana: World Wisdom, 2008.

"On the Margin of Liturgical Improvisations," "The Enigma of the *Epiclesis*," "The Question of Protestantism," "The Problem of Moral Divergences," "Alternations in Semitic Monotheism," "The Idea of the 'Best' in Religions," "Images of Islam," "Dilemmas of Muslim Scholasticism," "Paradise as Theophany," "Atomism and Creation," "On the Divine Will."

Du Divin à l'humain: Tour d'horizon de métaphysique et d'epistémologie. Paris: Le Courrier du Livre, 1981.

From the Divine to the Human: Survey of Metaphysics and Epistemology. Trans. Gustavo Polit and Deborah Lambert. Bloomington, Indiana: World Wisdom Books, 1982. New translation with selected letters, ed. Patrick Laude (trans. Mark Perry and Jean-Pierre Lafouge): Bloomington, Indiana: World Wisdom, 2013.

"Consequences Flowing from the Mystery of Subjectivity," "Aspects of the Theophanic Phenomenon of Consciousness," "Transcendence Is Not Contrary to Sense," "The Play of *Hypostases*," "The Problem of Possibility," "The Structure and Universality of the Conditions of Existence," "Outline of a Spiritual Anthropology," "The Message of the Human Body," "The Sense of the Sacred," "To Refuse or To Accept Revelation."

Sur les traces de la Religion pérenne [Tracing the Perennial Religion]. Paris: Le Courrier du Livre, 1982.

Survey of Metaphysics and Esoterism. Trans. Gustavo Polit. Bloomington, Indiana: World Wisdom Books, 1986, 2000. [English edition includes both this title and *Résumé de métaphysique intégrale* (see below).]

"Epistemological Premises," "Dimensions, Modes, and Degrees of the Divine Order," "Denominational Speculation: Intentions and Impasses," "Stumbling Blocks in the Language of Faith," "Outline for a Religious Typology," "Enigma and Message of Islamic Esoterism," "Universal Eschatology," "Synthesis and Conclusion."

Approches du phénomène religieux [Approaches to the Religious Phenomenon]. Paris: Le Courrier du Livre, 1984.

In the Face of the Absolute. Bloomington, Indiana: World Wisdom Books, 1989, 1994.

"The Decisive Intuition," "The Ambiguity of Exoterism," "Two Problems: Predestination and Evil," "Tracing the Idea of Eternity," "The Complexity of Dogmatism," "Christian Divergences," "The Seat of Wisdom," "Islam and Consciousness of the Absolute," "Observations on Dialectical Antinomianism," "Diversity of Paths," "Transcendence and Immanence in the Spiritual Economy of Islam," "The Problem of Delimitations," "The Mystery of the Prophetic Substance."

Résumé de métaphysique intégrale [Summary of Integral Metaphysics]. Paris: Le Courrier du Livre, 1985.

Survey of Metaphysics and Esoterism. Trans. Gustavo Polit. Bloomington, Indiana: World Wisdom Books, 1986, 2000. [English edition includes both this title and *Sur les traces de la religion pérenne* (see above).]

"Summary of Integral Metaphysics," "Creation as a Divine Quality," "The Onto-Cosmological Chain," "Dimensions of Omnipotence," "The Mystery of the Hypostatic Face," "The Irrefutable Religion," "Two Esoterisms," "Deficiencies in the World of Faith," "The Ambiguity of the Emotional Element," "The Psychological Imposture," "Anonymity of the Virtues," "Trials and Happiness."

Avoir un centre. Paris: Maisonneuve & Larose, 1988; Paris: L'Harmattan, 2010.

To Have a Center. Bloomington, Indiana: World Wisdom Books, 1990.

"To Have a Center," "Survey of Anthropology," "Intelligence and Character," "The Primacy of Intellection," "*Gnosis* is Not Just Anything," "Universal Categories," "Concerning an Onto-Cosmological Ambiguity," "Degrees and Dimensions of Theism," "Our Father Who Art in Heaven," "David, Shankara, Honen," "Fundamental Keys," "On the Art of Translating," "The Message of a Vestimentary Art," "Concerning a Question of Astronomy."

Racines de la condition humaine. Paris: Les Éditions de la Table Ronde, 1990.

Roots of the Human Condition. Bloomington, Indiana: World Wisdom Books, 1991, 2002.

"On Intelligence," "The Veil of Isis," "Problems of Space-Time," "*Mahāshakti*," "The Enigma of Diversified Subjectivity," "Traces of Being, Proofs of God," "Salvific Dimensions," "Man before the Sovereign Good," "Outline of the Christic Message," "Outline of the Islamic Message," "Pillars of Wisdom," "The Twofold Discernment," "Cosmic Shadows and Serenity," "Virtue and Way," "On Love."

Le Jeu des masques. Paris: Les Éditions du Seuil, 1990; Lausanne: L'Âge d'Homme, 1992.

The Play of Masks. Bloomington, Indiana: World Wisdom Books, 1992.

"Prerogatives of the Human State," "Man in the Cosmogonic Projection," "The Play of Masks," "*Ex nihilo, in Deo*," "Faced with Contingency," "Delineations of Original Sin," "On Intention," "Remarks on Charity," "No Initiative without Truth," "Being Conscious of the Real," "The Liberating Passage."

La Transfiguration de l'Homme. Lausanne: L'Âge d'Homme, 1995.

The Transfiguration of Man. Bloomington, Indiana: World Wisdom Books, 1995.

"Thought: Light and Perversion," "Reflections on Ideological Sentimentalism," "Usurpations of Religious Feeling," "The Impossible Convergence," "Art: Its Duties and Rights," "The Spiritual Meaning of Work," "Faculties and Modalities of Man," "Axioms of the *Sophia Perennis*," "The Mystery of Possibility," "The Ternary Rhythm of the Spirit," "An Enigma of the Gospel," "Characteristics of Volitive Mysticism," "Tracing the Principle of Sacrifice," "Dimensions of Prayer"; excerpts from *Le Livre des Clefs* [The Book of Keys].

The following English language collections were also published during Schuon's lifetime.

Language of the Self. Trans. Marco Pallis and Macleod Matheson. Madras: Ganesh and Company, 1959; Bangalore: Select Books, 1998. Revised edition: *Language of the Self: Essays on the Perennial Philosophy*. Bloomington, Indiana: World Wisdom Books, 1999.

"Orthodoxy and Intellectuality," "The *Vedānta*," "Self-Knowledge and the Western Seeker," "A View of *Yoga*," "Orthodoxy and Originality of Buddhism," "Principles and Criteria of Art," "The Meaning of Caste," "The Meaning of Race," "The Sacred Pipe of the Red Indians," "What Can the East Offer the West?," "*Gnosis*: Language of the Self."

In the Tracks of Buddhism. Trans. Marco Pallis. London: Allen & Unwin, 1968; Unwin & Hyman, 1989; Revised edition: *Treasures of Buddhism*. Bloomington, Indiana: World Wisdom Books, 1993; Bangalore: Select Books, 1993; New Delhi: Smriti Books, 2003.

"Originality of Buddhism," "Message and Messenger," "Charity and Existence," "The Question of Illusion," "A Buddhist Eye on Science," "Cosmological and Eschatological Viewpoints," "More About Human Destinies: The Function of Mercy," "What is Matter and Who is Mara?" "Some Fallacies and Facts concerning Buddhism," "Glimpses into Zen," "Science, Myth, and the Meaning of Ancestors," "Ethics and Mythology of *Shintō*," "The Noble Virtues: Some Lessons of *Shintō*," "Treasures of Buddhism," "Mystery of the *Bodhisattva*," "The Feminine Element in *Mahāyāna*," "Synthesis of the *Pāramitās*"; revised edition includes: "Remarks on the Enigma of the *Kōan*," "*Nirvāna*," "Christianity and Buddhism," "The Vow of Dharmakara."

Dimensions of Islam. Trans. Peter N. Townsend. London: Allen & Unwin, 1969.

"The Use of Hyperbole in Arab Rhetoric," "Dimensions of the Universe in the Koranic Doctrine of the Divine Names," "The Servant and Union," "Some Difficulties in the Koran and Other Scriptures," "Concerning the Phenomenon of Muhammad," "The Koranic Message of Sayyidna Isa," "The Virginal Doctrine," "*Al-Nūr*," "Implications of the Love of God," "Some Observations on a Problem of the Afterlife," "The Five Divine Presences."

Islam and the Perennial Philosophy. Trans. J. Peter Hobson. London: World of Islam Festival Publishing Company, 1976.

"Truth and Presence," "Form and Substance in the Religions," "The Human Margin," "Paradoxes of Spiritual Expression," "Seeds of a Divergence," "The *Sunnah*," "Dilemmas in Asharite Theology," "The Problem of Possibility," "The Problem of Theodicies," "The Sufi Paradise," "The Forbidden Fruit," "The Two Paradises."

The Feathered Sun: Plains Indians in Art and Philosophy. Bloomington, Indiana: World Wisdom Books, 1990.

"The Symbolist Mind," "A Metaphysic of Virgin Nature," "The Shamanism of the Red Indians," "The Sacred Pipe," "Symbolism of a Vestimentary Art," "The Demiurge in North American Mythology," "The Sun Dance," "A Message on Indian Religion," "His Holiness and the Medicine Man," "Excerpts from a Diary," "Excerpts from Correspondence."

The following articles were published in various journals and anthologies but not included in any of Schuon's books; titles appearing only in English were never published in French.

"Réflexions sur le symbolisme de la pyramide" [Reflections on the Symbolism of the Pyramid] (*Voile d'Isis*, February 1934); "La Démonstration des voies" [Explication of Paths] (*Voile d'Isis*, August–September 1934); "Poèmes soufis [de Mohyiddin Ibn Arabi]" [The Sufi Poems of Ibn Arabi] (*Études traditionnelles*,

August–September 1934); "*Rahimahu 'Llāh*" (*Cahiers du Sud*, August–September 1935); "*Al-Dīn*" (*Études traditionnelles*, March 1938); "Considérations générales sur les functions spirituelles" [General Considerations concerning Spiritual Functions] (*Études traditionnelles*, November–December 1939); "Communion et Invocation" [Communion and Invocation] (*Études traditionnelles*, May 1940); "La Vierge noire de Czenstochowa" [The Black Virgin of Czenstochowa] (*Études traditionnelles*, May 1940); "Fatalité et progres" [Inevitability and Progress] (*Études traditionnelles*, July–August 1947); "L'Œuvre" [The Work (of René Guénon)] (*Études traditionnelles*, July–November 1951); "Les vertus spirituelles selon Saint François d'Assise" [The Spiritual Virtues according to Saint Francis of Assisi] (*Études traditionnelles*, April–May 1953); "Caractères de la mystique passionnelle" [Characteristics of Passional Mysticism (of Saint John of the Cross)] (*Études traditionnelles*, July–September 1953); "Invocation of the Divine Name" (*Kalyana-Kalpataru*, October 1961); "No Activity without Truth" (*Studies in Comparative Religion*, Autumn 1969); "The Three Dimensions of Sufism" (*Studies in Comparative Religion*, Spring 1976); "A Belated but Still Timely Word about the Encyclical *Populorum Progressio*" (*Studies in Comparative Religion*, Winter–Spring 1978, under the penname Fidelis Sapientiae); "Il n'y a pas de droit sacré à l'absurdité" [There is No Sacred Right to Absurdity] (*Études traditionnelles*, April–June 1978); "Quelques critiques" [Some Observations (concerning the Work of René Guénon)] (*René Guénon: Les Dossiers H*, ed. Pierre-Marie Sigaud (Lausanne: L'Âge d'Homme,1984); "Note sur René Guénon" [A Note on René Guénon] (*René Guénon*, ed. Jean-Pierre Laurant (Paris: Les Cahiers de l'Herne, 1985); "The Perennial Philosophy" (*The Unanimous Tradition*, ed. Ranjit Fernando [Colombo: Sri Lanka Institute of Traditional Studies, 1991); "Normes et paradoxes dans l'alcheimie initiatique" [Norms and Paradoxes in Initiatic Alchemy] (*Connaissance des religions*, January–June 1995); "Le Mystère des nombres" [The Mystery of Numbers] (*Connaissance des religions*, July–December 1995); "Entre l'Orient et l'Occident" [Between East and West] (*Connaissance des religions*, January–June 1996); "Hagia Sophia" (*Connaissance des religions*, July–December 1996); "À propos de la spiritualité indienne" [Concerning American Indian Spirituality] (*Connaissance des religions*, January–June 1997).

POETRY

Sulamith [Shulamite]. Bern: Urs Graf Verlag, 1947 (German).

Tage- und Nächtebuch [Book of Days and Nights]. Bern: Urs Graf Verlag, 1947 (German).

Road to the Heart. Bloomington, Indiana: World Wisdom Books, 1995 (English).

Liebe, Leben, Glück, Sinn [Love, Life, Happiness, Meaning]. Freiburg im Breisgau: Verlag Herder, 1997 (German).

Adastra & Stella Maris: Sinngedichte / Poésies didactiques [Didactic Poems]. Sottens, Switzerland: Les Sept Flèches, 2001 (German–French).

Adastra & Stella Maris: Poems by Frithjof Schuon. Bloomington, Indiana: World Wisdom, 2003 (German–English).

Songs for a Spiritual Traveler: Selected Poems. Bloomington, Indiana: World Wisdom, 2002 (German–English).

Herbstblätter—Der Ring: Sinngedichte / Feuilles d'automne—L'anneau: Poésies didactiques [Autumn Leaves—The Ring: Didactic Poems] Sottens, Switzerland: Les Sept Flèches, 2002 (German–French).

Autumn Leaves & The Ring: Poems by Frithjof Schuon. Bloomington, Indiana: World Wisdom, 2010 (German–English).

Lieder ohne Namen: Sinngedichte / Chants sans noms: Poésies didactiques. Volumes I–III. Lausanne, Switzerland: Les Sept Flèches, 2002 (German–French).

Lieder ohne Namen: Sinngedichte / Chants sans noms: Poésies didactiques. Volumes IV–VII. Lausanne, Switzerland: Les Sept Flèches, 2003 (German–French).

Lieder ohne Namen: Sinngedichte / Chants sans noms: Poésies didactiques. Volumes VIII–XII. Lausanne, Switzerland: Les Sept Flèches, 2004 (German–French).

Songs without Names: Poems by Frithjof Schuon. Volumes I–VI. Bloomington, Indiana: World Wisdom, 2007 (English).

Songs without Names: Poems by Frithjof Schuon. Volumes VII–XII. Bloomington, Indiana: World Wisdom, 2007 (English).

Das Weltrad: Sinngedichte / La roue cosmique: Poésies didactiques. Volumes I–II. Lausanne: Éditions Les Sept Flèches, 2004 (German–French).

Das Weltrad: Sinngedichte / La roue cosmique: Poésies didactiques. Volumes III–V. Lausanne: Éditions Les Sept Flèches, 2005 (German–French).

Das Weltrad: Sinngedichte / La roue cosmique: Poésies didactiques. Volumes VI–VII. Lausanne: Éditions Les Sept Flèches, 2005 (German–French).

World Wheel: Poems by Frithjof Schuon. Volumes I–III. Bloomington, Indiana: World Wisdom, 2007 (English).

World Wheel: Poems by Frithjof Schuon. Volumes IV–VII. Bloomington, Indiana: World Wisdom, 2007 (English).

INDEX

Names beginning with the Arabic particle "al-" are alphabetized under the first significant element; thus "al-Ghazzali" is found in the Gs. For specific writings of Schuon, see under Schuon, Frithjof, writings of.

www.ingramcontent.com/pod-product-compliance
Lightning Source LLC
LaVergne TN
LVHW011959040926
847296LV00029B/280